PENGUIN BOOKS

THE NORTHERN CRUSADES

Eric Christiansen, a Fellow of New College, Oxford, is the author of *The Origins of Military Power in Spain* and works mainly on Northern history in the Middle Ages. Danish by descent and English by education, he has spent some time in and around the Baltic Sea, and has lectured in London, Copenhagen and Florida. He has translated the histories of Saxo Grammaticus and Dudo of St Quentin.

Acclaim for The Northern Crusades *:*

'This interesting, well-written book fills a major gap in historians' literature dealing with the late Middle Ages in northern Europe ... a worthy introduction to a complex area of history' – James Brundage in the *Journal of Ecclesiastical History*

'The author's many insights ... give the book an importance far beyond the circle for which it was intended ... For Mr Christiansen history remains an art as well as a science' – Peter King in the *Slavonic Review*

'His scholarship is wide, honest and exact ... Grounded in rigorous historical observation, not ideological fervour, military Christianity is explained with a brilliance which leaves the reader at once dazzled and sickened ... Valuable, learned and attractively written' – F. R. H. du Boulay

ERIC CHRISTIANSEN

The Northern Crusades

PENGUIN BOOKS

PENGUIN BOOKS

Published by the Penguin Group
Penguin Books Ltd, 80 Strand, London WC2R 0RL, England
Penguin Putnam Inc., 375 Hudson Street, New York, New York 10014, USA
Penguin Books Australia Ltd, 250 Camberwell Road, Camberwell, Victoria 3124, Australia
Penguin Books Canada Ltd, 10 Alcorn Avenue, Toronto, Ontario, Canada M4V 3B2
Penguin Books India (P) Ltd, 11 Community Centre, Panchsheel Park, New Delhi – 110 017, India
Penguin Books (NZ) Ltd, Cnr Rosedale and Airborne Roads, Albany, Auckland, New Zealand
Penguin Books (South Africa) (Pty) Ltd, 24 Sturdee Avenue, Rosebank 2196, South Africa

Penguin Books Ltd, Registered Offices: 80 Strand, London WC2R 0RL, England

www.penguin.com

First published by Macmillan
Published in Penguin Books 1997

11

Set in 10/12 pt Monotype Janson
Typeset by Rowland Phototypesetting Ltd, Bury St Edmunds, Suffolk
Printed in England by Clays Ltd, St Ives plc

ISBN-13: 978-0-14-026653-5

www.greenpenguin.co.uk

CONTENTS

LIST OF MAPS

ACKNOWLEDGEMENTS

The author owes more than he can repay to almost everyone else who has written on the subjects of crusades and the North, but in particular to Christopher Tyerman, Peter King, and Peter and Birgit Sawyer; and to the late John Fennell, the late Karol Gorski, and the late Karl Leyser.

960s–990s	Christian churches established among West Slavs, Danes, Poles, Russians.
997	Martyrdom of St Adalbert of Prague in Prussia.
1000	Polish archbishopric founded at Gniezno.
1050s	Building of cathedrals of Holy Wisdom at Novgorod and at Polotsk.
1066	Ousting of German missions and rule from West Slavs.
1070s	Adam of Bremen writes his *History of the Archbishops*.
1086	Martyrdom of King Canute IV in Denmark.
1096–9	First Crusade to Jerusalem.
1103	Pilgrimage of King Eric of Denmark to the East.
1103/4	Establishment of Lund as metropolitan of the North.
1108?	Appeal for war on Slavs in Magdeburg diocese.
1116	Russian outpost among Estonians at Odenpäh.
1118	Hospital of St Mary for Germans founded at Jerusalem.
1124 and 1127	Missions of Bishop Otto of Bamberg to the Pomeranians; bishopric at Wollin.
1129–36	Bernard of Clairvaux composes Rule for the Templars.
1135	Danes raid Rügen; Saxons build stone fort at Segeburg.
1139–43	Saxon conquest of Wagria and Polabia.
1143–4	Cistercians enter Sweden and Denmark.
1147	First Northern crusade, against the Baltic Slavs.
1164	Revolt and subjugation of the Abotrites by the Saxons and Danes.
1168–9	Conquest of Rügen by Valdemar I of Denmark.
1171	Alexander III authorizes crusade against the east-Baltic heathen.
1181	Fall of Duke Henry of Saxony.
1185	Pomeranian Slavs submit to Canute VI of Denmark.

1188	Estonians raid Uppsala. First mission to the Livs.
1198	Innocent III authorizes the Livonian crusade; Bishop Berthold slain.
1200	Bishop Albert establishes the see of Riga and Order of Sword-Brothers.
1200–1209	Conquest of the Livs and Letts by Bishop Albert and crusaders.
1215	Innocent III consecrates Christian bishop of the Prussians.
1217	Honorius III authorizes crusade against the Prussians.
1219	Valdemar II founds Reval and begins conquest of northern Estonia.
1225	William of Sabina's first legation to the east-Baltic churches.
1226	Frederick II's Bull of Rimini grants Prussia to the Teutonic Order.
1230	Gregory IX authorizes the Teutonic Order to conquer the Prussians.
1231–40	Teutonic Knights and crusaders conquer the western Prussians.
1236	Sword-Brothers annihilated by the Lithuanians at Siaulai (Saule).
1240	First crusade against the Russians; Swedes beaten on the Neva, Pskov taken.
1242	Teutonic Knights defeated at Lake Chud. Prussians revolt.
1249	Treaty of Christburg. Conquest of middle Finland by the Swedes under Birger Jarl.
1254–6	Conquest of Samland.
1260–83	Revolt and final subjugation of the southern Letts, the Curonians and Prussians.
1290	Conquest of Semigallia by Teutonic Knights of Livonia.
1292	Swedes establish outpost of Viborg (Viipuru) in Karelia.
1297	Civil war in Livonia.
1300	Swedes build fort of Landskrona on the Neva.
1304	Crusaders from Rhineland assist the Teutonic Knights against Lithuania.
1308	Teutonic Knights occupy Danzig.
1309	Headquarters of the Teutonic Order moved from Venice to Marienburg.

1318	Novgorodians raid Finland and burn Åbo cathedral.
1323	Treaty of Nöteborg ends Swedish–Novgorodian war. Peace of Vilnius between the Teutonic Order and Gediminas of Lithuania.
1329	King John of Bohemia's crusade; Prussia at war with the Poles and Lithuanians.
1332	Prussia makes peace with Poland.
1337	Emperor Lewis IV authorizes the grand-master to conquer Eastern Europe.
1343	Revolt of the Estonians against the colonists.
1346	Valdemar IV of Denmark sells Estonia to the Teutonic Order.
1348	King Magnus of Sweden invades Russia. Prussians beat the Lithuanians at Strawe.
1350	King Magnus's second crusade.
1362	Prussian Knights and crusaders capture Kaunas.
1364	Urban V's crusading Bull urges continued war on Lithuania.
1381	Cannon used by the Teutonic Knights on the Niemen.
1382	The Order takes Vilnius and Trakai.
1386	Prince Jogailo of Lithuania baptized and made king of Poland.
1392	The Order seizes the Polish duchy of Dobrzyn.
1398	The Order conquers Gotland and is ceded Samogitia by Witold.
1405	Dobrzyn returned to Poland. Samogitia subjugated.
1409	Samogitia revolts. Dobrzyn reoccupied by the Order.
1410	Poles and Lithuanians defeat the Order at Tannenberg.
1414	King Wladyslaw IV invades Prussia again, and retires.
1415	Poland and the Order appeal to the Council of Constance.
1423	The Order cedes Samogitia to Witold by the peace of Lake Melno. Last German crusaders reach Prussia.
1429	Detachment of Teutonic Knights sent to defend Hungary against the Turks, at request of Emperor Sigismund.
1433	Polish–Hussite army invades Prussia.
1435	Poles defeat the Livonian Knights at Wilkomierz; peace of Brest.
1444–8	War between the Livonians and Novgorod.

1454–66	Thirteen Years' War of Poland and Prussian towns against the Teutonic Order.
1466	Second peace of Torun; half Prussia ceded to Poland.
1471	Livonian–Lithuanian alliance frustrated by deposition of Master Wolthus von Herse.
1478	Submission of Novgorod to Ivan III of Moscow.
1480	Livonians fail to conquer Pskov.
1496	Swedes take Ivangorod.
1501	Treaty of Wenden unites Livonians and Lithuanians against Ivan III.
1502	Master von Plettenberg saves Livonia at the battle of Lake Smolina.
1519–21	Poles invade Prussia.
1525	Secularization of Prussia under Duke Albert.
1561–2	Partition and secularization of Livonia.

Denmark

Nicholas (1104–34)
Eric II (1134–7)
Eric III (1137–46)
Sweyn III (1146–54)
Canute V (1146–52, 1154–7)
Valdemar I (1157–82)
Canute VI (1182–1202)
Valdemar II (1202–41)
Eric IV (1241–50)
Abel (1250–52)
Christopher I (1252–9)
Eric V (1259–86)
Eric VI (1286–1320)
Christopher II (1320–26)
Valdemar III (1326–30)
Valdemar IV (1340–75)
Oluf (1375–87)

Sweden

Canute Eriksson (1167–96)
Sverker II Karlsson (1196–1208)
Eric X Knutsson (1208–16)
John Sverkersson (1216–22)
Canute (1229–34)
Eric XI (1222–9, 1234–50)
Valdemar (1250–75)
Magnus I (1275–90)
Birger (1290–1319)
Magnus II (1319–63)
Albert (1364–89)

Margaret I of Denmark (1387) and of Sweden (1389–1412)
Eric VII and XIII (1396–1439)
Christopher III (1439–48)
Christian I (1448–81 in Denmark, 1457–61 in Sweden)
John (1481–1513; with Sten Sture regent of Sweden 1470–97, 1501–3)

LITHUANIA (GRAND-PRINCES AND GRAND-DUKES)

Mindaugas (Mindowe) (*c.* 1219–63; king from 1253)
Treniota (Troinat) (1263–4)
Vaisvilkas (1265–7)
Traidenis (Troyden) (*c.* 1270–82)
Pukuveras (*c.* 1282–92)
Vytenis (1293–1315)
Gediminas (1315–41)
Algirdas (Olgerd) (1345–77)
Kestutis (Kynstut) (1377–82)
Jogaila and Vytautas (Witold) in dispute 1382–92
Jogaila (1382–92) becomes Wladyslaw IV of Poland (1386–1434)
Skirgaila (1387–96)
Vytautas (Witold) (1392–1430)
Svitrigaila (1430–32)
Sigismund (1432–40)
(*Note*: Lithuanian spellings given first, German forms in parentheses)

TEUTONIC KNIGHTS

(*Note*: many spellings vary; the *von* (v.) indicates either place of origin or family name, sometimes both.)

Prussia	*Livonia*
PROVINCIAL MASTERS	PROVINCIAL MASTERS
Hermann Balk (1230–39)	[as Prussia] (1237–8)
Heinrich v. Weide (1239–44)	Dietrich v. Grüningen (1238–42, 1244–6)
Poppo v. Osternach (1244–6)	Heinrich v. Heimburg (?)
Dietrich v. Grüningen (1246–59)	Andreas v. Stierland (1248–53)
Hartmut v. Grünbach (1259–61)	Anno v. Sangershausen (1253–6)
Helmeric v. Rechberg (1262–3)	Burchard v. Hornhausen (1256–60)

MASTERS OF PRUSSIA
(*continued*)

Johann v. Wegleben (1263)
Ludwig v. Baldersheim (1263–9)
Dietrich v. Gattersleben (1271–3)
Conrad v. Thierberg (1273–9, 1283–8)
Conrad v. Feuchtwangen (1279–80)
Mangold v. Sternberg (1280–83)
Meinhard v. Querfurt (1288–99)
Conrad v. Babenberg (1299)
Luder v. Schippen (1299–1300)
Helwig v. Goldbach (1300–1302)

Conrad Sack (1302–6)
Sieghard v. Schwartzburg (1306)
Heinrich v. Plotzke (1307–9) (then grand-commander)

MASTERS OF LIVONIA
(*continued*)

Werner v. Breithausen (1261–3)
Konrad v. Manderen (1263–6)
Otto v. Luterberg (1266–70)
Walther v. Nordeck (1270–72)
Ernst v. Ratzeburg (1272–9)
[as Prussia] (1279–81)

[as Prussia] (1281–3)
Willekin v. Schurburg (1283–7)
Cuno v. Herzogenstein (1288–90)
Halt v. Hohembach (1290–93)
Heinrich v. Dumpershagen (1294–5)
Bruno (1296–8)
Gottfried v. Rogga (1298–1306?)

GRAND-MASTERS AT
MARIENBURG (1309–1457)

Siegfried v. Feuchtwangen (1309–11)
Carl v. Trier (1311–24)
Werener v. Orseln (1324–30)
Duke Luder of Brunswick (1331–5)
Dietrich v. Altenburg (1335–41)
Ludolf König (1342–5)
Heinrich Dusmer (1345–51)
Winrich v. Kniprode (1352–82)

Conrad Zöllner v. Rothenstein (1382–90)

Gerhard v. Jocke (1309–22)

Johannes Ungenade (1322–3)
Reimar Hane (1323–?)
Eberhard Monheim (1328–40)

Burchard v. Dreileben (1340–45)
Goswin v. Hercke (1345–60)
Arnold v. Vietinghof (1360–64)
Wilhelm v. Vrimersheim (1364–85)
Robin v. Eltz (1385–8)

GRAND-MASTERS AT
MARIENBURG (*continued*)

Conrad v. Wallenrod (1391–3)

Conrad v. Jungingen (1393–1407)
Ulrich v. Jungingen (1407–10)
Heinrich v. Plauen (1410–13)
Michael Kuchmeister v.
Sternberg (1414–22)

Paul v. Russdorf (1422–41)
Conrad v. Erlichshausen (1441–9)
Ludwig v. Erlichshausen
(1450–67)

MASTERS OF LIVONIA
(*continued*)

Wennemar Hasenkamp v.
Brüggeneye (1389–1401)
Conrad v. Vietinghof (1401–13)

Dietrich Tork (1413–15)

Sievert Lander v. Spanheim
(1415–24)
Cisso v. Rutenberg (1424–33)
Franke v. Kersdorf (1433–5)
Heinrich Schlungel v.
Buckenvorde (1435–8)
Hei(de)nrich Vinke v.
Overbergen (1438–50)

GRAND-MASTERS AT
KÖNIGSBERG

Heinrich Reuss v. Plauen
(1469–70)
Heinrich Reffle v. Richtenberg
(1470–77)
Martin Truchess v. Wetzhausen
(1477–89)
Johann v. Tiefen (1489–97)

Duke Frederick of Saxony
(1498–1510)
Margrave Albert of Brandenburg-
Ansbach (1511–25); duke of
Prussia (1525–68)

Johann Osthof v. Mengden
(1450–69)
Johann Wolthus v. Herse
(1470–71)
Bernt v. der Borg (1471–83)

Johann Freitag v. Loringhoven
(1485–94)
Wolter v. Plettenberg (1494–1535)

Hermann Hasenkamp v.
Brüggeneye (1535–49)
Johann v. Recke (1549–51)
Heinrich v. Gallen (1551–7)
Johann Wilhelm v.
Fürstenburg (1557–9)

Gotthard Kettler (1559–62);
duke of Courland and
Semigallia (1562–87)

NOVGOROD (PRINCES ACCEPTED BY THE CITIZENS)

Yaroslav Vsevolodovich (1223, 1226–8, 1230–36)
Alexander Nevsky (1236–40, 1241–55, 1255–63)
Yaroslav, his brother (1265–7, 1270–71)
Yury of Suzdal (1268–9)
Alexander's sons:
  Dmitri (1272, 1277–81, 1284–93)
  Andrey (1282, 1293–1304)
Michael of Tver (1308–10, 1315–18)
Dmitri of Bryansk (1311–14)
Yury of Moscow (1314–15, 1318–24)
Ivan of Moscow (1329–39), with Narimont/Gleb of Lithuania in the
  western provinces (1333–45)
Simeon of Moscow (1346–53)
Dmitri of Suzdal (1360)
Dmitri Ivanovich of Moscow (1367)

Personal names are given in anglicized forms where they exist, but not necessarily in English forms: e.g. Casimir rather than Kazimierz, but Ivan rather than John. Otherwise, the spelling follows that used nowadays in the languages descended from the languages spoken by the persons named: e.g. Lithuanian rulers get modern Lithuanian spellings, however imaginary, except Vytautas, who is Witold because that is what he is called in English. Low Germans get High-Germanized; Baltic Slavs are left spelt more or less as in their own documents, not as in Polish.

Place names are ticklish, because most of the places mentioned have been claimed and settled by speakers of more than one language at different periods. Again, where anglicized forms exist, they have been used, and, if they happen also to be German forms, the coincidence is unavoidable. Otherwise, towns and villages are spelt as in the languages descended from the languages used by those who ruled them at the time: e.g. Prussian towns and Livonian towns in German, Finnish towns in Swedish. Great rivers get their English names; small rivers and small lakes the names used by the states in which they now lie.

Alternative forms – usually the post-1945 form – are given in brackets.

MONEY

Throughout this period, silver pennies of all sorts circulated in the countries round the Baltic. They were reckoned in notional totals of shillings, or öres, and marks, so that a Danish mark was made up of 8 öres or 240 pennies; a Prussian mark, of 24 scot or 720 pennies; a Riga mark of 36 shillings or 48 öre or 432 pennies. The Lübeck mark of 16 shillings or 192 pennies might equal 3 to 4 shillings sterling c. 1300. But there were also real weights of silver: up to c. 1300 the Gotland mark was predominant and later the mark of Cologne (8¼ oz: 234 g). From

1340 Lübeck minted a gold florin or gulden worth half a silver mark and upwards, which competed with the gold Hungarian ducat thereafter, while the new silver groat of Prague passed at 60 to the Cologne mark. North of Livonia pennies were reckoned by notional bundles of fur, so that 6 or 7 pence made 1 nogata, 20 nogaty 1 grivna, or 4–8 oz silver weight at Novgorod.

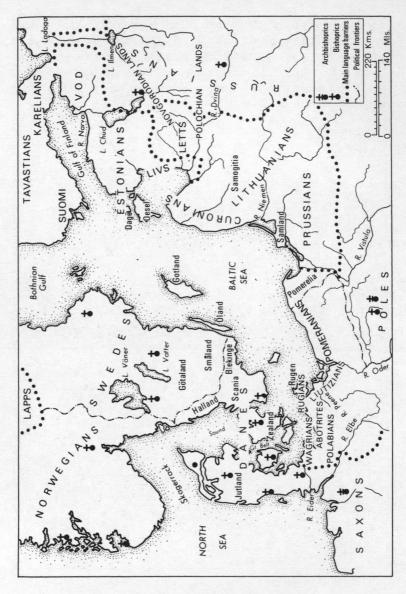

MAP I
The Baltic Region, 1100

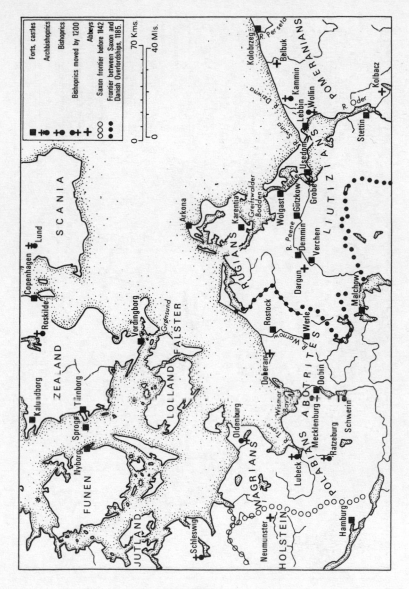

MAP 2

The Wendish Crusades, 1147–85

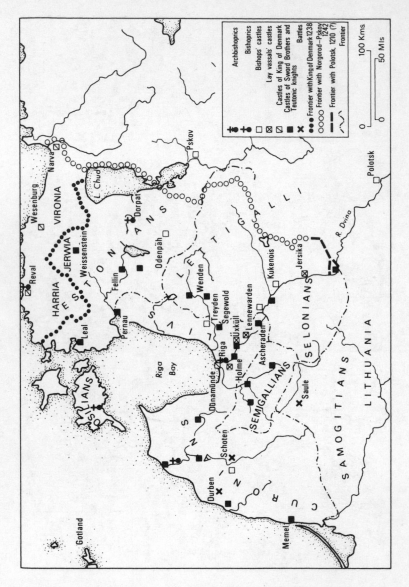

Archbishoprics
Bishoprics
Bishops' castles
Lay vassals' castles
Castles of King of Denmark
Castles of Sword Brothers and Teutonic knights
Battles
Frontier with King of Denmark 1238
Frontier with Novgorod–Pskov 1242
Frontier with Polotsk 1210 (?)
Frontier

100 Kms.
50 Mls

Polotsk

Pskov

Narva

Wesenberg

VIRONIA

L. Chud

Reval

HARRIA

JERWIA

Weissenstein

Dorpat

ESTONIANS

Odenpäh

LETTIGALLI

Leal

Fellin

Pernau

Wenden

Treyden

Segewold

Uxküll

Lennewarden

Kukenois

Jersika

R. Dvina

SELONIANS

LIVONIANS

Riga Bay

Riga

Dünamünde

Holme

Ascheraden

SEMIGALLIANS

LITHUANIA

Saule

LIVONIANS

Schoten

Durben

CURONIANS

SAMOGITIANS

Gotland

Memel

MAP 3
The Livonian and Estonian Crusades, 1198–1290

xxii

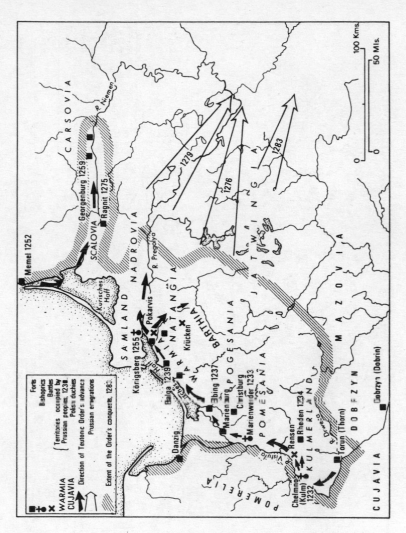

Forts
Bishoprics
Battles
Territories occupied by
Prussian peoples, 1230
Polish duchies
Direction of Teutonic Order's advance
Prussian emigrations

WARMIA
CUJAVIA

Extent of the Order's conquests, 1283

CARSOVIA

R. Niemen

Georgenburg 1259
Ragnit 1275

Memel 1252

SCALOVIA

NADROVIA

SAMLAND

Kurisches
Hoff

R. Pregolya

Pokarvis

Königsberg 1255

Kruicken

ERMLAND

Balga 1239

WARMINATANGIA

BARTHIA

NADROVIA

POGESANIA

Elbing 1237

Christburg

Marienburg

Marienwerder 1233

POMESANIA

Rheden

Rhensen

KULMERLAND

Chelmno
(Kulm)
1232

Danzig

POMERELIA

R. Drwęca

Torun (Thorn)

DOBRZYN

Dabrzyn (Dobrin)

CUJAVIA

MAZOVIA

SUDAVIA / JATWINGIA

1279

1276

1283

100 Kms.

50 Mls.

MAP 4
The Prussian Crusades, 1230–83

xxiii

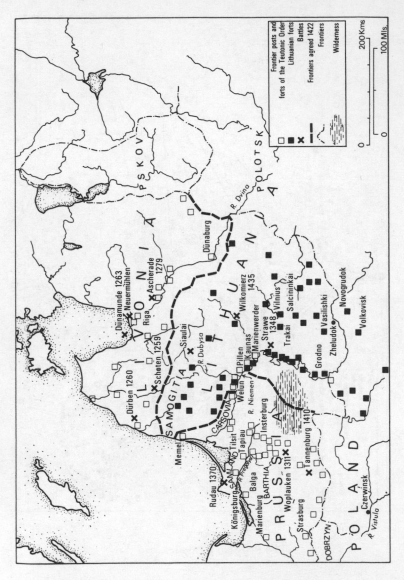

Frontier posts and
forts of the Teutonic Order ■
Lithuanian forts □
Battles ✕
Frontiers agreed 1422
Frontiers
Wilderness

200 Kms
100 Mls

PSKOV

POLOTSK

R. Dvina

LIVONIA

Dünaburg

Neuermühlen
Ascherade 1279
Dünamünde 1263
Riga
Scheten 1259
Siaulai
R. Dubysa
Dirben 1260

LITHUANIA

Wilkomierz
1435
Vilnius
Salcininkai
Vasilishki
Novogrudok
Volkovisk
Zheludok
Grodno
Trakai
Strawe
1348
Kaunas
Marienwerder
Welun
Pillen

SAMOGITIA

Memel

Rudau 1370
Königsberg
Marienburg
Balga
Strasburg
Tilsit
Tapiau
R. Pregora
SAMLAND
Woplauken 1311
BARTHIA
Insterburg
CAPSOVIA
R. Niemen
Tannenburg 1410

PRUSSIA

DOBRZYN

POLAND

Czerwinsk
R. Vistula

MAP 5
The Lithuanian Front, 1280–1435

xxiv

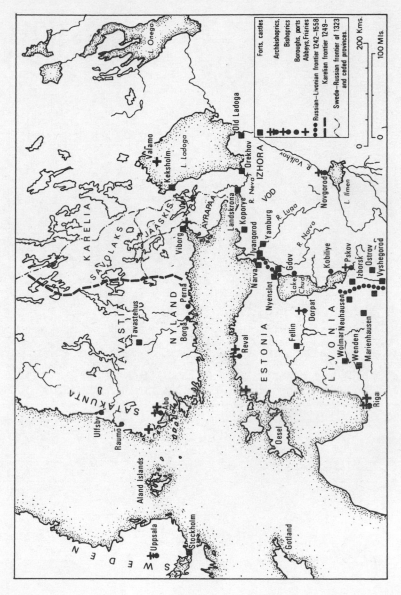

Forts, castles
Archbishoprics
Bishoprics
Boroughs, ports
Abbeys, Friaries
Russian–Livonian frontier 1242–1558
Karelian frontier 1249–
Swede–Russian frontier of 1323
and ceded provinces.

200 Kms.
100 Mls.

L. Onego
Valamo
Keksholm
L. Ladoga
KARELIA
Old Ladoga
Orekhov
R. Neva
IZHORA
R. Volkhov
Novgorod
L. Ilmen
SAVOLAKS
JAASKIS
AYRAPAA
Landskrona
Koporye
Yamburg
R. Luga
VOD
Viborg
R. Narva
Gdov
Kobiliye
Pskov
Izborsk
Ostrov
Vyshegorod
TAVASTIA
NYLAND
Pernö
Nyenslot
Narva
Lake
Chud
Tavastehus
Borgå
Dorpat
Wolmar Neuhausen
LIVONIA
Abo
S A T A K U N T A
Reval
ESTONIA
Fellin
Wenden
Marienhausen
Riga
Ulfsby
Raumo
Oesel
Åland Islands
Uppsala
Stockholm
Gotland
SWEDEN

MAP 6
The Russian Front, 1242–1500

xxv

The crusades to the Holy Land are well known, or, at least, widely heard of. The crusades against the Albigensian heretics, and against the Muslims of Spain, are familiar to students of medieval history. But the crusades of North-East Europe remain outside the scope of most English readers, and are remembered, if at all, as the subject of Eisenstein's haunting essay in nationalist propaganda, the film *Alexander Nevsky*. He is said to have chosen the subject because so little was known about it that the facts were unlikely to interfere with his fictions.

This book is an attempt to describe the struggles waged round the Baltic from the twelfth to the sixteenth centuries in the name of Christianity, and to explain the part they played in the transformation of Northern societies which took place at the same time. There is no room for more. The general history of the Baltic world will only be referred to in so far as it directly concerns the crusades, and the reader will have to look elsewhere for a proper account of the rise and fall of the Scandinavian kingdoms, the East European principalities, the Hanseatic League, the fish trade, the German colonization of the East, the development of cities, churches and shipping.

The starting point comes at the end of the Viking Age, when Scandinavian rulers found themselves shut off from the long-range overseas conquests of the past, and challenged by newly invigorated Slav nations in home waters. After a survey of the Northern world as it was in 1100, the story moves round that world, concentrating in turn on those areas and periods most involved with the crusades: beginning with the south-west Baltic in 1147, when the pope first authorized a Holy War against the heathen of the North, and ending with the Russian frontier at about 1505, when the very last Northern crusading Bull was sent from Rome. In the intervening period the lands the crusaders conquered had been changed almost out of recognition – in population, speech, culture, economy, government. It would not be altogether accurate to say that they had been civilized, or Catholicized, but these phrases express one part of what had happened: the part that involved the coming of the main components of medieval culture from their cradles in France, Italy and the Rhineland, and the development of trade and resources by imported skills. Describing this process in full would require a very different sort of book, and focusing on even the limited topic of the crusading ventures has made it impossible to say much that ought to have been said. I apologize for the gaps, and hope that the reader will recognize, even in the darkest passages, that there is a plan.

Telling this story means keeping at least three balls in the air at the same time: a narrative of campaigns; a survey of ideological developments; and a sketch of political history. The crusades can be understood only in the light of, for example, the Cistercian movement, the rise of the papal monarchy, the mission of the friars, the coming of the Mongol hordes, the growth of the Lithuanian and Muscovite empires, and the aims of the Conciliar movement in the fifteenth century. Dealing briefly with all these big subjects, and linking them to the far north of Europe, has not been easy; and an English reader may well ask, is it worthwhile?

There are several reasons for answering yes. In the first place, the Northern crusades were a part of a wider Western drive, and if that is to be studied it should be studied in full – in the most unlikely places, and in the most peculiar forms. The Holy Wars of the Mediterranean brought about spectacular conquests, and enduring obsessions, but amounted in the end to a sad waste of time, money and life. After 200 years of fighting, colonization, empire-building, missionary work and economic development, the Holy Places remained lost to Christendom. The Saracens won. The two faiths remained invincibly opposed, and if the cultures mingled it was not because the Christians had attempted to conquer the Near East; there were more enduring and less explosive points of contact.

The Northern crusades were less spectacular, and much less expensive, but the changes they helped to bring about lasted for much longer, and have not altogether disappeared today. The southern coast of the Baltic is still German, as far as the Oder; and it is not sixty years since the Estonians and Balts lost the last traces of their German ascendancy and fell under a new one. Western forms of Christianity survive in all the coastlands opposite Scandinavia, and the Finns remain wedded to

Western institutions and tolerant of their Swedish-speaking minority. The reborn republics of Estonia, Latvia and Lithuania look west for support and sympathy. For seven centuries these east-Baltic countries were colonial societies, bearing the mark left by their medieval conquerors whatever outside power tried to annex or change them. If ever the crusades had any lasting effect, it was here, and in Spain.

Secondly, the Northern crusades were a link between this region and Western Europe; they helped bring it into a common 'Latin' civilization. Not the only link, but a steely one, and difficult to ignore. New Catholic societies were founded in hostile and unfamiliar territory. How to run them, defend them and develop them were problems to be met with on all the frontiers of Europe, both in the Middle Ages and later, and they have an interest that is more than local. Here were the great central institutions – churches, manors, castles, boroughs, feudal law-codes, church law, guilds, and parliaments – translated into a cold, dark and inhospitable outer world, forced to adapt, grow, or go under. This was not a promised land, glittering with the allurements of Spain or Palestine; the victories, profits, and the harvest of souls had to be wrested painfully in the face of exceptional obstacles. The study of these institutions on their home ground, or in hot-house colonies, is well established and keenly pursued; but at least as much can be learned about them by looking at them under stress, beyond the pale. The story of the Northern crusades can provide one such insight, and make the picture of medieval culture a little clearer.

And, finally, the story concerns England more than many other countries. Despite the Norman conquest, and the involvement of English kings in France, England was never cut off from the Baltic world, and after 1200 became more and more firmly connected by trade, by political alliances and by the crusading movement. In the 1230s, Henry III granted a special privilege to the association of Baltic traders based on the island of Gotland, and a pension to the Teutonic Knights who had embarked on the conquest of Prussia; while at the same time an English bishop was leading the Swedes to baptize and annex the peoples of central Finland. Between 1329 and 1408 several hundred Englishmen served under the Teutonic Order in the crusade against Lithuania, and in 1399 one of them, Henry Bolingbroke, became King Henry IV of England. Quarrels and treaties between English kings, the Hanseatic League, the Teutonic Order in Prussia and the Scandinavian rulers recurred throughout the fifteenth century, and from the 1340s onwards the cloth-vending English merchant was a regular interloper in Baltic commerce, lured by tar, wax, fur, corn, longbows and timber. What happened in this distant world mattered in England, and mattered all the more by reason of the Northern crusades.

For these reasons the story deserves to be retold. Few subjects have been worked at more exhaustively by continental historians, mostly Germans, during the last 150 years. Few remain more impenetrable to the English reader unfamiliar with German. For the most part, what is presented here amounts to a small scree on the mountainside of German and Scandinavian *Ostforschung*, with a few pebbles from Russia, Poland, Finland and the liberated Baltic republics thrown in. But the reader must be warned that the author has made very little reference to the attitudes and general conclusions of his sources. This may obscure the fact that the issues involved are by no means all dead ones, and that contentiousness remains a dominant characteristic in the field of medieval Baltic history.

It has long been so, because the powers that dominated the region in the nineteenth century tended to justify current policies by rewriting the past, and identify themselves either with the crusaders or with their enemies. Thanks largely to the scholarship of Johannes Voigt, and to the journalism of Treitschke, the Teutonic Knights came to be seen as the harbingers of the Prussian monarchy, the Second Reich and German *Kultur*. 'What thrills us,' declared Treitschke, 'is the profound doctrine of the supreme value of the State, which the Teutonic Knights perhaps proclaimed more loudly and clearly than do any other voices speaking to us from the German past.' 'A spell rises from the ground which was drenched with the noblest German blood,' he intoned; and meanwhile, the foes of German imperialism denounced the Teutonic Knights and praised the rulers of Novgorod and Poland as champions of Slav national-ity. (For example, the great Polish antiquary J. Lelewel, who wrote of the Teutonic Order, 'They created a monastic state, which was an insult both to humanity and to morality.') When nationalist movements got under way in Estonia, Latvia and Lithuania, the polemical chorus grew louder; all that had happened in the distant past of these countries was either indicted as a crime against humanity or sanctified as a 'stupendous and fruitful occurrence'. By no means all historians followed these fashions, but they were so much in accordance with the spirit of the times that millions were affected by them. In 1914 the name 'Tannenberg' was applied to Hindenburg's repulse of the Russian armies in East Prussia, in deliberate 'revenge' for the defeat of the Teutonic Order in 1410; and, later on, Himmler's plan to mould the SS as a reincarnation of that Order proved yet again the irresistible strength of bad history. Many Soviet Balticists wrote under a cloud of pure nineteenth-century Panslavism, merely streaked with dialectical materialism of the same vintage. All the honest and meticulous work of modern scholars has made little impression on the versions of Baltic history commonly received.

This is understandable. The southern and east Baltic coastlands have had more than their share of misery in the twentieth century. The forces of the modern world – fascism, communism, total war, and industrialization – have smashed almost every town from Kiel round to the Arctic Circle at least once within living memory, and have crushed both their servants and their victims with an oafish destructiveness that makes the wars of the Middle Ages seem almost picturesque by comparison. At least 5¼ million inhabitants of these coasts fled or were driven into exile between 1939 and 1950; few will ever go home. The Baltic became a political backwater, but the cost of this tranquillity was an implacable grievance among the millions who have left, and a continuing series of wrongs done to the millions who stayed put. In such a climate, old wounds do not heal, and old quarrels are not forgotten, even by historians. The interpretation of conflicts between Christianity and paganism, between Western Catholicism and Eastern Orthodoxy, between German, Balt and Slav, still rouses passion after the ending of the Cold War.

The work on which the first edition of this book was based was composed in haste over twenty years ago, and the author has had time to repent of the many errors and misconceptions which it contained. The flowering of Baltic and Northern medieval research since then has made it necessary not only to correct mistakes, but to revise almost every conclusion drawn from the evidence. The very notion of 'crusade', as it existed in the 1970s, has been largely discredited, and dark areas of Lithuanian and North Russian history are being continually lit. These developments have resulted in a fuller section on further reading at the end of the book, although work published in English or French is still scarce.

I

NORTH-EAST EUROPE
ON THE EVE OF THE CRUSADES

This is where the great North Russian Plain stops. It ends with a horseshoe of mountains and plateaux, curving round from Finland into the Scandinavian peninsula, and with an interlocking barrier of water, the Baltic Sea. It is the presence of this sea which gives the region its peculiar character; that, and the great rivers which connect it with more temperate climes.

LAND AND SEA

The Baltic was not always a sea. In its underlying ooze there rest the shells of a little mollusc, *Ancylus fluviatilis*, which lives only in fresh water. Seven thousand years ago, the sea-bed was a lake, formed by water draining off the Scandinavian and Central European highlands: 'Lake Ancylus' to geologists. Round it was a marshy plain, stretching from the Atlantic to the Urals, until the ocean drowned the western area to form the North Sea. Then Lake Ancylus drained into this new sea through two channels. One, now blocked, is marked by the great lakes of central Sweden; the other consisted of the passages between the Danish islands and Scania, called the Sound and the Belts. Then the salt water began leaking into the lake through these channels, and it became the sea which has been known since medieval times as the Baltic, after the Belts.

But the salt water has never succeeded in filling it, because of the volume of river water being discharged into it from the south and the east. The Baltic drinks up four huge continental rivers: the Oder and the Vistula, which flow from the Bohemian and Carpathian mountains, 300 miles away, and the Niemen and Dvina, which drain off the Russian Plain. In the north, where the Baltic forks into the Bothnian and Finnish gulfs, the water comes off the Fenno-Scandian highlands in numerous smaller rivers, and remains almost fresh. So you have a brackish, mostly landlocked, half-sea, where the tide ebbs and flows very feebly, intruding sinuously into a region so austere that in very cold winters the ice has been known to cover almost the entire surface of water. As a result of this intrusion the region possesses several natural features which have influenced and partly determined the way local civilizations have developed.

In the first place, the link with the ocean through the Belts has softened the climate so as to make it possible to lead the sort of life we call civilized. If you trace the 60th parallel, which bisects the Baltic, round the world, you will go through Siberia, Yakutsk, Kamchatka, Alaska, Hudson's Bay – horrible places where until the nineteenth century no one was able to survive according to the rules of European (that is, Mediterranean) culture; and the sad story of the Norse colonies on Greenland shows what happened when they tried. Yet east of the Sound and the Scandinavian mountains there were peoples who were already recognizable members of the European family in the ninth century. They were enjoying a privileged climate, however harsh by Mediterranean standards. Thanks to their sea, they could raise crops, keep cattle, and live in homesteads and villages right up to the Arctic Circle.

At the same time, they lived on the edge of an intensely cold area, where animal life has to be thickly furred, and where large tracts of land are useless for agriculture; only the nomad can live there, and when the agriculturalists pushed north they had to learn some of the arts of survival in a cold climate from the hunters and gatherers who were there first. The Baltic provided easy access to these regions in summer, but the newcomers could only go so far, and then they had to stop or change their ways.

Climate made a frontier. In the early Middle Ages it ringed the Gulf of Bothnia, about a hundred miles from the coasts of northern Sweden and northern Finland. To the west it doubled back up the 'Keel' of high mountains in Norway to the Arctic Ocean; to the east it struck south-east to the tip of Lake Ladoga, then on across the North Russian Plain. On one side of this line, human existence depended on the plough and the tilled field and the grass meadow; on the other, the area called Finnmark by the Norse, it was the skills of huntsman, trapper, and herdsman which counted. Up there – or down there, since Bothnian means 'bottom', both to Finns and to Swedes – everything was different: there were no fixed villages, no harvests, no wheels, no kingdoms and no churches. The people moved with their reindeer and portable huts across areas that could not be fitted into political geography until modern times; they were Lapps, for the most part, with trading and hunting parties of Norwegians, Swedes and Finns moving among them in winter, and bargaining for their furs, their feathers and their children – or robbing them, for it was the southerners who were the human wolves of the sub-Arctic. The Vikings knew these wanderers well, and the authors of the sagas sometimes sent their heroes skiing across the Far North to do battle or business with the nomads or with other interloping frontiersmen; but they were never at home in Finnmark, and were convinced that the inhabitants were magicians, who could control the weather, change their shapes, and bring the dead back to life. Less northerly medieval writers peopled the Far North with freaks: amazons who made themselves pregnant by sipping the water and produced dog-headed male children, sold yapping on the Russian slave-market; white-headed savages defended by monstrous hounds; green men who lived a hundred years; and cannibals. Thus Adam of Bremen, in the 1070s; not until 1555, when the exiled Swede Olaus Magnus published his work *Historia de gentibus septentrionalibus* ('History of the Northern Peoples') at Rome, was educated Europe given a credible account of the Lapps.

The climatic frontier was a barrier to understanding, because those who lived beyond it had worked out a system of survival that meant organizing their lives in ways outsiders found alien. Small groups of families, amounting to 100–150 souls, would lay claim to a 'home', or *sit*, which consisted of a route and its resources between summer and winter camps. The reindeer-droving, trapping, fishing and fathering along the route were regulated by a council of heads of families, the *naraz*, and the adjustment of boundaries between each *sit* was left to a meeting of delegates from each *naraz* of the adjacent groups. Some fisheries and hunting-grounds would be exploited by teams from more than one *sit*, and such joint enterprises would establish bonds between the family groups they came from, but the cohesion was weak. Outsiders liked to think of kings, strongholds and armies among the Lapps, but they were using the wrong words; it was too difficult to explain.

However, the settled communities living on the edge of the frontier were deeply affected by the closeness of the alien world. It was a constant source both of profit and of danger: of profit, through trade and the direct tapping of animal resources by fishers and hunters who had learned their skills from the nomads; of danger, through hard winters that led to crop failures and death by starvation, and through depredations on their livestock by bears, wolves and smaller beasts of prey. In the Novgorod Chronicle we read how this often prosperous city too near the edge of the wild was brought to its knees by starvation again and again – in 1128, for example, when last year's frost had killed the winter corn:

This year it was cruel; three bushels of rye cost half a pound of silver; the people ate lime-tree leaves, birch-bark, pounded wood-pulp mixed with husks and straw; some ate buttercups, moss, horseflesh; and thus many dropped down from hunger, and their corpses were in the streets, in the market-place, and on the roads and everywhere. They hired hirelings to carry the dead out of the town; the serfs could not go out; woe and misery on all. Fathers and mothers would put their children into boats as a gift to merchants, or else put them to death; and others dispersed over foreign lands.[1]

It was just as bad in 1230, when 3030 were alleged to have died of starvation, out of a population that cannot have exceeded 5000, and the chronicler related how

some of the common people killed the living and ate them; others cut up dead flesh and corpses and ate them; others ate horseflesh, dogs and cats; but to those they found in such acts they did this – some they burned with fire, others they cut to pieces, and others they hanged. Some fed on moss, snails, pine-bark, lime-bark, lime- and elm-tree leaves, and whatever each could think of ... There was no kindness among us, but misery and unhappiness; in the streets unkindness one to another, at home anguish, seeing children crying for bread and others dying. And we were buying a loaf for a quarter of a pound of silver and more, and a quarter of a barrel of rye for a quarter of a pound of silver.[2]

And in 1413–14 the roving Burgundian knight Ghillebert de Lannoy discovered that 'in winter, no foodstuffs come to the market of Novgorod the Great, be it fish, pork, or mutton, and no game, because everything is dead and frozen'.[3]

It could be just as bad in all the Northern countries: the Baltic climate had brought grain-eating peoples to live on the edge of destruction. On the other hand, it was a region which was not ignored by the rest of Europe – again, thanks to its sea.

For the draining into the Baltic of five great rivers brought immense tracts of southern and eastern territory within reach of the Far North. In the Middle Ages, the Saxon marches of Brandenburg, Meissen and Lusatia, the Polish principalities and duchies of Silesia, and the Bohemian land of Moravia were all linked to the Baltic by the Oder. There were repeated contacts. For the Saxon princes it was a matter of expansion and alliance. The margrave of Brandenburg was trying to seize Stettin as early as 1147, and was raiding the surrounding territories in the 1190s; the duke of Saxony established a colony at Lübeck in 1158, and married two of his children to the offspring of the Danish king; the margrave of Meissen married his daughter to the king of Denmark in 1152. The bishop of Moravia went north to preach to Baltic Slavs in 1147, and the Silesian princes became regular crusaders in the ensuing two centuries. For the river was an economic artery, and the more of it a ruler controlled, the richer he got; the more he competed for power and wealth along its sources and tributaries, the more he was interested in the affairs of those who lived beyond its mouth.

The Vistula brought in the Polish rulers at an early date: Boleslaw the Terrible was already hoping to control its estuary at the turn of the tenth century, and this ambition remained a cardinal point in the policy of all his more active successors, even though the centre of their power lay hundreds of miles upstream, at Cracow on the edge of the Carpathians. But the Vistula also involved the Russian principality of Volhynia, and the world of the steppe; in 1241 it even brought an army of Mongols into the forests of Prussia.

Similarly, the Niemen involved the Russians of Minsk, as well as the Lithuanians, the Dvina brought in Polotsk, and the Lovat–Volkhov–Lake-Ladoga–Neva waterway brought in the whole area of Novgorod's influence, stretching to the Urals. The prime importance of river communications throughout Russia meant that here porterages between tributary streams extended the 'human catchment area' of the Baltic for immense distances – to the Arctic Ocean via the northern Dvina, to the Black Sea via the Dnieper, and to the Caspian via the Volga. All over this network Baltic commodities flowed outwards, and goods scarce in the North flowed in, and princes and merchants concerned themselves with what was going on in the region where the rivers ended. The prince of Polotsk had a marriage alliance with the king of Denmark in the twelfth century; the prince of Smolensk made a treaty with the merchants of Riga and Gotland in 1229; and with the rise of Moscow in the fifteenth century her landlocked rulers were irresistibly drawn to the Gulf of Finland and the Bay of Riga. By 1555, according to Olaus Magnus, 'Muscovite Russian' was one of the five current languages of the sub-Arctic world – like German.

The basins from which the great rivers flowed were penetrated by Latin and Byzantine civilizations far earlier than was the Baltic coast, and the differences between upriver and downriver societies were never greater than in the early Middle Ages. River contacts reflected the difference. Attempts at exploitation, conversion, conquest, even assimilation were added to the exchange of goods, immigration of colonists, and casual raids, which had been going on since Neolithic times. But it was the flow of water that made it all possible.

This leads to a third sea-determined constant of Baltic culture. The mixing of fresh and salt water in a large sheltered pool creates conditions that are very congenial to fish, and to fishermen. In spring, the Baltic becomes an inviting soup of plankton. Water from the middle of the North Sea flows in along the bottom and brings in the mackerel about May – in the Middle Ages, accompanied by seals, bigger fish and the occasional whale. Bank water, from the Dutch and German flats, comes in above this, and the herring ride with it. Until the fifteenth century they arrived in April or May, to spawn, and they stayed until November. The top layer of water, the brackish Baltic current, attracts salmon and eels from the rivers; and all the lakes and waterways of the surrounding countries once teemed with every kind of freshwater fish, from perch to pike. Olaus Magnus devoted a whole book within his work to fish, and another to monstrous fish, and all throughout the Middle Ages the catching, processing and vending or eating of these creatures played a large and growing part in the lives of the Northern peoples, radically affecting their economics and politics.

According to a fable in Knytlinga Saga (ch. 28) the harsh king Canute IV of Denmark (see below, p. 26) had tamed his Scanian subjects by threatening to take away their fishing rights in the sound, even before 1086. They submitted because they could not live without the herring; and by c. 1250, when the saga was written, that was a credible story. However, archaeology reveals a comparatively low fish consumption in Viking Age sites round the Baltic (compared with Norway), as well as rather sparse coastal settlement, and no sign of 'fishing communities', despite many hooks and traps. In the twelfth century and later, there was a change: stretches of coast in the western Baltic were transformed every summer by the setting up of bothies and tents in the temporary camps known as *fiskelejer*, where fishermen, driers, merchants and king's men came together and held markets. The most famous of these were situated on the south-western tip of Scania, at Skanör and Falsterbo, and in the thirteenth to fifteenth centuries they formed a virtually independent commonwealth, ruled by their own customs and laws and attracting buyers from all over Europe. The king of Denmark and his archbishop took their cut, and left the fishermen and merchants to run their own business; and meanwhile, every spring, the herring migrated south through the Sound in masses so dense that at times a man had only to scoop them out of the water in a pail.

Other fishing methods had changed the look of river mouths and shallow coastal waters. Off Scandinavian shores there were 'eel-yards', lines of stakes supporting platforms from which the eel-catcher could set and manage his traps, and herring-weirs, or enclosures of stakes which could be made secure by sealing them with nets or wickerwork (there is a surviving example at Kappeln). In the running water of the great Slav river mouths there were fish-fences and weirs (*jazy*) so numerous that the Danish raiding fleets of the 1160s and 1170s were continually obstructed by them, and destroyed them as they advanced; in Danish and Swedish rivers there were V-shaped salmon-traps (*laxakar*).

The organization and development of fisheries was a matter of politics. It meant competitive exploitation of water resources and manpower, and here the princes and the landowners stepped in; already in the twelfth century the *piscatura* was a form of lordship along the coast, on rivers and lakes, jealously guarded against encroachments by poachers, and protected from overfishing by bans on certain kinds of net. The fish itself was an acceptable token of power, and could be paid in tribute or tithe; the islanders of Öland, off south-east Sweden, made their sole acknowledgement of loyalty to the king at Uppsala by sending him an annual present of herring, and in the 1170s Bishop Absalon of Roskilde let the Slavs of Rügen present him with a single fish in recognition of his sea-patrols, which enabled them to bring in their catch unmolested. When the warriors of the king of Poland reached the Pomeranian coast in 1107 they sang of their conquest in these terms:

> Salted fish and stinking, once they brought us from afar,
> Now the boys have caught 'em fresh, and all alive they are![4]

Thus the introduction of new fishing and preserving methods, and the rise and fall of demand on the international market, were matters of life and death to the Northern peoples – for Lapps, Finns, Balts and, later on, Germans were as concerned in the business as Scandinavians and Slavs.

The last point worth stressing in this survey of the natural peculiarities of the North concerns transport and communication; and for the most part that meant boats.

It was possible to move over North-East Europe by land, even at this date, but the fewness and badness of the trackways made it slow going and left large tracts of country out of reach. In the 1070s Adam of Bremen reckoned that the overland journey from Hamburg to Wollin took a week; it was something over 200 miles. The sea-voyage from Oldenburg to Novgorod was five times as far, and was expected to take only twice as long. If you went from Denmark to Sigtuna, in eastern Sweden, and took the land-route, the journey was estimated at four weeks; by sea, five days. In winter the difference might be more, or less, depending on whether the snow was deep – since it was then possible to take short-cuts across rivers and lakes, and the traveller might well be equipped with skis or a sledge; but, on the whole, nobody travelled in winter unless he had to, or was drawn by the profits of raiding or hunting. May to October were the months for moving, and during that period the sea was preferable to the land.

It was a very navigable sea, once the ice melted. Nowadays Danish coastal waters freeze only one winter in three, and never for longer than three winter months. The average duration of ice in south-Baltic harbours varies from three days in Flensburg Fjord to three weeks at Stralsund. Riga and St Petersburg are closed by ice about six months a year, the Estonian ports about four, like the Bothnian coast. Then the good weather begins, with easterly winds frequent from April to midsummer, and prevailing Westerlies from July to September. The mariner then faces a long stretch of water, never more than 200 miles across, along which his course is made easy by numerous islands and shallow anchorages.

The art of navigation was the art of staying within sight of the coast, knowing the landmarks and taking soundings of dangerous shoals; above all, of reading weather from the sky. Compasses were not used in the Baltic until the sixteenth century, and were hardly needed then, except by strangers, for the previous 300 years had seen the coastline punctuated with tall spires and crosses, immediately recognizable ten miles out to sea, and the difficult channels marked out by 'booms' and stakes. The dangers were dense fogs, sudden high winds, and pirates; and the proximity of shelter made it easier to avoid at least the first two of these than in the North Sea, the Channel or the Mediterranean.

The earliest Baltic sailors were probably the Finns, who erected birch-bushes in skin boats to catch the wind. The Germanic peoples developed the techniques of oar and sail, until the 'Viking ship' became the dominant sea transport over the whole of Northern Europe, both for warriors and for goods. Whoever controlled the men who knew how to build and manage such craft got wealth and power; and from the ninth to the eleventh century Viking leaders tended to apply this rule in the regions where wealth and power were greatest: the British Isles, Western Europe and the Russian riverways. By 1100 the opportunities for this kind of adventure were much reduced, but, within the Baltic region, power and the warship still went together, and a ruler's importance depended on the size of his fleet. The kings of the Danes and Swedes had attempted to provide themselves with vessels by imposing military duty on their more powerful subjects. They met with little success, and had to appeal for the crews of their raiding fleets. After c. 1170 Danish kings relied on a public contribution by ship-districts to man defensive levy-fleets, and for this the whole kingdom was assessed at some 860 ships. No more than 250 could be expected for offensive campaigns.[5]

However, there were many varieties of ship, and each one brought a different reward to its owner and crew, and influenced social organization in a particular way. There were at least two classes of warship: the large sixty-oar 'dragon', or *skeiðr*, which the Norwegians had perfected, and which was usually too deep in the water for effective use in shallow seas and river wars, and the ordinary forty-oar levy ship, *snekke* to the Danes, *snækkja* to the Swedes, which the Slavs built somewhat lighter and lower than the Scandinavians. These needed crews of trained warriors, provisions for overseas expeditions, and a complicated technique of building and maintenance; therefore the kings and pirate chiefs who controlled them had to be landowners, lords of retinues, the masters of populous communities. Their ships had room on board for slaves, cattle and loot, but it was restricted, and such cargoes limited the movements of the crew. When it came to trading, there was another kind of ship, long, but wide and deep amidships, with fewer or no oarsmen, relying on wind power – the *byrthing*. Behind the *byrthing* was the partnership of two or more owners, pooling their resources and risking shipwreck and piracy for gain; and in the twelfth century the makers of such partnerships appear to have been associating into guilds and companies to protect themselves against a hostile world. The men of Gotland, or those who enriched themselves by trade, ran their island through an association of this kind, without the interference of the Swedish king; in the 1150s the landowners and merchants of Zealand safeguarded themselves from piracy by maintaining a small fleet of raiders under a privateer called Wedeman. The vulnerability of the *byrthing* made self-help a necessity, until princes could be got to assume responsibility for its safety.

Then there were the small ships, a whole variety of types used by families or groups of neighbours for raiding, ferrying, trading, fishing and transport: the four- to fifteen-oared *skude* of the Danes, a keeled vessel that could accompany warships, carry bowmen, scout upriver, or be used for small-scale depredation on its own; the flat-bottomed *pram* of the Slavs, for riding over marshes and lakes – not found in early sources, but soon to be imitated all over the Baltic; the small keeled sailing-boat that plied between villages with local produce; the *haapar*, built for speed and resilience on the rivers flowing into the Bothnian Gulf, held together with green roots, poplar twigs and deer sinews; the *strug* and *ushkui* of the Russian rivers; and the *bolskip*, the *skute* and the *kane*, which carried merchandise up and down the Peene. For every shore- and river-dweller in North-East Europe, the boat was a vital part of his life and livelihood; changes in the technique of boat-building, and in the balance of sea-power, would have momentous effects.

'Sea-power' is the wrong term. It has come to mean the hegemony that depends on the naval power of a state; but what concerned the medieval North was more like ship- or boat-power, the ability of any group, from an individual to an association of traders or a king, to achieve a variety of ends through ownership or control of the appropriate type of craft. At no time could a fleet of big warships dominate the whole range of Northern waterways; at most they could patrol certain areas, routes and harbours, such as when Canute the Great and Valdemar the Great policed the waters of Denmark, but such periods of limited sea-power were exceptional. At most times, pirates, levy-ships, slavers, traders, fishers and river transports carried on their various businesses in a state of wary co-existence, with battles, pursuits and deals recurring as occasion served. In the 1070s the king of Denmark had an arrangement with the pirates who infested the Great Belt: they robbed, he took a cut and looked the other way. At the turn of the fourteenth century things were not much better: the queen of Denmark waged open war with an association of pirates based on the north German coast, the *Vitalienbrüder*, but Danish, Swedish and Mecklenburg landowners connived at their robberies and bought and sold with them. Nobody could rule the waves when nobody could rule more than a share of the coasts and rivers that hemmed them in so closely.

In these various ways, the conjunction of a temperate sea and intractable hinterlands of forest, mountain and bog, of mild summers and dreadful winters, of nomad and farmer, had given the Baltic and North-Eastern world of the early Middle Ages a character of its own, which marked it off from other regions and compelled the people who lived there to work, eat, fight and even think in similar fashions. It was a world to some extent separated from others by natural barriers, although, even in the case of the brutal climatic frontier, there was a way in and out for those who knew the rules. To the south, east and west, access was more open, but there were still difficulties, and these difficulties could be greatly heightened by peoples interested in keeping intruders out.

The coastal areas of the North German Plain, for example, were detached from the big rivers that ran through them, and riddled with small streams flowing directly into the sea from sodden infertile plateaux – the Mecklenburg lakes, the Masurian lakes and the bogs of Hither Pomerania. Here are the Danes trying to get through the 'wide, obstructive and filthy marsh' north of Demmin in 1171, as described by Saxo Grammaticus:

Its surface was covered by a thin layer of turf, and, while it could support grass, it was so soft underfoot that it swallowed up those who trod there. Sinking deep into the slime, they went down into the muddy depths of a foul morass ... To ease their progress, and avoid becoming exhausted, the cavalry then took off their armour, and began leading them from the front. And when the horses got bogged down too deeply, they hauled them out, and when the men sank as they led them along, they kept themselves upright by holding on to their manes; and they crossed the little streams, which meandered about the marsh in great numbers, on wattles of woven reeds ... and, while the horses were pulling themselves out of the hollows into which they sank, now and then they crushed under their hooves one of the men who were leading them. The king himself, who had thrown off everything except the shirt next to his body, and was carried on the shoulders of two knights, hardly managed to escape from the soft mud. Seldom has Danish valour sweated more![6]

South of these marshes, and south of the barren highlands of Outer Pomerania, stretches a belt of sandy forest and heathland, also interspersed with lakes and bogs, leached, acid and intractable. It runs from the North Sea to the Vistula, and baffled the cultivator until modern times. The missionary Otto of Bamberg crossed it on his way to the coast in 1124 and 1127. On the first occasion, going from Poznan to Pyrzyce, his disciple Herbord claimed that.

the route is as hard to describe as it was to follow. For no mortal man had been able to get through this forest, until in recent years ... the duke [of Poland] had blazed a trail for himself and his army with lopped and marked trees. We kept to these marks, but it took us all of six days to get through the wood and rest on the banks of the river which is the Pomeranian frontier, and it was very hard going, on account of various snakes and huge wild beasts, and troublesome cranes that were nesting in the branches of the trees and tormented us with their croaking and flapping, and patches of bog which hindered our waggons and carts.[7]

That was about ninety miles in six days; and in 1127 Otto took five days covering the thirty-five miles between Havelburg and Lake Müritz. It was not surprising that most travellers kept to the riverbanks, or went by boat.

That was Slav country, and its western limit was marked very firmly, at least between the ninth century and the 1140s, by the *Limes Saxonicus*, a no-man's-land of dense forest and hedges which covered the sixty miles between Kiel Fjord and Lauenburg on the Elbe. Weak sections could be manned from the nearest villages to keep out raiders, and, while merchants and armies could get through, it was never a safe journey as long as this remained a political barrier.

Also to the west, if you came by land, there was an ancient trackway running from Saxony northwards up the length of Jutland to the Limfjord; this was the *ochsenweg* or *Hærvej*, and it was used every now and then by invaders from the south who sought to conquer the Northern world. However, since the eighth century there had been an earth-wall, extending west from Schleswig, which could be used to block this entrance; here the track had to keep to a narrow neck of dry land. After Henry the Lion had ridden through with a Saxon army for a brief raid in 1157, King Valdemar of Denmark began lengthening and strengthening this defence with a mighty brick wall, and by the end of the century his sons had secured control of the roads that led to it, down to Hamburg and Lübeck.

The western approaches by sea – the Skagerrak, Kattegat, Belts and Sound – could not be sealed off, even by the forts at Nyborg, Sprogø and Copenhagen built in Valdemar's reign, but the terrors of the North Sea and the treacherous sandbanks of the north Jutland coast still kept most English, Flemish and French mariners at a distance in the early Middle Ages; they preferred to anchor at Ribe, on the west coast of Jutland, or unload at Hollingstedt, up the Eider. Norwegian shipping was more adventurous, and had long formed part of normal Baltic traffic; but the kings of the Danes made it their business to deter the raids on Danish islands which had enriched so many Norwegians in Viking times, and they appear to have met with success in the twelfth century.

To the east, the obstacle was mainly forest, which covered thousands of square miles between the Vistula and the Gulf of Finland and clogged the drainage of thousands more. Swedes had penetrated this region by navigating the rivers, and had set up a network of colonies and tribute-collecting chieftaincies stretching as far south as the Steppe; these became the Russian city-states. By 1100, the Rus blocked the way east for Scandinavians other than merchants and mercenaries, and were sending raids westwards, towards the Baltic coastlands. Russian traders came to Gotland, Wollin, and Schleswig; but centuries of water-borne traffic had caused no large immigration from the East.

Nature thus presented certain obstacles to the intruder into this world. They were not insuperable; but they needed labour and organization to be overcome, and in the early twelfth century no outside invader or settler had been able to secure a permanent foothold for six hundred years. Ever since Roman times, the Baltic region had been an exporter rather than an importer of men.

PEOPLES

The peoples settled in North-East Europe *c.* 1100 can be divided into four main groups by language: Norse speakers, Slavs, Balts, and Finno-Ugrians. The first three spoke languages of the Indo-European family, the last are classified as Uralian. Affinity of speech within these groups never kept them apart or led their components to merge with each other; in economic and political matters, their culture was not much affected by such differences. Nevertheless, each group seems to have had certain distinctive characteristics shared by its component peoples in matters of social organization, religion, diet and dress, and these seem to provide a fair-enough principle of arrangement. This is to walk in the footprints of the first great Northern geographer, Adam of Bremen, the schoolmaster to the cathedral community of the metropolitan of the North, who was writing his *Gesta Hammaburgensis ecclesiae pontificum* ('History of the Archbishops of Hamburg') in the 1070s, and collecting much of his information first-hand – from King Sweyn II of Denmark, among others.

The first group (called Scandinavian) consisted of the people called Swedes, Götar and Danes, who spoke a variety of languages usually lumped together as 'East Norse'; and the Norwegians, the 'West Norse' speakers. In those days the Norwegians occupied the coastlands of what is now Norway, as far north as the Lofoten Islands; and in addition, to the south, the shores of the Kattegat down to where Gothenburg now stands were theirs. They played a part in Baltic affairs both by trekking over the mountains into Lapland and by sailing in from the west; but the bulk of the population lived away from the inland sea, on the Atlantic side of the dividing central Scandinavian range they called 'the Keel', and during this period were more involved with the British Isles, the Faroes, Iceland and Greenland than with the great North-East. The events of the next 300 years were to draw them increasingly away from the West, and more deeply involve them in the politics of Danes, Germans and Swedes, but for the time being they can be left to one side.

The Swedes and Götar, who had been joined into one commonwealth for centuries, were by contrast almost wholly east-facing; they had no western coastline until the thirteenth century, only an upriver port at Gamla Lödöse, and their coastline on the other side began round Kalmar and went north as far as the Bothnian Gulf. Inland, the Swedes were settled most thickly in the area of modern Stockholm and Lake Mälar; the Götar in the area of the two great lakes Vätter and Väner. South of them there was a mountainous and forested region called Småland, where settlements were very sparse and political affiliations somewhat unclear, and the coastal district called Blekinge, over which the king of Denmark had had some sort of authority since the time of Old Canute – which was how Canute 'the Great' was usually described. Then came the Danes: the Scanians and Halländingar, inhabiting the fertile and temperate coastal valleys of what is now south-west Sweden; the Danes of the islands, of whom the most numerous were the Zealanders; and the Jutlanders, who occupied the whole peninsula down to the Eider and Kiel Fjord.

Most Danes and Swedes were peasants, living in small rural communities, raising grain crops – chiefly barley, sometimes wheat, oats and rye – and keeping cattle, swine and ponies. The pattern of agriculture varied, but on the whole the resources of a village were shared out in much the same way as you would find in southern England at this period: two- or three-field crop-rotation, cleared grazing land in commons, fenced or unfenced according to season, with collective responsibility for keeping boundaries and respecting local custom. Outside this pattern there were the 'fringemen', who lived off the forest, coast and mountain by fishing, trapping, hunting and mining, and the burghers – artisans, tradesmen and innkeepers settled in boroughs and ports. This was the working population.

Foreign observers, such as Adam of Bremen, were moderately impressed by the prosperity attained at least in Denmark: they could see abundance of corn, cattle, horses and butter, and tall, well-favoured people, if somewhat uncouth and boozy. However, medieval writers tended to judge a nation's prosperity by the level and style of the consumption of its ruling class, and they have to be corrected by referring to other standards. The archaeology of medieval Danish villages reveals little trace of fatness: the villagers were living close to starvation, in the shadow of the three great menaces of the time – bad years, bad health and greedy landlords. For the peasants were to a large extent unfree:

either thralls, or villeins owing service to lords or poor men working for others.

The village and its inhabitants were sometimes owned by one man; sometimes the economic units into which its resources were divided – the *bøl* – were separately owned, or halved and quartered among owners; but in any case it was landownership, great or small, which sorted people out. All over the fertile districts of Denmark and Sweden villages were overlooked from far or near by the ring-fence and high-roofed hall of the landowner or bailiff, who took some of what the others could raise, and by the rather similar-looking church, which took a little more. In other places, the village freemen kept the biggest share of the community's land in their own hands, and set their few slaves or hired men to work it. Out in the woods, particularly in Sweden, there were many communities of free peasants who both ploughed for themselves and carried the sword or spear of respectability; but, on the whole, where there was a freeman, there was also a slave. And, despite the huge differences in wealth between poor and rich freemen – between the owner of half a *bøl*, and the owner of 500 *bøl*, as we find in twelfth-century Denmark – they shared a legal status: they were the *bøndær* ('dwellers, inhabitors'), who made up the political nation, whose forebears had done well from military service, piracy, trade or, perhaps, good husbandry.

Most Danish and Swedish *bøndær* owed some form of allegiance or respect to the powerful dynasties, the kingly lines, which personified the peoples and exercised public authority as well as owning private wealth. They were newly rich families which had clothed themselves in royal traditions that went back to the legendary past; the Knytlings of Denmark copied English and German rulers. However, despite the importance of the kings, for most practical purposes the *bøndær* were self-governing, in peace if not in war. Each local district (*herred* in Denmark, *hundrad* in Sweden) was run by an assembly of landowners, the *ting* or thing, which could meet as often as once a week; and each province, group of *herreder* or island lay under the jurisdiction of a larger assembly, meeting perhaps twice a year, the *landsting*.

The *landstinge* were used by kings as military musters, and political councils, and the smaller assemblies were expected to hear the king's representative and follow him to war or peace-keeping duty, but in both cases the *ting* was normally ruled by local opinion and local grandees, the 'honourable' men. Social stability rested on these sessions – peace between kin-groups, collective intimidation of the unfree, pursuit of the outlaw, fair dealing in trade, demarcation of boundaries, the deterring of intruders. And, when the king died, plenary gatherings of the *bondær* assembled to acclaim or reject members of the royal families with a claim to succeed – even if this sometimes only meant ratifying, or anticipating, the verdict of battle. In the early twelfth century the freeman and his lord were still running Denmark and Sweden without much interference from above, and kings who fell foul of assemblies were badly treated. In 1131 the son and heir of King Nicholas of Denmark was accused of murder and publicly defamed by the *ting* at Ringsted, and the King had to exile him to Sweden to avoid bloodshed; in 1153 Sweyn III was assailed by jeers, hisses and stones at the Scanian *landsting*.[8] In Sweden it was worse: if the king wanted to attend an assembly among the Götar, he had to be formally inducted, and when King Ragnwald rode up unasked to the *ting* at Karlaby in the 1120s he met 'a shameful death'.[9] However, times were changing; kings were growing stronger.

They were much richer than other landowners. In both countries they held accumulations of royal estates and the right to stipulated amounts of food, drink, silver and transport in each district. They could ride or row from place to place with armed retinues, 'eating their way round their kingdoms', and spending the great festivals at their larger halls entertaining the great men; the gluttony and drunkenness of which they and the Slavic princes were accused must have been in part a consequence of this form of social control. In addition, the Danish king had rights over his burghers – mint money, a 'midsummer-geld' from town property-owners, tolls, protection money from guilds and foreigners – plus a right to take fines from certain kinds of malefactor, a right to appropriate wrecks on the kingdom's shores, and rights over various natural resources; and he took the inheritances of heirless men. All this brought in wealth, and his position was further strengthened by a qualified right of command over the two national organizations which all men were bound to obey: the *lething*, or military levy, and the Church. The *lething* has been mentioned above (p. 15), and its working will be described below. The Church had taken a long time to get established (*c.* 815 to *c.* 1020), but by the 1070s there were seven bishops carrying out their duties under the protection of the Danish king, and these duties included attendance at local assemblies, helping in local defence and assisting the ruler with advice, hospitality, writing and prayer. Until

1103 they acknowledged the archbishop of Hamburg–Bremen as their spiritual overlord, although it was the king who put them into their sees; after 1103 the bishop of Lund became metropolitan archbishop of the Scandinavian churches, and the king of Denmark had a *Reichskirche* of his own, like the Emperor.

Denmark was beginning to look like the other kingdoms of Latin Christendom, and under the rule of Nicholas (1104–34) and Valdemar I (1157–82) the resemblance was to become much more marked. The first charters and stone churches had appeared in the 1070s; the first monastery shortly afterwards. Pope Gregory VII had written to the Northern kings as members of the Christian commonwealth, and Paschal II recognized the murdered Canute IV (d. 1086) as a martyr for the Catholic faith. St Canute's brother, Eric I, went on a pilgrimage to Byzantium, and the great nobles were following the example of the kings in endowing churches; sometimes they became bishops, and it was no longer necessary to import most of the senior clergy from Saxony or England. In the tenth century the kings had accepted the name of 'Christian' on behalf of their subjects; now this inoculation had taken effect.

The process of assimilation to Western models took longer among the Swedes – there was a time-lag of about fifty years – but it went in the same direction. The last openly heathen king died at the end of the eleventh century, and until then the shrine of the old god Frey stayed open at Uppsala; the backwoodsmen of Småland were said to have been untouched by Christianity in the 1120s, and pockets of resistance survived much longer in other remote areas. However, in about 1120 a papal scribe was able to list seven out of the nine main districts of Sweden as bishoprics, and in 1164 the kingdom was granted an archbishop of its own, albeit subject to Lund. The consolidation of royal power also took longer – partly as a result of the weakness of the Church, partly because of the rivalry between competing dynasties between 1156 and 1250, and at first because of the continuing division between Swedes and Götar. Sparser settlement, poorer communications, colder winters and huger forests made control harder to establish; but the essentials were there.

Christianity had not pacified these peoples. They were still dominated by fighters, brought up to kill and be killed, whether they lived as princes, landowners or swordsmen; and between the fighting classes and the rest there was a barrier of birth, breeding and outlook reinforced by heroic tradition and law. 'By law shall the land be built' ran the new saying, but the landowners made, remembered and administered the law, and foreigners found it brutal and un-Christian. When Canute IV had tried to soften it in the 1080s, he had met with fierce hostility; it was not until the second half of the twelfth century that it could be written down and humanized to some extent. It was not solely a matter of legalized oppression. The outrageous offender, even if he were rich, could be outlawed – as with King Nicholas's son in 1131; the king had an interest in settling cases of open violence and feud, since he stood to gain his fine; and the procedures by which feud, pursuit of stolen goods, and inheritance could be carried on, were governed by notions of right. Until the 1130s there were no walled towns, private fortifications or extensive private jurisdictions to favour the strong yet further. Church law had to be modified and justified before it became binding in the courts for the Scandinavians, who had accepted Christ without rejecting their ancestral voices. They showed it in many ways. They persisted in using the old names: among the Danes, Sven, Erik, Harald, Aki, Toki, Bovi were still much commoner than Nigles, Pæter, Kristoffer. They listened to the old poems and paid Icelanders to recite. They continued to practise divorce, and, above all, displayed ruthlessness in revenge. Between 1131 and 1135 the numerous Danish royal family was almost wiped out in a war of vendetta, and on one occasion King Eric 'the Unforgettable' is reported to have had eight children, his own nephews and nieces, murdered in cold blood to round off a quarrel with his brother, whom he had already killed;[10] six bishops had died in battle against this Eric, yet he gave land to the canons of Lund and the monks at Ringsted, he was said to rule 'by the favour of divine clemency'[11] and he was reckoned a righteous man by the historian Saxo at the end of the century. Such men worshipped success; Christ would grant it, and give shelter to the blood-stained soul after death, and in return he expected baptism, liberality to his priests, penance, burial in hallowed ground – little more.

Landowners and hired swords who lived by these rules were as much a terror to their neighbours across the Baltic as had been their Viking ancestors, but by 1100 the pattern of their overseas enterprises had changed. In the East there was employment for warriors at the Russian and Byzantine courts, and war-bands continued to take that road; but opportunities for acquiring hegemony and land were fewer. We read of no Swedish kings leading raids into Finland between the 1050s and the 1140s; the Russians kept an increasingly tight hold on the trade-routes and on the tributary peoples who supplied the furs, and the Swede who hoped to make his fortune had either to engage in trade as a merchant or to serve his time as a paid mercenary in the Varangian Guard, along with Danes, Norwegians, Icelanders and Englishmen. The money was there, but the competition was stiffer.

In the West, the alluring prospects which had led so many Danes to put to sea between 800 and 1075 were no longer so inviting. In 1069, 1075 and 1086, Sweyn II and Canute IV made serious attempts to begin the reconquest of England, but each attempt met with diminishing success; the last never sailed at all. The recalcitrant crews disbanded without permission, and, rather than pay a fine for neglect of duty, rose up and hunted their king to his death. As an English chronicler put it, 'the Danes, who were once regarded as the most loyal of all peoples, became guilty of the most faithless and treacherous conduct imaginable'.[12] There may have been many reasons for this, but it will be enough to consider three.

In the first place, the captains were probably able to profit as much by staying at home as by risking a dangerous voyage to a well-defended island. The great families had accumulated too much land and money at home to go on adventures; the man who could get his own way in the *ting*, work his peasants or finance a trading-ship had no need to go to England for gain, and the hungry fighter would find ships enough to prey on in home waters. Even the fleets which reached England in 1069 and 1075 behaved as if they were out for a quick profit and a safe journey home, rather than the territorial conquest of 1016.

Secondly, Danish kings were no longer rich enough to keep pace with the cost of effective warfare in the West. Sweyn Forkbeard and Old Canute had kept a large mercenary army, but, when Canute's successors lost England, they lost their main source of revenue, and were only able to maintain a small retinue of trained fighters. Sweyn II had begged Edward the Confessor for the loan of fifty ships' crews in 1052, and had been refused. When his son Canute IV was killed at Odense in 1086, he had only twenty warriors about him. The great fleet that had deserted him had been a fleet of the wrong sort, its crews not trained in siege warfare, or equipped for a cavalry campaign. Other kings were wiser: his brother, Harold 'the Soft', and his Norwegian contemporary, Olaf 'the Quiet'.

Thirdly, there were more immediate military problems at home: the coasts and frontiers of Denmark were being regularly raided and despoiled by the Baltic Slavs. The Danes had become a *Herrenvolk* on the defensive.

Of the three remaining groups of Northern peoples, the closest to the Scandinavian was the Slavonic, and in particular those West Slavs who occupied the coastlands and hinterland from the bay of Kiel to the Vistula, including the islands of Fehmarn, Poel, Rügen, Usedom and Wollin. They were divided into a number of nations. From the Saxon and Danish frontiers to the Trave were settled the Wagrians, and from the Trave to the Warnow the Abotrites – two kindred peoples loosely united with the Polabians of the Elbe basin under one dominant dynasty. From the Warnow to Rügen, round the Oder mouths and up the Peene, was an unamalgamated group of tribes which was given the collective name of Liutizians or Wilzians – 'terrible' or 'wolf' people; the northern-most, on Rügen and the coast facing, were the Rugians or Rani. The languages spoken by the Abotrites and Liutizians were somewhat differ-ent from those of their Sorb and Lusatian neighbours to the south, and are classified as the West Lechic; the East Lechic include the languages of the Poles and the nation which peopled the remainder of the West Slav coastland from the Oder eastwards to the Vistula – the Pomeranians, or 'dwellers on the shore', later differentiated towards Danzig by the names Pomerelian and Cassubian ('shaggy-coatmen').

The Baltic Slavs were the most recent arrivals in the North. They had moved in from the south-east, and occupied areas left vacant by migrating Germans at various dates from the first to the sixth centuries. By the eighth their boundaries were stable, although the struggles for supremacy within each nation led to some adjustments later. Adam of Bremen recognized that they were related to the Bohemians and Poles, and could therefore be described as forming part of the population of the large Central and East European area he called Slavia. Latin writers called them Slavs, but distinguished them from the Poles, Russians and Czechs, whom we also call Slavs; Scandinavians and Germans called them Wends. At this period they differed in some respects from all their neighbours, but they also had much in common, and this deserves to be emphasized.

For the Wends were mostly peasants, like the Scandinavians: tillers and herdsmen living in small villages and raising corn, flax, poultry and cattle, with fishing, bee-keeping and trapping as side-lines. The common unit of land value was the *kuritz* or ploughland (always *uncus* in Latin, as opposed to the *mansus*, or German *Hufe*); the peasant paid a grain tax on this, and additional renders on any other kind of work he was engaged in. He appears in the early charters as a thrall, appendant to the *unci* he worked, or a contributor to the many payments owed by his village; and other evidence suggests that he was often a captured or purchased prisoner, held in hereditary servitude.

As in Scandinavia, the agricultural surplus maintained a landowning class: either country magnates living in forest strongholds with their retainers, or communities of warriors and burghers settled in towns. Slav society was intensely militarized. It had developed in the ninth and tenth centuries under pressure, between the hammer of the Vikings and the anvil of the Reich, and for long periods the Abotrites and Wagrians had been obliged to pay tribute to Danish kings and German bishops and marcher lords. The dominant class that emerged had held on to its territories and peasants by learning from the enemy and exploiting its own people to maintain effective armies, fleets and fortifications. The wider settlement areas were subdivided into small territories organized round one or more earth-walled, stockaded and moated forts, usually under the control of the ruler's governor, or *voivot*. The *voivot* exacted military service from the warriors, and taxes from the peasants, and supplied the prince with hospitality when he came on his visits, which could be either occasions of prolonged feasting and public assembly, or shows of force and punitive intimidation. The prince was called *knes*, and as in Scandinavia acted as the leader of his people in general, and as the chief of an extended family of princely kinsmen, all of whom had claims of some kind to land and jurisdiction; but his power was limited.

For there were territories and territories. Some were hinterland forest areas, where the *knes* had land of his own and his *voivot* was unchallenged; others lay along the great waterways and inlets, and formed the 'town-lands' of thriving communities with a will of their own and the power to assert it. Alongside the geography of tribe, territory and principality lay the geography of urban communities. In the tenth century the Wends had already been grouped round small circular or oval earthworks, which early texts refer to as *civitates*. The effects of war, trade and reclamation tended to favour a small number of these at the expense of the rest, and the result, in the eleventh century, was a line of precocious town communities lurking crab-like a few miles up every estuary from Denmark to the Vistula. They reveal the stages of their growth in their plans. At the highest points came the *gard* (*grod*) or *palatium*, a barracks, citadel and residence, usually reinforced with a moat, earth-wall and wooden towers. Below it, within a ring-wall, was the *urbs*, or *suburbium*, originally a place of refuge for the district, later a space crammed with the houses of nobles, artisans and merchants, except for one or more patches of holy ground where there were small timber temples. Outside the walls there was often a further concentration of dwellings, for fishermen, peasants and small traders, and a market. The pattern varied according to local terrain (the three hills of Stettin, for example) and according to the stage of development reached, but it formed a marked contrast to the simple quadrangular town-plotting of Denmark.

None of these towns was built directly on the coast; they were on inlets, rivers and lagoons – on top of a cliff, in the case of Arkona – where the balance between accessibility and security had allowed them to grow. Following the line from west to east, we begin thirty miles from the Danish and Saxon borders, with the 'old fort' of the Wagrians, Stargard to them, Brandehuse to the Danes, Oldenburg to the Germans. This coast was far too exposed to raiders for settlement, and Oldenburg could only be approached from the sea by going round to the east and sailing in along a fifteen-mile series of interconnecting lakes. Nevertheless, it was a sizeable port, and the inhabitants had grown rich on trade and piracy. A Saxon bishop had lived there in the tenth century, but the people had rejected his faith, and in the twelfth century the church was a ruin outside the walls and the temple served as the cult centre of the Wagrians.

From there a track ran southwards – not by the coast, but inland, through dense forest – for thirty miles, to the Trave, where an embryo town, Liubice or Old Lübeck, was beginning its existence under the protection of the *knes*; it was no more than a fort, some huts and an anchorage at this date, when the chief Polabian 'city' was the lake settlement of Ratzeburg, connected with the Baltic by a tributary of the Trave. The 'great city' of the Abotrites was Mecklenburg (Veligrad), five miles upstream from Wismar Bay, dominating the outfall of a wide network of lakes and rivulets. On the next large inlet to the east, the Warnow, there were the beginnings of the future city of Rostock – a temple, anchorage and merchant settlement seven miles upriver that was soon to outgrow the large fortifications where the Kissini took refuge nearby.

Here the Abotrites ended; here the Rugians began, and the traveller would look in vain among their marshy and forested continental domains for places larger than villages and forts. However, on their island fastness of Rügen there were two remarkable townships: Arkona, on the very north-eastern tip of the island, looking out to sea over tall white cliffs; and Karenz (modern Garz), a lake town in the southern part of the island. Arkona appears to break the normal rule of keeping away from the shore, but the appearance is deceptive: the cliffs were too steep and the shore too dangerous for a direct approach from the sea, and all shipping had to go round by the shallow inlets which flood the central part of Rügen, or risk a landing to the south, where the cliffs are lower. Much of this town-site has since been eroded, but excavation has borne out the description of it given by the twelfth-century Danish historian Saxo. It needed no *castrum* or citadel, thanks to the headland on which it stood, but this was cut off by an earth and timber wall rising to some 100 feet, penetrable only through an even taller fortified gate-tower. Then came a curved sector of housing; then an open space; and then – probably on ground now washed away – the temple of the god Svantovit, which served as an international centre of pilgrimage and contribution, and a treasury, as well as the focus of public worship. Here came merchants from all over the Baltic; here the Rugian warriors met in council, and took their orders from the high-priest and his miraculous horse, which no man was allowed to ride. The defences of Karenz, in the south, were lake, river and marshland, reinforced by a more conventional ring-wall. By 1168 it appears to have been developing from a refuge fort into a populous settlement; Saxo describes densely packed housing, stinking to heaven, and archaeologists have found three small spaces left clear for the temples on the higher part of the town.

The Liutizians settled along the Peene had several well-protected towns, of which the most important was the furthest upriver, Demmin (the 'smoke-place'). That was where three rivers met, and where overland traffic from Mecklenburg and Holstein could embark on the thirty-mile downriver voyage to the sea; a key stronghold of the Pomeranian dukes and princes after they conquered it in the early twelfth century, it had been formerly the citadel and cult centre of the Redarii, the home of the god Radigost.

The mouth of the Oder was dominated by the old city now called Szczecin (pronounced 'Schet-sin') by the Poles, Stettin by the Germans; it may have been Szcztno to the Pomeranians, and the Danes called it Burstaborg, 'Bristle-borough'. This was 'the mother of the cities of the Pomeranians',[13] with walls enclosing three temple-crowned hills in pagan days (before 1127), and a reputation for impregnability: 'as safe as Stettin wall' ran the proverb, according to Saxo.[14] Here the missionary, Otto of Bamberg, found a community of 900 families, and among them a great man rich in relations and retainers, Domislav, who was reckoned to have a household of 500 and laid down the law for his fellow citizens. Another magnate was able to put to sea with his own fleet of six ships, and the multitude of slaves brought in by such adventurers must have swollen the population to several thousand, among whom the temple priests formed a powerful clique. For this was a place to grow rich, where four trade-routes met and river boats met sea-going vessels and exchanged cargoes; a city that in 1127 could fight, and win, a war with the Rugians.

The daughters of this mother were Wolgast (Vologost), Usedom (Uznam), Lebbin (Liubin), Wollin (Wolin) and Cammin (Kamien), to put the German forms first. They lay on the reedy channels by which the Peene and the Oder push out to the sea from the Gulf of Stettin – all defensible places with markets and ports, competing with each other for trade and able to defend themselves with fleets and armies. Wollin had once been the greatest of them, the Jomsborg of the Vikings, ruler of the Oderine islands, but had declined with the silting up of the Dziwna outflow and the diversion of overseas trade to Stettin, and by 1100 was rivalled by Cammin. Nevertheless, the earliest missionaries baptized 2156 citizens there in 1124, and founded two churches to serve them. Wolgast levied toll on the Peene traffic, and controlled the surrounding districts both on the mainland and on the island of Usedom; the *viovot* had a two-storey house in 1127, and there was a temple, a city magistracy and conspicuous riches.

East of the Oder, along the empty Pomeranian coast, and up the river Perseta, you came to Kolberg (Kolobrzeg), a town of unique importance on account of its salt-works, and, further upstream, Belgard (Bialogard), where the Polish ruler had established a short-lived bishopric in the tenth century, and where the *knes* of the Pomeranians now had his chief residence. From there to the south of the Vistula the coastlands were empty, and a track ran through hill country towards the port of Danzig

(Gdansk), then overlooked by a *grod* and *suburbium* on an offshore islet, and governed by an agent of the duke of Poland.

This catalogue includes the most important of the Wendish towns, and, even if their average population may not have been comparable with the numbers of Rhineland or Flemish boroughs in this period, it was most impressive by the standards of the thinly settled Baltic region. Only Schleswig (Slesvig), in Denmark, could compare with these places, and other ports and market-places among the Scandinavians would have looked small beside them. Moreover, they had a special influence on the societies in and round them.

Consider the power of the prince once more. He was a great landowner in the countryside, the lord of the biggest retinue of mounted warriors in the land, and receiver of taxes and food supplies from his people; he also appears to have commanded abject reverence, in excess of what a Dane or Swede would have shown his king, with kneeling, acclamation and foot-kissing. His blood was sacrosanct, and in the case of the Abotrite princes had been inherited from a line going back at least to the early tenth century. Yet the powerful men who accepted his authority, and served him with their own retinues, were often town-dwellers, who met together either with the whole citizenry in open assembly, or in the 'senates' and 'magistratures' mentioned by Latin authors, to settle their own affairs, even to decide on peace or war. The business of these magnates was often raiding foreign coasts or rival cities, and it could lead to warfare involving the whole nation. In such cases the *knes* would be summoned to help, and give command of the city forces, but normally it appears that the relationship between urban communities and princes – especially between the Liutizian cities and Pomeranian princes – was a fairly loose one. The prince sent in his *voivot* to hold the fort and gather the tolls, taxes and services; the strong men of the city minded their own business and followed policies dictated by local interests.

Among the Abotrites, it would appear that in the period 1083 to 1127 the *knes* was able to build up such a strong private army, with the help of Saxon and Danish mercenaries, that his hold on the towns was a tight one. It is noteworthy that this ruler, Henry, was a Christian, educated abroad. And, when his dynasty was overthrown after his death, civil war, Danish and Saxon incursions, and losses of territory in Wagria made the warlord an indispensable leader. By contrast, among the Rugians, the *knes* was merely a landowner deputed to lead the troops whenever the 'senate' decided; and the senate was dominated by the high priest of Arkona.

For the paganism of the Wends was bound up with their civil organization. Their whole country was studded with holy places – groves, oaks, springs and rocks – where the peasants made offerings and held rites of propitiation and festivity; and they envisaged the world as peopled by a numerous holy family of gods, subordinate to a divine patriarchal spirit in the sky. Such rural shrines were also to be found among the Danes, Swedes and Saxons, in out-of-the-way districts, and were able to co-exist for centuries with the official Christianity of the parish church; it was too deep-rooted to erase completely. What gave a different dimension to Slav paganism was the existence of a priesthood able to elaborate and intensify worship by constructing images, cult objects and temples, and the development of master cults within the cities, where special skills in augury and ritual made the priests leaders of the community. Out in the woods, they cannot have done too well; Otto of Bamberg found one of them living almost entirely on the fruit of his single sacred nut-tree.[15] But in the city temples it was a good life. The men of Gützkow had spent 300 marks on putting up a temple to their god, and regarded it as so beautiful that they could not bear to pull it down, even after they had accepted baptism. At Stettin there were four temples, and sacred houses where the nobles met to feast off gold and silver. And at Arkona the shrine of the four-headed idol Svantovit was enriched by a tax levied on all the Rugians, and by voluntary contributions from overseas, from worshippers seeking luck or advice. The whole nation was said to attend the harvest festival in front of his temple, bringing cattle to sacrifice; and the high-priest – the only Slav allowed to grow his hair long – decided whether they were to have war or peace. He had his own war-band of 300 horsemen, all the bullion taken in war, and his own estates.[16]

This rampant idolatry was to receive a setback when the Pomeranian princes accepted baptism and authorized German missionaries to destroy the temples and build churches; the missions of 1124 and 1127 administered a shock from which the temple organizations of the Oderine cities never recovered. And in the same period, *knes* Henry of the Abotrites was allowing Saxon priests to attack some of his people's shrines with axe and fire. But, after Henry's death, the rising war-leader Nyklot fully identified himself with the old faith, and remained heathen until his death in 1160; and the Rugians, strong and independent, kept up their cults, temples and sacrifices till 1168. In no case did a city abandon its gods without pressure from the prince, and even with this pressure the reaction was sometimes fierce and bloody.

Why then should some princes have attacked paganism, and others favoured it? They all wished to increase their power; and substituting a princely church, and priests who were in their service, for city-run temples and local priesthoods would be an obvious advantage to them. Nevertheless, as they said in Stettin, the new god was a German god, and a prince who was holding the frontier against the Germans might well object to letting him through; the Wagrians and Abotrites probably remembered the dark days of the tenth century, when they had been made tributary to Saxon bishoprics and forced to pay 'Slav tithe'. Behind the somewhat unassuming Saxon missionary Vizelin (active among the Abotrites *c.* 1125–54) there was a land-hungry crew of Saxon frontiersmen, who were now trying not merely to tax the country of the Slavs, but, further, to steal it. The old gods who had inhabited it for so long might prove better allies than enemies to a *knes* who had determined to fight for his independence. The military situation made paganism attractive to Nyklot; on Rügen the prince appears not to have been important enough to interfere with the religion of his people. Not until the Danes had destroyed the idols in 1168–9 do the Rugians appear to have accepted the sole leadership of a secular ruler and his family.

Thus, by 1100 the West Slavs living along the Baltic were a vigorous and thriving people with a peculiar form of political organization which represented a compromise between the interests of town communities and the interests of territorial princes. The compromise appears to have been successful, in that both powers continued to grow, and were able until the 1140s to defeat foreign aggression. The princes needed the long ships of the cities to wage war, and the cities needed the protection of the princely land forces; when they combined, the other Northern peoples had reason to fear. A Slav war-fleet looked very similar to a fleet of Vikings, and might, as in 1135, range as far north as the southern Norwegian town of Konghelle, and be mistaken for an armada of Danes.[17] But, when the ships got near, the onlookers would recognize the cropped heads of the crews, and hear the characteristic shrieking and jeering of the Wends preparing to fight; it was time to run, or be brave. On land, they were experienced cavalrymen, wheeling and charging unexpectedly on small horses which would be called ponies nowadays; the magnates appear to have owned studs and stables of these animals – as they owned the ships – and to have mounted their dependants on them in time of war. These horsemen were not as heavily armoured as Saxon or Danish cavalry, and relied on speed and surprise rather than on sword- or spear-play in close combat. The lack of heavy horse was to prove a disadvantage, but, for the purposes of raiding, ambushing, and pillaging, the Wendish 'rough-rider' was good enough.

Four hundred miles east of Danzig, another branch of the Slav people had settled in the Northern world and become an important political and economic force. The 'East Slavs' of Polotsk and Novgorod had entered the region before the ninth century, cleared themselves a space for settlement in the forest and along the great rivers, and accepted ruling dynasties and Christian missions from Kiev in the course of the tenth and eleventh centuries. The name of 'Rus', whatever its origin, was applied to them in this period (Adam of Bremen calls them Ruzzi), but they themselves saw Russia as the country to the south, where the great prince lived and the bishops came from. For what distinguished them both from the Baltic Slavs, and from the surrounding peoples, was their Christianity, symbolized by the cathedrals of the Holy Wisdom at Novgorod (built 1045–52) and at Polotsk (c. 1100), and the Holy Trinity at Pskov (c. 1137). As Christians, as city-dwellers and as subjects of a prince (*kynaz*), the Russians of the North were representative of Byzantine civilization; as traders and farmers they depended on what they could extract and sell from the forest peoples that surrounded them: slaves, fur, wax and honey. Novgorodian society at this period was already more complex than that of the Balt and Fennic peoples in the same region, involving the organization of peasant labour on large estates, and dominant cadres of nobles, landless warriors, merchants, monks and priests. It was an expensive complexity, which could not have been sustained solely on the proceeds of the arable land, which the Slav peasant was tilling and slowly enlarging, along the rivers and lakes. Regular imports of foodstuffs and forest products from the entire North-East region were a necessity, and the Russians had established themselves as the economic masters of this region by peopling the vital points where all trade-routes met and crossed. The Novgorodians round Lake Ilmen commanded the porterage to the upper Volga, with a hold on lakes Ladoga and Chud through the towns of Ladoga and Pskov; the Polochians on the upper Dvina commanded the porterage to the Dnieper. By holding these corridors they ensured that the whole volume of Baltic–Black Sea–Caspian trade would pass through their hands, and that the products of the whole surrounding region would come to their markets. It was a hegemony built on communications by a smaller nation of monopolists. Their wealth depended on the river boat and the sledge. So far, they had established no firm political control over the peoples living round them; but their hold on the eastern threshold made Novgorod potentially as dominant a force in the eastern Baltic as the Saxons and Poles on the southern shore.

East of the Vistula a dense deciduous forest stretched most of the way from the Baltic coast to the west Russian uplands. In the Wendish woodlands, the going was difficult; here, for the most part, there was no way through at all. Layers of dead wood, luxuriant undergrowth, lakes, bogs and hills confined human settlement to the coastal strip and the valleys of the Vistula, Niemen and Dvina; and among the oaks, ash, elms, linden-trees and maples that hemmed in the cleared ground grazed the aurochs, the bison, the bear and the elk.

This area, of some 400 miles from north to south, 300 from east to west, was the home of a group of peoples known nowadays as Balts. They seem to have arrived as the earliest westward migration of the Indo-European family, and by 1100 had lived there for at least 3000 years, during which they had lost ground outside the forest to later immigrants. Their languages were archaic, and are divided into an East and West Baltic group; their common civilization and religious belief make it possible to treat them as a unity similar to that of the West Slavs, but whether they considered themselves in this light is uncertain. From the earliest times, they had lived as separate peoples, occupying defined geographical limits. They were

1 the Prussians, first named as such in the ninth century (by the 'Bavarian geographer'), who lived between the Lower Vistula, the Narew, the Niemen and the Baltic coast;
2 the Lithuanians, who lived north and east of the Niemen, within the watershed of its tributaries the Nevezis and the Viliya;
3 the Latvian nations, who lived on the lower Dvina and were called Lettigallians north of the river and Semigallians and Selonians to the south (they are now known as Letts); and

4 the Curonians (first named in the ninth century by Latin sources, and called *Kurir* by the Scandinavians), who lived on the peninsula between the Baltic and the Gulf of Riga, spoke a tongue akin to Lettish, but had become mixed with settlers of Fennic stock, and adopted some of their ways.

These larger nations were associations of smaller groups, which may be termed tribes, and which were the effective political units until historical times. The tribe could mobilize as an army (*karya* in Prussian, *karias* in Lithuanian) and assemble in a meeting (*wayde*); it had its own defensive refuge forts, and took collective responsibility for keeping its frontiers. Some tribes were remarkably ancient (Ptolemy mentioned two south-east Prussian tribes, the Galindians and Sudovians, in the second century AD, and they survived into the thirteenth century), but their ability to maintain their autonomy and manpower was evidently unequal. Some tribal armies had bigger forts and more effective war-leaders than others. Some combined, as did the Zemaiciai (Samogitians) and Aukstaiciai, who made up the Lithuanians. Some throve at the expense of their neighbours. Some lost land to outsiders – as the Pomesanians and Pogesanians of Prussia had been pushed back from the Vistula by the Poles before 1200, and the Letts of Jersika had been subjugated by the Russians. Tribes could combine in warfare, but there is no evidence that the whole collection of tribes we call a nation ever came together for a common purpose until after the twelfth century. The Prussian tribes never acted as one, perhaps because until the crusades any one or two were able to deal with outside aggression; the Lithuanians were welded together by the vigorous leadership of a line of rulers that came to power in the early thirteenth century. What gave the nations their identity before that was their exploitation of broadly homogeneous settlement areas, a common language and common religious cults. The discernible social developments of the period 1000–1200 – militarization, lordship, class-distinction, accumulation of heritable wealth – were not necessarily leading to greater cohesion or solidarity between the tribes. For example, the five 'jurisdictions' we find among the Curonians in the ninth century had become eight in the thirteenth century, and as late as 1219 the Lithuanians obeyed five great chiefs and sixteen lesser ones.

Like the Slavs, the Balts were farmers, clearing land by burn-beating and tree-cutting, ploughing it both with wooden and with iron-tipped ploughs, and raising crops on a two- or three-field rotation: mostly inferior wheat (spelt), rye and millet, but they knew about legumes, oats and barley. They harvested both with sickle and with scythe, raised cattle and horses, grew flax and wove linen. They had been settled in this region so long that they had little to learn about getting a living from it, and they had mastered the art of winning valuable commodities and foods from the surrounding forest and sea: from the forest, honey, wax and furs; from the sea, amber, the petrified resin of the fir-tree washed ashore along the coast of the Prussian peninsula of Samland. Since Neolithic times this substance had been exported to southern Europe and exchanged *en route* for Mediterranean artefacts; it remained for centuries the most profitable product of the Baltic. The exhaustion of rival deposits on the west coast of Jutland left the Prussians a monopoly, and Scandinavian merchants, also interested in furs and slaves, dealt with them, and even settled among them, at the ports of Truso and Wiskiauten in the period 700–900. During those years the Vikings may have secured the sort of lordship over some Prussians that they were to gain over Slavs and other Eastern peoples, but the evidence for this is slender, and King Alfred's informant Wulfstan reported the Prussians to be a strong and independent nation. The Curonians appear to have been tributary to the Swedes in the ninth century, but, long before 1100, both they and the Prussians had emerged as redoubtable seafarers, trading and raiding on their own account, in vessels not unlike those of the Vikings.

The leaders of the coastal Balts took to the sea; but all the Balt nations were strengthening their defences by building large earthworks topped by wooden walls and towers, and by accepting the authority of warlords. These leaders – 'kings', 'captains' and 'dukes' in foreign sources – were the organizers of the tribal aristocracy, the warriors who could equip themselves with horses and weapons, or knew how to use them. Such fighters, at least before 1200, probably consisted of most of the able-bodied men of the tribe, and must therefore have included small cultivators who would have been classed as unfree or unmilitary peasants among the Danes and Slavs; they went to war in clothes of linen and wool, their bodies protected by shields and helmets, and were familiar with both the stirrup and the spur. Their leaders decked themselves in more elaborate equipment, and enhanced their position by accumulating loot and slaves, but it would appear that in 1200 the building-up of large private estates of land had not got very far among them. According to Wulfstan, the Balts of his day competed for a dead man's wealth by horse-races after his death; in the thirteenth century landownership was vested in extended kin-groups rather than in individuals.

Slave-ownership and accumulations of silver currency bars were the most important differentials of wealth; perhaps wives were as well. The Curonian chiefs appear from the archaeology of their graves to have enjoyed as high a standard of living as any other Northern social group at this period; they could certainly dispose of iron, precious metal, jewellery, women and manpower in as much profusion as the Scandinavian landlords whom they preyed on and bargained with, and the size of the great earthworks at Impiltis (12½ acres) and Apuole attest their military potential. The price for this prosperity was paid mostly by the peasants of Sweden and Curonia, who for fear of raids and captivity were unable to live along their fertile coastlands, and by the prisoners the Curonian chiefs imported for ransom, forced labour or trade.

The Lettish chiefs maintained their hold on the Dvina valley by setting themselves up in similar huge fortifications, which served as settlements and trading-posts for their dependants; their remains can be seen at Lielupe, Tervete, Daugmale, Jersika and elsewhere. They had recently learned how to conserve fuel by using stone or clay stoves rather than open hearths, and the Dvina supplied them with a constant flow of customers for their wares, and of the silver, wool and weapons they took in exchange. There were Russian tribute posts at Jersika and Kauguru (Kukenois, Kokenhusen), but the Letts were not Russified, and for the most part they held their own against all comers. It could be said of them, as Bartholomew the Englishman wrote of the Lithuanians in the 1230s, that they were

stalworth men, strong werriours and fers. The glebe of the cuntrey ... bereth wel corne and fruyte and is ful of mores and marys in many places, with ful many woodes, ryvers and waters and wylde beestes and tame; and is strengthede with woodes, mores and marys, and hath litel other strengthe but woodes, mores and marys. Therefore unneth that londe maye be assailed in summer, but on wynter, when waters and ryvers ben yfrore.[18]

This tendency to dig in, fight back and grow rich had not endeared the Balts to Christendom, or opened their country to Christian missions. Boleslaw the Terrible of Poland had sent St Adalbert of Prague to the

Prussians in 997 and they had martyred him; Sweyn II of Denmark told Adam of Bremen that he had had a church built among the Curonians, but nothing more is heard of it. The cult of holy places, plants and animals, the cult of the dead (*veles*) and the cult of gods were the essential guarantees of the health, security, success and identity of the family, village and tribe, and the wise men and women who understood the rites were treated with the utmost respect. Festivals of fecundity, and funerals involving the sacrifice of horses and humans, were the high-points of the year, and the lesser domestic rituals were to survive in some areas down to the eighteenth century. And, just as the paganism of the West Slavs appears to have gained in vigour under assault from outside, so the paganism of the Balts was to reveal remarkable powers of development wherever it was saved from the first impact of the Church Militant by determined war-leaders. The sacrificial fire-place and four-headed pillar under the cathedral cemetery of Riga were not the end of the story.

North of the Dvina valley, the country changes. First come the boggy highlands and rocky coasts of Estonia, where the oak, the ash and the elm no longer predominate, and pine grows thicker; 'the glebe thereof bereth menelich corne', wrote Bartholomew. 'This lond is moyste with waters and pondes. There is plente of fyshe of the see, and of layes and pondes: there ben many flokkes of bestes.' East of Lake Chud (Peipus, Peipsi), where the last swans nested, and then north, lies the great coniferous forest, drained by wide rivers in north-western Russia and threaded by a complicated pattern of bogs, lakes and streams in Finland. We approach the climatic frontier, where arable soils dwindle and the calendar defeats the farmer; flour is eked out with ground pine-bark, there are no bees and no orchards, hen's eggs are a delicacy. Gathering, trapping and hunting play a much larger part in the life of the farming communities. Summer is sometimes brilliant, always brief; the shadow of winter lies over the whole year.

In this region, Swedes and Norwegians came and went, and the Slavs had settled; but the true natives were the nations speaking Finno-Ugrian languages, the least numerous of the old Northern peoples, though the ones spread over the widest homeland, a belt 500 miles deep running a thousand miles from the Bothnian Gulf to the Urals, interrupted only by a Slavonic finger pointing north from Polotsk to Pskov and Novgorod. These peoples appear to have migrated westwards before 1400 BC and to have reached Finland via Estonia in Roman times; at least, some went there, and others, the Livs, pushed south to the mouth of the Dvina, while the Estonians (Chuds to the Russians) kept to the highlands and southern coast of the Finnish Gulf, and settled the islands of Dagö and Ösel (Hiiumaa and Saaremaa). They settled in tribes with defined territories, like the Balts; there were three among the Livs, fifteen or sixteen among the Estonians, and each territory encompassed groups of settlements called *kilegunde* – *Kilegund* being the word later used for 'parish'.

At the head of the Gulf of Finland, between Novgorod and the river Narva, lived the Vods. North of the Gulf were four separate peoples, usually named Finns by later Western sources. The *Kainulaiset* were settled round the Bothnian Gulf. On the south-west tip of Finland were found the *Suomi*, or Finns proper (called *Turci*, as in the port of Turku, by Adam of Bremen), a partly baptized and semi-tributary *gens* of experienced tillers and fishers keeping to the edge of the great inland forest. To the east of them came the Hämäläiset (Tavastians to the Swedes, Yam to the Russians), who lived by the lakes of middle Finland and used the empty southern coast for their summer hunting trips. Then came the Karelians (Korel to the Russians, Biarmians to the Norwegians), who settled and hunted along a wide strip from Lake Ladoga to the White Sea and the north end of the Bothnian Gulf. They moved north in summer for the fishing and fur-gathering from tributary Lapps, and south again in winter to trade with the Russians.

These were the westernmost members of the great Fennic family; but even Adam of Bremen was aware that further east came a whole new Fennic world, which, by the twelfth century, Russian writers liked to regard as their own. The author of the Primary Chronicle, a monk of Kiev, tells us their names: the Ves, the Eastern Chud, the Pechera, the Perm, the Cheremis, the Merya, the Mordva and others – all these were reputed tributaries of Novgorod, as were the Vods, Estonians and Karelians in the west. It appears that they did sometimes pay tribute – and sometimes they killed the collectors; but what bound them to the Russians was the attraction of the Novgorod fur market, and the goods the Novgorodian concessionaires were able to offer in exchange for furs when they met them at their trading-posts. It was a relationship that left both parties to go their own way for most of the year; indeed, it depended on their doing so. And this was the kind of link that most

Fennic peoples accepted either with outsiders or with each other; in no case, by this date, does it appear to have hampered their autonomy or interfered with their distinctive cultures.

Consider the life of the nations living in Finland. The Tavastians and Suomi had adopted a pattern of settlement that consisted of a log-hut and smaller buildings, surrounded by a stockade, where an extended family and its slaves lived under the authority of its head, the *talonpoika*. A group of such family hamlets would have a common identity as a clan, *suka*, and a group of clans would share the use of a hill-fort and call themselves a tribe; but the word used, *heimo*, was borrowed from the Balts and did not represent the same all-absorbing unity as among the Letts, or even the Estonians. It was an association for more limited purposes, including war; and, in so far as invasions by the Swedes and Russians seem to have been unsuccessful before the twelfth century, these purposes were achieved. There were no kings or chiefs to rule the tribes; but in each *suka* the heads of families convened to make the necessary distribution of arable, hunting and fishing rights in the home fields and extended range of forest and lake exploited by the clan. A rich paterfamilias with a horse and armour might be deputed to lead a war-band drawn from a whole tribe, and a 'chief father', *isänta*, would head the more restricted associations of hunters who went north in search of game, furs and slaves. This was a system not dissimilar to that of the nomadic Lapps, described in the first section of this chapter, and among the Karelians the resemblance was more marked, down to the use of the bark or skin wigwam. It represents a cunning adaptation of the group existence necessary to farmers to meet the exceptional asperities and opportunities of the Finnish landscape, unable to provide the regular grain surplus that would be needed by a caste of military specialists. It was not primitive.

Both the Suomi and the Estonians had been raided and enslaved by Swedish Vikings, and had learned how to defend themselves, retaliate, and trade on their own account. The Norwegian hero Olaf Tryggvason was supposed by his twelfth-century biographers to have been held in Estonia as a slave while he was young; he fell to the share of an Estonian Viking called Klerkon, along with another boy and an older man, and 'Klerkon thought Thorolf too old to be a thrall, and unable to do slave work, and killed him; but the boys he took with him and sold them to a man called Klerk, in exchange for a good goat. Still a third man bought

Olaf, purchasing him for a good cloak or garment.'[19] Henry of Livonia reported how in the early thirteenth century the Estonians on Ösel 'were accustomed to visit many hardships on their captives, both the young women and the virgins, at all times by violating them and taking them as wives, each taking two or three or more of them'.[20]

Slaves and furs came to market at Reval (Tallinn) on the coast, or at Dorpat (Tartu) inland, already noted as important places in the geography that Al-Idrisi wrote for King Roger II of Sicily in 1154; or they could be carried across to Gotland and marketed at Visby. There were also trading-posts in Finland, and Al-Idrisi described one of them as a 'great and flourishing town'; but his informant was not impressed by the prosperity of the people round about; and he thought the Estonians spent the winter in caves. They did not, but some had underground refuges, and they were notoriously difficult to attack. 'The men were sometyme strange, fyerce, and cruelle, and unsemely,' wrote Bartholomew the Englishman, 'and far from good beleve';[21] for most Estonians were resistant to Latin Christianity until the twelfth century, worshipping trees, ancestors, and the army of spirits with which they peopled the woods. The wise-man of the family, and the shaman, held the gates of the invisible world; sacrifice brought health and success.

INTERACTIONS

All these peoples were linked to each other primarily by the exchange and purchase and transportation of goods and slaves. The volume of portable wealth which it paid to carry depended to some extent on local demand and consumption, but also on the appetites of a much larger world; hence the dominance of the Danes, Wends and Russians, who held the gates to Western, Central and Eastern Europe. They carried the furs, wax, amber, dried fish, and slaves to the markets of the borderlands, or attracted foreign merchants to their own, and they accumulated the biggest share of silver and imported luxuries.

Their contacts with each other, and with their richer customers, had therefore to be peaceable – up to a point: the point at which trading of goods ended, and competing to obtain them began. Thus we find certain places and conditions in which merchants and others agreed to live and deal together according to established rules, despite the fact that when they travelled between these places they had to go armed and ready to fight all comers. At Schleswig, for example, there were fixed communities of Danes and Frisians, and a continual coming and going of Saxons, Wends, Swedes, Norwegians and Russians; at Stettin market you would meet Poles, Germans, Danes, Rugians, and at Wollin, according to Adam of Bremen, these and 'Greeks' as well – it was the same on Gotland, at Sigtuna, and at Novgorod. In these places there was a market-place embracing all comers, whether by arrangement among merchants, as with the old Swedish Law of Birka (named after a market town abandoned after 1060), or by negotiation with the territorial ruler, as with the Law of Schleswig and the commercial sections of the earliest Russian codes. At Schleswig the king's agent exacted certain law-fines, tolls and annual renders from the settled artisans; in exchange the burghers could fix the weight of their money, admit any foreigners not at war with the king, and have peace; skippers had full rights over their crews and cargoes.

The intervention of the king is significant. Rulers stood to gain by increase of trade, and in the twelfth century they took an increasing share in it. They patronized foreigners who could bring them wealth, information and military skills or entertainment, and tried to create conditions which would attract them and favour their own merchants. The adventurer from Iceland, Norway or Saxony would usually get a welcome at the court of the Danish king; the *knes* of the Abotrites was surrounded by Saxons. The Russian princes insisted that, if a Russian borrower went bankrupt, his foreign creditors were to get satisfaction first, and that rates of interest for long-term loans should be low, to suit the long-distance trader, who would have to travel far before he got a return on the money he had borrowed. If a trader lost his goods through shipwreck, he was allowed to make good his debts in instalments, instead of having to sell up at once. And already, by 1117, the Danish king claimed a right to wrecks on his coast, rather than letting them be broken up and pillaged by the shore-dwellers as in ancient times.

This common pursuit of wealth was the privilege of a small class of specialists, the international trading elite which could provide itself with transport, goods, languages and weapons. Between them and their less-privileged suppliers of wealth there was continual suspicion and hostility, tempered by occasional compromise.

Such, for example, was the case with the link between the Scandinavians and Russians on one side, and the fur-providing tribes of the Far North; this was formalized by the Norwegians in the arrangement known as the *Finnkaup*, a monopoly granted by the king to one of his northern magnates, who was entitled to travel into Lapland with a small army each winter and collect a tax from the nomads while selling them goods (*finnferth*). The army was necessary to punish the Lapps for defaulting on their *skatt* payment and to drive off Karelians who were attempting the same kind of exploitation with an eye to the Novgorod and Finnish market. By such means, the Norwegians were reputed to have made enormous profits; but it was a business that involved continual robberies, burnings and killings, and had to be kept going by punitive expeditions, sometimes led by the Norse king. It was the same for Novgorod: to reinforce the Russian trade monopoly with the surrounding Fennic nations, the prince would periodically have to go out and slay, burn and terrorize until the chief men bowed the knee and sent in the *vykhod* of fur bundles. There was no love and little trust on the fur trail. In 1193 the Chronicle tells how a force under Captain Yadrei rode all the way to the Yugra, on the lower Ob, took a fort, and camped by another settlement to wait for the submission of the Yugrians; but one of Yadrei's men, Savko, conspired with the Yugra chief, and the captain was persuaded not to attack.

'We are gathering silver, and sables, and other precious goods: do not ruin your serfs and your tribute,' said the Yugra, but in fact they were collecting an army. Then they said, 'Select your bigger men and come into the town.' And the captain went into the town taking with him a priest and Ivanko Legen, and other bigger men; and they cut them down on the eve of St Barbara; and they sent out again and they took thirty of the bigger men; and these they cut to pieces, and then fifty, and did the same to these.

Then more were killed, at Savko's own request, and the weak and exhausted remnant was cut to pieces by an attack from the fort; eighty men got back to Novgorod the following spring, but misfortune had turned them against each other:

Their own fellow-travellers killed Sbyshko Volosovits and Zavid Negochevits and Moislav Popovits, and others bought themselves off with money; for they thought they had held counsel with the Yugra people against their brothers, but that is for God to judge.[22]

On the Baltic and its coastlands there was a no-less-deadly state of war brought about by competition between the elite slavers and traders of Denmark, Sweden, Curonia, Slavia and Estonia. In the period 1100 to 1250 this was to escalate into a series of full-scale wars involving the whole military resources of these countries and the permanent subjugation of peoples. The reason for this escalation is not altogether clear, but in the case of the Danes and the Wends an unequal distribution of resources between the nations appears to have much to do with it. The Slavs were increasing in numbers, as the size of their cities testifies, and therefore needed either more abundant crops or larger territories; but their soils were for the most part markedly poorer than those of lowland Scandinavia, and their land boundaries could be neither held nor pushed back without constant exhausting warfare against Saxons and Poles. To bring more land under cultivation they needed the cheapest form of labour – prisoners of war; to increase the supply of foodstuffs to their towns they needed the profits of trade and pillage, which included cattle, sheep and grain as well as bullion and slaves. Moreover, they had to fill the gaps in their own herds and workforce left by Danish raiders. More and more, the Slavs were compelled to keep their economies going by overseas raiding; while the Danes, who had better land and a population more evenly distributed over it, were finding that the balance of power was turning against them. Danish traders could compete successfully with Wends in the market, but they could not defend their coasts; this needed concerted action by king and landowners, preferably with the assistance of the Saxons, and required a greater degree of political cohesion than they possessed in 1100.

Thus trade was leading to a new kind of war; but war was an old story in the Northern region, and at all times it tended to follow a pattern, even rules. This pattern must be examined as the second most important interaction between the peoples.

Like trade, it was the pursuit of elites, and in its simplest forms could be merely an extension to a family feud. In the early 1040s an Abotrite prince sent his sons on a raid to Denmark; they were captured and killed. To avenge them, he collected a large army and marched overland to devastate Jutland. The invaders happened to be intercepted by the Danish king Magnus the Good, and were destroyed in their thousands on Lürschau Heath, north of Schleswig. In the 1120s another Abotrite prince, Henry, had a son killed by the Rugians. He marched to avenge them with a force of Slavs and Saxons, but there was no fighting: the Rugians paid compensation and the army marched home. In 1152 the

Swedish king's son abducted the wife of a Danish noble, and her sister, and slept with both of them in turn. The king of the Danes, Sweyn III, decided that the dishonour was national, and led a full-scale invasion into Sweden with the intention of conquering the country, despite the fact that the king of Sweden was suing for peace and his son was dead. These examples indicate how normal modes of upper-class behaviour – private raiding, wife-snatching – could in certain circumstances generate enough heat to bring about full-scale war; but not always. To turn a private into a public quarrel, there had to be a shared interest between the war-leader of a people, his magnates and the available trained manpower, and this was not always there. It had not been present in 1086, when Canute IV of Denmark wanted to attack England; nor, a generation later, when King Nicholas wanted to invade the Abotrites, and his chief officer, Elef, stood by at Schleswig with his horses and let him be defeated. With these loosely organized countries, wars tended to be transient intensifications of the constant and casual friction between ruling classes, and rarely produced long-term effects.

Even when rulers were able to organize armies to serve political ends, they were seldom able to gain territory or subjugate populations. Canute the Great had seen Norway slip from his grasp before he died, and his son Hardacanute lost first England and then Denmark. The devastating campaigns led by the Polish rulers into Pomerania from 1090 to 1128 led to nothing more than an uneasy arrangement between the two sides, with the Poles keeping their distance in future. They fared no better on the right bank of the Vistula; 'let us leave the Prussians with the brute beasts', wrote the first historian of Poland.[23]

This apparent inconclusiveness of Northern wars was partly owing to the limited aims of the men who fought them. Rulers were content with a show of submission and the payment of tribute; if that was not obtained, they would burn and loot and withdraw, and their poets would assure them that they had achieved a great victory. They were not trying to change political geography.

In addition, techniques of warfare were limited by natural obstacles which made large-scale campaigning and annexation virtually impossible. All over the North, it was accepted that there were two kinds of campaign. One was the summer raid, which went out either before or after the harvest, usually within the periods May–June and August–September. Since land communications were at their worst in March–

April and October—November, with melting snow and autumn rains, it was essential not to exceed these limits, and the preferred method of fighting a summer campaign was always by sea, when this was feasible. Winter campaigns usually went overland, taking advantage of frozen bogs and rivers, and went out and back either before or after the Christmas or Midwinter feast; cold spells and shortage of foodstuffs usually made them either small or short affairs.

There were good reasons for these conventions. The Russian Primary Chronicle tells how in 1103 the prince of Kiev's retainers advised him not to set out on a full expedition in spring, because this would mean requisitioning the peasants' horses while they were needed for ploughing: advice which could have been given even more forcibly in Novgorod, where horses were scarcer. And a winter force that was too numerous, or ran out of supplies, was in for a disaster – as when the Danes invaded Sweden early in 1152, deliberately waiting for the frost in order to be able to take short-cuts over the lakes. But, when they reached the interior, according to Saxo,

an unusually deep fall of snow had covered the entire countryside, and the cold was so intense that when frost-benumbed children were put to the breast they died even as they drank the milk, and mothers, on the verge of a similar fate, clutched their dead offspring in their expiring embraces. The Danes were also hit by the same inclement weather, and failed to spend the night in camp or keep military watch; some looked after themselves by the camp-fire, some under roofs, dreading the cruel climate, not the war. They all kept a better watch on the skies than on the enemy.

After some fighting, the king wanted to advance,

but the excessive cold, and the lack of horses, which had been caused by the bad roads and no fodder, prevented him. Then those who had been reduced from cavalry to infantry loaded their fellow-soldiers' horses with their baggage, and these, being overburdened, stole back home without the king's knowledge.[24]

Such campaigns were better fought by the Karelians, and the partisans of the Norwegian pretender Sverrir in 1175–9 – by small bodies of picked men using skis and hunting skills; but those forces could do little in densely populated lowland areas, where their fewness would tell against them, and it was lowland areas that it paid to raid.

Expeditions by sea were also much restricted by weather and season.

The open-decked warship was apt to be immobilized by contrary winds, and foundered in gales. To assemble a great fleet took time and planning; to have the fleet set sail in the right direction before it had consumed its own provisions required luck. This was what compelled King Valdemar I of Denmark to put to sea in a cross-wind in the summer of 1159; he had waited so long for calm weather that he had to risk his men's lives by drowning, or go home. Their ships took such a battering that most were compelled to put back; the king had to leap from his to another, sword in one hand, standard in the other, and the few crews who kept going had to keep rowing while they ate their rations.[25] It was a heroic crossing, but a risk that most levy-captains preferred not to take.

The longer the campaign lasted, the greater the chances of running into bad weather; a large amphibious operation was perhaps the most risky of all undertakings, given the combined chances of disaster on land and sea. It was not until the 1130s that the Danes and Slavs began transporting horses with their levy-ships, and thereby increasing the range of landing-parties; and, both before and after that innovation, there were good reasons for not putting to sea with a large proportion of a country's warriors too often; as King Valdemar was reminded when he led his levy-fleet literally up a creek in the marshes of the Dziwna, the kingdom might lose its whole ruling class in one go.

Thus the effectiveness of both summer and winter raids depended on their overcoming problems of transport which could not be solved, as elsewhere in Europe, by the accumulation of vehicles, supplies and draught-animals. The combination of raid and conquest which Canute and William I had achieved in England, for example, was not feasible in the early medieval North; large armies could not survive a whole winter in enemy territory, or prefer the long-term gains of lordship and annexation of land to the quick advantage of a blackmail payment, loot and a safe journey home.

Trading and marauding were of course not the only ways the Northern peoples interacted: by the year 1100 there were negotiations between rulers, Christian missions, and marriage alliances, but these can wait till a later chapter. It was in trade and raids that most friction was being generated, and it was this friction that would lead to the Northern crusades.

2

THE WENDISH CRUSADE IN THEORY AND PRACTICE, 1147–1185

THE CRUSADE OF 1147

Crusades are difficult to define, because there were many different types of warfare conducted in the name of Christianity, and none of them was called a crusade at the time. 'Taking the cross' became a preliminary move towards embarking on or contributing to a 'holy war' designated as such by the pope; but medieval lawyers and theologians were slow to work out what made such wars holy in general terms. The beast was born not because of an ideological development but because of a political adventure by dedicated clerics and warriors at a moment when the usual 'defenders of the faith', the kings and emperor, were at war with each other or with the pope himself. This detachment from the church militant was not a permanent state of affairs, and rulers were soon to take the cross in respectable numbers; but it happened that in the 1090s no great king was interested in avenging Christ's honour overseas.

So Pope Urban II was able to take the initiative that caused the muddled international raid of 1096–9 to be known as the First Crusade. It resulted in the conquest of Jerusalem from the Muslims, and in the founding of new Christian governments and colonies in the Near East. But what set this enterprise apart from other wars were its objectives and results, the way the armies were recruited and led, not the conditions of service. The troops fought under vows of fidelity which freed them and theirs from secular cares and vexation, and obtained remission of sins for their souls – the same terms as were granted to pilgrims and to combatants in lesser campaigns for the defence of the church or good causes. Once Jerusalem was taken, there was no need for further action on this scale until the end of the twelfth century, and no need to define or institutionalize the holy war more precisely. It was agreed that what we call 'the first crusade' was beyond the normal scope of human endeavour. It was the result of *Gesta Dei*: God's Own Achievement.

At no stage was there general agreement about what exactly were the religious objectives that justified the first or later crusades. The rank and file went on believing that they were joining in a sort of pilgrimage, but it was difficult for raids on Alexandria, Tunis and Constantinople to be identified with pilgrimages in the ordinary sense. The defence of Christian communities on the Muslim frontier and under Muslim rule was a constant need, but this could usually be achieved more easily by negotiation and treaty than by war – as Frederick II was to demonstrate in 1227. Christian frontiersmen were seldom as eager for intervention by Western armies as the crusaders imagined; and, when the crusaders won new territory or recaptured lost ground, their achievements tended to conflict with traditional doctrines of the primacy of spiritual over temporal concerns. After the loss of Jerusalem in 1187, the need to regain the Holy City and to repeat the glories of 1099 led to the creation of a firmer concept of the crusade, and of machinery to make it real. It became a way of winning spiritual merit, by fighting or otherwise, instigated by popes through a system of persuasion, threat, and reward, aimed at recruiting warriors to serve Christianity wherever the faith was in danger. Its rhetoric, law, ritual and finance were 'routinized'. But until then, holy war was an imprecise term.

Why, then, did the papacy decide to bring this weapon to bear on the pagans of North-East Europe in 1147? This region had known many previous invasions by Christian armies, usually under the leadership of the imperial dynasts; Carolingians, Ottonians and Salians had subjugated Danes and Slavs and forced them to accept baptism and obey bishops. But by the end of the eleventh century this tradition had run out of momentum. The Danes had become an independent Christian people; those Slavs who had rejected Christianity no longer had a strong claim on the attention of the emperor, since he was now preoccupied with the Rhineland, southern Germany, and Italy. The great north-German archbishoprics of Bremen and Magdeburg were left to fend for themselves, and did so by encouraging peaceful missions – those of Vizelin, Norbert, and Otto of Bamberg in the 1120s. The Saxon counts and dukes who had once profited by eastward imperial expeditions were alienated from the later Salians and unable to wage wars of conquest on their own. They had not forgotten their 'imperial destiny', or their claims to

Wendish territory, but their pugnacity now took the form of frontier raids and reprisals between evenly matched and somewhat ineffective warlords. In 1108 there was an appeal in Magdeburg diocese for westerners to come and grab land from the Wends, and the Saxon duke Lothair made at least three vigorous inroads into Slav territory between 1110 and 1124, once reaching as far as Rügen; but the result of his wars was not to extend either the Empire or the Church. His captain Adolph of Schauenburg was left to hold Holstein as best he could, and this was only possible in alliance with the powerful Abotrite ruler Henry. Lothair became king of the Germans in 1125, and his attention was drawn to the south; the north-eastern frontier was largely left to the frontiersmen, and when Lothair died in 1137 a succession dispute left them without their traditional war-leader, the duke, for some years.

By 'frontiersmen' I mean the Saxons living across the Elbe, in 'Holsatia' or 'Nordalbingia' – the Western half of Holstein, behind the hedges and woodlands of the Limes Saxonicus. Saxons had a carefully nurtured reputation for bigness, bravery and brutishness; the Holsatians were reckoned lawless, fearless and ferocious even among Saxons. As might be expected along a frontier, a large proportion of them were free, technically noble, skilled at arms, and apt to make up for the poor living they got from their war-stricken farmlands by mercenary service or raiding. Dukes and kings had employed them, but seldom trusted them; they were kept in hand by distributions of spoil and the threat of Slav invasion. Whether to avenge a Slav raid on Segeburg, or because of rivalry between faction-leaders within Saxony, a group of these men suddenly decided to establish themselves as landowners in the country east of their ancient frontier. Between 1140 and 1143 some dozen noble families pushed into Wagria, displaced the Wendish Chiefs, built forts and halls, and settled. Their count, Adolph II, and his rival, Henry of Badewide, a claimant to the county, advanced further east into the lands of the Polabians, and took possession of the forts and towns of Lübeck and Ratzeburg. After 300 years, the Limes was no longer a political frontier. This was land-grabbing, not crusading, but, since the missionary Vizelin, who had been working in the area for fifteen years, could now be set up as a bishop (at Oldenburg; later at Lübeck) the result was a gain for Christendom; and the methods used by the invaders to grab and hold their land indicated how future 'holy' wars might be fought. Small forces of heavily armed knights, and small stockaded blockhouses were sufficient to open up and subjugate the new territory; then colonists were brought in to clear unsettled areas and increase the revenues of the new landlords, and with the colonists came mission-priests to 'tame' and tithe the Slavs. This breaking-up of traditional Slav patterns of authority and society was something new, since the German conquerors of the tenth century had merely levied tribute and military service from the countryside and had lived much like the Slav warlords whom they had ousted. Their bishops had taken money in lieu of baptism, and life had gone on as before; now the Slav peasantry were detached from their hereditary lords and religion, and compelled to surrender grazing and forest lands to immigrant cultivators. By 1145 the Wendish overlord Nyklot had lost his western provinces for ever; and, further south, the Slavs of the old Nordmark had partly accepted the rule of the Saxon margrave Albert the Bear.

At this point the news that the Muslims had conquered the Christian principality of Edessa reached Western Europe, and Pope Eugenius III proclaimed an expedition to save the Holy Land. The main propagandist and organizer of the crusade was the influential Cistercian abbot St Bernard of Clairvaux. In the course of the year 1146 he succeeded in persuading large numbers of knights in France and southern Germany to take the cross and prepare for the journey eastwards under their kings, Louis VII and Conrad III, but outside these countries the response was less satisfactory; neither his golden voice, nor the brazen tongue of his letters, could stir up the Spaniards and north Germans to join him in the multitudes he had hoped for. Eugenius saved the situation in Spain by authorizing Alfonso VII of Castille to attack the Spanish, instead of the Syrian, Muslims; a similar measure occurred to Bernard on 13 March 1147, when he attended a *Reichstag* at Frankfurt and found the Saxon nobles clamouring to be allowed to attack the pagan Slavs on their own eastern frontier. He referred the matter to Eugenius, and on 13 April 1147 the Bull *Divina dispensatione* authorized the Christians of Northern Europe to make war on their own heathen, under Bishop Anselm of Havelburg, instead of marching to Jerusalem. The privileges, merits and insignia of these crusaders were to be exactly the same as those of the rest, but their aim was quite different. For St Bernard, the crusade was defined not by where it went, but by what it did. He urged crusaders to fight the heathen 'until such a time as, by God's help, they shall be either converted or deleted'. There was to be no truce, no taking of tribute from the unconverted; baptism or war were the alternatives.

Neither the idea of the crusade nor that of compulsory baptism was new to the Danes, Saxons and Poles who responded to this appeal. Contingents from all three peoples had gone to Jerusalem either to fight, or as pilgrims, or both, and had received the remission of sins and other benefits that such journeys earned. Their ancestors had themselves sometimes had Christianity imposed on them, under threat of death if they refused. The Danes may even have followed this rule in 1135, when they captured Arkona and baptized the garrison, although the results had not been encouraging. The Poles had tried to bring the Pomeranians to the Church in the same way. However, they were not accustomed to waging war on their own neighbours for spiritual rewards, or to rejecting offers of tribute. When the Saxons demanded to be let loose on the Slavs, they did so for good old-fashioned reasons, either to get submission and tribute, or to seize more land; for the Danes it was an opportunity for revenge and retaliation against the pirates and slavers, and for the Poles a chance of intimidating the Prussians. The fact that *knes* Nyklot and his people were heathen was a secondary consideration; what stiffened the sinews of the assembling armies was his sudden invasion of Wagria in June 1147, when he devastated the new settlements and made it plain that he meant to have his own again.

So the late summer of 1147 saw an imposing attack on the Abotrites by two Danish fleets and two Saxon armies. The contenders for the Danish throne, Canute V and Sweyn III, sank their differences for the time being, and co-operated with Archbishop Adalbero of Bremen, the young Duke Henry the Lion of Saxony and one force of Saxons in a pincer-movement directed at Nyklot's new outpost at Dobin; the other Saxon army marched under the legate Anselm from Magdeburg to the Liutizian stronghold at Demmin, a distance of over 135 miles. Nyklot seems to have played his hand very shrewdly. Dobin was a small place, off the beaten track, surrounded by marsh and lake, when he himself drew attention to it by fortifying it that very summer; yet it kept two armies busy, while a third had to keep watch on the Danish fleet in Wismar Bay. Nyklot got the Rugians to attack this fleet by sea; the other army of Danes was mauled by a sally from Dobin, in a position where the lake cut them off from Saxon aid, and before long the two kings were racing back to Denmark to continue their civil war. Duke Henry and the archbishop stayed by the fort until the garrison agreed to accept baptism, then quickly withdrew, without doing further damage. When some of the more enthusiastic crusaders wanted to lay the countryside waste to force a surrender, the Saxon knights objected, 'Is not the land we are devastating our land, and the people we are fighting our people?'[26] They did not want to kill the goose that laid the eggs, even for the good of their souls.

The army that marched to Demmin was full of bishops (Mainz, Halberstadt, Münster, Merseburg, Brandenburg and Olmutz, as well as the legate, Anselm of Havelburg), and succeeded in burning one heathen temple and its idols at Malchow; but it also contained two land-hungry Saxon marcher barons, the margraves Conrad and Albert the Bear, and on their instigation was diverted eastwards to besiege the Christian city of Stettin. Crosses appeared on the walls; the Pomeranian bishop, Albert, and prince, Ratibor, came out to explain: wrong bird! The leaders parleyed, the men grumbled, and, grumbling, trailed off home.

So the first Northern crusade was not an unqualified success, whether as a military enterprise or as the fulfilment of an ideal. Prince Nyklot was left in control of the Abotrites east of Lübeck, a heathen warlord in a heathen country, who had bought peace from the Saxons by a token submission. The baptism of his warriors had no visible effects: the idols, temples and sanctuaries remained. The experiment in co-operation between Christian rulers had misfired. Not a foot of ground had been added to Christendom. 'We did what we were told, but it didn't work',[27] wrote Abbot Wibald of Corvey, who had marched to Demmin in the hope of staking a claim to the island of Rügen. The baptisms were 'false', said the chronicler Helmold, and even when the Slavs liberated some of their Danish captives, as stipulated, they kept back all those who were still fit for work. There was bad blood between the different nations: the Saxons thought the Danes useless as allies, and there was a rumour that they had been bribed by the Slavs to stand by and let the Danish contingent be massacred. There was disunity between the bishops, who wanted souls as well as land, and the barons, who wanted land or tribute. There was disunity between the leaders, who went home as soon as they could patch up a treaty, and the rank and file, who wanted to fight on, presumably to get bigger shares of loot.

On the other hand if this campaign had not been undertaken as a holy war, it would have seemed fairly successful. It rounded off the Saxon occupation of Wagria and Polabia, and made Prince Nyklot a tributary and ally of the Saxons; it produced a certain amount of loot, freed a certain number of slaves, and suffered only one serious defeat, when the Danes were thrown back at Dobin. This was not bad for one late summer behind the Slav frontier. There had also been a demonstration of the strength of Christendom in the old-fashioned sense. A temple had been burnt, heathen warriors had been dipped in the waters of salvation, and a wide range of peoples had been seen co-operating in the cause. For the war on the Wends, which was waged by the Saxons, the Danes and contingents from imperial Burgundy, Poland and Moravia, was at least, in the words of a Czech chronicler, a *commotio christianorum*: a rally of the faithful. And the following year, the Pomeranian prince Ratibor came into Germany to reaffirm his Christianity in public.

It was only from the point of view of St Bernard and the clergy of the Slav missions that the campaign appeared a failure. It was they who had decided to make the permanent conversion of the Slavs the main aim of the undertaking, and it is worth asking why they imagined that this could be achieved through a military campaign. On the face of it, the assumption was absurd, and the Pomeranian bishop who saw the crusaders off from Stettin said so: 'If they had come to strengthen the Christian faith ... they should do so by preaching, not by arms.'[28]

There were two answers to this. One was the belief that, before the preachers could have their say, and touch the hearts of their pagan listeners, the devil had to be physically defeated and sent about his business. He had visible agents in this world: the dark spirits who inhabited the idols and groves worshipped by the heathen, and the free-ranging spirits of the air, who spread their wings over pagan armies and assisted in their battles. For idols were vain, but not empty: from Roman times onwards, Christian missionaries who destroyed them had glimpsed their dusky tenants as they slipped back to Hell, sometimes in the shape of beasts (as at Arkona in 1168), sometimes as a swarm of flies (as at Gützkow in 1127); and the diabolic army that marched in the sky was sometimes visible to all. Smashing an image, or routing a force of heathens was an act that could be interpreted as a blow against the spiritual forces that misled mankind. Such blows had to be struck, or the truth would never become visible to the heathen, for the bigger demons were captains in an army that included myriads of smaller ones, each billeted in the soul of an unbeliever and holding his senses and his mind in thrall. Before baptism came exorcism; if this ceremony meant anything, it meant that the unregenerate pagan was possessed, and the lives of the saints afforded many examples of the possessors leaving the mouths of converts in the shape of small black men, visible to some, if not all. Like all explanations of human behaviour, this one had pretensions to scientific status; and, like all scientific explanations, it had its comic side; but the sources make it clear that until the eighteenth century large numbers of educated people took it seriously, and saved their laughter for the deluded heathen who worshipped base matter and vile spirits when they might be worshipping God. The whole idea of diverting some crusaders to attack Northern 'barbarians', while others marched to the Holy Land, depended on a global strategy against the army of darkness; St Bernard knew that even if the devil were humbled by the defeat of his Near Eastern army, his rule on earth would continue until all the nations were converted, and he concluded that the battle for the North was a necessary prelude to the Last Days. How did he know this? The accumulated libraries of Christian teaching on the subject of idolatry, conversion and eschatology were on his side; the new-found freedom of church leaders to put doctrine into practice gave him confidence and credibility.

This doctrine was perfectly compatible with the belief that the heathen ought to be reasoned into Christianity, by preaching, teaching and example – 'weaned on the milk of learning'. Once the superhuman forces had been defeated, the humans would be receptive to gentle words; but first things first. There was no missionary among the Slavs or Prussians so mild that he was not prepared to take his axe and his torch to a sacred tree, image or temple, regardless of the protests of the local people; and any weapon was good enough to discredit or dismay a heathen priest. You could not be nice to Satan. His 'bonds' had to be forcibly snapped before those who had been his slaves could be taught to use their limbs. And there can be little doubt that in some cases this worked. There is a story about Otto of Bamberg's mission in Stettin (1127) which sums up the way these preachers set about their work:

... one day he found boys playing out in the street. He greeted them in their barbaric tongue, and even blessed them with the sign of the cross in the Lord's name, as if joining in their fun, and when he went on a little way he noticed that they had all left their games and gathered together to stare; as boys of that age will, they followed behind the bishop admiring the appearance and dress of the strangers. The man of God halted, and addressed those round him in a kindly way, asking if any of them had been baptized. They looked at each other, and began to point out those among them who had been baptized. The bishop called them to one side, and asked them if they wanted to stick to the faith which goes with baptism, or not. And, when they affirmed that they wanted to hold fast to their faith, the bishop said, 'If you want to be Christians, and keep the faith of baptism, you should not allow those unbaptized infidel boys to join in your game.' Immediately, like joined together with like, as the bishop had suggested, and the baptized boys began to reject and abominate the unbaptized, and stopped them from sharing in any of their games. And so it was beautiful to see how these boys gloried in their profession of the Christian name, and became more friendly and keener to pay attention to their teacher even in their games, while those boys used to stand off at a distance as if confused and panic-stricken by their infidelity.[29]

In the end, says the narrator, Herbord of Michelsberg, the excluded boys begged to be baptized. The anecdote illustrates how a conscientious missionary was prepared even to demoralize children in order to win them over to Christ; if it took fire and sword to work the same change in adults, that fire and sword were also blessed. In this way the pious soul-seeker and the freebooting warrior could be yoked together as partners.

And it was these missions which provided the other main justification for wars of conversion. By 1147 they had met with some success in Pomerania, and were active among the Abotrites and Wagrians and Polabians, but their work was unfinished: paganism was resistant and hostile throughout Nyklot's country, and among the Liutizian cities. Nevertheless, both these areas had once been tributary to the Christian empire of the Ottonians, and the memory of earlier attempts at conversion was kept alive by ecclesiastical tradition, and by Adam of Bremen's great *Gesta Hammaburgensis ecclesiae pontificum.* Adam had pointed to the past – the ruined churches dating from the period 930–85, the martyrdoms and persecutions of converts and missionaries – to awake the modern age to its responsibilities; and it was tempting to construe this tradition as ground for a territorial claim on the lands inhabited by those who were still heathen. Reconquest was the objective of some Spanish crusaders of the twelfth century, although the lands they invaded had been lost nearly 500 years before; in the North, there developed among churchmen a similar belief that soil irrigated by martyrs' blood had been marked out for Christian rule, and that this blood cried aloud for vengeance. From this point of view, the heathen had no right to occupy their territory in peace: they were usurpers, who ought to be punished quite apart from their service as conscripts in the army of Satan. Many had been baptized and had then relapsed; they were guilty, not merely ignorant. The war waged against them was therefore defensive – of established Christian interests; and, if it was defensive, it was 'just'.

These ideas encouraged one group of ecclesiastics to expect great things of the crusade of 1147, and the partial failure of the experiment disappointed them. Events had shown that it was not enough to recruit an army, sign it with the cross and send it into battle, because only a small number of those involved were prepared to put conversion and territorial annexation in front of the other possible gains from such a war. At this date the number included St Bernard himself, Pope Eugenius, Legate Anselm of Havelburg and the more reform-minded of the Saxon bishops, and the lower clergy engaged in Slav missions; it would be necessary to increase the size of the group, and make their ideas more popular before further success could be expected. It would also be necessary to elaborate the system by which crusaders were recruited and led.

SUPPORTERS AND CHRONICLERS

St Bernard died in 1153, a disappointed man, but thereafter the influence of his teaching spread. The process was helped by the founding of Cistercian and other houses in Northern regions where monks and nuns had hitherto been rare or unknown, and by the promoting of bishops who were members of the order, or friendly towards it. Between 1150 and 1200, Denmark, Sweden, Saxony over the Elbe, and the Wendish lands underwent the shock of monastic colonization, which had been spread over centuries in Western and Mediterranean Europe, and absorbed in a short period much of the civilization that came with it: new ways of praying, educating, reasoning, building and writing. In these regions, the Cistercians, Premonstratensians and other 'modern' movements did not have to fight for their place within an old-established framework of monkish life, as in England or France; they were largely free to create monastic life from nothing, according to their own rules, and to intervene boldly in worldly affairs to 'cut corners'. Among other things, these monks and their friends were agreed that to wage war on heathendom was among the first duties of Christian rulers and their subjects, and to promote conversions among the heathen a laudable aim for all monks.

Three men may be singled out as examples. The most influential was Eskil, a Danish nobleman who succeeded his uncle as archbishop of Lund in 1138 and ruled there for the next forty years. One half of him was a prelate of the old school: he had been married, he built castles, led armies, made kings and tried to unmake them, accumulated vast treasures and fought for the privileges of his see and family with vindictive zeal. The other half was different. He had met St Bernard and had visited Citeaux. He was so impressed by the man and his order that he swore to join Clairvaux before he died, and lived out most of his archiepiscopal reign under the shadow of this future renunciation of the world, which finally took place in 1177. He encouraged Cistercians to settle in his province, and sank his differences with King Valdemar whenever that ruler was prepared to back the causes he believed in, especially the war on the heathen. He was an invaluable ally on crusade, because he talked the language of the soldiers and carried with him a network of noble kinsmen, as well as believing in the spiritual value of what he was doing. It was the threat of his anathema and the example of his personal participation which got Valdemar's first attack on the Rugians under way in 1159; it was his rebuke that stopped the Danes from resting under their ship-awnings while pursuing the Rugians in 1160 ('What! Buried before you're dead?'[30]); and it was he who in 1168 insisted that Valdemar stop his men from plundering Arkona, once the inhabitants had agreed to accept baptism and pay tribute. He probably had a hand in the sending of monks across the Baltic to Kolbacz and Dargun in the 1170s, and certainly assisted the consecration of the first missionary bishop to the Estonians, Fulk, in 1167.

Eskil's successor, and somewhat uneasy partner in war and the encouragement of monasteries, was another magnate's son turned bishop, Absalon of Roskilde (1158–92) and Lund (1178–1202). Absalon was also a patron and friend of the new orders, and a fanatical enemy of heathendom, but his approach was simpler than Eskil's: he had been brought up with King Valdemar, and believed that the Church's best interest lay in supporting the king's, and in extending his power as widely as possible.

This meant fighting all his wars, not merely those against the heathen, and spending most of his life in the saddle or on the gangway of his ship; tactics, reconnaissance, raiding, military discipline, coastal patrols, espionage, subversion and terrorism were an essential part of his public duty as he saw it. From the start, according to the historian Saxo, who described much of his life and served him, 'he deemed it vain to foster religion inwardly, if he let it founder outwardly, and he acted the pirate as much as the prelate. For it is no less religious to repulse the enemies of the public faith than to uphold its ceremonies.'[31] This is a long way from what is generally thought of as the Cistercian ideal, and, indeed, Absalon was no monk and never renounced the world; but his obsession with defeating and converting the unbeliever made him a powerful exponent of the crusading idea, and his ability to back this idea with the whole military strength of his king and country gave it a gruesome reality. He was no mere Slav-hater: he appears to have enjoyed good relations with those Wends who were not at war with him, and to have willingly served them as liaison-officer with his king. But, when it came to war, he outdid his comrades in arms; he was even prepared to prevent peace offers from being interpreted to the king if he thought they were not worth listening to, and might interrupt a successful assault.

Among the Saxons there were equally aggressive clerics, but the occupation of Slav lands by Saxon invaders made the problem of conversion as immediate as that of military power. The work of Vizelin was carried on after his death in 1154 by several disciples, but perhaps his most influential successor was Bern, a Cistercian monk from Amelungsborn in Saxony who became a mission-bishop among the Abotrites from 1158, first at Mecklenburg, then at Schwerin. Bern persuaded the local ruler, Nyklot's son Pribislav, that he had more to gain by fostering the Church and joining in the war on heathendom than by opposing it as his father had done. This achievement was all the more remarkable as between 1160 and 1167 Pribislav was driven out of his ancestral lands by Bern's patron, Duke Henry the Lion; and, when reinvested as the prince of Mecklenburg, he had nothing to thank for it except his own hard fighting and political shrewdness – it was not a reward for his conversion, which had taken place in 1160, before his disinheritance. Pribislav became an ally of the Saxon duke, an enemy of the pagan Rugians, a friend of the Cistercians (who came to Doberan, the abbey where he buried his wife in 1172) and an active assistant in Bern's work of conversion. In a sense,

Bern achieved by diplomacy and persuasion what the crusaders failed to achieve by war; but not really. He believed in fighting for the faith, and in the violent extirpation of paganism, as is shown by his joining in the 1168 campaign against Rügen, but the prestige he enjoyed among the Abotrites was not due only to the knowledge that the Saxon duke and his armies were behind him. He merely learned by bitter experience that conversion is much easier when the local ruler is on your side, and took pains to bring this about; as a result, the landless mission-bishop whom Pope Adrian IV had sent out in 1158 died in 1191 a rich and powerful prelate with a thriving and expanding diocese, covering all the mainland territory of Rügen as well as the Abotrite lands. There was a Saxon count at Schwerin, Gunzelin, who made his fortune on a small share of conquered Slav territory, but the bishop did better, in terms of both wealth and political importance; it cannot have harmed the popularity of the idea of converting the heathen to demonstrate that missionary work brought material rewards.

These three examples will be enough to give an idea of the sort of church-leader that fostered the crusade against the Wends in the period after 1147. The belief that fighting the heathen was good for the soul was older. It appears in the 'Magdeburg Appeal' of 1108, and in the *Song of Roland* (*c.* 1135). Saxo has a story about an old German knight who, in about 1166, reproached Duke Henry the Lion for not pursuing the war on the Slavs with sufficient vigour. He reminded the duke that he had been 'dedicated' to fight this war by his guardians while still a child, and would incur God's anger by neglecting their vow. 'For my part,' he claimed, 'I have received three wounds in my body while serving in that war promised long ago. And, if, while fighting in the same cause, I had added two more to these, I would presume at the Last Judgement to look with audacious eyes at the wounds of Christ, which would be the same number as mine.'[32] The story is an obvious invention, but it shows the sort of attitude the veteran crusader might have been expected to have, and the writers who describe these wars are apt to decorate their narratives with miraculous incidents that proved the spiritual value of the fighting.

The most important of these writers are Helmold and Saxo Grammaticus. Helmold, a Saxon priest working in the frontier parish of Bosau in Wagria, wrote his *Chronica Slavorum* ('Chronicle of the Slavs') in two stages between 1167 and 1172, as a continuation of Adam of Bremen's

Gesta. He had been trained under the influence of Vizelin, in his house of regular canons at Neumünster (Faldera), and was chiefly concerned with tracing the conversion of the Slavs to Christianity. This aim provided him with an inflexible standard of judgement: the peoples, princes and policies that aided conversion were good and worthy of record, and all that impeded or ignored it was bad and fit only to be condemned. The wars on the Wends were not always to his liking, because they often failed to win souls; and the reason for this, he insisted, was that they were waged not primarily to extend the Church, but in accordance with the 'selfish' political ends of the duke, his vassals and the king of Denmark. In the old days, the emperors had neglected their duties in the North, and thus 'the imperial Henrys certainly retarded the conversion not a little'; in more recent times, Christian princes were either too friendly with the heathen, or too greedy for their lands and silver to care about their souls – 'the princes used to protect the Slavs for the purpose of increasing their incomes', and until 1167 'no mention has been made of Christianity, but only of money',[33] in all Duke Henry's Slav wars. Nevertheless, Helmold was not against war; it merely had to be the right kind of war, fought with the right motives against the right target. If Henry and Valdemar would only combine and attack the heathen, all would be well; if they would only follow up victory with religious indoctrination, there would be rejoicing in heaven. Helmold was a firm believer in a crusade that never happened. He is interesting both because of this misplaced idealism and because of his interest in the Slavs themselves, their beliefs and reaction to Christianity; nearly every generalization about the paganism of the Wends goes back to his text.

The Danish historian Saxo wrote his 'History of the Danes' (*Gesta Danorum* is the title of the most recent edition, probably wrongly) between about 1185 and 1215, using the reminiscences of Bishop Absalon for the period after 1150 or so. Nothing is known about Saxo, except that he was a cleric of vigorous literary pretensions whose father and grandfather had fought for the king, and who served Absalon and glorified him. For Saxo, the war on the Wends was the Punic War of the Baltic, a wholly magnificent effort by a warrior nation under the leadership of two heroic saviours: Absalon and Valdemar. He was interested in the spiritual regeneration of the heathen Slavs, but much more interested in the political regeneration of Denmark, and he seems to have believed that both aims were equally acceptable to God. He was writing at a time when Denmark was a powerful and prosperous kingdom, and his concern was to give this kingdom a past as glorious as the present. He is, therefore, a highly tendentious and selective writer. However, his blind faith in the rightness of war and *Realpolitik* makes him an excellent witness, both of campaigns and of the attitudes of campaigners; he is not, like Helmold, embarrassed by spiritual reservations.

The two main reasons he gives for the war on the Wends are retaliation and imperialism, and there is no reason to quarrel with this interpretation. By 1158 a generation of coastal raids had brought Denmark low:

piracy was so unchecked that all the villages along the eastern coast, from Vendsyssel to the Eider, were empty of inhabitants, and the countryside lay untilled. Zealand was barren to the east and south, and languished in desolation. The dearth of peasantry made it the home of robbers. Pirate raids had left nothing of Funen, except a few inhabitants. Falster was bigger in courage than in size, and compensated for the disadvantage of its smallness by the bravery of its natives. For it was untouched by the yoke of tribute, and kept the enemy away either by treaty or by force. But Lolland, although bigger than Falster, nevertheless sued for peace and paid tribute. Other places were desolated. Thus there was no confidence either in arms or in forts; and the inlets of the sea were obstructed by long pales and stakes, so as not to let the pirates in.[34]

Helmold testifies that the Wendish slave-markets were thronged with Danish captives at this time, and condemns the Danish kings for doing nothing about it. Thus the natural desire to 'get their own back' must have led many Danes to join in the campaigns of King Valdemar both before and after the conquest of Rügen in 1168–9; but the king himself was increasingly concerned to acquire new territory and vassals along the south coast of the Baltic, and become the ruler rather than the scourge of the Wends. Saxo approved of both these ambitions; good servant, bad master, was his view of the Slav. Nevertheless, he atttached importance to the religious consequences of the wars, and was fully convinced that the Danes were fighting the devil as well as the visible enemy. The destruction of idols and the rooting out of 'vain superstition' were the by-products of Danish aggression, but none the less admirable for that, and he justified the continuing of the war against the Christian princes of Pomerania in 1170–85 by claiming that their subjects were not true Christians, but still half sunk in heathendom. The argument is specious, but it is interesting that he thought it worth making; and he even explains the downfall of Henry the Lion in 1181 as the result of the duke's failure to respect the Church at home or extend it among the Slavs. His work shows how the crusading fleece had become wearable by even the most self-confident wolf; why, for example, Valdemar had a pilgrim's palm-frond stamped on one of his coin-dies, and appears to have used the white-cross flag of the Hospitallers as his war-banner.

THE SLAV WARS OF HENRY THE LION AND VALDEMAR THE GREAT

After 1147 the war on the heathen Slavs was fought without the benefit of papal authorization, or any of the apparatus of a formal crusade; there was no vow, no *ad hoc* legatine commission, no special preaching or promises of crusade privileges. Pope Alexander III congratulated Bishop Absalon on the conquest of Rügen in 1169, but the news had come to him out of the blue; it was not part of papal strategy. When Alexander did send a crusading Bull to the Christians of the North, probably in 1171, its wording suggests that he thought the Slav wars were over, and that the new target should be the Estonians of the east Baltic. And the next appeal was *Audita tremendi*, calling all the faithful to the defence of the Holy Places and the reconquest of Jerusalem (Christmas 1187); there was no allowance there for collateral action in the North, and in the event it brought a force of Danes and Norwegians to Palestine. However, the campaigns of Henry the Lion and Valdemar against the Wends may be viewed as wars carried on successfully in the shadow of the unsuccessful 1147 crusade.

Both rulers were religious enough. Henry went on an arduous pilgrimage to Jerusalem in 1172-3, and Valdemar donated half his patrimonial lands to Danish churches. But neither could afford the luxury of a religious war. They fought to increase their wealth and prestige, and did so by fighting each other, if necessary, the heathen Slavs at other times, and the Christian Slavs also. For ten years after the 1147 crusade, Henry and his Saxon vassals, Adolph of Holstein and Henry of Ratzeburg, appear to have enjoyed good relations with Prince Nyklot of the Abotrites and Prince Ratibor of Pomerania, while heathen pirates from both principalities ravaged the Danish coasts and grew rich. Some of the profits passed into Saxon hands as tribute and blackmail. The situation changed when Valdemar began paying Henry to help him and Nyklot got out of hand. A brief punitive expedition by the duke in 1158 failed to cow him, and the success of Valdemar's two seaborne raids on the Rugians in 1159 must have suggested to the duke that combined operations might produce better results than letting things remain as they were. Hence the joint campaign of 1160, in which Valdemar worked along the Abotrite coast, keeping the Rugians busy, while Henry led an army deep into the hinterland; Nyklot was killed and his sons were driven across the Warnow. Most of the Abotrite lands were partitioned among the duke's henchmen and bishops.

The next time the two rulers co-operated was in 1164, after Nyklot's son Pribislav had briefly regained his father's lands through a general Abotrite revolt, and had destroyed one Saxon army at Verchen, near Demmin. This time Henry marched to Demmin, and the Danes sailed up the Peene to cow Pribislav's Liutizian allies; Pribislav was driven out, and the Danes attempted to colonize the Peene port of Wolgast. Neither victor held on to his gains: the Liutizians began to harass the Danes as before, and, according to Saxo, a further Abotrite revolt, engineered by Bishop Absalon, drove the Saxons back to the west. A treaty between Henry and Valdemar stipulated that they were to share future conquests; in 1168 – or possibly 1169 – Valdemar conquered the lands of the Rugians, destroyed their temples, carried off their treasures and made their prince his tributary. Henry wanted half, and in the ensuing war he encouraged the Wagrians, Abotrites and Liutizians to fight the Danes for him, until Valdemar bought him off, in midsummer 1171.

This left the Danes free to raid the Oder mouths at will, and drive the Liutizians off the sea; in 1177 Henry joined Valdemar in a last joint campaign, anxious not to miss the pickings which were now falling to his rival, and in the following year the Pomeranian princes Kazymar and Bogislav, who protected the Liutizians, were compelled to make peace.

The downfall of Henry the Lion, and the dismemberment of his duchy in 1181, left the Pomeranians and Abotrites without a protector to save them from Danish aggression, and the rulers of both peoples became vassals of Valdemar I's sons, along with the Saxon frontier counts of Holstein, Schwerin and Ratzeburg, who had done well out of the war and had held on to the western Abotrite lands annexed in the 1140s, entrenching themselves by importing colonists and Germanizing their territories. But the possibility of further conquest towards the east appeared slight.

However, in the period 1159–68 the Danes were learning how to fight a different sort of war. They were using the old technique of the Viking raid – a surprise landing on the shore or upriver, a quick sweep inland for slaves and booty, an embarcation rapid enough to forestall enemy retaliation – to pursue strategical aims. In 1160 and 1164 these aims were dictated by Duke Henry, whose land army needed diversionary action and transport; but, at the same time, King Valdemar and Bishop Absalon were working out a way of forcing Rügen and Wolgast to make peace, by devastating their territories at home while hunting down their shipping in Danish waters. The Danes had little experience in siegecraft, and found difficulty in taking any fortress that could resist direct assault. The number of their heavy cavalry was limited by the allowance of four horses to a ship. Nevertheless, by repeatedly burning the unwalled suburbs of Slav forts, and by going through territories at harvest time burning the grain on the stalk and driving off cattle, they could do enough economic damage to bring the cities to their knees. In times past, the Slavs had been able to recoup such losses by counter-raids on the Danish coast, and Helmold had written, 'they think nothing of the attacks of the Danes; in fact, they think it sport to measure arms with them';[35] but by 1170 Denmark was protected by new stone and brick towers (Nyborg in Funen, Sprogø in the Great Belt, Kalundborg and Tårnborg in western Zealand, Vordingborg in the south and Copenhagen in the east) and by continuous coastal patrols – at first organized by Absalon and his kinsmen, later made a permanent obligation on bachelors liable to *lething* service. After their defeat off Falster on 6 December 1172, Slav raiding fleets never ventured into Danish waters again. And in their own coastal waters and rivers their warships could do little to deter the invading *snekker*, which had the advantage over them in height and length, and were not much deeper in the water. They could be hindered by archery from disembarking, and Duke Henry appears to have sent the Pomeranian dukes two experts to improve their men's shooting in the 1170s, but there was an answer to this: both the crossbow and the Norwegian longbow were used to return fire from ship to shore. Bridges, fishing-weirs and underwater obstacles could be used to block rivers for a while, but they were dismantled or cleared without much difficulty, and permanent booms or bars would have been as harmful to the Slavs as to their enemies; furthermore, the shore-forts which the Pomeranians put up at the mouth of the Swina were swept away by storm floods. Therefore, when the Danish and Rugian fleets began operating in concert against the Liutizian cities, the land armies of the Pomeranian princes could do little to protect them.

At this stage of the war, the raids alternated with the arrival of Danish monks to occupy Pomeranian abbeys. Cistercians from Esrum in Denmark came to Dargun on the Peene (1172) and to Kolbacz near Stettin (1175), and Premonstratensians from Lund to Belbuk (1177) and to Grobe. This spiritual penetration meant co-operation between Danish clerics and Slav princes, but never lessened the savagery of the raiding fleets. While the monks sang, the warriors so devastated the lands round the mouths of the Oder that the cities of Wolgast, Usedom, Wollin and Cammin became temporarily uninhabitable. A great sea-fight in the Greifswalder Bodden (19 May 1184) destroyed the Liutizian–Pomeranian fleet in its last effort to regain control of the Wendish littoral by invading Rügen, and thereafter both 'Hither' and 'Hinter' Pomerania were defenceless. At Cammin, in 1185, Prince Bogislav made one sally against the invaders, wheeled to avoid an unexpected counter-attack, fell off his horse and raced back to safety on foot. He had had enough. The following day he opened negotiations with Archbishop Absalon, and that night he was carried back to his tent from Absalon's ship, dead drunk.[36] There was nothing left for him to do but surrender the whole of Pomerania to Canute VI, and trust the king to let him continue ruling there as his vassal; yet he had never once been able to meet him on land with fairly matched forces, nor had the Danes successfully besieged one of his strongholds.

The later stages of this war made it clear that the destruction of heathenism and the implantation of Christian churches and abbeys had been only one of several ways in which Slav populations were made politically subject to outside invaders. But Slav rulers themselves made use of the same method, and were thereby able to survive as effective territorial princes. The Pomeranian prince Vartislav had understood this in the 1120s, when he sent Otto of Bamberg to baptize his recently annexed Liutizian subjects, and when in 1140 he got Innocent II to appoint an independent Pomeranian bishop. His brother Ratibor and his sons Kazymar and Bogislav, Prince Pribislav of the Abotrites, and

Prince Jaromar of the Rugians all followed the same policy, as far as the Danish and Saxon raiders would let them. The fight for power and the fight against heathenism were related, but they were carried on by Slavs, Saxons and Danes indifferently.

On two occasions it appeared that combined operations by Christian powers had succeeded in overthrowing 'the forces of darkness'. That was in 1160, when Prince Nyklot was killed and the idols of his people at Mecklenburg, Rostock and elsewhere were broken by the invaders, and in 1168, when the Danes, aided by the Pomeranian princes, overthrew the gods of the Rugians and baptized their worshippers. So in November 1169 Alexander III wrote to Absalon of his joy on hearing that King Valdemar

inspired with the heavenly flame, strengthened by the arms of Christ, armed with the shield of faith, and protected by divine favour, has defeated those hard-hearted men by the might of his valiant arm, and has strenuously recalled them from their most scandalous enormities to the faith and law of Christ, and has also subjected them to his dominion.[37]

And Saxo gives graphic descriptions of the 'scandalous enormities': the religious practices of the Rugians, the cult of the four-headed god Svantovit, and the worship of the lesser idols Rugievit, Porevit and Porenitz. In their place the king founded churches and manned them with Danish priests; the purpose of Alexander's letter was to place Rügen under the bishop of Roskilde, as part of his diocese.

It is worth noting the differing political consequences of the two victories. From 1160 to 1166 Henry the Lion, probably in accordance with the wishes of his Saxon vassals, tried to diminish or root out altogether the native Slav dynasty, and bring the people under direct Saxon rule. Since 1143, some frontiersmen, including Bishop Gerold of Wagria and Count Henry of Ratzeburg, had been inclined to tame their Slav subjects by forcing them to emigrate from favoured areas, and introducing Saxon and Flemish settlers. There was a feeling that Slavs were untrustworthy and incorrigible, and for a while the duke appears to have shared it. But the great revolt of 1164, and the ensuing wars, convinced him that the policy of dispossession was too troublesome to continue; besides, many Saxon leaders also revolted against their duke in 1167−8, and it was always convenient to have Slav allies to keep them in check. Therefore Henry reinstated Pribislav as 'prince of Mecklenburg, Kessin and

Rostock' and in effect restored the principality of Nyklot which he had destroyed in 1160. Valdemar seems to have learned by this example. When he had conquered Rügen, he set up the existing prince, Jaromar, as immediate ruler of the people, and left him to govern as he pleased provided he supplied the Danes with tribute and military service; the bishop of Roskilde and the new priests were given lands that had formerly belonged to the heathen gods and their priests, but otherwise the Rugian nobles were left in possession. The war on the Wends was in one sense a competition between duke and king for reliable Slav vassals, and in this competition the destruction of pagan regimes was merely a preliminary to the building-up of more amenable political structures.

The idea of the war of conversion therefore emerged unscathed and strengthened from the brutal power-struggle of 1147–85. Northern rulers were made aware of its value as a key to political aggrandizement and greater wealth. From baptized communities came tithes of silver and grain – the bishop of Roskilde got seventy tons of corn a year from the faithful of Rügen – and the new abbeys and churches reimbursed their patrons with taxes and hospitality. A converted country could be 'opened up' to settlers from Christian lands, who came voluntarily rather than being captured and driven in as slaves, and paid for their plots and houses in rent. The monks led the way. 'Whereas it is well known,' runs a charter of Bogislav of Pomerania, 'that the greatest part of the common people subject to our jurisdiction are rude and uninstructed in the discipline of the Christian faith, we have no doubt that if we support good provosts and men of holy life we shall succeed in making our unbelieving people recognize the true faith.'[38] His brother Kazymar's charter to Dargun abbey points to the other advantages. He granted the monks

full power and perfect freedom in calling to themselves and settling wheresoever they wish, on the possessions of the aforesaid church of Dargun, Germans, Danes, Slavs or people of any nation whatsoever and men of all callings, and of exercising those callings, and setting up parishes and priests, and opening taverns just as they please whether after the custom of our own people, or as the Danes and Germans do.[39]

'. . . setting up parishes and priests, and opening taverns' were to be part of the same process, which early in the thirteenth century was to include the founding of new towns on the Lübeck model along the 'Wendish coast' – Wismar, Rostock, Stralsund, Greifswald; all stood on attractive sites which the slave-traders and pirates had made uninhabitable before. With such prospects in mind, Germans, Danes, Swedes and converted Slavs viewed with relish the prospect of further 'wars of conversion' in the east Baltic.

The papacy also began to take a more continuous interest in this prospect. Alexander III had congratulated and rewarded Valdemar I of Denmark not only as a 'crusader' but also as a recent adherent in his struggle with the Hohenstaufen emperor and his antipope. Archbishop Eskil and the new crop of Cistercian abbots drew his attention to the difficulties and dangers of the Northern churches, troubled by unruly magnates and lawless parishioners, and still hemmed in by the pagan world of the east Baltic. Wars between kings, piracy at sea, violent disputes over land-titles, vengeful outlaws and ruthless brigands made the whole Northern world seem stony soil for the ideal of Christian harmony which Alexander shared with the clerical elite of Scandinavia. It would encourage a better order if the weapons of secular society could be turned outwards against the heathen; and in the crusade the papacy possessed the means of bringing this about. Therefore, in either 1171 or 1172, the pope issued the crucial Bull *Non parum animus noster*, which placed the war against the pagans of the North – Estonians and Finns, in this case – on exactly the same footing as pilgrimage to the Holy Land:

We therefore grant to those who fight with might and courage against the aforesaid pagans one year's remission for the sins they confess and receive penance for, trusting in God's mercy and the merits of the apostles Peter and Paul, just as we usually grant to those who visit the sepulchre of the Lord; and if those who perish in the fight are doing their penance, to them we grant remission of all their sins.[40]

The fighting was not only to be defensive. They were to fight 'intending to spread the religion called Christian with a strong arm'.

For the time being, the princes of the North were too busy fighting each other to pay much attention; it was not until 1184 that the Danes made ready to go on a large-scale raid to Estonia, and then they were distracted by the outbreak of their last war with the Christian Pomeranians. Once this was over, both the victors and the victims of the Wendish wars looked east for profit and salvation. For the assault on east-Baltic heathendom involved not only Germans and Danes, but also members of the surviving Slav dynasties – the princes of Rügen in 1219 and 1279, the prince of Mecklenburg in 1218. The crusade had become an integral part of the Christian culture they had been forced to accept.

3

THE ARMED MONKS:
IDEOLOGY AND EFFICIENCY

The story so far has been of the conquest of the west-Baltic heathen by Saxons and Danes. With the thirteenth century, the warships and field-altars set out for the eastern Baltic, and the picture becomes more complicated. In this chapter and the two following, parallel events and themes will have to be dealt with successively. New forces and people from outside the North make their appearance in this region, and the first thing that must be dealt with is an element that came to shape the whole history of Prussia, Livonia and Estonia: the religious military order.

VARIETIES OF MONASTIC KNIGHTHOOD, 1128–1237

These associations of monkish knights were not originally intended to colonize, domineer, convert the heathen or make profits. The first aims of the Templars, for example, were to live lives of poverty and chastity while defending or recovering the Temple and Holy Sepulchre of Jerusalem. The German Order of St Mary began in the same way. However, the accidents and adjustments which led them to become conquerors and rulers involved their committing the worst excesses of the world they had renounced. The atrocities of the Teutonic Knights fill books, if not this one.

Violence and religion had long been friends before this particular merger was arranged, even if only metaphorically. 'Thou art God's soldier' wrote St Paul (2 Timothy 2.3); but 'the weapons we fight with are not human weapons; they are divinely powerful. Yes, we can pull down the conceits of men . . .' (2 Corinthians 10.4): by prayer, not by the sword. But later, the term God's or Christ's army was applied to conventional fighters engaged in a meritorious cause, such as a crusade. This perpetuated a very old tradition from the days when, in Gibbon's words, 'the attachment of the Roman troops to their standards was inspired by the united influence of religion and of honour'.

These, like other, pagan traditions, had been refined and transformed when the Christian emperors took over the old imperial army and civil service in the fourth century. The army had been united in its dedication to the divine emperor; now it was dedicated to Christ through the emperor. Military service was resanctified; by serving Rome with the sword, the legionary served the Church and saved his own soul. A priest was not allowed to become a soldier, because a mediator between God and man had to be free of the taint of blood; but, as late as the twelfth century, the Romans of the Byzantine Empire accepted that a professed monk could continue to serve in the imperial army.

This set of beliefs was extremely durable. It was good enough for Justinian and his successors at Constantinople, and it was good enough for Charlemagne, and the Ottonian and Salian emperors of the west. But here, in the eleventh century, it broke down. By this time the Western emperor was only one among hundreds of military paymasters; anyone who could afford a warhorse, armour and weapons was liable to exercise the military art without respect for the old conventions of what was called 'public war' – that is, war on behalf of the emperor. There had always been such men, but Roman lawyers had dismissed them as brigands, and the Church had condemned them. Now they were so numerous that, if the clergy were to continue moulding society to a Christian model, they would have to come to terms with them. Bishops and abbots could only maintain their rights and property by waging private war, which meant employing whatever warriors they could get, and sometimes leading them in person; it was no longer realistic to bless imperial troops and curse all the rest.

Therefore the clergy had to try and harness the amenable, and suppress or correct the noxious. Monastic knighthood emerged as one of three ways in which this was done.

The first was by encouraging discipline and taboo – to begin with, by restrictive agreements among the princes and prelates who employed the warriors. The Truce of God, the Peace of God, and some aspects of the *Bann* or King's Peace of individual rulers were examples of this. Oaths and treaties also limited the occasions of warfare to certain stated grievances, and the sanction of excommunication was applied to those who broke the rules. The second way was by promoting Holy War, which meant the recruitment and organization of warriors and clerks to serve what they considered to be the common cause of Christianity, whether in Spain or in Palestine.

However, these two devices did not succeed in turning military service into a Christian calling. Most clerics agreed that it was better not to fight at all than to fight with restraint and honour. By the early twelfth century it was clear that spiritual propaganda had not transformed the knights of Western Europe; only that the rising cost of equipment had made them a more exclusive class, with occasional crusades providing an outlet for the more adventurous, guilty or desperate. And most of the persistent fighting could not be fitted into the two acceptable categories of Just War and Holy War.

The third way came into being thanks to the encouragement and publicity of St Bernard of Clairvaux. He believed both in limiting home warfare and in crusades, but he wanted more; and in the 1120s he believed he had found it, in the shape of a small force of knights who had bound themselves to serve in the crusading kingdom of Jerusalem for life. In effect, they had taken to religious life without ceasing to be warriors. He was so impressed that he wrote his treatise *De laude novae militae*[41] to inspire these knights and publicize what he took to be their ethos.

For he believed that they had reconciled spiritual and earthly warfare. The 'new knighthood' fought two manifestations at once: the Satan in themselves, represented by the imperfections in their bodies and minds, which were repressed by vows of chastity, poverty and obedience; and the outward Satan, manifested in the troops of Islam, whom they encountered in battle. Both were sacred duties; each was assumed to support the other. For St Bernard's concern was both with the 'cause of Christendom' and with the soul of the individual warrior. He was a firm believer in the ruling class, but he wanted its members to be aware of their responsibility to God for the position of power in which he had placed them; since this position involved fighting, fighting had to be justified. Too often, a knight lost his soul in a meaningless private war, or even a tournament; but such dangers could be avoided if the battle was against both self and enemy at the same time. The Cistercians had made labour, as well as prayer, a path to God. Why not war?

It was a subtle view, but rested on clumsy and conventional assumptions. One was that the end justified the means. Another was that war for the defence of the Holy Places was, or could be, a spiritually meritorious occupation. Another was that Muslims were merely robot agents of Satan's foreign policy. Such beliefs were both popular and respectable at the time, particularly among crusaders. The author of the *Chanson de Roland* summed it up by making Charlemagne's archbishop bless the Christian host before battle with the Saracens, and, 'as their penance, he ordered them to strike'. 'If you die, you will be holy martyrs. You will have seats in Paradise the Great.'[42]

This attitude had no clear theological foundation. From the time of Gregory the Great, a long line of churchmen had argued in favour of a kindly, rational and accommodating approach to the unbeliever, and Bernard himself was later to claim that, since the Church was destined to bring the whole world to Christ through conversion, it was better to argue with the heathen than to fight them. To justify the New Knighthood he assumed that the Templars would only be fighting defensive wars, but on the whole he preferred to avoid the problem. He sanctioned the current detestation of Saracens, and let the prevailing obsession with Jerusalem carry the armed monks on its back.

Thus even in the title-deeds of military monasticism – Bernard's *De laude*, and the Rule composed for the Templars (1129–36) – there were ideas which set the new Orders at an angle from some Christian traditions; but this was no disadvantage. By 1200 the Templars, Hospitallers and Spanish Orders were rich, famous and effective, for in addition to St Bernard's theoretical advocacy they enjoyed three further advantages.

The first was the continuing support of the Cistercian Order and its friends, which assured them of patronage and encouragement from a whole international complex of abbots, bishops and scholars – the dominant spiritual force of that century. They were ivy on the oak that sprang from Citeaux. But equally important was the second advantage, their military efficiency, particularly noticeable in a precarious military situation. Their Rules gave them the discipline, dedication and morale which other crusaders lacked. They were able to recruit selectively, train systematically, replace casualties automatically, and demand lifelong service as a matter of course. It so happened that the Rule of the Templars was a marked advance in military organization, although this was not its main purpose. And, thirdly, the Orders were given lands and money for which they were not accountable to anyone except the pope. Since they were fighting a war, they invested much of this wealth in castles, and castles brought *dominium* – political power over the surrounding territory.

With these assets the Templars and Hospitallers became the backbone of the Latin cause in Palestine, and therefore an essential component of what was thought to be the right order of things. Which is not to say that they were above criticism. They were complained about almost from the beginning, and their success attracted increasing hostility, but the substance of these criticisms was that the Orders were not living up to the high ideals that they professed – not that there was anything wrong with those ideals. It did them little harm, because at least they could be seen to be shedding their own and Saracen blood in Palestine. They may not have succeeded either in keeping or in recovering Jerusalem, but without their help Outremer would fall.

Therefore, when the emperors Henry VI and Frederick II planned crusades of recovery, it was natural that they should invest in the military Orders, and that they should favour a small group of German knights and priests that had come together at Acre during the Third Crusade. It was accepted that crusading kings should be responsible for recruiting national contingents for crusading armies, and these Hohenstaufen rulers seem to have hoped that a German brotherhood would help them in their task of focusing and maintaining German interest in the Holy Land.

So the Teutonic Order of St Mary's Hospital in Jerusalem was singled out for development by a group of influential princes, and by the popes, at a time when its late arrival and puny growth would seem to have earmarked it for amalgamation with one of the two big Orders. It began about 1190 as a makeshift field-hospital at Acre, apparently using the title of St Mary's, Jerusalem, as an allusion to the German hospital in the Holy City, which had been lost to Saladin three years earlier. These hospitallers were later given property in the city of Acre and round about, and recruited a small police force of knight-brothers; there were probably no more than a dozen to twenty until after 1210. Henry VI got them a charter of incorporation from the pope, and permission to use the Rule of the Templars without having to obey the Master of the temple, but his sudden death in 1197 stopped his crusade, and the Order was left idle.

His son, Frederick II, took the cross in 1215, got the Order's privileges confirmed and extended, and promoted its master, a Thuringian knight

called Hermann of Salza, to the rank of a prince of the Empire –
presumably so that he could work with born princes on a footing
of social equality. Both emperors and their friends, but particularly
Frederick, made donations of land in Italy, Greece, Germany and
Palestine. From 1190 to 1210 the Order received eighteen recorded
donations; from 1211 to 1230 sixty-one, of which seventeen came from
Frederick and his son.[43] At the end of this period the Teutonic Order
was a thriving institution, a sturdy miniature version of the other two
Orders, with only one important difference: its knight-brothers and
priests were all, or nearly all, German. However, since its estates lay all
over the Mediterranean, as well as north of the Alps, it could still be
described as an international Order.

Both the Hospitallers and the Templars were still inclined to regard
it as a potential candidate for incorporation. In the 1240s its master,
Gerhard Malberg, went over to the Templars, and the Hospitallers were
urging the popes to assign them the Teutonic Order as a dependent
brotherhood. And throughout the first century of their existence, to 1291,
the knight-brothers of the Teutonic Order remained a copy of the
Templars and were dedicated primarily to the defence and advancement
of the Latin colonies of the Near East. Their headquarters was the
hospital at Acre, their chief citadel the castle of Montfort or Starkenberg
thirty miles inland, which was built to dominate the territory gained in
1229 by Frederick's crusade. When they assembled in general-chapters,
the venue was always Palestine. The *Magister generalis*, whom the Germans called *Hochmeister*, and we 'grand-master', spent much of his time
at the papal and imperial courts, where crusading policy was formulated,
but his deputy, the grand-commander, *Grosskomtur*, remained at Acre
administrating the order through four local officers: the marshal, the
hospitaller, the treasurer, and the *Trapier*, literally 'master-draper' or
quartermaster. The names of these officers, and the whole administrative
structure, were borrowed from the Templars; and when, in about 1220,
the Teutonic Order was authorized to make its own statutes, the result
was a virtual transcription of the Rule of the Temple.[44] The Order
assisted crusaders of all nationalities, and attracted donations from all
over Europe: from the kings of Castile, Sicily, Armenia, England, Sweden
and France, as well as from German princes. When in 1258 it at last got
the Templars and Hospitallers to acknowledge it an independent equal,
it was because it was at one with the other Orders in their commitment

to the Palestine crusade, and rich enough to hold its own in this field. The fact that it had already begun developing in a rather different fashion in other arenas, on the Vistula and Dvina, was irrelevant: it was essentially the same as the other big two, and would perhaps have remained the same, if the fall of Acre in 1291 had not deprived it of its original Palestinian base.

Nor was this the Teutonic Knights' only front against the Muslims. They were also given land near Tarsus in Armenia, a result of the alliance between King Leo II and the Emperor Henry VI, and in 1236 accepted from King Hethum I the huge fief of Haronia, a white elephant that involved them in the defence of his eastern frontier for the time being, and might have drawn them in further, but for his overthrow by the Sultan Baibars in 1266. The bailiwick of Armenia remained their senior territorial grouping outside Palestine until well into the fourteenth century.

Similarly, the patronage of King Ferdinand III of Castile (married to a Hohenstaufen princess in 1219), brought them three castles in Spain and considerable estates north-east of Toledo, and elsewhere in the south, which could only be enjoyed at the cost of assisting in the Spanish *reconquista*.

The price of international recognition and prestige was thus an expensive commitment to the general policies pursued by the other major Orders, and conformity with the ideals which had sustained the whole crusading adventure in Palestine. At the same time, the Teutonic Knights were becoming linked with a different sort of policy, and a variant ideal, which had been fostered by two much smaller and less successful Orders.

These were the Brothers of the Knighthood of Christ in Livonia, *Fratres Militie Christi de Livonia*, commonly known as the Sword-Brothers, and the Knights of the Bishop of Prussia, called Knights of Dobrzyn, or in the German form, Dobrin.

They were different because they were primarily associated not with crusades, but with missions. The Sword-Brothers began at Riga, about 1202, in the household of a German bishop, Albert of Buxtehude (Bekesho-vede), who was trying to persuade the Livs to accept Christianity. The mission had already been going for about twenty years by then, but its progress had been continually hampered by two obstructions: the Livs refused to take baptism very seriously or heed what their bishop told them, and the area at the mouth of the Dvina was continually raided and disorganized by the surrounding peoples. Preaching was not enough; the bishop needed an army. Crusades were tried, and found wanting: the crusaders went home and their work was undone. Albert therefore persuaded a small group of knights to prolong their crusading vow into a religious profession, and take service under him as a permanent garrison. They were to hold the fort at Riga while he went back to Christendom to recruit more crusaders, and while his priests carried on the work of catechism and church-building in the security which their presence would give. If further crusades secured him wider control of the Dvina valley, they were to garrison what had been won. They wore white mantles, like the Templars, with emblems on their left shoulders: a red sword and a small cross.

Some five years later, another missionary bishop, probably a Pomeranian of noble birth, who was attempting to convert and pacify the Prussians, who lived on the lower Vistula, started a similar group. This prelate was Bishop Christian, a Cistercian who had begun his mission in 1206 and was finding the going even harder than Albert of Riga, even when he had the Danish king and the local Polish dukes to protect him.

He never managed to get very far into Prussian territory, and he and his dukes were continually harassed by raids from the pagan interior. He needed an efficient body of cavalry to enable him to hold his ground; and the Duke of Cujavia agreed. They recruited some fourteen north-German knights, swore them to the same service as the Sword-Brothers, and gave them a fort at Dobrzyn on the Vistula to defend. By 1222 they were calling themselves *Fratres Militie Christi de Livonia contra Prutenos* and wearing a similar emblem to that of the Sword-Brothers – only, instead of a cross, their sword was surmounted by a star: perhaps the star of Bethlehem that originally led the Gentiles to the truth.

These new Orders differed from the others, and from the Teutonic, in three main respects. First, they were not autonomous: they were servants of their bishops sworn to obey and protect them. Secondly, they had very little land other than what they could conquer for themselves; they had no influential patrons outside their own impoverished and underpopulated marcher lands. Thirdly, their function was to assist the conversion of the heathen, rather than to recapture the Holy Places.

Popes Innocent III and Honorius III took both of them under their protection, and sent letters of encouragement and approval; for a while, they were *personae gratae* with papalist ecclesiastical opinion. It was questionable whether this new function was compatible with the ideology of military knighthood as it had developed hitherto, but the popes were prepared to stretch the concept of the crusading vow to cover military action in defence of missions, as well as warfare in Palestine. Hence *Non parum animus noster*; hence the appointment of the first bishops to the Estonians and Finns; hence the crusading forces which set sail from Sweden and Lübeck in the 1190s to aid the new mission on the Dvina. Like the 1147 venture, these expeditions were not very efficient either at conquering or at aiding the conversion of the heathen. If they were run by kings, they were little different from the coastal raids that had been carried on by Viking leaders of all beliefs for centuries past. For example, the 1195 'crusade' of Earl Birger of Sweden was destined for the Dvina, but the wind carried it to Estonia, and, when the Estonians offered tribute after three days' harrying, the earl forgot that he had promised to baptize them, and sailed off well pleased with what he had got. Expeditions organized by local bishops did no better. Neither the crusade to Livonia in 1198 nor those from Poland to Prussia in 1222 and 1223 achieved anything durable for the missions they were intended to support. But the Sword-Brothers did.

What was needed was not periodic visitation by forces of undisciplined military amateurs, but a permanent garrison of professionals which would sit out the winter year after year. The rewards of campaigning in the eastern Baltic were not tempting enough to attract secular warriors to such a life, but for military monks the prospect was not nearly as daunting, because they had chosen to live in hardship and labour. Thus, for purely military reasons, new forms of monastic knighthood were instituted on the Vistula and the Dvina, and St Bernard's ideal had to be developed to meet a new situation.

The armed monk of the Baltic had to deal with two classes of people that presented him with problems not solved by the Rule of the Templars: the heathen, or non-Muslim infidel, and the convert, or neophyte. The heathen was not in possession of land or shrines that could be viewed as rightfully Christian, like Palestine and the Holy Places, and he was not necessarily at war with Christendom; could he be left in peace, or must he always be attacked? Ought a Christian warrior to make truces or alliances with him? Was it sinful to accept conditional surrender, or to grant peace on terms? Was the convert to be made use of, and governed, or given complete freedom? Was he the responsibility of the monks who had conquered him, or of the priests who had baptized him? Could their claims be reconciled? These questions were not merely academic, because both priests and monks were agents of ecclesiastical authority, and for the thirteenth-century clerics authority came from doctrine, and doctrine had to be orthodox. The solutions adopted by the Knights of Dobrzyn and the Sword-Brothers were not altogether orthodox, and, when the Teutonic Order took over what they had conquered and continued their work, it inherited a number of theological problems as well. The part it was called on to play in the North was very different from that required in Palestine.

THE MONASTIC WAR MACHINE, 1225—1309

Between 1225 and 1229 the Teutonic Order was pulled in two directions. The emperor wanted to use it for the crusade to Palestine, and a Polish duke, Conrad of Mazovia, wanted it to defend his duchy against the heathens of Prussia. Duke Conrad had taken part in the unsuccessful crusade against the Prussians of 1222—3, but his main aim was to subjugate other Polish dukes with a view to becoming possessor of Cracow and senior prince of the Polish realm. By intimidating his Northern neighbours, the Order would leave him free to pursue this aim. By entrusting the task to a military Order, he merely followed the example of other East European rulers: the Templars and Hospitallers were already established east of the Oder, and even the Spanish Order of Calatrava held lands near Danzig by this date. However, these Orders were reluctant to fight outside Palestine or Spain; Hermann of Salza's knights may have appeared more biddable, since they had already done notable service for the king of Hungary.

But the Hungarian episode had made Hermann wary. From 1211 to 1225 his men had defended the eastern frontier of Transylvania against the Cumans on the invitation of King Andrew; they had built five forts, and pacified the region known as the Burzenland. But, as soon as they had served their turn, the king accused them of disobeying both him and his bishops, and turned them out. Honorius III had protested, but to no avail. Therefore Hermann decided not to commit the Order to fighting the Prussians until he was guaranteed autonomy; while Conrad waited, he led his men to Palestine with the emperor, and only sent a detachment to the Vistula in 1229, after he had received full authorizations from Frederick and Conrad to hold the province of Chelmno and future conquests as lordships of the Order. He made no decision to abandon one type of crusade for another; the Prussian venture was training for further Jerusalem crusades as cubbing is for fox-hunting.

Thus the Teutonic Knights had several advantages which their precursors had lacked. First, they entered Prussia with a free hand. The Bull issued at Rimini by Frederick II, the charter sealed on the bridge at Kruszwica by the duke of Mazovia, and the Bulls of Gregory IX were agreed that the Order's main field of activity, fighting the heathen, was to lie outside the scope of any other authority, although the mission was to remain under Bishop Christian. But in 1233 the bishop was captured by Prussian raiders, and he was not released until 1239; he was not there to interfere with the first conquests, and it was not until 1243 that the Order had to share what it had won with other mission-bishops.

Secondly, they were allotted a bigger share of crusading recruitment. This was vital, because without secular crusaders they could attempt no big offensives. Gregory IX put official crusade-preaching for Prussia in the hands of the Dominicans, an Order expanding rapidly throughout Germany in the 1230s, and in 1245 Innocent IV granted full indulgences to all who went to Prussia, whether in response to a papal appeal or the Order's; this was extended to all who stayed at home and merely contributed money in the 1260s. In addition, the whole clergy of Northern and Central Europe was repeatedly instructed to preach for the Prussian war, and the Order was allowed to remit sins on its own account. Whereas Bishop Albert of Riga had been obliged to search out reinforcements for Livonia, the Teutonic Order was overwhelmed with assistance. The first contingent, in 1232, included seven Polish dukes, and in 1233 Margrave Henry of Meissen arrived with 500 knights. The margraves of Brandenburg, the dukes of Austria, and King Ottokar of Bohemia came later. They came because they were already connected with the Order as donors and allies, and because they were Easterners[45] – Prussia was much nearer than Palestine, and full redemption of the crusading vow could be earned in a few weeks. On at least five occasions the opportune arrival of such princes saved the Order from disaster, but the master and marshal of Prussia always had a papal warrant to use the reinforcements as he wished. The moment they ceased to be of use, after the submission of the central Prussians in 1273, they were no longer sent for. There were to be no Bohemunds coming out as crusaders and setting up states of their own.

Moreover, the Order's liaison with the papacy was much better than that of the Sword-Brothers. While the master was fighting in Prussia, the grand-master kept a close watch on the Curia. When the Prussian Brothers deviated from papal policy, there was usually someone at Rome to deny awkward rumours, correct misunderstandings, and put in a word at the right moment. In the course of the thirteenth century, only Alexander IV and the eccentric Celestine V publicly reproved the Order for its misdeeds; exposure such as the Knights in Livonia had faced in 1235–6 was deferred until the early fourteenth century. Papal legates were not so easy to appease (see chapter 5), but even they could not be in two places at once, and the Order was.

And, finally, the Teutonic Knights were to acquire a vast network of estates outside the Baltic region. Loss of territory and manpower at the front had no serious economic consequences. By 1250 there were already twelve bailiwicks or complexes of lands, revenues and rights within Germany, and the total of commanders who assembled at the general-chapter was over a hundred. There were also bailiwicks all over the Mediterranean, but it was from Germany that the knight- and priest-brothers were recruited, particularly from Westphalia, the Middle Rhineland, Franconia and Thuringia, and, although the Holy Land acted as a counter-attraction to Prussia, it was a diminishing one. Where the knight-brothers held land, they reaped recruits; between 1210 and 1230 the total of recorded donations trebled, and the total of 1230 had doubled by 1290. There were no overall totals of manpower for the medieval period, but it seems likely that in the fourteenth century there were some 2000 knight-brothers and 3000 priests, nuns and sergeants at any given time.[46]

Such were the Order's assets. It remains to ask who joined it, and why.

In 1216 Honorius III had insisted that entrants should be 'military persons' – that is, anyone capable of exercising the profession of arms; but that was a vague category. At the time, it embraced both the rich and the poor, both the territorial prince and the landless mercenary. Of the first fifteen grand-masters, four appear to have been the sons of *minsteriales*, men whose status came from their administrative office in the service of a ruler; five were the sons of knightly landowners, whose rank came from inherited fiefs; one was the son of a burgher; one was a territorial prince; and four have origins that cannot be traced. Roughly the same proportions seem to have prevailed during the thirteenth century, but, since German society was far from homogeneous at this period, it is difficult to draw general conclusions about the class, status and rank of recruits as a whole. Most were from 'ministerial' (service) families; but, as time went on, and the line between noble and non-noble was drawn more firmly, recruits came from above, if not far above, that line. However, it was not until the 1340s that the grand-master insisted that all postulants must be *wolgeboren*, unless specially exempted. At all times, geography and family tradition were the chief determinants of who became a knight-brother. Thus, between 1250 and 1450, fifteen of the senior officers serving in Prussia came from five noble families owning land in the proximity of Wurzburg, and throughout the period 1200 to 1525 enlistment in the Wurzburg–Nuremberg region was heavy. Hessians and Rhinelanders only rose to prominence in Prussia from 1300 onwards, and Bavarians after 1400; Westphalians and Lower-Rhinelanders always tended to make for Livonia. When factions developed within the Order, they went by 'tongue' or dialect rather than by social origin. When it came to class, the thirteenth-century Brothers were a mixed bag, although none could have been peasants by birth; but they were nearly all Germans.

The national exclusiveness was not insisted on from the beginning. The Sword-Brothers, Knights of Dobrzyn and Teutonic Knights just happened to be three among many small bands of superfluous German warriors looking for employment outside Germany, like the Saxons who served the kings of Denmark, Hungary and Bohemia, and the Polish and Pomeranian dukes. The patrons of the Teutonic Order hoped to use it as a means of attracting such warriors further afield, to Palestine, Italy and Armenia; they were more interested in stimulating than in restricting recruitment. As a result, some Poles, Swedes and Franks were admitted.

No similar groups developed in Scandinavia, because in fighting the Northern pagans Scandinavian warriors were enlisted by their kings, and could not embark on independent state-building. Those who were attracted to military monasticism were provided with an outlet by the Hospitallers, who were already established in Denmark and Sweden before the Teutonic Order went to the North.

The Spanish and Portuguese military Orders which developed out of earlier fraternities of knights, priests and townsmen in the period 1150–1220, were similar to the Teutonic Order in being committed to a local crusade against the infidel, and in their nationally biased recruitment, but very different in other ways. They were founded because Spanish kingdoms and churches were already irretrievably committed to a Holy War; the Teutonic Order was developed because most German princes were not. Thus the Spanish Orders served their kings and bishops; the Teutonic Knights attempted to make rulers and prelates serve the crusade. Their original purpose was to use Germans to extend Christendom, not to expand Germany.

The Rule laid down that candidates for admission as knight-brothers should be able to give satisfactory answers to the same five questions that were asked of postulant Templars. Do you belong to any other Order? Are you married? Have you any hidden physical infirmity? Are you in debt? Are you a serf? Five noes, and then the candidate had to give five yeses. Are you prepared to fight in Palestine? Or elsewhere? To care for the sick? To practise any craft you know as ordered? To obey the Rule? Then he made his profession:

I, Cuno von Hattenstein, do profess and promise chastity, renunciation of property, and obedience, to God and to the Blessed Virgin Mary, and to you, Brother Anno, Master of the Teutonic Order, and to your successors, according to the Rules and Institutions of the Order, and I will be obedient to you, and to your successors, even unto death.[47]

He was then admitted, and subjected to a regime that was intended to ensure that at all times he played two roles, that of monk and that of knight, with equal efficiency. His life was governed by the Rule (approved by the legate, Cardinal William of Sabina, before 1245), by the Institutions, and by the *Consuetudines maiores*, sets of regulations inspired by the Rules of the Templars, Hospitallers, the Order of the Holy Spirit and the Dominicans. Further ordinances were added by the grand-masters, so that the whole collection formed a sizeable law-book; copies had to be kept in every commandery, read out in full three times a year, and sections expounded every Sunday.

These texts insisted on a full routine of religious observances. The knight-brother was expected to recite the offices throughout the day, both inside the convent and on active service, using the somewhat streamlined form of liturgy which the Dominicans had adopted, to give them more time for their ministry. It seems that this practice was rigidly enforced. In 1344, Grand-Master König got the pope's permission to begin the first mass just before dawn, while on campaign, because the days were so short in winter that the knight-brothers had to be ready to move while it was still dark. Nevertheless, the hallowing of the sacrament had to be timed so as to coincide with the first rays of the rising sun.[48] In camp, the master's or the marshal's tent became the church of the army, and the full cycle of hours had to be performed within hearing of the guards, at a portable field-altar. Whereas the Templars had been made to receive the sacrament only three times a year, the Teutonic Knights had to communicate seven times, and the incidence of their fasts was painfully heavy. There was Lent, and a further meatless season lasting for most of November and December; nor could meat be eaten on any Monday, Wednesday, Friday or Saturday, or any one of twenty other stated fast-days. Eggs, milk, porridge and water formed their staple diet.

Military and monastic discipline went together. They were expected to perform all the duties of knighthood, and allowed few of the privileges. Their equipment and armour were uniform, each man being issued with a pair of shirts, a pair of breeches, two pairs of boots (neither loose nor tight), one surcoat, one sleeping-bag, one blanket, one breviary and one knife. He could have two or four mounts as ordered, but they were not his own; they belonged to the convent. He was not allowed to consort with laymen, and his fur-coat had to be cheap: goatskin or sheepskin. He had to sleep in his shirt, breeches and boots, and was not allowed to put a lock or fastening on his box. He had to remain silent at meals and in dormitory, on the march and in the latrine; his only lawful amusement was the solitary one of wood-carving. All the courtesy and conviviality of secular knighthood was forbidden. He could not display his own coat of arms, if he had one: argent, a cross sable, was good enough for all. He was not allowed to joust, or to hunt most forms of game; he could kill only wolves and bears, but without the assistance of hounds. He could let his beard grow, but his hair had to be short and neat.

The only objective was efficiency, to get the squadron of knight-brothers acting as one man under the absolute authority of the marshal. Therefore the marshal could use his club on the Brothers in battle, and his rod in camp. Mobilization, parades, route-marches, pitching camp, guard-duty, and conduct in the field were all regulated by an undeviating routine, and carried out in silence. As there could be no individual shares of booty, no individual cuts of ransom money, and, as a knight-brother could own neither his horse nor his sword, he was not like his secular counterpart. Although he had no property, he was allowed and encouraged to trade for the profit of his house, at a time when this was not considered a proper occupation for worldly warriors.

Nevertheless, he was expected to kill, intimidate and govern. Since he believed that he was advancing Christianity thereby, he could reconcile these activities with his religious vocation; whether they could be reconciled with religious conduct is another matter. As for chastity, the knight-brother was exposed to strong temptations, because war and power continually put women at his mercy. They were booty, and the expectation of raping them was what kept his native auxiliaries up to the mark. Some Brothers must have joined in, as witness the partisan but not unbelievable evidence of Polish deponents describing incidents in the war of 1329–32. A knight testified that the Brothers of the Order had raped more women than had their Old Prussian underlings, and a burgher had watched the women being dragged to their tents.[49] The temptations of active service must often have proved irresistible, but it does not follow that the vow of chastity was ignored or taken lightly. It may well have been taken all the more seriously. The chronicler Peter of Dusburg quoted with approval the example of the commander of Königsberg, Berchtold Bruhave (1289–1302), who went through the reverse of a trial marriage before joining the Order. He chose the prettiest girl he could find, and slept with her for a year without touching her. 'Ecce, mira res et stupenda', wrote Dusburg.[50] Those who lacked Bruhave's strength of mind had to use pain as an antidote, wearing their mail-shirts next to the skin until the raw flesh rusted the metal. Some were said to have been helped by miracles. The terrible Johann von Gilberstedt of Halle had been so vigorous in secular life that even after receiving the last rites he had been moved to rape his nurse. However, devils had then picked him up and thrown him into a distant marsh, from which he had crawled into the Order as a humbled penitent. It seems that in the minds of most Brothers sexual passion and the cult of chastity fought a continual war, which neither could win; but it is worth noting that Commander Albert of Meissen composed a special prayer to avert incontinence: 'O highest joy, give us a true love of thee, and a pure life, give us a clean conscience, and protect us from lust.'[51]

The spiritual motive of the Teutonic Knights, and of all crusaders, was the desire for atonement through service. The method chosen may seem bizarre, especially when contrasted with the ministry of love carried on by the Franciscans for the same purpose, but the Teutonic Knights and the friars worked together, and had this in common: they were both trying to achieve redemption and holiness without cutting themselves off from the practical world. Their Orders expanded most vigorously at the same time, between 1220 and 1250, and were seen as complementary; they shared a monastic dedication to an unmonastic way of life. And, as long as most Latin Christians accepted the fight against the heathen as a laudable and holy enterprise, it made as much sense to become a knight-brother as to become a Friar.

While the knight-brothers were the dominant caste within the Order, they were not the only members. The task of running their parishes and hospitals was left to Priest-Brothers, Half-Brothers, and sisters, so that the ministries of charity, education and preaching were affiliated to the war machine. By 1400 the order ran one hospital at Elbing, where the duty of attending – but not treating – the indigent sick was performed in accordance with the regulations established by the Order of St John, which required hospitallers to treat the inmates as 'our lords, the poor'. This meant providing alms, asylum and masses, rather than medicine, and in towns, hospitals were run by burghers, not Brothers. The success of this ministry may be judged by the fact that in 1229 the Order's Rule was adopted by the English hospital of St Thomas of Canterbury at Acre, at the request of the bishop of Winchester.

Just as the Teutonic Order was able to exploit and adapt various strains of religious feeling, so its Northern crusade was greatly assisted by Germans who were drawn to the same region for purely secular reasons. The Gotland association of German merchants engaged in the Russia trade had led the way in the later twelfth century, and Bishop Albert of Livonia had made use of German emigrants to reinforce his see at Riga with a new borough, and to help hold down the country by accepting rural fiefs. This pattern of town-building and enfeoffment was followed by the Teutonic Knights from the beginning; each newly gained Prussian district was given a settlement of burghers and a sprinkling of knightly vassals, to act as a source of income and military service for the Order.

As early as 1233, in the charter issued for the settlements at Chelmno (Kulm) and Torun (Thorn) – the *Kulmischer Handfest*[52] – Hermann of Salza laid down what he considered the right political conditions for his burghers. This charter granted a measure of independence to the townsmen, but reserved for the Order a share of the profits of justice, an annual rent, the right of coining money, military service, and ownership of the territory round the town. This 'law' – derived from the town-law of Magdeburg, and conceded by all colonizing princes – was less favourable to the townsmen than the *Lübisches Recht* granted to the coastal cities of Riga, Reval, and Elbing, which allowed them control of their own districts and an independent militia, and it was not until 1255 that the Order was strong enough to insist on Kulm Law for all future incorporations; but thereafter it provided an acceptable arrangement for co-operation between the Order and its towns, and encouraged further immigration. The alliance was crucial, because it linked the conquests of the Order to the most powerful social catalyst in the east Baltic region: the German borough. The wealth, industry and ingenuity of these new settlements made them the *taches d'huile* of Prussia and Livonia, from which trade, culture and technology seeped out into the forest and marsh and transformed the tribal societies round them more effectively than conquest and baptism.

During the conquest, both the Sword-Brothers and the Teutonic Knights had the advantage of innovations made available to them largely as a result of their close contact with the merchants, colonists and craftsmen of Germany. These men had been entering the Baltic world in increasing numbers since the chartering of Lübeck in 1158, and the destruction of Wendish sea-power by the Danes gave them free and profitable access to the Novgorod trade route in their own ships. The most important of these innovations was the bigger ship, whether the enlarged Scandinavian *byrthing*, quadrupled in capacity and fitted with inboard rudder and decks, or the well-rounded high-sided *kogge*. 'Cog' had originally been the name given to any ship with a straight stem and stern, set at an angle to the keel, but towards the end of the twelfth century the Germans appear to have discovered a way of using this shape for a pre-eminently capacious vessel, steered by a true rudder rather than a starboard oar. A cog could carry 500 passengers, or a town's supplies for a whole winter; it could be used as a fighting ship, and outmatch the raiding-craft of the Balts (see page 101) and, in time, compete with the long-ship. It was the perfect transport for carrying reinforcements through pirate-infested waters, and the essential economic link between new merchant communities and well-established markets. In combination with the river-boat – the *bolskip* and other forms of lighter – it gave the knights a great logistical advantage, even if they had no cogs of their own until later.

Another innovation was the stone tower. The Teutonic Knights were experienced castle-builders in Palestine, but in the North they had to begin without labour, without local skills and with few deposits of workable stone; they had to make do with wooden blockhouses ringed by pallisades. Valdemar I had proved how effective brick towers could be as coastal defences, but the art of brickmaking was not yet widely known in the North outside Denmark, and, in any case, it needed manpower and settled conditions not available in the east Baltic. The alternative was masonry, a skill well established among the Saxons since counts began putting up stone castles in the early twelfth century; and it appears to have been emigrant masons from Germany who enabled the Knights to replace their first blockhouses with towers, and thus escape their enemies' most dangerous weapon, fire. There were probably no more than five such towers in Prussia by the 1250s, and perhaps ten in Livonia, but their importance was crucial: they kept small garrisons alive when they would otherwise have been overwhelmed. In the fourteenth century brick would succeed stone as a cheaper and more readily available material.

And, finally, there was artillery – especially the crossbow, which had become a favourite weapon of the German merchant-venturer by 1200, and an indispensable arm of city militias. It was not a knightly instrument, and it was not the Sword-Brothers or Teutonic Knights who brought it to the North, but without it they would not have won their early struggle for survival; its accuracy and penetrating power shortened the odds considerably in the battle between many and few. Magnified into the ballista, or giant catapult, and mounted on a tower or wall, it became a weapon that could fell groups of men in close-packed assault, and deter attackers from otherwise flimsy defences.

These three examples are chosen for their immediate usefulness in the waging of war, but there were other innovations, in the fields of building, tool-making, ironwork, pottery, husbandry, fishery and carpentry, which gave material substance to the claim of the armed knights that they were making new societies out of barbarian lands. These changes did not come out of mass-books, or from Rules that bound their observers to lives of material austerity; they came from a necessary partnership with secular Germans obsessive in the pursuit of profit, land and lordship, and infectiously ingenious at getting what they wanted. North-East Europe was about to succumb to a combination of religious and economic forces which its home-grown civilizations had few means of resisting, but to which they adapted with variable success. By 1300, Low German, the language of Lübeck but not of the Prussian Knights, had become the common language of business throughout the region, from the North Sea to Novgorod, and all the peoples round the Baltic were competing for shares in the increasing wealth of the North. In this scramble, Teutonic Knights, crusaders, colonists and natives were competitors, unequally matched.

4

THE CONQUEST OF THE EAST BALTIC LANDS,
1200—1292

During the thirteenth century, the east Baltic world described in chapter 1 was transformed by military conquest. First, the Livs, Letts and Estonians, then the Prussians and the Finns, underwent defeat, baptism, military occupation and sometimes dispossession or extermination by groups of Germans, Danes and Swedes. Four new countries were born: the 'dominions' of Livonia and Prussia, and the 'duchies' of Estonia and Finland, all firmly anchored to Latin Christendom and open, to a greater extent than ever before, to the influx of people, ideas, trade and technical innovations from the West. In 1200 the limit of Latin Christendom could be taken as a line running 700 miles north from Danzig, by way of Gotland and the Åland islands to the mouth of the Umea river on the Swedish coast. By 1292 it ran between 150 and 300 miles east of that line, including a land-mass equal in area to the whole of Britain and supporting a population probably less than a quarter of the supposed 5 millions then inhabiting Britain. All this conquering was in some sense a fulfilment of the programme first put forward by Alexander III in *Non parum animus noster*. A new archbishopric and eight new bishoprics shared responsibility for these souls, many of them new converts or still unbaptized, and garrisons of knights and armed monks were posted along the new frontier to keep them from the world of heathendom and Greek Orthodoxy that lay to the east. For knights and armed monks had carved these lordships and bishoprics on the backs of indigenous populations for whose benefit all holy writ had been simplified into the catch-phrase 'Compel them to come in.'

LIVONIA

The best-documented conquests were those undertaken by the military Orders, and the first of these was the subjugation of the peoples who were brought together under the authorities of Livonia by the bishop of Riga and his armed monks, the Sword-Brothers. This process marked the coming of a new concept, and a new technique of subjection, to the Far North, and made the old systems of supremacy obsolete. Before 1200 the Dvina-dwellers had already been subject to outsiders. The Russians of Polotsk had established a principality at Kukenois, and were obeyed by a Lettish under-king at Jersika (Gercicke), halfway downriver from Polotsk to the sea. The princes of Novgorod and Pskov took tribute from the northern Letts and the southern Estonians at the forts of Odenpäh (Otepää), founded in 1116, and Dorpat (Tartu), founded in 1133; and the Lithuanians had a hold on the Selonian Letts south of the river. These overlordships were discounted by German invaders after 1200 as in some sense spurious or illicit, and were subverted wherever possible. By 1250 most Russian princes had acquiesced in their exclusion from these lands, and had come to terms with the new masters, who were good customers if bad neighbours.

There are two main sources, both contemporary, full and representative of the German groups to which their authors belonged. The earliest is Henry's *Chronicle of Livonia*, written in Latin between 1225 and 1229 by a mission-priest who had shared in the birth-pangs of the colony and was still alive in 1259, working in the church he had founded at Papendorp among the Letts. Henry was interested in warfare, and described the annual campaigns in detail; but he appears also to have loved the indigenous peoples who submitted to the rule of his church, and to have seen this submission as an act that gave them the chance of a new and better life in both worlds. Before baptism they stole, robbed, murdered, broke oaths, committed incest and polygamy and behaved like fools; after, they came to their senses, went to judges for wrongs to be righted, and, after some backsliding, settled down to lives of virtue. Therefore he approved of whatever methods were used to secure baptism.

Some methods were humane; as when in the winter of 1205–6 the bishop of Riga put on a miracle play to explain Christian doctrine to the Livs. But for the most part he gathered in his flock by war, and even in the miracle play the battle-scenes were so well done that the audience panicked and tried to run away.[53] In 1211 the Sword-Brothers and the Christian Letts marched to destroy the Estonians in the fort of Fellin (Viljandi). The besiegers first showed the garrison their Estonian captives, and offered to spare their lives if they would surrender and be baptized.

The garrison refused, and the prisoners were all killed and thrown into the moat. The siege continued for five days, with heavy casualties on both sides; then the Brothers repeated their offer. The Estonians answered: 'We acknowledge your God to be greater than our gods. By overcoming us, he has inclined our hearts to worship him.'[54] They surrendered, and the survivors were sprinkled with holy water and catechized. Henry's comment is that the clergy were right to postpone full baptism for a while, since so much blood had been shed. He saw nothing wrong in this approach to conversion, because for him voluntary adherence to the faith and baptism under threat of death were both God's will; it did not matter by what means the number of the baptized increased.

However, he believed that after baptism the convert should be carefully instructed in the meaning of his faith and fairly treated by his new rulers. He had no time for colonial profiteers – tribal judges who took bribes, knights who encroached on native property, extortionate priests – because such men undid God's work. The new order had to be better than the old, not only because it was Christian, but also because it was meant to give subject populations peace, plenty and self-confidence; and Henry was writing during a peaceful interlude which he took to be proof that the previous bloodshed and devastation had been worthwhile.

As it turned out, he was wrong. During the next sixty years all the early battles had to be fought over again, the land resubjugated, the martyrdoms reiterated. His illusions about the peaceful transformation of the Letts were to be shattered again and again in his own lifetime; and the Sword-Brothers, whom he liked to see as the obedient agents of the bishop and his missions, were to be exposed as an international scandal, and taken over by the Teutonic Knights. The armies of the Blessed Virgin were to suffer twelve great defeats before her people could live in security. And the voice which came from Livonia at the end of the century was much harsher.

It spoke Middle High German, and belonged to the anonymous knight – perhaps a member of the Teutonic Order – who wrote a rhyming history of Livonia.

The *Livländische Reimchronik* gives the viewpoint of the monastic knight, rather than that of the missionary. The Virgin, whom Henry saw as the universal mother, is here a war-goddess. God is a hard master, whose service is military. The pay is salvation, but the only sure way of earning it is martyrdom: death at the hands of his enemies. Success in battle is one proof of his goodness, but he bestows it capriciously. What God likes best is martyrdom, and, next to martyrdom, the killing of heathen men, women and children, the burning of their houses, the lamentations of the bereaved.

Therefore the Teutonic Knights and their masters are continually going into battle against hopeless odds, in search of death rather than victory, and they set out on gratuitous (and often unsuccessful) expeditions against peaceful tribes because God's lust for empire will not give them rest. He reveals himself in blood and fire; to kill and burn is to reveal him. The Rhymer even describes the mendicant Orders as joining the knight-brothers in this kind of mission. When the Order devasted Samogitia in 1255, he claims,

> The first fire that burned that land
> Was lit by a Preaching-friar's hand,
> And a Greyfriar followed after.[55]

For, while God welcomed the voluntary adoption of the faith by heathen peoples, the only way of ensuring that the conversion was genuine was by bringing them to unconditional surrender, or, as with the Semigallians in 1290, by allowing only those who surrendered to remain in their country. A truce never paid; it was always better to fight, even unsuccessfully. The work of the unarmed missionary was always suspect, as in Lithuania during the 1250s, when the king accepted baptism and then allowed his people to attack the Order's troops. The Teutonic Knights are never presented as preachers, and it is implied that their willingness to undergo martyrdom is worth more to the Church than any amount of verbal proselytizing.

The attitude of the Rhymer towards the natives is less paternal than Henry of Livonia's, but not wholly unsympathetic. If they opposed the Order, they deserved no mercy whatever, but their valour as enemies was not denied. Their warriors go by the same epithets – *vromer helt, degen* (noble hero, man of valour) – as those of the Christian armies, and their successes are never played down. If they assist the knight-brothers they pass muster, and win unstinted praise for their deeds if they stand their ground in battle and not much blame if they run away. The Rhymer appears not to care much whether they go to church; but he likes to describe the loyal Curonians marching home laden with justly earned booty and celebrating the Order's victories. Even during peace-time, Christian allies such as Mindaugas of Lithuania are regarded as honourable men, entitled to respect, and, when the Lithuanians decide to break this peace, their motives are presented as rational: they want to prevent their country from being taken over by outsiders.

Nevertheless, just as God compels his servants to fight, so the devil drives the heathen Samogitians into battle by the inflammatory words of his agents, the sacrificer or *bluotekerel*. The war is really between two sets of war-gods, both using brave and honourable men as their pawns, and it so happens that God and his Mother, who use Christians, are the stronger. Battle is therefore inevitable; there is no other way of demonstrating to the enemy that his gods are wrong. The Christian wins both ways: by martyrdom, through defeat, and by converting the enemy, through victory. Therefore the Rhymer can look back on ninety blood-stained years without regret. Not, like Henry of Livonia, because war had led to peace and conversion, but because his side had come out top in the end.

These two sources, and many others, represent the opinions of the conquerors; none come directly from the conquered. What these thought can only be deduced from the number of times they tried to shake off their masters and the new religion, but this is inconclusive evidence. Some remained loyal at all times; others, like the Estonians of Fellin, accepted the verdict of battle as just, and served in the armies of the newcomers as a more effective way of pursuing longstanding local quarrels, or of excluding other invaders. German traders were, after all, a source of profit, and the natives' own tribal chiefs had schooled them in devastation long before the foreigners moved in.

The Riga mission began as a family enterprise. The head of the family was Hartwig II, archbishop of Bremen (1185–1207), who spent his reign trying to regain lost territory for his once-glorious see, and reassert his rights. When he heard that an ancient canon of the house of Segewold in Holstein (a part of his diocese) had settled on the distant river Dvina to preach the word, he had the imagination to make him bishop of the Livs. After all, there had been a time, before 1103, when Hamburg–Bremen had exercised spiritual authority over the entire Northern world. Meinhard, the newly appointed bishop, made little progress. He bribed the Livs to accept baptism, by showing them how to build stone-walled forts at Üxküll and Holm, and then found that they had no intention of staying baptized. The pope wrote to him and advised him to use compulsion, but how? The German Dvina merchants wanted only to trade, the Swedes only to plunder; Meinhard died in 1196 after a harassed old age, and Hartwig sent out a younger man to replace him, the Cistercian abbot Berthold of Loccum, but Berthold sailed back the following year and reported that the situation was untenable. He had tried winning over the Livs with presents and entertainment; they had made it clear that they wanted to get rid of him.

Hartwig already had an answer: the continuous crusade. In 1195 he had got Pope Celestine III to authorize full crusading privileges to all who took the vow to make a pilgrimage to the Dvina, and in 1198 Innocent III reiterated the offer; that year, Berthold sailed back to the Livs with a fully equipped force of Saxon crusaders. These knights proved effective in battle, and would have been more so if the bishop had not let himself be surrounded by the enemy and torn to pieces. The crusaders ravaged the countryside, forced some Livs to accept baptism, and then sailed off, leaving things as they were. However, Livonia had her first martyr, an almost essential component in the paradigm of conversion. To replace him, Hartwig appointed his own nephew, Albert of Buxtehude, who spent a year recruiting more crusaders, and arrived on the Dvina with a force of over 500 warriors in twenty-three ships.

The response to Hartwig's appeals was not solely the result of sympathy with his aim of extending the power of his archbishopric; he had as many enemies as friends in Saxony. But the appeals came at the end of a decade of crusading propaganda, when there were many in Northern Europe who had taken the vow in the expectation of sailing to the Holy Land, and had been disappointed by the collapse of the Emperor Henry's crusade before it could set sail, in 1197. The unrest and local warfare which had broken out in Germany after the emperor's death had also produced a larger crop than usual of men with murder and bloodshed on their consciences, or reasons for leaving home; for those who lived near Cologne, Soest, Bremen or Lübeck and had connections with the eastern trade, the route to the Dvina, via Gotland, was a well-known way to riches, and therefore a not-unattractive path to salvation. Hartwig and Albert merely had to tap these reserves of manpower, and organize them, and then repeat the process year by year, as authorized by Innocent III in 1204; thus the Lübeck–Livonia run became a steady source of profit and absolution for skippers, knights, burghers and princes. Those who came and went made things better for those who stayed overseas; and pre-eminent among those who stayed were the kinsmen of Archbishop Hartwig.

Albert, the bishop, was their chief; he moved his see downriver from Üxküll to the more accessible port of Riga, where cogs could anchor, and built a new town there for German settlers. He went back to Germany every year until 1224 to drum up support, and secured his position by frequent contact with Innocent III and King Valdemar II of Denmark. He put his brother Dietrich in charge of a new Cistercian abbey at Dünamünde, and also persuaded him, in time, to marry a Russian princess and act as castellan of the fort at Odenpäh, which kept the Russians out. He enfeoffed his brother-in-law, Engelbert von Tisenhusen, with lands round Riga, and recruited his influential second cousin, another Dietrich, from Stade, as one of the military retainers. When Dorpat was captured, his brother, Rothmar, became bishop there, and another brother, Rothmas, became Hermann's provost (dean). The families founded by these men, the von Tisenhusens, von Üxkülls and von der Ropps were to count for much in Livonia, but Albert's most enduring legacy was his monastic family, the Sword-Brothers, who were to emerge as the dominant political force in the country even during his own lifetime.

The Sword-Brothers appear to have been men of mixed social origins. In the eyes of a hostile chronicler, they were 'rich merchants, banned from Saxony for their crimes, who expected to live on their own without law or king'.[56] But some were members of Albert's own noble kin-group, and the most important, Folkwin, may have been a son of the count of Naumburg, a district in north Hesse; those whose origins can be traced come either from this area or from the Bremen–Lübeck region, where most of the bishop's connections lay. There were probably never more than 120 of them, dispersed among six convents, but they were not easy to control. Folkwin took over as master in 1209, when a brother called Wigbert, from Soest, killed the first master with an axe, and as time went by there was almost no crime of which they were not accused; they were a rough and ready lot. However, both under Wenno and under Folkwin they fought successful wars in conditions that left no room for mistakes.

The secret of their military success lay in the limited role which they played in the overall crusading strategy worked out by the bishop and their masters. They were a heavily armed and heavily mounted elite, and had to be used sparingly in battle, both because of their fewness and because the terrain of the Dvina valley was not ideally suited to cavalry action. Their main duty was to organize crusaders and indigenous levies during the summer campaign, and to hold defensive positions in winter. Bishop Albert and the crusaders of 1200 managed to establish Riga as a base, enfeoff the first German landowners and win over half the Liv nation under their kinglet Caupo; after that the Sword-Brothers were required to press on upriver and consolidate what was gained. The Semigallians, south of the Dvina, came over in 1205, to share in a victory over Lithuanian raiders, and the kinglet of Kukenois gave the bishop half his land in 1207, also for help against the Lithuanians. Both Kukenois and Jersika were occupied in 1209, and most of the Letts brought under the rule of Riga; in 1212 Prince Vladimir of Polotsk conceded his former tributaries to the bishop, for the sake of a military alliance and free passage for his merchants on the Dvina.

From 1209 to 1218 a series of campaigns subjugated the southern Estonians, who inhabited the provinces of Sakkala, Ungaunia and Rotala, and beat off counter-attacks or rival bids for supremacy by Russians and Lithuanians. The arrival of Danish crusaders in northern Estonia set a limit to expansion in this direction for the time being, and in 1222 the Estonians were partitioned between King Valdemar and Bishop Albert. From 1223 to 1224 both Danes and Saxons were busy reconquering ground lost in an Estonian revolt. After a brief interlude, while the country was being set in order by the papal legate William of Sabina, the islanders of Ösel were subdued (1227), and the Curonians capitulated by the treaties of 1230–31.

The outlines of 'Livonia' were drawn. During these grim campaigns the Dvina served as a lifeline between a series of fortified convents and stone blockhouses: Dünamünde, Riga, Kirkholm, Üxküll, Lennewarden, Ascherade, Kukenois. The cogs unloaded men and supplies at Riga, and reinforcements could be carried forward by the river-boats that plied between Polotsk and the sea. South of the river lay heavily forested country from which Lithuanian and Curonian raiding parties period- ically struck; these had to be attacked out in the open by the garrison troops, preferably on their way home, when slowed down by the herds they were driving with them. They could not be pursued into their own countries without grave danger. To the north, the country was more open and mountainous, threaded with small rivers and approachable by well-worn invasion routes. There were more fields and villages to be won in this direction, and the ground could be held by hill-forts: Segewold, Treyden and Wenden on the Treiden Aa; Pernau (Pärnu) on the coast; Fellin, Dorpat and Odenpäh, and eventually Leal (Lihula) and Weissenstein (Vissuvere) in the far north. In penetrating these areas, the Sword-Brothers used every technical advantage they had. The forts themselves were the most important: square stone barracks for man and horse, usually planted on a captured earthwork, and crowned by a watchtower in one corner. Body armour, crossbows and large catapults were decisive in the early stages, and in 1207 the Brothers broke a Polotskian invasion by using calthrops, spiked devices that lamed cavalry. Siege-towers, trebuchets and fascines forced Fellin to surrender in 1211; a 'great machine' recaptured Kirkholm in 1220. After a defeat by the Curonians in Riga Bay in 1210, the Brothers stopped fighting in small ships and used the cogs, which drove back the Osilians from Riga in 1215 and could not be built by the enemy.

But the heathen always had the advantage of numbers and experience in local conditions, and soon began to copy the siege-machines and put on captured armour, or buy it from merchants undeterred by papal bans. The invaders could not rely on superior weapons alone. What made them more formidable was their ability to enlist the support of indigenous peoples, and for this intimidation was not sufficient. Nor was persuasion by the word: Henry of Livonia makes it clear that there were never more than a few who were prepared to renounce the old gods and fight for the new without other inducements. In the course of the wars, baptism became the consequence, not the cause, of adherence to the crusading army. The adherence came about because of material inducements. One was protection against Russians and Lithuanians, the bishop's competitors. Another was the aid the crusaders were prepared to give to Livs and Letts in raiding the Estonians – a chance to settle old scores and get rich. And another was the fact that the bishop was in partnership with everybody's best customers, the German merchants who brought silver and weapons and luxuries in exchange for furs and wax; and if necessary he could close the mouth of the river. Thus the peoples of Livonia were first either won over as allies, or conquered with the help of these allies; next, baptized, garrisoned and subjected to an occupying elite of priests and landlords. But would they accept the second phase?

Many had revolted against it, even before 1237; and many would revolt later. The next fifty years tested to the utmost the strength of this colonial superstructure.

These protracted disorders were largely the responsibility of the Sword-Brothers. They had won most of the country on the understanding (of 1204) that they could keep a third for themselves and must hand over the rest to the bishop. But the land produced small yields, and the wars were expensive. Their attempt to get more out of their peasants contributed to a widespread revolt in 1222, and they were rebuked by Pope Honorius III. They tried to compensate themselves by seizing the king of Denmark's land in Estonia, but the papal legate made them return it. When he left, they took it back, started encroaching on the bishop's share, and began levying tolls on the Dvina. Complaints reached Rome, and by 1230 the Sword-Brothers were becoming an Order of ill repute; another legate, Baldwin of Aulne, decided that they had outlived their usefulness, and reported that they ought to be suppressed. But, when he tried to recapture the Danish fort of Reval from them, with his own force of knights, he was defeated and made prisoner, and could only go back to Italy and begin a lawsuit against them. Master Folkwin began to feel the cold, and tried to persuade the unimpeachably respectable Teutonic Order to admit his knights as brethren; after a tour of inspection, a party of Teutonic Knights reported back to a chapter-meeting at Marburg that the Sword-Brothers 'were people who followed their own inclination, and did not keep their rule properly, and merely wanted to be given *carte blanche*, and not have their conduct looked into unless they agreed to it'.[57] They must have found out that the Sword-Brothers had even arrested their own master during the trouble with the legate.

The lawsuit at Rome went against Folkwin's Order, and the Teutonic Knights refused to assist him without papal permission. Then, in the summer of 1236, the master was persuaded by his crusading reinforcements to launch an invasion into Lithuania. Assisted by the prince of Pskov, he marched as far south as Saule (Siauliai) and then discovered that the crusaders were unwilling to fight, for fear of losing their horses in surrounding swamps. The Lithuanians attacked, and the entire host was annihilated – 'cut down like women', according to the Rhyme-Chronicler. Folkwin and fifty of his brethren were killed, and the Sword-Brothers were finished. They had made enemies of the king of

Denmark and the pope, the only powers that could help them, and in May 1237 the survivors were placed under the rule of the Teutonic Knights. Hermann Balk, the master of Prussia, took over the defence of Livonia.

Master Balk and the papal legate, William of Modena, set about saving the province. A crusade was preached, reinforcements marched north from Prussia, the king of Denmark was pacified by the return of Estonia, and the archbishop of Riga was persuaded to rest content with one-third instead of two-thirds of the conquered country. By 1255 the Livonian masters had won back the territory south of the Dvina that had been lost in 1236. They had persuaded King Mindaugas of Lithuania to accept baptism and an alliance, and they were co-operating in the subjugation of the Prussian province of Samland.

This ascendancy was based, as before, on alliances with the frontier nations. Force was used to show the Curonians, Semigallians and Samogitians who was the stronger, but the terms of the ensuing submissions were not harsh. They had to accept baptism, but they could keep their forts and govern themselves; the Order would fight for them, if they fought for the Order. Hostages were the only guarantee of their good faith.

This system collapsed in 1259, when the Samogitians broke the truce and defeated Master von Hornhausen of Livonia at Schoten in Curonia, killing thirty-three of his knight-brothers. The Semigallians and some of the Lithuanians changed sides, and, when von Hornhausen tried to take a short-cut into Prussia in search of reinforcements, his army was ambushed and destroyed at Durbe (1260). He was killed along with 150 knight-brothers, and the news of his overthrow made all the Lithuanians and most of the Prussians reject Christianity and declare war on the Order. The Estonians of Ösel followed suit, and the Russians recaptured Dorpat with Lithuanian help.

This revolt seems to have been the result of political calculation, rather than of resentment at racial oppression; the peoples governed directly by the Order in the Dvina and Vistula valleys remained loyal. The rebels were those least burdened by garrisons or services. But an Order that let itself be defeated by Samogitians was an Order that had been discredited. So for the next thirty years the Livonian knight-brothers fought on with unremitting savagery to achieve two goals: first, to regain unchallenged military supremacy; second, to deprive their former client-nations of political independence. The latter was long delayed, because the former was elusive; in 1262, 1270, 1279 and 1287 the Livonian knight-brothers met with heavy defeats, and four of their masters were killed in battle, as well as their marshal, Willekin, who was captured and burned alive. Their enemies could outnumber and outfight them; therefore, they had to impose permanent military garrisons on conquered territory, and protect them with a wide band of scorched earth. The Curonians were subjugated by 1263. The Semigallians were never subdued. Most of their nobles were kidnapped and beheaded; the people were driven from their lands into Lithuania, leaving a marshy waste overlooked by lonely castles. The Selonians continued to inhabit an unfortified forest, debatable between Livonian and Lithuanian raiders. The Samogitians remained unconquerable and aggressive enemies of the Teutonic Order. However, by 1290 there was a line of a dozen forts running from Dunaburg to Memel, and a 'wilderness' to the south of it. It was a stabilized frontier which kept the Lithuanians out, and the missionaries in, and committed the Order to a literal enactment of Luke 11.21: 'When a strong man armed keepeth his palace, his goods are in peace; but when a stronger than he shall come upon him . . .'

PRUSSIA

The Christian 'land of Prussia' began c. 1200 as a mission by monks from Lekno in Poland; was fostered by Innocent III; furthered by Bishop Christian with Danish help; but won by Teutonic Knights in two simultaneous wars: one against the heathen Prussians, the other against any possible Christian competitors.

The second war was sometimes open, as in 1242–8, when they were fighting Duke Swantopelk of Danzig (Pomerelia), but it was usually diplomatic. Throughout the conquest, the knight-brothers had to manoeuvre carefully lest any other power gain a claim or a foothold in their territory. Lübeck wanted to found colonies on the coast, and succeeded in doing so at Elbing. The Knights of Dobrzyn wanted to retain their lands on the southern Prussian frontier. The princes of Poland wanted shares of conquered Prussia in return for their help, and German princes hoped for dominion over all of it. Papal legates wanted to reserve more land for the bishops, and more liberty for converts, than the Order was prepared to give. German colonists were not always docile. And, without help from Lübeckers, Poles, papal legates and colonists, the conquest would have been impossible; yet such was the luck and acumen of the Order that in the end it was achieved with only a minimal sharing of sovereignty to placate the bishops.

Nevertheless, it took fifty years. The Prussians were more numerous and better led than the peoples of the Dvina, and before the Order arrived they had successfully resisted all Polish attempts to subdue and convert them. 'Tanto brevior, quanto coactior'[58] was how the Polish historian Vincent Kadlubek described such efforts in about 1220: 'the harder pressed, the shorter lived'. From 1217 to 1223, Pope Honorius III and Bishop Christian made strenuous efforts to organize an invincible crusading army against the Prussians, but the result was a futile convergence of German and Polish knights on the Chelmno side of the frontier, followed by a devastating heathen retaliation. This was why the duke of Mazovia, Conrad, then sent for the Teutonic Knights. The example of the Sword-Brothers in Livonia gave the Teutonic Knights the key to success. Their first task was to establish a line of river-forts. These they had to use as bases, from which crusading allies could intimidate or attract the riparian and coastal tribes. After that, they could conquer, garrison and open up the interior, and push east up the Niemen.

They began at the Polish fort of Chelmno in 1230.

All previous invasions had gone eastwards into the forests of the interior, but the captain of the Knights at Chelmno, Hermann Balk, concentrated his efforts in the west, along the Vistula. His first expedition, in 1231, secured the river above Chelmno by building a small fort at Torun (Thorn) opposite the mouth of the river Drweca (Drewenz), which flows into the Vistula from central Prussia. An army of Polish and German crusaders mustered there, the following year, and pushed north-east of Chelmno to found a new fort at Marienwerder (Kwidzyn); another fort at Reden (Radzyn) protected the 'Kulmerland' east of Chelmno. The next crusade, under the young margrave of Meissen, harried the nearby Pomesanian Prussians until they made peace, and supplied Hermann with two large river-boats. With these he pushed north from Marienwerder and founded Elbing (Elblag) on the delta of the Vistula, and Christburg on Lake Dzierzgon, which dominated the country east of Marienwerder. The Pomesanians and Pogesanians found themselves cut off from their main trade-route, and made their peace with the Order. By 1239 there was a garrison at Balga, thirty-five miles north-east of Elbing on the Frische Haff, and the master was waiting for the next wave of crusaders, to continue the encirclement.

So far, most of the fighting had been done by Polish and German crusaders, and the Order had merely built small timber forts. Losses had been light, and Hermann had been able to detach some of his men to occupy Livonia. But, when the duke of Brunswick arrived with more volunteers, harried the tribes round Balga into submission and left colonists to make settlements in their country, the Order found itself overwhelmed by a concerted attack from both sides of the Vistula delta. A former ally, Duke Swantopelk of Danzig, discovered that the new trading communities at Torun, Marienwerder and Elbing were competing with his own merchants, and that Balga threatened his hold on the sand-spit which enclosed the Frische Haff; in 1242 he came to an understanding with the Prussians, and together they destroyed all but three of the Order's forts and settlements, and ravaged the Kulmerland.

This was the beginning of a ten years' war. Swantopelk had a river-fleet of over twenty ships; he built counter-forts to contain the Order's garrisons, and kept up a continual harassment of German populations. The Prussians soon discovered how to deal with the Order's offensives, and annihilated two marshals and their armies at Rensen (1244) and Krücken (1249). Heavy-armed knights, big horses, and crossbows gave the Order an advantage on level dry ground within reach of a stockade. Elsewhere, the knight-brothers could be pinned down, cut off, and ambushed. But the Prussians could only attack forts by direct assault or by blockade, and crossbowmen and supply-boats frustrated these attacks. It looked like stalemate, especially when Swantopelk failed to destroy a force of knight-brothers which he had ambushed outside Torun in 1246.

What turned the balance against Swantopelk was the help given the Order by the papal legate and other Polish princes. The Poles wanted to dislodge him from the mouth of the Vistula, and the legate wanted him to co-operate with the Order against the heathen. A crusade was preached against him, and he agreed to make peace and share the Vistula delta with the Teutonic Knights. The Order was saved, but only at a price. In return for papal and German assistance, Master von Grüningen had to promise to endow three independent bishoprics out of his conquests, and to grant civil liberties to all converts. To get help for further conquests, he had to promise shares to Lübeck and the Polish princes; he could not prevent the pope offering the peninsula of Samland to

King Håkon IV of Norway, if he were to succeed in subduing it first. Three unexpected allies saved the Order from having to honour these promises. One was King Ottokar of Bohemia, who came on crusade in 1254, and paid for the building of the Samland fort named Königsberg in his honour. The other was King Mindaugas of Lithuania, whose conversion allowed the unopposed founding of two more forts up the Niemen river, Memel and Georgenburg. By 1259 the Sambian Prussians had been forced to submit – to the Teutonic Knights, rather than to Poles, Lübeckers, papal legates or Norwegians; but whether Samland could be kept free of outside Christian powers in future had yet to be settled.

The third 'ally', the Russian prince Daniel of Galicia, had no intention of assisting the Order: he wanted Prussia for himself. Nevertheless, between 1248 and 1254 the elaborate invasions which he and the Polish dukes Semovit and Boleslaw conducted up the Narew river from the Bug basin occupied the most powerful Prussian people, the Yatwingians, while the Order was gaining ground in the North. This pressure also helped drive Mindaugas of Lithuania into his *rapprochement* with the Germans, and in the subsequent decade it was the Russian, and occasionally Mongol, presence on the Bug which prevented the takeover of Prussia by Mindaugas's successors.

For the defeat of the Livonians at Durbe in 1260 was followed by the military collapse of the Prussian Brothers in the face of a general revolt by their indigenous subjects. Many of their garrisons and colonies were massacred, and the first reinforcement of crusaders was wiped out at Pokarwis. Pope Urban IV, who had been trying to organize a crusade against the Mongols, urged all who had taken the cross to turn north and save the Order, promising full remission of sins for any length of service at all; but by 1264 two Prussian masters had been killed in battle and the Brothers were reduced to a few of their strongest forts. Even Marienwerder had been captured, and Königsberg only survived thanks to reinforcements from Livonia.

This time the Prussian nations were organized by *capitanei* and equipped both with siege-machines and with crossbows. Their knowledge of German enabled them to infiltrate the enemy camp, and they were helped by Duke Swantopelk's son Mestwin and by the leadership of the Yatwingians, now free of Russian lordship. They showed mastery of river warfare, open battle and sieges. The knight-brothers were very nearly ousted; but, once again, they were saved by German crusaders, in particular by the duke of Brunswick (1265), the landgrave of Thuringia (1265), the margraves of Brandenburg (1266) and the margrave of Meissen (1272).

The forts were relieved, the waterways reopened, and the bases of the *capitanei* were impoverished by systematic ravaging. Nations were forced either to submit or to emigrate, and if they submitted they had to accept garrisons and the demotion of their chiefs to feudal vassals of the Order. Meanwhile, the chief forts were rebuilt as brick or stone castles: Königsberg in the 1260s, Marienwerder and Marienburg in the 1270s. No papal legate intervened to moderate the process of resubjugation, and no deals had to be made with Polish and other neighbouring princes; all the Lithuanians could do was welcome and resettle those Prussians who fled to the east. All the central nations had submitted by 1277. Some of the Barthians, some of the Scalovians and all the Nadrovians had left their homelands for new lands on the Niemen, where they were joined by Pogesanian refugees, who had made a last bid for independence that year. By 1283 even the Yatwingians had been ravaged beyond endurance. One of their leaders came in with 1500 warriors to live under the Order's rule, and another took the road to Lithuania with the rest of his nation. The war had become an affair of small guerrilla raids over no-man's-land, for which the Order employed not German crusaders but bands of converted Old Prussians, who specialized in surprise attacks and furtive massacres. The converts made two more forlorn attempts at revolt, in 1286 and 1295, hoping in both cases that external enemies of the Order – the prince of Rügen and the rulers of Lithuania – would intervene on their behalf; but it was too late. The Teutonic Knights were firmly in the saddle.

The third phase of conquest was thus completed, and the Order was left in undisputed control of the lordship of Prussia, apart from enclaves held by the bishops of Warmia (Ermland) and Pomesania. The see of Samland was held by a nominee of the Teutonic Knights.

This control would have been much harder to establish if the Order's chief patrons, the pope and the emperor, had not been more intent on fighting each other than on supervising the conquest. Each had a policy that would have brought the Prussian nations and their monastic conquerors under his own lordship; but so suspicious of each other's interference were they that they preferred to keep outbidding each other for the friendship of the Order than risk alienating the grand-masters by inhibiting their freedom of action. This was how Hermann of Salza got his initial grants of lordship both from Frederick II and from Gregory IX in 1226 and 1230, and why he was subsequently allowed to take over both the Knights of Dobrzyn and the Sword-Brothers; why the Bull *Pietati proximum* (1234), claiming Prussia for St Peter, and the Imperial Bull of Verona, claiming Courland, Semigallia and Lithuania as fiefs of the Empire (1245), were never made effective, and why the treaty of Christburg (1249) granting liberties to Prussian converts was enforced only up to a point. While papalists and Hohenstaufen fought each other to the death, the grand-masters took their pick of privileges, and thereafter their gains were confirmed and reconfirmed by succeeding popes and emperors, who liked to think of them either as a 'flourishing limb of the imperial court, the tender plant and creation of the emperors' (Rudolph of Habsburg's Privilege of 1273) or as 'our beloved sons and brothers, who, for long years past have exposed their minds and bodies for the cause of the faith' (Boniface VIII, 1300).

ESTONIA

The story of how the Danish kings reorganized their military system to conquer the Wends has already been told. After 1185 it remained to be seen how far their method of extending lordship through parallel campaigns of coastal devastation and church-building could be stretched. Pope Alexander III had pointed the way to the east for all Scandinavian believers; the growing volume of trade with Novgorod and Polotsk made the destruction of Sambian, Curonian and Estonian sea-power desirable aims, and the subjugation of the homelands of these pirates seemed a feasible way of going about it. Denmark was now a prosperous and united kingdom, well stocked with merchants, knights and monks, and able to bear the expense of war. Accordingly, kings Canute VI (1182–1202) and Valdemar II (1202–41) organized a number of eastward probes to follow up the raid of 1170 which their father, Valdemar I, had sent against the Estonians. Danish fleets attacked Finland in 1191 and 1202, Estonia in 1194 and 1197, Ösel in 1206, and Prussia in 1210. These raids may have done some damage, and intimidated a few heathen for a while, but that was all. There were no territorial princes in those parts with whom permanent ties of vassalage could be created and in whose lands monks could be settled; no Danish missionaries or settlers were prepared to found independent outposts like Meinhard's at Üxküll. And it may be doubted whether the conquest of the eastern Baltic came high on the king's list of priorities until after 1216. Before that the Danes were busy with the more rewarding task of winning control of the lands between the Elbe and Pomerania. Once the whole Baltic coast from Lübeck to Danzig acknowledged Valdemar II as overlord, it was time to think of annexing less accessible areas in the east.

All this while, the idea of the crusade gained ground. Gregory VIII's appeal for the reconquest of Jerusalem, *Audita tremendi*, inspired seven of the flower of the Danish nobility to make the journey to Palestine in 1191, and many had joined the north-German contingent which sailed in 1188. The Norwegian author of the work which describes the 1191 expedition (*De profectione Danorum in Hierosolymam*) puts into the mouth of Archbishop Absalon's brother Esbern a speech to the king and nobility which criticizes the sordid materialism of his own times and conquests undertaken for mere glory, and exhorts the Danes 'to greater and more profitable contests'. 'Let us be "partakers of the inheritance of the saints" and share in their labours', he demanded,[59] and in the end over a thousand were said to have responded to the appeal. Further contingents sailed in 1197, 1216 and 1225. Meanwhile, the king and the archbishop were keeping an eye on Hartwig of Bremen and the Livonian mission, and wondering whether sordid materialism and the labours of the saints might be brought together, nearer home.

They learned some useful lessons. In 1206 Valdemar II and Archbishop Andrew, Absalon's kinsman and successor, sailed to Ösel with a well-prepared force, and forced the Estonian islanders to submit. They put up a timber fort, but no one volunteered to man it, and it had to be burnt down before they re-embarked. When the fleet sailed home, Andrew and Bishop Nicholas of Schleswig went south to Riga for the winter, and when they got back to Denmark they were evidently wiser in the techniques of subjugation: timber forts and summer cruises were not good enough. However, a claim had been staked: henceforward Valdemar regarded the Estonians, and perhaps the Livonians as well, as his by right. The fact that he did virtually nothing about it for twelve years, while Bishop Albert and the Sword-Brothers were steadily advancing into Estonia, made little difference to his claim; he controlled Lübeck and the western Baltic, and they could do nothing without his permission.

Saxo, who was still writing his history of the Danes at this time, was livening his narrative with far-fetched stories of how the king's forebears had populated Prussia and conquered the Dvina, the Estonians and the Finns; Innocent III was writing encouraging letters, and treating Valdemar as the favoured champion of the Church.

In 1218 Honorius III promised Valdemar that he could annex as much land as he might conquer from the heathen, and in the same year Bishop Albert, alarmed at an invasion from Novgorod, went in person to beg the king to attack the Estonians. In 1219 he mobilized his fleet, joined forces with the Rugian navy and arrived off the north-Estonian coast with his archbishop, three bishops and Prince Wizlav of Rügen, Jaromar's successor. They landed in the one first-rate harbour of Lindinisse, in the coastal district of Revele, which was part of the land of Harria, and began building the fort which the Estonians called Tallinn, the Danes and Germans Reval, and the Russians Kolyvan. When the Estonians attacked, they were defeated with heavy losses, and, when the fort was ready, a garrison of knights, priests and bishops moved in and stayed behind when the king sailed home. The following year, the king returned with reinforcements and Dominican friars, and both Danes and Sword-Brothers harried and subjugated the northern Estonians, while King John of Sweden conquered the north-western coast (Rotala) and built a fort at Leal. The result was an ugly quarrel between the conquerors over jurisdiction, and an appeal to Rome. Henry of Livonia describes how the Danes went about putting up large crosses as tokens of their lordship, and distributed holy water to village headmen to sprinkle promiscuously over their people, while the German missionaries did their work conscientiously,[60] but Henry was committed to Riga. The situation was simplified when the Swedes were pushed out of Leal by the Rotalians, and Valdemar closed Lübeck to Livonian crusaders; Bishop Albert had to surrender the whole of north Estonia to him (Harria, Vironia and Jerwia) as the price of opening Lübeck, and was only prevented by the intransigence of his burghers from handing over Livonia as well. The Sword-Brothers did him fealty for the lands they had conquered in southern Estonia. Sea-power had compensated Valdemar for the lack of other advantages. He had no military monks, no time for persistent campaigning in the east, and comparatively few would-be colonists to hold the land for him, but as long as he had command of the Baltic there was no getting rid of him.

Several attempts were made, and, thanks to the king's unlucky kidnap-
ping by a German prince in 1223–7, they almost succeeded. His garrison in
Jerwia were caught and disembowelled by rebels, who ate the governor's
heart; a Novgorodian army besieged Reval for four weeks, and in 1225
the Sword-Brothers seized Harria and Vironia for a while. Reval fell
to the Sword-Brothers in 1227, but was handed back by the Teutonic
Knights at the treaty of Stensby in 1238, along with Harria and Vironia.
The popes still expected Denmark to take the lead in the Northern
crusade, and Denmark still had the largest naval resources; the only way
of keeping Valdemar interested was to let him have his Estonian
dependency.

So he kept it; not by the diligence of his missionaries, not by the
dedication and prowess of his garrison, not by the number and loyalty
of his colonists, but because with some 200 ships at his disposal he was
able to apply the requisite force at exactly the right moment, and outbid
his rivals for papal approval. Much of his territory was subjugated for
him by Bishop Albert's men, and colonized by Saxon immigrants, many
of whom were expelled after 1238 and replaced by more dependable men
– also Holsteiners and Westphalians, for the most part. The new town
of Reval was as German as Riga, and the continuation of the war against
the 'heathen' Russians east of the Neva was left to the association of
vassal landowners, without much interference from Denmark. But, as
long as the king's captain held Reval castle, his taxes could be collected
and the proceeds of his large private estates were guaranteed. For this
citadel commanded a spacious harbour on a rocky and treacherous coast,
and sea-communications kept it safe when the hinterland was lost. Here
were the arsenal, stables and treasury that constituted the heart of Danish
rule; already by 1227 it contained a store of 400 hauberks, and stabling
for 250 war-horses and 200 hacks. Most of the arms and troops were
in the 'lesser castle', where the captain lived; this was built in the
south-western corner of the 'greater castle', containing the bishop's
palace, the vassal's houses and the cathedral of St Mary – the cathedral
gave the whole acropolis the name of 'Domburg'. Below the walls, and
across the moat lay the new town, the house of Dominicans, the Cistercian
nunnery of St Michael, eight churches, two chapels, a leper-house, a
hospital, guild-houses, bath-houses – all the amenities of a Christian
city, ready to stand siege. Halfway along the road to Narva, which the
besiegers would be using, stood the castle of Wesenburg (Rakvere), built

by 1252; Narva was not successfully fortified until 1329. Only in these three places could burghers live together in safety.

After Valdemar II had sorted out his difficulties with the Teutonic Knights, and his archbishop had settled with the Livonian bishops the boundaries of his new suffragan diocese of Reval, there still remained the question of how far the king's authority could be pushed towards the east, into the Vod country dominated by Novgorod. The papal legate got Valdemar to co-operate with the Teutonic Order in the anti-Russian crusade of 1240–42, and it appears that at first the king had hopes of winning at least a slice of Russia for himself. He sent his sons Abel and Canute to accompany his Estonian vassals on the campaign, and with them a fleet of men and women 'to till the lands devastated by the Tartars, and settle them';[61] according to Matthew Paris, these preparations led to a rumour that the Danes were about to invade England again. But the failure of the invasion kept the king's men to the west of the river Narva in future.

In 1244, Valdemar's son Eric IV took the cross, and until 1254 there was hope at Rome that there would be another Danish push to the east. In the event, the Estonians were hard put to it to hold on to what they had gained, and the Danish fleets that sailed to Reval in 1268 and 1270 were needed to meet serious incursions by Russian and Lithuanian armies. Valdemar II's successors had too much to occupy them at home for aggression into Russia; the once united monarchy was slowly disintegrating in conflicts between rival princes, kings, barons and bishops. They were content to remain absentee landlords of a fairly profitable colonial investment, and leave the problems of holding down and converting the indigenous Estonian population to local landlords and clergy. The combination of spiritual obligation and political opportunity which had produced the crusades of 1219 and 1220 were not to be repeated.

FINLAND

Denmark was not the only country with a levy-fleet and an interest in the eastern Baltic. The Swedish kings had a similar system of mobilization, and their subjects had to face a much more dangerous threat from the sea. Denmark's eastward shipping and outermost province of Blekinge may have been preyed on, but the whole length of Sweden's coast was liable to devastation and pillage by enemies living directly across the water, a mere 150 miles away, with halfway anchorages off Gotland and the Åland islands. Curonians, Osilian Estonians and Karelian Finns had been plaguing these shores for some time before Swedish rulers began to embark on serious wars of conquest and retribution.

It was suggested in chapter 1 that the balance of loss by piracy and profit by reprisal and trade was not so unequal that Swedish kings had much incentive to disturb it. The only three eastward expeditions in the twelfth century for which there is reliable evidence suggest that these kings were more interested in practising and profiting by piracy than in suppressing it.

In 1142, according to the Novgorod Chronicle, 'a prince of the Swedes with a bishop in sixty ships attacked merchants who were returning from overseas in three boats. They fought, and accomplished nothing, and they carried off three of their ships and they killed 150 of them'.[62] This brush could have happened anywhere in the eastern Baltic. In 1164 the Swedes, with a fleet of fifty-five ships, tried to take the fort of Ladoga, but failed, and were routed by the prince of Novgorod on the Voronezhka; and in 1195 or 1196 they set out to assist Bishop Meinhard in Livonia, but followed the wind instead and ended up by pillaging Estonia, until the inhabitants bought them off with tribute. These were old-fashioned Viking raids, and the Swedes were not alone in making them: in 1186 King Sverrir of Norway's brother Eric ran short of money, and 'went to the Baltic to plunder heathen lands'. He plundered Rotala and the mouth of the Dvina, then sailed back to Gotland and captured two cogs from the Saxons and returned home with immense wealth.

Later tradition has it that in about 1155–60 a Swedish king, Eric 'IX', led a full-scale expedition into Finland which conquered and converted the country, and has since been known as the 'first Finland crusade'. The story was told in the *Vita Sancti Erici*, ascribed to Bishop Israel Erlandsen of Västeras, who died in 1328–9, and was associated with circles committed to missions and crusades; as it stands, it is an obvious literary construct, which cannot be accepted as historical. It tells how the king embarked for Finland with a Bishop Henry from Uppsala, and began his campaign by offering the people peace and the Christian faith. They refused, and attacked him; he defeated them in battle (after which he was found weeping because so many potential converts had been killed), and then preached to them again, with greater success; when he sailed back to Sweden he left behind a Christian community.[63] The legend of Bishop Henry relates that after a short ministry he was axed to death by a convert; and at least it is certain that in the thirteenth century Eric and Henry were worshipped as the patron saints of Sweden and Finland respectively. But the legend is crusade propaganda, not fact.

There is some reason to believe that King Eric did raid Finland, because Innocent III addressed a letter to his grandson, Eric X (1210–16), in which Finland is referred to as 'the land which your predecessors of famous memory snatched from the hands of the pagans';[64] and some years earlier Alexander III had written to the Swedish archbishop and earl that he was distressed to hear that 'the Finns always promise to obey the Christian faith whenever they are threatened by a hostile army, and eagerly ask for preachers and teachers of the law of Christ, and when the army retires they deny the faith, despise the preachers, and grievously persecute them'. If this is a reference to 'St Eric's crusade', it suggests that it was not the only one, and that all had failed; but the pope clearly expected further developments, and proposed that in future the Finns should be made to hand over their forts 'if they have any' or other securities for their good behaviour. However, there is no clear evidence that the king of the Swedes actually ruled any part of Finland before 1200. It was still an open country.

When in 1209 Innocent III wrote to Archbishop Andrew of Lund thanking him for the news that 'a certain land, called Finland ... has lately been converted to the faith by the exertions of certain noble personages',[65] it would appear that he refers to the raids undertaken in 1191 and 1202 by Danish fleets, or, rather, to missions established after them. The pope allowed Andrew to consecrate a bastard as bishop of the 'new plantation', since nobody else wanted the job. It was said to be more likely to entail martyrdom than earthly honours. Nevertheless, a community of Christians had been established among the Suomi (south-west Finns), and in 1215 there was a Finnish convert, Peter Kakuwalde, working as a priest among the Estonians.

Denmark lost interest in Finland once territory had been gained in Estonia, and at the same time the Swedes stopped raiding the Estonians and began to show an interest in Finland. A number of Swedish peasants and landowners settled in the territory known as Satakunta, and joined the Suomi converts and priests as a Christian community under a bishop. This emigration was not the result of royal policy, but it was to have political consequences once attempts were made to extend Christianity beyond the limits of this original 'Finland' into the central lake-district.

The motives of the Swedes who went into Suomi lands, and of the Suomi who accepted their faith and paid tithe to their bishop, can only be conjectured. That part of the country was fertile and temperate, and easily accessible, by way of the Åland Isles, to villagers in small boats. There was a harbour at Åbo (Turku) where merchants of both nations might have settled, under the usual conditions of shared independence; the trades in fur and fish may have accounted for smaller settlements, at first seasonal, then permanent. The wilderness inland offered summer pasture for the herds of the immigrants, as well as hunting grounds for the Suomi. And the priests and later friars who went among the Finns may have been taking their only chance to get away from the excessively landowner-dominated churches of their homeland in Sweden; according to Archbishop Andrew, 'there is no church established anywhere in the world which is so oppressed by the insolence of the people'[66] – by the local freeholders, that is, who paid for the church-building and were allowed by law to treat the parish priest as their own hired man. Among the Finns, a priest might find martyrdom, but he would also find freedom. And the Suomi themselves had long been familiar with the Swedes, and may have seen Swedish communities as desirable sources of profit which presented little obvious threat to their independence or prosperity; perhaps they even looked on them as a guarantee that there would be no more punitive raids by the king and his warriors.

However, the Suomi were one people, the most agricultural of the Finns; the Tavastians were another, far less amenable to the Swedish way of life, and prone to supplement their gains by fur-trading with raids on the Karelian, Vod and Russian settlements of the eastern wilderness. As a result, the princes of Novgorod had built up connections with Vods and Karelians which by 1200 amounted to virtual overlordship, and resulted in an intermittent state of war between the Finnish nations. Were the Swedes to gain control of the Tavastians, they would find themselves committed to joining in this war; and they were already under attack from Karelian summer raiding parties, which put to sea on the north-eastern shores of the Bothnian Gulf and sailed southwards into the Swedish skerries. In 1227 Prince Yaroslav of Novgorod 'sent priests to baptize the Karelians, and soon all the inhabitants were baptized'.[67] This venture was followed by a corresponding mission to the Tavastians, undertaken by an Englishman, Bishop Thomas of Finland; but by 1237 Pope Gregory IX had been informed that the Tavastians had rejected Christianity, and called on all Christians to join a crusade against them. Both the Church and the Swedish king suddenly found it desirable to use force in order to maintain the balance of power and religion in Finland.

Their first joint venture was the expedition of 1240, which was decisively defeated by Prince Alexander Nevsky of Novgorod at the confluence of the Neva and the Izhora. After that it must have seemed all the more urgent to bring the Tavastians into the Latin Church, and the arrival of the Dominican friars ensured that Gregory IX's appeal for a Tavastian crusade would not be forgotten. The friars were committed to missionary work, and were befriended by Bishop Thomas, by Archbishop Jarler of Uppsala, and by the rising magnate Birger Magnusson, a brother of the Earl Charles who had been killed by the heathen at Ösel in 1220; thanks to this combination, King Eric XI, 'the Lisper', was persuaded to call out a full levy-fleet and sent it to Finland under Birger, his brother-in-law and now earl, in 1249.

The story of the 'second' and 'third' Finnish crusades was told in a Swedish rhyme-chronicle called *Erikskrönikan*,[68] which was written (probably between 1322 and 1332) by an unidentified follower of one of Birger Jarl's grandsons. The author expresses the attitudes of the new knightly landowning class which dominated Sweden at the time, and these attitudes to a large extent correspond to those of the crusade-minded European chivalry – always allowing for a dash of xenophobia and social realism. He believed in the crusading ideal, and had the greatest respect for the Teutonic Knights – 'God's knights', to him; but when he describes the Finnish crusades it becomes apparent that he has simply superimposed the opposition 'Christian–heathen' on the opposition 'us–the enemy', and regards Tavastians, Karelians and Russians as promiscuously pagan. Birger Jarl took command of the 1249 expedition 'because he wanted to increase his fame'; but it was assumed that God's reputation increased with the Earl's. The effect of the Dominican mission on lay society at home seems merely to have consisted of giving Sweden's enemies a new name. *Erikskrönikan* never refers to the expeditions of 1249 and 1292 as crusades, or implies that the participants expected full remission of sins for joining them; the author hopes that, by analogy with the Holy Wars of the Teutonic Knights, those who died will go to heaven, but the analogy is somewhat strained. It would appear that he, and the circle to which he belonged, were using the example of the crusade against the Balts as an encouragement to fight the Finns and Russians. In the narrative of the 1249 expedition, the attractions of loot, adventure and spreading the faith are given equal weight.

> Their loud lament the ladies sang
> And hands most piteously wrang,
> And still rejoiced when out men rode
> To magnify the honour of God.
> And many an old ancestral sword
> That long the walls had cumbered
> Was snatched from the nails where it slumbered.
> Then down to the sea they went in their bands
> And each hailed the other, clasping hands,
> And many a lad was kissed by the shore
> That never was kissed in this world more . . .
>
> The heathen did gird themselves, for they
> Knew well that the Christians were coming their way
> To deal them destruction, and little cheer.
> To harbour the Christians did steer,
> And gilded prows uncountable there
> Made all the infidels to stare . . .[69]

The harbour may have been Helsinki. There the Swedes landed and pushed upriver, driving the Finns before them.

> And well I trust, those men did win
> Gold and silver, and herds of kine.
> And off the Tavastian warriors run:
> The heathen lost – the Christians won . . .[70]
>
> And he who was fain to bow the knee
> And go to the font and a Christian be,
> They left him his life and goods to enjoy,
> To live at peace, without annoy,
> But the heathen who still denied Our Lord
> They gave him death for his reward.

The Christians built a stronghold here
And manned it with their kinsmen dear –
A place Tavastehus they call
Which did the heathen much appal;
They settled the land with Christian men
And there I trust they will remain,
And the land was turned to our belief
Which gave the Russian king much grief.[71]

So it did: not because the Tavastians had been subject to him, but because now they and the Suomi were under Swedish rule and were reinforced by castles at Åbo and Tavastehus. Novgorod and her Karelian allies would be liable to attack by combined armies of Swedes and western Finns. The Tavastians had gone raiding from the southern Finnish plateau down to the mouth of the Neva; if the Swedes built another fort there, they would be able to levy toll on all Russian and German merchants using the Gulf route to Novgorod, and drive a wedge between the city and the Karelians, who supplied a large proportion of her exports. If Swedish missionaries had their way, attempts would be made to win these Karelians from the Greek to the Latin faith and in 1257 Pope Alexander IV authorized the king of Sweden to conquer them. This was particularly annoying as the Karelian fur-traders were showing signs of independence – not only by driving out Norwegian tax collectors from Lapland (1271 onwards), but also by concluding separate treaties with German traders, which meant that they could supply furs direct to the Western market and bypass Novgorod.

Prince Dmitri reaffirmed Russian supremacy by an invasion of Karelia in 1278; five years later, Swedish raiders were fighting the men of Ladoga on the Neva again. 1291 was a bad year for Novgorod – flood, frost, loss of grain and horses – and the following spring a party of adventurers went on a raid into Tavastia to restock; in reply, Birger Jarl's grandson, King Birger, launched the expedition of 1292 which is known as the third Finnish crusade. The popes had authorized action against the Karelians, as disturbers of the Christian Finns, but only half the invasion force was directed against them (400 men, according to the Novgorod Chronicle); the other half went against the people living on the Izhora, a tributary of the Neva some seventy miles north of the city. Their leader was the largest landowner in Sweden, Tyrgils Knutsson, a relation of the king and bearer of the newfangled title of 'marshal'. Neither war-band appears to have met with much success; but, before the marshal sailed home, he had laid the foundation of the third centre of Swedish power in Finland.

On 4 March 1295 King Birger was able to announce to the traders of Lübeck and other Hanseatic towns that he had converted the Karelians to Christianity and 'with an immense army and laborious preparations we have erected the castle of Viborg, to the honour of God and the glorious Virgin, both for the protection of our kingdom and for the safety and peace of sea-farers'.[72] According to this document, that safety and peace had long been disturbed by Karelian pirates, who had not only robbed, but also flayed and disembowelled Christian prisoners of both sexes; in future, the Gulf would be open to all merchants free of toll, provided that they were not carrying arms to Novgorod, or that there were more than three Russian passengers to a ship. In other words, King Birger hoped to establish himself as the protector of the main north-east trade-route, and thus make himself indispensable both to the Russians and to the Germans. Supremacy in this crucial area would ensure that he held the upper hand in dealing both with Hanseatic merchants in Swedish towns, and with Russo-Karelian fur-traders in the Far North. For the sake of justifying and legalizing the annexation, the king claimed the conversion of the infidel and the protection of persecuted Christians – even the unity of the Catholic faith – as his motives.

The majority of Swedes can have derived little advantage from this conquest, although it was an escape for some small freeholders who were feeling the pinch of the new seigneurial landownership. These were the men who populated the southern coastlands in the period 1250–1300 and turned them into Nyland, or 'new country'. The profits, if any, of fighting in Finland went to the knights, bishops and magnates; the expenses were borne by their peasants. The commercial advantages that came from holding land along the main Novgorod trade-route are difficult to assess. Where they assume tangible form, in new markets and harbours, the king would seem to have been the chief gainer. Otherwise, it was a section of the nobility and clergy which benefited from the territorial annexation – in tithe, the cure of souls, and rent. The enterprise was essentially the work of a political elite and turned out to have side-benefits for larger and less favoured groups, including many of the Finns themselves. In bringing it about, the king and his advisers had to mobilize both summer levies and forces of occupation from a military class that had little experience in fighting overseas, and probably feared the risks of meeting 'wild Finns' and Novgorodians in alien and treacherous country.

These dismal and isolated struggles against starvation and smoke were endurable to professed monks trained in self-denial and discomfort, but the warriors who were fighting in Finland were not monks. They were used to their butter and beef, their fresh salmon, barley bread and unstinted beer; not for nothing were they called 'food Swedes' by the Finns on whom they were quartered. By this date the knights were hearing stories of the chivalry of Alexander the Great, King Arthur and Charlemagne, winning prizes at tournaments, and feasting on imported luxuries at the expense of ostentatious magnates. Those who wanted to leave home in search of redemption, to rid themselves of an unbearable load of sin, had little reason to go to Finland. The pilgrimage to Jerusalem was a more attractive and fashionable alternative. Monasteries would advance loans to would-be pilgrims on the security of their land; thus Gisli Petersson set out in 1259, the bishop of Linköping went with a party of pilgrims in 1282; and in 1293 many took the cross at Uppsala in response to Pope Nicholas's appeal for crusaders to the Holy Land. Two landowners are known to have joined the Teutonic Knights. Karl Ulfsson was killed fighting in Livonia in 1260 or 1261, and much praised by the Eric-Chronicler for his Christian heroism; Johan Elofsson, brother of the pilgrim-saint Ingrid, appears as a Knight of the Order between 1281 and 1295. There were many reasons, both spiritual and material, for not fighting the king's war against the Russians and the Karelians.

It was, therefore, all the more important to invest this war with a religious significance of its own. Hence the promotion of the cult of St Eric through the translation of his relics in 1257 and 1273, and the composition of his legend not long afterwards; in this just warrior, compounded from the English prototypes of Oswald, Ethelbert and Edmund, the Swedish clergy laid down a pattern for all campaigners in Finland to follow. He had gone to war for the salvation of the souls of those whom he conquered, and had thereby won a glorious victory over sin. His bishop Henry, who lay buried at Nousiainen, north of Åbo, had been murdered for trying to enforce the ecclesiastical penalty for homicide on a convert. Both the royal family and the prelates of Uppsala had thereby pledged themselves to the conversion of the Finns, and the fight must be continued by all devout Swedes. The papal bulls that authorized wars against the Tavastians and Karelians reinforced this tradition, and the papal rhetoric that construed Novgorodian raids as attacks on the Christian faith extended it to cover the gruelling frontier-wars of 1292 onwards. The Eric Chronicle was itself a statement of propaganda in this cause, and attempted against the evidence to prove that both knightly and religious values were upheld in fighting the Russians.

Thus, from one side of Lake Ladoga: 'God grant his heaven to those souls/Who suffered death in that dire slaughter.' And from the other: 'Grant rest, O Lord, in thy kingdom, to the souls of those who laid their heads at that fort for St Sophia's sake.'[73]

5

THE THEOCRATIC EXPERIMENT,
1200 – 1273

POPES AND LEGATES

The Lord gives proofs of his kindness towards his faithful servants by reserving for them enemies (whom he could destroy by his word alone) in order that they might come to the aid of the many who dwell near those enemies, for love of him, and that they might have a means of atonement and salvation by repaying to him something of what he did for them.

Not an easy sentence to follow. It comes from the Bull, dated 12 September 1230, by which Pope Gregory IX authorized the Teutonic Knights to move into Prussia, and it will serve as a sample of the devious rhetoric through which the institutional master-mind of the crusading movement communicated with its agents. Bureaucracies have their jargons, and the eloquent Italian lawyers who formulated papal policy in the thirteenth century were presumably able to sleep the sounder for knowing that the chancery clerks would convey instructions in this rhythmical flow of officialese. It was a prosy counterpoint which linked day-to-day politics with the eternal truths of the faith.

A comparison between these charters reveals the way in which the Curia worked its way towards each new Holy War by laying stereotype upon stereotype to form a paradigm. It went something like this: first, there are missionaries who 'spread the net of their preaching for a catch of barbarian souls', so that 'the trumpet of sacred eloquence resounds in the innermost recesses of the minds of those barbarians', and 'the fountain of the faith distributes its streams among various provinces deluded by idolatry'. Then, some barbarians join 'the household of God' in the 'new plantation of the faith' and may be expected to become 'equals in the love of good things, and harmonious in effective works' with true

believers. Sometimes, however, 'the Beast rises up, swallowing the multitudes with his gaping mouth, confident that Jordan may flow into his
jaws, against whom it is necessary that Christian people gird up their
loins', for 'the heathen do rage' and 'capture youths whom they wear
out with continuous and horrifying labour, and immolate in demoniacal
fires along with virgins crowned in mockery with flowers, and slay the
old men, and slaughter the boys, some piercing with darts, some dashing
against trees'. In that case, those 'who take up arms against the barbarity
of those pagans' and 'fight back with manful potency', 'protected by the
armour of God on the right hand and on the left', at the behest of 'the
Apostolic See which is the general mother of all, and grants the shield
of her protection at the request of believers', must bear in mind that 'the
exercise of piety is the more strenuously to be pursued in such places,
in order that the greater impiety may be prevented', and they must
exercise their 'ministry' of warfare so that the Church may spread 'into
the place of their encampment, where they stretch the ropes of their
tabernacles', and they may 'call the poor, the maimed, the lame, and the
blind to the wedding-feast of the king of kings' and 'green shoots and
reeds may spring up where formerly dwelt the owls'.

By such language the crusade was generated and guided. It was not
used simply for show. All over Europe there were men trained to
respond to such words, and translate them into action, because they
were committed by their professions, beliefs, and self-interest to do what
the pope wanted. How the twelfth-century popes came to authorize the
Northern crusade has already been described. After Alexander III, the
Curia was increasingly concerned with North-East Europe, and under
Innocent III (1198–1216) this concern took the form of intervening
wherever possible in accordance with the theory of papal monarchy –
the theory that as the vicar of Christ the pope had responsibility for the
spiritual and political welfare of all mankind, and a duty to use both
worldly and other-worldly powers to bring about the salvation of all
men. Innocent's successors continued to act according to this belief in
the face of strong opposition by the emperors and certain kings; and, in
spite of many proofs that the actual power of Rome was limited and
inadequate, Honorius III (1216–27), Gregory IX (1227–41), Innocent IV
(1243–54), Alexander IV (1254–61), Urban IV (1261–4) and Clement IV
(1265–8) were all determined to regulate the Northern world, and
ready to employ war, diplomacy, propaganda, administrative action,

bargaining, blackmail and bribery to achieve their ends. The Northern crusade was one of their instruments, although it also served the interests of others, and could be put to use only by compromise and co-operation. The setting up of new governments modelled on hierocratic principles was another; for in societies founded on the indoctrination of newly converted innocents, and governed by monks and bishops, there was in theory a better chance of saving souls.

The old-established churches of Scandinavia were better attuned to these policies than in previous centuries – less subservient to the wishes of their kings, more aware of the doctrine of ecclesiastical liberty. In the twelfth century, a French immigrant, Abbot William of Æbelholt, had been surprised at the way Danish churchmen actually respected the pope and handed over money without grumbling when he asked for it; but there were good reasons for this. In societies that still grudged the payment of tithe, and sometimes bullied and rejected their clergy, the papacy could represent freedom, justice and stability. In the newer colonial churches of the Wendish coast Rome also found servants. The archbishops of Bremen were no longer walking in fear of the great Saxon duke, since the old duchy had disintegrated in 1181. The bishop of Cammin, who governed the Pomeranian churches, was linked to the papacy by an exemption from intermediate ecclesiastical jurisdiction. Throughout the Baltic region, church courts had been established to regulate the discipline of the clergy and the morals of the laity, and, where canon law was respected, so was Rome, as the highest court of appeal. In addition, the popes could count on the new orders of mendicant friars. Both Dominicans and Franciscans were well established in the North by 1250, and were entrusted with the duty of preaching and collecting for the crusades.

Besides these local components of the great ecclesiastical machine, the pope could also make use of commissars sent out to bring the wishes of the centre direct to the periphery. Before the twelfth century, Roman legates had been sent to carry out restricted missions in specified provinces. By 1200 full power to represent the pope was being delegated to *legati a latere*, or cardinal–legates, who were entitled to continue functioning even after the death of the pope who had sent them. Favoured prelates could hope to become 'perpetual legates', with the power of deciding appeals from the highest provincial church courts, but it was the legates *a latere* who were 'part of the body' of the pope. They were co-ordinators, inspectors, reformers, judges, generals and ambassadors, and they were usually given particular instructions about the problems of the Northern crusade and the military Orders. Four of them made a deep impression on the Northern world in this period.

There was William, cardinal bishop of Sabina, an Italian ex-papal notary, ex-Carthusian monk, Dominican sympathizer and bishop of Modena, who held legatine commissions in 1225–6, 1228–30 and 1234–42. There was the Cistercian Baldwin of Aulne, who functioned between 1231 and 1234, first as nuncio, then as full legate, and was sent to clean up Livonia. There was James Pantaleon, archdeacon of Liège, who reorganized Prussia in 1247–9. There was Albert Suerbeer, ex-archbishop of Armagh, legate to Russia and the Baltic countries in 1246–50, and legate–archbishop of Riga from 1254 to 1273. When these men reached the Baltic, the pope himself was there; even kings and Teutonic Knights had to listen, and sometimes obey. It was no good pretending that they were 'false legates with false Bulls', as the Sword-Brothers claimed of Baldwin of Aulne. They carried commissions which the papal bureaucracy confirmed in messages to the local authorities, and their coming was usually welcomed by all who had outstanding ecclesiastical or political business to settle.

By these various instruments the papacy could, at times, get its way in the North-East as in other quarters of Europe – perhaps more so, given the way political and economic power was distributed. The popes could establish special protection over seafarers, pilgrims and merchants and humanize the law of wreck and salvage; could issue embargoes on the arms trade with pagans and Russians; discourage debt-peonage among the Rugians; divert tithe from church-maintenance to the crusade, or books from old libraries to missions. These are a few random examples of Rome's intervention. In sum, they amount almost to a power of universal supervision, even if power was exercised mainly at the request of local authorities.

At this point the reader may ask, 'But were the popes really interested in what happened in North-East Europe?' Surely they had enough to do defending their own states in central Italy, fighting the emperor, maintaining church rights in the more civilized parts of Christendom, and taxing the more taxable? Surely the crusade against Islam had priority?

The answer, I suggest, is that the popes were so deeply involved in their Italian problems that they could not afford to ignore anything that affected those problems. The 'propagation of the faith' in the Baltic could not be left to itself, because the Germans most concerned in the enterprise, whether monks, merchants or princes, were all connected to Emperor Frederick by interest and lordship; and from 1236 to 1250 he was the foe. As more territory was converted to Christianity, new sources of papal revenue were created, in a century when the popes made financial demands on a much wider range of countries and institutions than ever before. New churches could mean new money, and fresh patronage, and it was not long before fee-paying litigants from these regions began appearing at the Curia and making contributions to the papal treasury – and, so, to the wars in Italy. Relations with the Greek Christians of northern Russia could not be left to arrangements between local interests, because, if these Russians could be made to give up their allegiance to the Eastern Church, the day when the leaders of that church submitted to Rome would be brought nearer, and an effective and Latin empire in the East would redress the balance between the papacy and the disobedient empire of the West. The religious filaments that led from Novgorod to Kiev led on from Kiev to Constantinople, and so connected with the struggle for power in the Mediterranean. The crusade against Islam still had priority. Honorius III expected the bishop of Riga to send money for the reconquest of Jerusalem, even before Livonia was subdued; it was conceded that the Northern crusades were second-best, cut-rate enterprises, for the benefit of penitents with limited resources. However, this very fact made them an essential part of the crusading movement; they filled a yawning gap between the means of most German *crucesignati* and the expense and labour of a passage to the Holy Land.

For these reasons, the popes made a determined bid for power in the Baltic world between 1198 and 1268. Their concern showed itself most clearly in two ways: in their attempts to mould the conquered lands on theocratic lines, and in their attempts to coerce the Russians into adopting Latin Christianity.

THE BATTLE FOR THE CONVERT

Innocent III made it clear that, in the case of Livonia and all future crusading conquests, the bishop was to have supreme political and spiritual authority, and the monk–knights were to act as his agents and servants, keeping a third of the land and booty they captured for their own use. All conquered pagans were to be placed in the keeping of unarmed missionaries, and converts were to be given political liberty within the framework of a new theocratic state, where power would be exercised only in so far as it served the purposes of Christian law and teaching. In 1212 he claimed that Livonia had been 'subjugated for us'.[74] From 1224 to 1234 his successors attempted, through their legates, to turn all or the greater part of this territory into a 'land of St Peter' – a state ruled by vassals of the papal see.

But this programme was never realized in Livonia. The Sword-Brothers were already taking more than their share of land and power before Bishop Albert died, and thereafter they became a terror to friend as well as foe. In 1234 Gregory IX was informed that, among their other misdeeds, they had recently killed a hundred of the men enlisted by his legate to enforce papal policies, and that

they had heaped the bodies into a pile, and had stuck one of the slain who had been too faithful to the Church on top of the other dead to represent the Lord Pope, and had subverted the Church by roundly refusing to allow the Master to hand them over for burial, so that, in due course, converts and others might come and behold this manner of spectacle, and the Brothers might thus be seen by converts, Russians, pagans and heretics to be greater than the Roman Church.[75]

They had themselves enlisted those Russians and pagans to hold Dorpat for them against the bishop of Leal. They had killed 401 converts, beaten up the Cistercians of Dünamünde, pillaged the bishop's lands, prevented would-be Christians from receiving baptism from the bishop, and reduced others to slavery. In sum, they had done 40,500 marks' worth of damage to their Christian neighbours and to the pope himself. For such deeds, the Sword-Brothers were never effectively tried or punished, and the results of their unruliness could not be wiped out, even after the Teutonic Knights had replaced them. Livonia remained an inharmonious concert of Christian authorities, where the masters quarrelled and the servants groaned.

In 1253, the see of Riga was raised to an archbishopric and given to Albert Suerbeer, who as legate and archbishop of Prussia had been fighting to reduce the power of the Order for the previous six years. He tried to continue the struggle in Livonia, but was unable to make headway on his own.

In 1267 he went to the length of forming an alliance with a north-German prince, Count Gunzelin of Schwerin, against both the heathen and the Teutonic Knights. He had seen his position of supreme spiritual authority in the east-Baltic region steadily undermined by the Order, and he evidently preferred to share his power with a lay *advocatus* of his own choosing than with a monastic Order. The allies prepared for war, but in the following year the Livonian master had to face a Novgorodian invasion under Alexander Nevsky's son Dmitri. Once he had saved the province from subjugation, he was able to use his influence with the Gotland merchants to rob Gunzelin of the recruits and sea transports he needed for his *coup d'état*. The count went home; the master arrested the archbishop, and released him only after he had promised not to appeal to Rome for redress, or oppose the Order in future. Suerbeer had been made archbishop and legate as a zealous champion of papal power, episcopal immunity and the rights of the convert; he ended his reign in 1273 as a spent force, unable to control either his castles or his chapter, let alone the Teutonic Knights. Riga remained a thorn in their side, but the archbishopric could no longer serve as the keystone of the edifice of papal power in the Baltic provinces.

Prussia was made 'St Peter's patrimony' in 1234, but Innocent IV gave more to the Order than Gregory IX would have approved of. By the second half of the century, the Order was independent of two of the local bishops and controlled the third. It had imposed military service, labour service and legal jurisdiction on all converts, and would only grant political freedom as a privilege to a favoured elite. It aimed to keep two-thirds of any future conquests, and was accused of rejecting all means of converting the heathen other than conquest in war and forcible baptism. Something had gone wrong. But it was not just a case of an unruly Order defying papal instructions, for neither the knight-brothers, nor the missions, nor the succeeding popes were able to keep to the pure doctrine of Innocent III; both local conditions and political realism at the Curia led to its modification.

Innocent's programme for Livonia had not solved the problem of how to maintain an unwelcome mission. He believed that force should be used only to protect it, and repudiated the old-fashioned idea of conversion at the point of the sword. But at Riga, and on the Vistula, the missions were situated among peoples for whom raiding and plundering were normal incidents in the annual routine. The choice for the missionary was either to dig in, surround himself by a stockade and a military escort, and hope that prospective converts would come to him (in which case, as Bishop Christian found in Prussia, progress would be extremely slow) or else to join in, take sides, offer weapons and military help along with baptism, and establish a lordship (in which case progress of a kind could be spectacular, as with Bishop Albert in Livonia). But, if the mission took the second course, there was little chance of a state run for the benefit of converts. Instead the convert became a recruit in a society organized for war, where the priority was victory rather than justice or indoctrination.

Nevertheless, the Curia tried to ensure that in that kind of society the native populations enjoyed a measure of freedom. In 1225 the legate William of Sabina went round Livonia explaining to converts what their rights actually were, and to the Sword-Brothers how far they could go in exploiting their conquests. There were to be tithes, but no other taxes; the conquerors would have the power to judge, but not to impose ordeals or capital punishment; they could exact labour services but not to excess. Such was William's interpretation of the general instructions given him by Honorius III: 'You are to preserve all those who have been brought to the faith under the special lordship of the Roman Church, and promise a measure of liberty to prospective converts.'[76] This was reaffirmed by Gregory IX: 'If any slaves, or any under the sway of other rulers shall accept baptism . . . you must get the weight of their servitude somewhat reduced, and secure for them the freedom to confess their sins, go to church, and hear mass.' In recommending this minimal programme, the Curia was supported by the self-interest of the ruling elites; if they were to maintain themselves against numerically superior pagan forces, they had to win the loyalty or at least the quiescence of their subjects. As Gregory IX wrote to William in 1239, 'men signed with the mark of Christ must not be worse off than they were as limbs of the devil'.[77]

This was the lesson which the legate James drew from the rebellious state of the Prussian converts in the 1240s. He made the Order safeguard itself by conceding a 'bill of rights' to converts at Christburg in 1249. They were allowed to own freehold property, and bequeath it to near kinsfolk instead of letting it be taken by the tribe in default of male issue, as under paganism. They were to sell, buy, litigate and worship on a footing of equality with Germans and Poles. They were to be eligible for knighthood and priesthood. They were to be subsidized by the Order when they built their own churches. As a result, the conversion proceeded steadily until 1259. The knight-brothers gained allies among the unconquered Balts, and the friars reported success in instructing would-be Christians. Churches were built inland, as well as along the rivers and coast. An attempt to establish an archbishopric in Prussia failed, but in 1251 a papal court at Lyon arranged a general settlement between the Order and the bishops so that all parties would, in future, be able to co-operate in the work of conversion without quarrelling over lines of demarcation. This was the last achievement of the former legate, William of Sabina.

However, the rebellions of 1259 to 1263, and the twenty years' fight for survival that followed, put an end to the active intervention of papal legates on behalf of Prussian and Livonian converts. The result was that the Teutonic Order granted the Christburg liberties to a smaller number of Prussians than had originally been intended – only to the most loyal and powerful native families, not to whole tribes. For these favoured collaborators, Christianity brought great material advantages – property rights, rights of inheritance, freedom from tribal or communal discipline; and, if the conquered peoples were not better off under the Teutonic Knights, this was not simply because the knight-brothers wished to oppress them. As the wars dragged on, the real choice facing the Baltic nations was not between subjection to the Order and liberty but between two forms of dependence, either on the Order or on the Lithuanians. In either case, they had to fight or work for a military machine that was not greatly concerned about their souls.

Therefore the papal attempt to supervise and regulate the conversion of the heathen in this corner of Europe was not successful. On the whole, baptism remained a consequence of defeat in battle, and admission to the Church meant subjection to the victors. Neither Livonia nor Prussia became a 'land of St Peter'; but neither became the exclusive property of the Teutonic Order. What the popes had done to preserve the independence of the archbishopric of Riga and its suffragans, and to establish the Dominicans (at Chelmno, Elbing, Riga and Reval) and Franciscans (at Torun, Chelmno and Braunsberg) could not be undone. While these churches and houses remained active, the Order's treatment of its converts continued to be scrutinized and criticized.

THE WAR ON THE SCHISMATICS

Until about 1200 the differences between the rites and religious outlooks of the Eastern and Western Churches seem to have meant little in North-East Europe. They did not prevent marriages between the ruling dynasties of Russia, Scandinavia, Germany and Poland, or the coexistence of Orthodox and Latin churches in the mixed communities of Gotland and Novgorod. They did not prevent a Russian prince from allowing Canon Meinhard to set up his Latin mission on the lower Dvina.

The expansion of this mission into a militant lordship first brought home the danger of expanding Roman Catholicism to the north Russians. Not only was Russian hegemony over the Letts and Estonians pushed aside by armed force, but, in addition, the Latin insistence that these peoples should pay tithe to the clergy of Riga made it impossible for Orthodox churches to take part in their conversion. However, there is no evidence that the Russian clergy had yet made much effort to spread Christianity here, and the Riga priests justified their exclusiveness by sneering at their inactivity: to them, the Greek Church was 'always a sterile and unfruitful mother'.[78] This lack of serious competition for converts meant that Bishop Albert and the Sword-Brothers had no immediate interest in turning their occasional wars with Russian princes into wars on the Eastern Church. The Russians were too valuable as customers, and too troublesome as invaders, to be antagonized more than was necessary; if they could be persuaded to keep away from the Letts and Estonians, Riga was content. Similarly, the Russian princes were more concerned with pursuing their own internal quarrels than with the loss of unreliable tributaries on their western frontiers – a loss made up by gains through trade with the newcomers. Neither side could afford to maintain a properly defended frontier.

Meanwhile, Constantinople fell to Latin crusaders, and Innocent III attempted to impose his own authority and the Latin rite on the whole Eastern Church. He failed; but his successors were committed to following his example, especially on the western fringes of the Byzantine world, and where the see of Riga and the archbishopric of Novgorod shared a frontier.

In 1222 Honorius III insisted that the Greek rite was not to be allowed in any lands controlled by Latins.[79] In 1224 Dorpat was captured and made a Latin see, dedicated to St Peter, and the legate William of Sabina instructed the bishop to enter what he considered the promising mission field of Russia. Despite repeated invitations to turn Catholic, the Novgorodians were obdurate; in 1234 Prince Yaroslav devastated Dorpat, and then began obstructing the Latin mission in Finland. When William reappeared in 1237, as the agent of Gregory IX, he decided to use force rather than persuasion, and began organizing a crusade of Latin powers against Novgorod.

It has been argued that he was encouraged by the irresistible advance of the Golden Horde of Mongols, which reached the Volga in 1236, and wound its way towards Novgorod throughout 1237 and early 1238. But this argument assumes that the Curia had a better knowledge of what was going to happen in the interior of Russia than the Russians had themselves. The complete unpreparedness of the central Russian princes in Vladimir and Riasan shows that they had no idea where the Horde was going; it might have turned south to Kiev at any moment, and the fact that it had got to within sixty-six miles of Novgorod before it did so was something that no one could have foreseen. As it was, Prince Alexander Nevsky was so unconcerned by the Mongols that he did nothing at all to meet them; according to the Novgorod Chronicler it was prayer that saved the city, not the prince. In 1239 it emerged that the Horde had turned south, and had left Russian territory; it was not until 1240 that Gregory's crusade got under way, with the Swedish raid up the Neva and the conquest of Izborsk and Pskov by the Danes and the Teutonic Order, and there it stopped. When Alexander Nevsky led his troops into Livonia in spring 1242, the boot was on the other foot: the Horde had penetrated far into Poland and Hungary, and the papacy was begging the Teutonic Order to come south and help resist its progress.

It is not unreasonable to conclude that William of Sabina timed the crusades of 1240—41 to coincide with the weakness of Novgorod; but this weakness was caused by the quarrels of Prince Alexander with other Russian princes, and with his own subjects, who expelled him after he had defeated the Swedes. These dangers were more immediate than the incalculable menace of the Golden Horde, and they gave Gregory IX's plan at least a chance of success. The other factor in his favour was the desire both of the Teutonic Order and of King Valdemar II of Denmark to take over all or part of Livonia and Estonia after the collapse of the

Sword-Brothers in 1237. Only the pope could dissolve that disreputable Order, and dispose of the lands it had occupied; by granting half of Estonia to Valdemar in 1238, and Livonia to the Teutonic Knights, he satisfied both parties and put them in his debt. Assistance given to his crusade against the Russians was evidently part of the deal, although neither could well afford it. The Order was fully committed to another Holy War in Prussia, and had barely enough knights to hold Livonia; Valdemar was more immediately concerned with restoring his authority in Estonia by disseising unreliable vassals than with pushing on to the east.

However, the campaign began. The Swedes sailed up the Neva towards Ladoga, and were repulsed, in July 1240. In September, armies under the Teutonic Knights occupied Izborsk and Pskov. A friendly Russian governor was put in charge of Pskov, and early in 1241 the crusaders occupied Vod (Watland) and Ingria, the lands between Novgorod and the Finnish Gulf. Then the citizens recalled their prince, and the tables were turned. By the autumn of 1241, the invaders had been driven out of Vod; early in 1242 (according to the First Novgorod Chronicle),

Prince Alexander occupied all the roads right up to Pskov, and he cleared Pskov, seized the Germans and Estonians, bound them in chains and sent them to be imprisoned in Novgorod; and he himself went against the Estonians. And when they came to their land, he let loose his whole force to provide for themselves ... and the prince turned back to the lake [Peipus–Chud], and the Germans and Estonians went after them. Seeing this, Prince Alexander and all the men of Novgorod drew up their forces by the lake, at Uzmen, by the Raven's Rock; and the Germans and the Estonians rode at them, driving themselves like a wedge through their army. And there was a great slaughter of Germans and Estonians. And God, and St Sophia, and the Holy Martyrs Boris and Gleb, for whose sake the men of Novgorod shed their blood – by the great prayers of those saints – God helped Prince Alexander. And the Germans fell there, and the Estonians gave way, and they fought with them during the pursuit on the ice seven versts short of the Subol [north-western] shore. And there fell a countless number of Estonians, and 400 of the Germans, and they took fifty with their hands and they took them to Novgorod. And they fought on 5 April, on a Saturday, the commemoration day of the Holy Martyr Theodulos, to the glory of the Holy Mother of God.[80]

The Livonian Rhyme-Chronicler saw it differently. He claimed that the Order had left only two knight-brothers to hold Pskov, and that Alexander triumphed by the lake because the Order's forces were outnumbered sixty to one and surrounded. Some of the Estonian contingent – from Dorpat, apparently, not from Danish Estonia – were lucky enough to get away, but the loss of life was not severe: twenty brothers were killed, and six were captured. It was a disaster because it meant the abandonment of Pskov – not because the Order was decimated, or because Novgorod was saved; by this time, the eastward offensive appears to have halted. If the legate had planned to occupy Novgorod itself, he had failed to muster enough men, and he had underestimated the military potential of his enemy.

Gregory IX's successor, Innocent IV, made no attempt to resume the war of conquest against the Russians; he hoped to bring them into the fold by other means. From 1245 he was busy conducting a curious diplomatic dance with the ruler of the lands on the river Bug, Prince Daniel of Galicia and Volhynia, whom he tried to entice into the Latin Church by offering him a crown and military assistance against the Mongols. Daniel was not unduly worried by the Tartars, since his principality was also under attack from Lithuanians, Hungarians, Poles and other Russian princes. However, he was disinclined to throw away the chance of any advantage, and it was not until 1257 that it became clear that he had got his Latin crown, but intended to remain 'Greek' in religion. Until then there was a good chance that the whole west Russian region would be won over to Rome without fighting, and for most of that period the Curia left Novgorod alone.

When Innocent died, an attempt was made to revert to a policy of aggression. On 19 March Alexander IV ordered the new archbishop–legate, Suerbeer, to baptize the heathen east of the river Narva, and set a bishop over the Novgorod provinces of Vod, Ingria and Karelia.[81] Two Estonian vassals of the king of Denmark had informed him that these peoples were eager to enter the Latin communion, and Suerbeer wrote back agreeing. Canon Frederick Hazeldorf was appointed bishop of Karelia, and in 1256 the Dominicans were instructed to preach the crusade for Prussia and Livonia, in preparation for a new offensive. But the ensuing campaign revealed a large gap between the Pope's information and conditions on the spot. The 'heathen' gave no sign that they wished to join the Latin Church, and the only crusaders to appear were a small band of Swedes, Finns and Estonians, led by one of the landowners who had originally written to the pope, Dietrich of Kiwel. Dietrich's estates lay on the eastern frontier of Estonia, and he had a private interest in terrorizing the Vods on the other side of the Narva. He made no attempt to baptize or invade the schismatics, but used his troops to build a fort on the right bank, and went home before winter. By the time Prince Alexander arrived with an army from Novgorod, there was no Latin army left to fight; the prince ignored Estonia, and took the opportunity of leading a raid north into Swedish Finland. Bulls, preaching and 'crusade' had all been manipulated by one adventurous marcher baron, who was shrewd enough to play on the papal infatuation with the idea of a Latinized Russia.

From this time onwards, the Curia turned to the kings of Sweden for assistance in realizing that idea, and in 1257 Alexander IV entrusted them with the conquest of Karelia – a project they carried out in part over the following century. On the whole, Novgorod and the Livonian colonies were too closely linked by trade to wage war on each other for long; papal intervention had succeeded only in giving the Latins a pretext for invasions which they seldom dared or wished to undertake, and in reinforcing the Novgorodians' adherence to the Greek Church. Having failed to conquer them, the popes lost any chance they ever had of persuading them. The memory of the crusade of 1240–41 became part of the civic consciousness of Novgorod, proving to the citizens that political and religious independence were one and the same.* Nor were the Livonians anxious to pursue the crusade further south, against Polotsk, up the Dvina; fear of interrupting the river traffic kept the peace for most of the thirteenth century, and by 1305 this principality had fallen under the control of the Lithuanians.

Not that either pope or emperor had abandoned his interest in the north-eastern Catholic front: throughout the fourteenth and fifteenth centuries, they both continued to assert their responsibility for the spreading of the faith into Russia and Lithuania. However, the ways in which this responsibility could actually be exercised were reduced in

---

* The Byzantine version of holy war, waged for Orthodoxy by the ruler, with patriarchal blessing, icons, relics and sacred banners, reaches Novgorod in the early fourteenth century in the eulogies of Alexander Nevsky and the living prince Dovmont of Pskov. But see below, chapter 7, for the relative passivity of Novgorod clergy.

practice to either helping or hindering the Teutonic Knights; and, as each supreme authority went on outbidding and countermanding the other, neither could do very much. Nevertheless, while the going was good, the popes had been able to establish three of the institutions that shaped the Baltic world for the future: the crusade against the heathen, the crusade against the Russians, and the monastic crusading states. Round that tideless sea lay the stranded flotsam of papal ideology – partly dried, partly rotting, and partly fertile.

6

THE LITHUANIAN CRUSADE,
1283–1410

So, by the end of the thirteenth century, the Baltic had become a Latin sea, and a new religious frontier had been drawn. The balance of Northern civilizations described in chapter 1 had been upset by new ideas, new settlers, new governments and new inventions, all drawn in by the rivers and seaways that connected this region with Western and Central Europe. The North Sea, the Rhine, the Elbe, the Oder and the Vistula had all contributed to this change, and would continue to supply men, wealth and innovations. But the new Baltic provinces were now pressing against the dense forest of the great eastern river-basins: the Niemen, the Dvina, and the rivers that feed lakes Chud, Ilmen and Ladoga. Here they met a natural barrier, as already described; here they also met resistant and alien societies that barred the way. The Novgorodian and Lithuanian empires were built on manpower and resources drawn from vast contributory areas, and applied with skill to the service of the state. In each case, the state was drawn towards the Baltic by the drainage of its forests and plains, and by the momentum of its trade along these waterways. The Latins could not be left to enjoy their conquests in peace, nor were they prepared to let the two upriver empires develop unmolested. There was a partly blind, partly organized increase of pressure on the frontiers from either side, and the Holy War continued.

The next two chapters will describe in turn the attempts made by the Latin powers in the fourteenth century to revive and adapt the crusading ideal in the conflict of forces along the frontier: first, against the Lithuanians; then, against the Russians. No attempt will be made to give a full account of the wars and alliances of the Teutonic Order's Prussian state in this period, of the long-drawn-out quarrel with Poland, or relations with the Hanseatic League and Scandinavian princes. These matters affected the crusade, but deserve much fuller treatment than there is room for in this study.

THE ROADS TO COLLISION, 1203−1309

In 1283, according to the chronicler of the Teutonic Knights, Peter of Dusburg, the conquest of the Prussians ended and the war with the Lithuanians began.[82] It was still going on when he was writing, in the 1320s, and would continue intermittently until the peace of Lake Melno in 1422, when the Order was compelled to surrender for good its claim to northern Lithuania and Samogitia. Moreover, Dusburg's opening date of 1283 is not entirely accurate: the Sword-Brothers of Riga had first crossed swords with the Lithuanians in 1203, and throughout the conquests of Livonia and Prussia there had been clashes with the same enemy. Thus, for over 200 years there was either war or rumours of war, with a power judged in some circles to be founded on a denial of the Christian religion; and for most of that period crusaders from Germany and Western Europe were prepared to join in and fight for the Teutonic Knights in what they took to be the cause of Christendom.

But who were the Lithuanians? They were described in chapter 1 as Balts − members of the same language group as the Prussians and Letts − and in 1200 their way of life and political importance were about the same as that for the other Balt peoples. They consisted of a peasantry living under the rule of a mounted warrior-class in the densely forested basins of the rivers Niemen, Neris and Viliya, east of Prussia; five to eight homesteads, each with a holding of family land, made up a hamlet community − strictly exogamous, it appears − and the hamlets paid food rents and hospitality to the landowner, later called 'boyar'. The boyar recruited his kinsmen and the more substantial peasants into his military retinue, where they were known as 'friends'; led by the hereditary prince or kinglet of one of the nine districts of ancient Lithuania, groups of such retinues would go out raiding every spring, and return with cattle, slaves, silver and weapons. If their neighbours retaliated, they took refuge in the district fort, built like the Slav *gorod*, from which it took its name, *garadas*.

The Lithuanians had no coastline, no native supply of salt and little iron; they were probably fewer in number, and certainly less prosperous, than their Prussian cousins. Their strength lay in their inaccessibility, and in their horses − pampered chargers for the rich, promoted plough-ponies for the less fortunate warriors. In the period 1200−1250 their raiding-grounds were increasingly taken over by well-organized military powers: the Teutonic Knights and Alexander Nevsky's Novgorod to the north, and the feudal princes of Mazovia, Little Poland and Volhynia to the south. To make matters worse, the Mongols of the Golden Horde, better armed, mounted and trained than the Lithuanians, began making forays into their homelands in the 1240s and 1250s. The future looked bleak; but in the midst of continuous devastation and bloodshed a remarkable dynasty was able to hold the people together, organize them to wage effective war on their neighbours, and begin the annexation of surrounding territory.

The leading member of this family was Mindaugas (Mindowe, Medovg), who ruled from the early years of the century to his murder in 1263. According to the Volhynian Chronicler,

he was autocrat over all the Lithuanian land ... when he had begun to reign in Lithuania he had tried to kill off his brothers and nephews; he drove others out of the land and began to reign alone over the entire Lithuanian land. He became very proud and vainglorious – no one did he consider his equal ... [83]

In 1219 he was one of about twenty Lithuanian princes; by the end of his life he was supreme among a much smaller group, and had mobilized the whole free population to fight for him or his sons, either as cavalry or as infantry. His horsemen copied the tactics of the Mongols, but used short throwing-spears, and swords instead of bows, and protected themselves with mail. His infantry carried spears and axes, and his Lett auxiliaries made use of the crossbows they had got from the Sword-Brothers. An alliance with the Yatwingians brought him reinforcements skilled in combating the Teutonic Knights, and both the wealth and the technology of the Polish and Russian princes were pressed into his service. He fought for, and against, all the East European powers, involved them in his family quarrels, and allowed none of them to live in peace for long. They all tried to get the better of him, either by war or by offers of friendship, and sometimes he appeared to give way, either to superior force, or to diplomacy.

In 1249 his brother went over to Prince Daniel of Galicia, while his nephew allied with the Teutonic Knights of Livonia and accepted baptism. 'Now is the time for us to go and fight the pagans', said Prince Daniel to the Poles, 'for they are warring among themselves.'[84] But Mindaugas sent to Riga, and opened negotiations that led to his own alliance with the Teutonic Order, and baptism. He made large grants of land to the knight-brothers, and appointed the Order his heir, should he die without surviving issue. He accepted a crown from Innocent IV, and invited German merchants and friars and settlers to enter his country. Continuing wars with Prince Daniel, the Tartars, Novgorod and the Poles and the continued disaffection of the Samogitians made the advantages of this German connection seem less apparent in 1260, and in the last years of his rule Mindaugas could not prevent his kinsmen from waging war on all his Christian neighbours indifferently. Lithuanian forces drove the knight-brothers out of Courland, Samogitia and Yatwingia, and penetrated to the mouth of the Dvina in 1263. There, Mindaugas's nephew Treniota (Troinat) defeated the knight-brothers and burghers of Riga in a moonlight battle, and went on to devastate all Prussia and Mazovia. The king's policy of intimidating or killing all his kinsmen had turned most of the survivors against him; his brother-in-law killed him the same year, and Treniota was killed in the bath-house the year after.

Mindaugas's career followed the familiar pattern of 'modernizing' autocracy. His elimination of Lithuanian rivals, his importation of foreign ways, his use of foreign allies and his persistent aggrandizement of his country were policies that unified Lithuania, and left an indelible mark on Lithuanian society. Henceforward, his successors were to push their armies down all the great rivers that rose in the centre of their territory in order to construct a vast tributary system that absorbed the wealth of all the western Russian principalities. In the fourteenth century, the comparatively prosperous urban and manorial civilization of Pskov, Polotsk, Pinsk, Kiev and Volhynia–Galicia were yoked to the wooded heartlands of Lithuania proper and made to support a larger and larger military establishment: the grand-prince, his sons and vassal princes with their forts and retinues, the boyars and their retinues, the foreign technicians, and the court officials. The grand-prince rode round his own estates and his fortified towns at Trakai and Vilnius, secure in his ability to satisfy his princes with grants of conquered land, and in his personal control of the military machine. While he advertised his prowess and entertained his ruling class with herculean bouts of feasting and hunting (twelve hours eating a day, and a bag of a hundred bison, for example), his retainers were boarded out on the peasants, and his forts were manned by relays of recruits; in time of war, he or his kinsmen led rapid and well-equipped armies to the frontier, and then penetrated deep into hostile country and conducted battues which brought home every living thing, leaving not a house or crop behind them. The threat of these raids brought in a steady stream of silver, wax and furs, but otherwise subject peoples were left to practise their trades and religions unmolested. Settlers of all races were brought in to develop the forest-lands and increase the size and prosperity of Vilnius and the other princely strongholds. Success in war brought prosperity to the boyars, and a sharpened appetite for more; as consumers of wine, salt, sea-fish, woollens and fresh vegetables they greatly increased the volume of imports along rivers and caravan routes, and directed the attention of their rulers towards all the nearest sources of supply, either to trade with them or to annex them.

From the point of view of the Teutonic Knights and their subjects, this expanding Lithuania was both good and bad. Good, because it provided a lucrative market up the Vistula, Niemen and Dvina for their home products and Baltic cargoes. In about 1275 Mindaugas's son Vaisvilkas (Voishelg) made some kind of trade agreement with the burghers and knight-brothers of Riga, and thereafter there is evidence of continual buying and selling between the two sides; the Lithuanians supplied furs, wax, honey and silver (from the Mongols, the price of slaves) and the Germans horses, salt, weapons, bread, cloth, cabbages, horseradish, onions and fruit. Such exchanges continued throughout the fourteenth century, in war and peace, and were largely conducted by German merchants benefiting from the favourable conditions established by the Hanseatic League in the west and the Golden Horde in the east.

However, the military might of Lithuania was always a threat, as both the Order and the grand-princes were trying to absorb territory along the great river routes, and incorporate it into their colonial systems. Since Lithuanian raiders had reached the sea, both in Prussia and in Livonia, it was evidently possible to bring both areas under Lithuanian rule, and, as the empire expanded, the territories of the Teutonic Knights became a conspicuous exception to the prevailing order in Eastern Europe. Mindaugas's territory had occupied a rough circle, centred on Vilnius, with a radius of some 120 miles. A hundred years later, his descendant Algirdas dominated a huge semi-circle, radius over 400 miles to the south and east, with Poland and the Order's lands forming a segment to the west and north, still in close proximity to the grand-prince's homelands. Both systems had grown by absorbing tribes and principalities along their frontiers, and had come into competition over the conquest of Yatwingian, Samogitian, Curonian and Semigallian peoples. Even after this competition had been ended by the creation of the belt of devastation in the late thirteenth century, there was a chance that either might be able to muster sufficiently effective forces to capture the centre of the other's political system, and fall heir to the whole lot.

Moreover, the grand-princes and warriors of Lithuania remained pagan. Mindaugas had accepted baptism but the Galician Chronicler was not impressed: 'this christening was only for appearances. Secretly he made sacrifices to the gods – to Nenadey, Telyavel, Diveriks the hare-god, and Meidein. When Mindaugas rode out into the field, and a hare ran across his path, then he would not go into the grove, nor dared he break a twig. He made sacrifices to his god, burnt corpses and conducted pagan rites in public.'[85] Nevertheless, many of his subjects and kinsmen were displeased by his nominal conversion, and, according to the Livonian Rhyme-Chronicle, Treniota and the Samogitians sent to him at the end of his life and said,

The Samogitians sorrow for you and for your renown; now take their advice, and you will be the better for it ... all that the Brothers have taught you since they turned you from your gods is a pack of lies. Your father was a great king, and in his day there was not his equal to be found; now do you want to make a yoke for yourself and your children, when you might live in freedom for evermore? You've been making a big mistake. If the Christians conquer the Samogitians, all your honour and wealth will be taken away; in the end, you and your children will become serfs. How hopelessly blind you are ... If you want to be free of the Christians, then stand by the Samogitians, who are loyal to you; to this you must consent and turn away from Christianity ... [86]

By the mid-thirteenth century, the Samogitians were being sandwiched between Livonia and Prussia. They became intensely suspicious both of the Teutonic Knights and of the Christian faith, and the grand-princes had to be more careful in future about which religion they professed. There were always inducements to become Christian, since most of their subjects were orthodox White Russians, and the popes showed a periodic interest in bringing them into the Latin fold by gifts and diplomatic persuasion; but as long as their power depended on Lithuanian horsemen they avoided committing themselves either to

Greeks or to Latins. Although they never became high-priests of a public and official paganism that fulfilled the social and political functions of the Christian churches, the great princes avoided baptism however often their kinsmen and daughters took the plunge. As a result, their religion was viewed by outsiders as a sort of militant paganism; quite wrongly.

Both Prussians and Lithuanians had numerous gods, personifying and regulating every aspect of life and death. The four mentioned above, in the passage quoted from the Galician Chronicle, will serve as a selection: a god of ill fortune, a 'far-spirit' protecting the dead, a sky-ruler, and a goddess of the forest. When in 1258 a force of Lithuanians was disappointed of the chance to loot a town, 'they grieved and spat, shouting *yanda*, invoking their gods Andai and Diveriks and others',[87] and both they and the Prussians were also reported to venerate Percunos, ruler of fire and lightning, Picollos, ruler of the underworld, and Potrimpo, god of rivers and springs. A seventeenth-century collector, Hartknoch, was able to list thirteen separate categories of minor gods, and folklore preserved details of what they were supposed to look like, although they were never worshipped in idol shape.[88]

To keep this god-world and our world together, the Balts had developed public rituals of sacrifice, propitiation and rejoicing. It was the policy of their rulers to put themselves and their armies at the centre of these rituals, and to exploit the whole complex of belief and action by linking them with their political and military success. Supernatural powers were easily attributed to successful fighters. It was said of the Yatwingian captain Skomond that he 'was a fortune-teller and a magician and quick as a wild beast'. The most successful devoted a sizeable proportion – perhaps a third – of their booty to ritual cremation, and publicly invoked the gods to join the feast of blood and fire. While his warriors consumed the 'victory banquets', the ruler was drawing strength from the whole range of what Christians called 'heathendom', from sun-worship to the practice of keeping lucky snakes in the cow byre. When, like Algirdas in 1377, and Kestutis in 1382, he was cremated with immense piles of grave goods, and a whole stable of horses, he reaffirmed the reality of the kingdom of spirits (*veles*) in the sky, and ensured their blessing on his dynasty. When captured commanders of the Teutonic Order were burned alive or suffocated by smoke (as reported of Gerhard Rude in 1320, Henzel Neuenstein in 1365, and Marquard von Raschau in 1389), the inferiority of the Latin invader could be demonstrated in public. When doomed Lithuanian garrisons had themselves killed by their own wise woman rather than fall into Christian hands (as at Pillen (Pilenai) in 1336), the power of Lithuanians gods and ancestors to reward their servants after death was asserted in the extremest possible way.[89]

It has been alleged since the thirteenth century that the Lithuanians were deterred from becoming Christians because of the brutality and greed of the Teutonic Knights. This view may have its merits, but it ignores the fact that the Lithuanian religion was successful in its own right. It was more successful than the similar religions of the Prussians and Letts, because the Lithuanian political system was more effective: each helped the other, and the Teutonic Knights could do little about either except contain them. Since the Lithuanians were not a small tribe, they could not be brought to the Church by intimidation or conquest. Since they were prosperous and well organized, the example of the neighbouring Christian peoples was not in itself seductive; the example of the Mongols was perhaps more to the point. Paganism allowed the Lithuanians to govern Latins, Greeks, Jews and Tartars impartially. If it was true that the Teutonic Order insisted on conversion by conquest, and by the subjugation of the convert, it hardly affected the issue of Lithuania's belief, since the Order failed to conquer in this case. When Grand-Prince Jogaila finally accepted baptism in 1386, he was moved by the prospect of winning the Polish kingdom, and of depriving the Teutonic Knights of their *raison d'être*. The slow progress of the missionaries within Lithuania after 1386 suggests a deep-rooted and much-valued alternative religion which survived the baptism of the boyars.

The Order and the Lithuanians were first brought into conflict because both wanted to exploit the same Lettish and Prussian peoples. This phase of their relations was brought to an end in the years before 1283, when the Order subjugated or drove out the easternmost Prussian peoples, and created a no-man's-land between their vassals and those of the grand-prince. During this period, Lithuanian expeditions broke into Livonia several times and won signal victories (over Master Otto von Lutterberg at Karki, near Sworbe, in 1270, and over Master Ernest von Feuchtwangen at Ascherade in 1279) and suffered signal defeats (on the Dubenaa in 1272, and at the new fort of Dunaburg in 1278) but were unable to stop the Order from consolidating its territory. However, the land frontier was vulnerable; the river Niemen flowed through it, and river-boats could carry an army. Only if the Niemen were controlled at least as far up as the confluence of the Viliya would Prussia be safe; and the security of Livonia depended on a similar push up the valley of the Dvina. So from 1283 to 1296 there was a series of encounters along these rivers while each side tested the other's strength. The Livonian Knights managed to occupy Semigallia, and the Prussian Knights established two or three forts on the left bank of the Niemen and destroyed a few Lithuanian forts on the right. The Lithuanians raided Courland and Samland, and provoked a brief Prussian rising in 1295. This war was not regarded as particularly critical by the grand-masters: there were no appeals for crusaders.

Then in 1297–9 Grand-Prince Vytenis (Withen), great-great-grandson to Mindaugas, made an alliance with the burghers of Riga. He occupied Livonia, defeating and killing Master Bruno, and sent a diversionary raid to devastate central Prussia. The entire population of the new settlement of Strasburg (Brodnica) was massacred in 1298, and 250 captives were carried off in 1299. It was then that the knight-brothers realized that the future of their colonies was at stake, and they called on the grand-master and the German princes for a crusade. They had themselves conquered Prussia by a skilful use of the rivers, and they would need all their resources to prevent the operation being repeated: and the only land-route connecting Livonia and Prussia was the new coastal road from Memel to Courland that ran through a strip of country defenceless against Samogitian raids.

But it was not as simple as that. Prussia was certainly under attack, and no doubt needed reinforcements. However, it was in Livonia that the Order was in real trouble, and the source of it lay not only in Grand-Prince Vytenis's raids, but also in the state of civil war which had developed between the knight-brothers, the archbishop, and the burghers of Riga. This was one of several great scandals in the history of the Order, and one of the biggest rows of the Middle Ages. It is worth investigating.

Events had made Livonia into a pentarchy, where power was shared between the archbishop, his three bishops (of Courland, Ösel, and Dorpat) and the Teutonic Knights. Both bishops and knight-brothers had enfeoffed secular vassals, who tended to form an increasingly independent class, and the archbishop had chartered a community of burghers at Riga which increased in size, wealth and power until it formed a further ruling authority. Competition both for land within the province and for shares of trade on the Dvina prevented their living together in harmony, and weakened the military organization, which was the responsibility of the knight-brothers. In 1290 Master Halt von Hohembach wrote to the Prussian master, who wanted him to co-operate in a *winter-reysa*, that 'you should know that on six separate occasions this summer we have gone to the lords of this province and begged them most urgently for their help in sending out an expeditionary force'. And, after three days' pleading with the assembled province, he had been met with a blank refusal by all except the archbishop himself, who could only put 18 German knights and 300 natives in the field. 'And on our part, the strength we can lead over the Dvina, including Courland, Estonia and the river lands, amounts as we reckon to 1800 men, both Germans and natives.'[90]

In the ensuing years, friction grew worse. Violence broke out when the archbishop went away and his burghers decided to build a weir upstream to prevent spring floods from drowning their property at Riga. The barrier would impede the pack-ice and let the water through, but it would also hinder river-boats and prove detrimental to the knight-brothers' lands and markets upriver. It also meant trespassing on the archbishop's own land, and it happened that the Order had been appointed to oversee his property while he was away. The knight-brothers broke down the bridge which led to the construction site; the burghers retaliated, and there was bloodshed. Houses were burnt, and goods impounded. Then the archbishop came back, and took sides with the burghers. The Order hung on to his lands, and closed the river.

This was the sort of quarrel that could be expected between any expanding municipality and the surrounding landlords. The burghers needed more land, and the Order was not going to be satisfied with less; the archbishop wanted to keep some hold on his townsmen, and supporting them against the Order was one way of doing this. What made the situation explosive was that all three parties had their head-quarters within Riga, so that each was in a position to strike mortal blows to gain limited ends. Then the burghers called in Grand-Prince Vytenis to help them. The Lithuanians entered Riga and destroyed the Order's castle, and the following year (1298) did further damage to the knight-brothers and their lands. The Rigans never denied that they were responsible for the incursions of 1297–9; but they complained all the more when they were defeated by the knight-brothers at Neuermühlen after their allies had ridden away.

Their complaints, the complaints of the Order and the complaints of the archbishop all went to Pope Boniface VIII, and the Curia had the task of deciding between them. According to the burghers, the knight-brothers had tried to steal Riga from its rightful lord, the archbishop. When they tried to appeal to Rome, the knight-brothers had said, 'We will be pope enough for you'; they had killed citizens and burnt their houses, devastated the surrounding farmlands, threatened to force their wives to work at their mills grinding corn, and murdered eight poor pilgrims. They had built a new castle to oppress the citizens, and had tried to corner the Lithuanian trade for themselves: they were not interested in fighting the heathen, only in making money out of them.

Archbishop John III took up this theme. The Order was given Livonia, he claimed, to assist in the work of converting the natives and to keep out the pagans; instead of which it had oppressed the converts, hindered the work of conversion and refused to fight the Lithuanians. They were responsible for the failure of the church to keep King Mindaugas within the fold; they had deterred the Semigallians from the faith by their 'savagery, cruelty and tyranny'. They had shown themselves friendlier to the king-elect of Germany than to the pope; they had rejected the authority of the Livonian bishops; they had besieged and imprisoned the archbishop himself, and fed him on bread and water for eight months; they had pillaged and impoverished him. The bishop of Ösel claimed that they had invaded his island, arrested eighty of his flock under flag of truce, besieged him at Leal until he agreed to surrender all his castles and temporal rights, destroyed altars, sacred images, hospitals and almshouses. The bishop of Courland had his own list of grievances against the commander of Goldingen. He had killed the bishop's people, stolen his grain, his wardrobe, thirty pairs of shoes, and a flask of communion wine; he had even given the bishop's corporal-cloth to his maid, to make into a head-dress.[91]

It sounded bad, but it was only one side of the case. The grand-master was summoned to the Curia to answer the accusations, and Boniface began trying to reconcile the litigants. He seems to have believed that, whatever the knight-brothers had done, Livonia had to be defended, and this would only be possible if the Livonian authorities co-operated.

From 1300 to 1303 he made the Order give back what it had taken, and compensate its victims, without pressing charges. There was a lull in the quarrel, broken when Benedict XI sent a new archbishop to Riga, and an even more comprehensive indictment of the Order arrived at the Curia. This had to be answered, and from a document produced in mid 1306 [92] we hear the other side of the story.

The knight-brothers claimed that they had merely been asserting rights granted to them by papal Bulls over the previous sixty years. It was the popes who had given them the lands and wealth they were accused of coveting so eagerly, and they had paid for them with their own blood – 200 knight-brothers and 2000 of their dependants had died in Courland alone, where the bishop was complaining about his shoes. The vacancy at Riga had given them the duty of looking after the archbishop's lands, and the archbishop's castle had been occupied as security for a loan to one of the archbishop's vassals. The misconduct they were accused of – which by now included burning their dead, killing their wounded, and witchcraft – was mere slander; and, as for obstructing missions, they had co-operated with the archbishop in building forty new churches. They had built the castle of Mittau in Semigallia at their own expense, and had waged war on the natives only after they had massacred the garrison; and the bishops and burghers had helped them in the war. They had only taken over the archbishop's lands on the Dvina to protect the country against the Lithuanians, at the request of converts. It was true that they traded with the Lithuanians – a papal charter of 1257 [93] authorized them to do so – but not in time of war; whereas the burghers of Riga supplied these heathen with weapons and foodstuffs in both war and peace, and had actually formed a military alliance with them. As for their neglect of the task of conversion, let anyone ask a Livonian native 'Do you believe in God?', and he would reply, 'I believe in God, in the holy virgin Mary, and in the teachings of Holy God and the Holy Roman Church, and in the catechism, like other true and good Christians.' In any case, their record spoke for itself: over 100,000 Christians in Livonia, won for the Church in less than a century, while in Estonia, Russia, Ösel and Semigallia, where the Knights had no power, there was nothing but apostasy, schism and paganism.

This was not the end of the argument. However, it shows how tensions within the Order's lands made it essential that the knight-brothers should continue, whenever possible, to carry out the task they had been sent there to perform: to fight and convert the heathen and the schismatic. Without papal approval, they would be unable to hold their own against their Christian neighbours, or keep out the Lithuanians; the only way to keep this approval was to press on with the crusade and attract from outside as many crusaders as possible to assist them, both to gain ground and to enhance their international standing.

Two startling political events irrevocably committed the whole Order to the Lithuanian war. One was the fall of Acre in 1291, which made it impossible for the knight-brothers to continue fighting in the Holy Land, and led to the setting up of a new headquarters at Venice. Venice was the usual embarkation point for all Germans bound for the East, and was chosen in anticipation of a crusade of recovery; but the crusade never came. Meanwhile, the knight-brothers in Prussia did their best to divert more of the Order's resources to the North. Grand-Master Conrad von Feuchtwangen had served both as master of Prussia and master of Livonia, and made a personal visit to Prussia in 1295 to help morale; Master Sack of Prussia and his eleven commanders wrote to von Feuchtwangen's successor that the grand-master must stop ignoring reports of the danger their province was in, and take their problems seriously, or they would not be answerable for the consequences. When Grand-Master Gottfried von Hohenlohe did come north in 1302, he tried to make the Brothers keep their Rule more strictly, and met so much opposition that he resigned his office. His successor, Siegfried von Feuchtwangen, found himself beset on all sides, both by Lithuanians and by Livonian litigants, and when his Prussian knight-brothers seized the Pomerelian port of Danzig in 1308 it seemed that Poland and Brandenburg were likely to join in against the Order.

This was particularly alarming at that moment because the grand-master of the Templars had been arrested at Paris the year before, and on 22 November 1307 Clement V authorized the arrest and dispossession of the Templars throughout Europe, pending the results of an inquiry into their conduct. The estates of France pronounced against them the following May, and that summer Clement V took up residence in France apparently on the best of terms with Philip IV, the persecutor of the Templars. The absurdity of the charges, and the ease with which that Order was destroyed in all countries other than Spain and parts of Germany, put the Teutonic Knights in jeopardy; if Templars could be hunted down and burnt alive merely on suspicion of collaborating with the Muslims and disregarding their Rule, what would happen to an Order with a dossier of accusations against it ranging from genocide to the murder of pilgrims? Moreover, since 1305 King Philip IV had been urging that all the military Orders should be abolished, and a new one set up with himself at its head. Von Feuchtwangen prepared for the worst by leaving Venice, and in September 1309 he established the headquarters of his Order at Marienburg Castle (Malbork) within his own territory of Prussia, beyond the reach of any secular ruler.

He was just in time. The following June, Clement V issued the Bull *In vinea domini*, which ordered the archbishop of Bremen and Canon Albert of Milan to investigate all the outstanding charges against the Teutonic Knights, who

alas, insulting our Redeemer, shaming all the faithful, and damaging the faith, have become domestic enemies and familiars of the enemy, not fighting in the name of Christ against the enemies of the faith, but rather, astounding to hear, waging war on behalf of such people against Christ, with various cunning ruses.[94]

In 1312 Clement's inquisitor excommunicated the Livonian knight-brothers from Riga, and, although the excommunication was removed the following year, the knight-brothers had evidently escaped dissolution only by a narrow margin. It cannot have been an accident that, when von Feuchtwangen died, they elected as his successor Carl von Trier, who 'knew the French like his own language, and was able to talk to the pope and cardinals without an interpreter; he was so affable and eloquent, that even his enemies delighted to listen to him'.[95] But his own knights drove him back to Trier in 1317.

Prussia became the main concern of the whole Order, and the whole apparatus of the crusade was applied to the Russian and Lithuanian frontiers. The grand-master was now a sovereign lord with three main political preoccupations: extending his sovereignty to include the surviving enclaves of episcopal and civic power in Prussia and Livonia; securing Danzig and Pomerelia against reconquest by Poland, and working towards the overthrow of Lithuania and the independent Russian princes – the heathen and the schismatic. At the same time he had to fight the propaganda battle and the continuous wars of litigation in the Curia, and prove to the world that the Teutonic Knights were doing their job as a military Order – winning converts and defeating the heathen. The war had to go on.

THE MORALITY AND RECRUITMENT OF THE CRUSADE

One question remained unanswered. Was warfare a lawful means of getting converts? The Schoolmen had been debating the subject for some time, and many were convinced that the answer was no. Friar Roger Bacon was one of them. In his *Opus maius*, completed in 1268, he argued that preaching was the only way of securing the minds of the heathen, and that the military monks were hindering the process 'owing to the wars that they are always stirring up, and because they wish to have entire sovereignty'. He condemned the Teutonic Knights in particular: 'many years ago, they deceived the Roman Church with subtle arguments'; and since then, he alleged, their record had proved the falsity of these arguments. He held (on astrological grounds) that

when Christians discuss matters with pagans like the Prussians and the other adjoining nations, the latter are easily won over, and perceive they are in error … they would become Christians very gladly if the Church were willing to permit them to retain their liberty and enjoy their possessions in peace. But the Christian princes who labour for their conversion, and especially the brothers of the Teutonic Order, desire to reduce them to slavery, as the Dominicans and Franciscans and other good men throughout all Germany are aware … [96]

At the time of the great council of Lyon in 1274 the morality of the crusade came under fire from many quarters, and Humbert of Romans, former general of the Dominican Order, wrote to Pope Gregory X in his *Opusculum tripartitum*, that the war against Muslims ought to be continued,

but about the idolaters who are still with us in northern parts, the Prussians, for example, and those like them, it must be said that there is still hope that they may be converted in the same way as many of their neighbours … the Poles, the Danes, the Saxons and Bohemians, and many others. In any case they are not in the habit of attacking us, nor can they do much if they attack … And so it is quite enough for Christians to defend themselves manfully when they invade.[97]

Such arguments carried a certain weight in Rome, and filtered through to the Baltic by way of the friars and the educated clergy not attached to the Order. How could they be countered?

One objection came in the report sent in to the pope by a more impartial witness, the bishop of Olomouc.[98] Neither the Lithuanians nor the Prussians, he pointed out, were harmless: they had inflicted grave damage on the Church in Poland, and the Polish churches 'are walls next door to our own house, and when they catch fire we observe that our interests are clearly involved'. The princes of Germany were too divided among themselves to go to the assistance either of their own frontier lands or of the Holy Land; if they were persuaded to set sail for Outremer they would leave their own country in danger. This was the 'domino theory' of the time, and to those living within reach of Lithuanian armies it was more attractive than Humbert's argument that the heathen of the North were 'enervated' and harmless. According to the Volhynian Chronicler's continuator, before the treaty of 1305 'the Lithuanians and Samogitians had done a great deal of harm to the Poles and had taken into captivity whole squadrons of Poles and Masurians, so that Poles were sold in Lithuania and White Russia for a *grivna* [four ounces of silver] or ten Lithuanian *groshi*, and the Lithuanians swapped them among themselves for horses and oxen.[99] The Order had its own chronicle of Lithuanian raids to recount.

Another objection lay in the attitude of Lithuanian princes to Christian missionaries. At times, they were tolerant and apparently sympathetic. Between 1322 and 1324, Grand-Prince Vytenis's brother and successor, Gediminas, who had let his daughter be baptized for the sake of a Polish alliance, made several friendly overtures to Catholic powers. He sent letters to the friars, to the Hanseatic cities and to the pope, inviting settlers, merchants, artisans, soldiers and missionaries to enter his country and dwell there under his protection. He asked the pope to be his father, and expressed a great desire to live at peace with the Church. On the other hand, he remained entirely unconvinced by arguments in favour of Christianity, however mildly they were put, and, when papal emissaries finally asked him to join the Church, in November 1324, all he said was 'May the devil baptize me!'[100] In the following January two Cistercian abbots[101] testified that Gediminas had since killed or enslaved over 8000 Christians residing in or near his territory – and this at a time when he was at peace with the Teutonic Knights. His incipient conversion had been a sham; or, rather, a sensible diplomatic manoeuvre. The episode hardly demonstrated that warfare was a better method than preaching for securing conversions, but it did show that neither method was likely to have much effect on a powerful and intelligent heathen ruler.

From the Order's point of view the strongest argument against the peaceable approach to conversion lay in their archive. They were there because papal Bulls had authorized them to fight the heathen and rule the convert, and because the whole of Scripture and the Fathers had been combed for texts and opinions that justified what they were doing. Tradition and the *status quo* were on their side, whatever the intellectuals might say. St Bernard had justified monastic knighthood, Gregory IX had sent them to Prussia, and the canonist Hostiensis had proved that the heathen had no right to liberty or independence: these were not names that could be brushed aside. Nor could the charters, the Rule and the treaties; nor could the blood and money that had been spent in the cause. If it were objected that the Order had exceeded its documented rights and duties, by oppressing its partners and subjects, especially converts, it could be replied that there was a war to be won, and imposing discipline and even excessive labour-services on the whole Christian community was a necessary means of achieving this end. And in fact, from 1299 onwards, the knight-brothers in Livonia were evidently determined to put an end to the division of power within the province, and, by establishing themselves as the sovereign body over the whole territory, prevent the possibility of another civil war. If they were entitled to run a war-machine, it was their duty to run it as efficiently as possible – at least as efficiently as the grand-prince of Lithuania ran his, and it was not run on brotherly love.

The flaws in these two sets of arguments are hardly worth pointing out; the arguments themselves are worth repeating because they are what people believed at the time, and help explain why they acted as they did. The Order's case may have been weak, but it satisfied thousands of crusaders who made the journey to Prussia in the course of the fourteenth century.

It is surprising that the Order should have attracted more secular crusaders from a wider field in that century, after Prussia and Livonia were conquered, than in the thirteenth, when its life depended on such assistance. Part of the explanation is that there were many fewer crusades to the Near East; or, rather, that the doctrine of the crusading vow was still flourishing at a time when opportunities for its redemption in Palestine were few. There were collection boxes in every church, crusading taxes in every kingdom, regular reminders from the pulpit, and a continuous distribution of indulgences, letters of protection and special privileges. There was a great deal more planning and theorizing on the subject, now it became clear that the old ways of conducting crusades were inadequate. At the same time, continuous conventional wars in France and Germany meant that there were more professional and semi-professional fighting men than ever before; whenever there was a truce, or a treaty, these men had to face the question 'Where next?' The Teutonic Order made sure they came to Prussia, both by developing friendships with rulers and warriors in many different parts of Europe, and by offering their 'guests' all the advantages that went with the status of crusader.

Some kings and princes bought shares of merit by making donations. These begin with the emperors, and include most of the kings of Europe, including Edward I and Edward III of England. They wanted to be regarded as crusaders, even if they never went on a crusade. Rulers were apt to find it expedient to take the cross, but inexpedient to fulfil the vow; a gift of any kind to a crusading order was one way out. A friendly act would do as well; thus in 1329, all the brother dukes of Silesia were admitted as *confratres* of the Order, in recognition of their hostility against the king of Poland. Such allies were bought for the time being; others were more or less wedded to the Order from birth, by family tradition or by the proximity of the Order's estates to their own. All the German kings and emperors held on to Swabia and the upper Rhine, and the strength of the Order in this area cemented the special relationship that Henry VI and Frederick II had begun. All the kings of Bohemia inherited the bond established by the crusading king Ottokar; they had the Order's bailiwick of Bohemia to remind them of it. With Central and East European dynasts such as King John the Luxemburger (king of Bohemia 1310–46) and his son the emperor Charles IV (of Bohemia and Germany, 1347–78) the friendship was close and mutually profitable. These rulers made use of knight-brothers from the Order's convents in Germany, while the Order employed them and their subjects in Prussia.

The first crusaders to arrive in Prussia at the beginning of the four-teenth century, after a thirty-year interval, were Rhinelanders, under the count of Homberg. Their lands lay round the grand-master's private bailiwick of Coblenz, and their trip may be attributed to the influence of the Order as a local landowner. Rhineland princes were soon afterwards much involved in the wars of the Valois and Edward III, and in the enterprises of John of Luxemburg, and through this network of interests the habit spread. Bohemians reached Prussia in 1323, Alsatians in 1324, Englishmen and Walloons in 1329, Austrians and Frenchmen in 1336, Bavarians and Hollanders in 1337, Hungarians and Burgundians in 1344, and in the second half of the century Occitanians, Scots and Italians.

The leader of the fashion was King John of Bohemia, who made three expeditions to Prussia and brought many lesser princes in his train. He went in 1328–9 partly in order to strengthen his claim to the kingdom of Poland by helping the Order against the reigning Polish ruler Wladyslaw Lokietek; but he also believed in what the Order stood for. As he put it in the preamble to one of his charters,

their praiseworthy state and their memorable holiness of life and worship attract us; they suffer heavy and unbearable labours and expenses for the extension of the orthodox faith, and have made themselves into an unbreakable wall to defend the faith against the Lithuanians and their partisans, whoever they may be – pestilential enemies of Christ! – as we have seen ourself; every day they expose themselves fearlessly to danger and death, hemmed in, divided, hopelessly slaughtered and afflicted![102]

That was how the brothers liked to see themselves; it was a help if such a personage as King John made a public affirmation in favour of this view. In 1328 he had brought the French poet Guillaume de Machaut in his retinue; Guillaume's references to the conquest and conversion of Lithuanian *mescreans*[103] were the sort of publicity the Order needed, and could have reached a wide audience. In 1341 the dying grand-master Dietrich von Altenburg consigned the Order to John's protection; the king was nearly blind, he had very little land or money to spare, and his own subjects had rejected him, but his reputation as a knight was so high that such an association was bound to encourage similar enthusiasts to make the journey to Prussia.

Duke Henry of Lancaster, Edward III's cousin, was one of these; he took advantage of the truce in the French war to set out for Prussia, but there was no *sommer-reysa* in the year he chose, 1352, and he redeemed his vow when he got to Stettin. His grandson, Henry, Earl of Derby, later Henry IV, made two expeditions to Prussia, in 1390 and 1392, and the detailed account of what he spent on these trips brings out the enormous financial saving made by the Order on the military service provided by such magnates. Between August 1390 and April 1391 Henry maintained a retinue of thirteen knights, eighteen squires, three heralds, ten miners and engineers, six minstrels and sixty other ranks – about 100 in all, with perhaps fifty more volunteers. He spent a total of £4360, or 13,000 Prussian marks (more than the Order was to pay for the whole isle of Gotland), and, of this, £564 went on wages and over £400 on gifts. In 1392 he spent £239 in six weeks. He received presents and entertainment, but these were not worth anything like what he handed out; he was a big spender for the honour of his father, John of Gaunt, and his cousin King Richard II. He had his silver and his kitchenware made locally, to the tune of £75, and he hired boats, horses, and waggons to carry his stuff. His father had to help him with the payments, but the Lancaster estates could afford it.[104]

The disadvantage of this system was that princes sometimes tried to use their association to advance their own political interests through the Order, or else demanded a say in how the fighting was to be conducted. The first was not a serious threat, since it could be averted or mitigated by bargaining, but the second was: a prince who brought 500 knights with him, as did the margrave of Meissen in 1391, could hardly be ignored if he had views on what the marshal of the Order ought to be doing, but the conditions of the Lithuanian war left no room at all for mistakes. If it was too wet, or too cold, there could be no campaign, however many crowned heads were strutting impatiently round the yard at Marienburg castle; yet some of them would always be prepared to chance it, and court disaster. Wigand of Marburg relates how in 1378 von Kniprode went on a *Winter-reysa* 'in honour' of the duke of Lorraine, who had just arrived with seventy knights. This campaign was a success, but, when the duke of Austria and the count of Cleves arrived, a little later, he was obliged to lay on a special raid for them in early December, which was really no more than a week's safari to give them a chance to accomplish their vows before Christmas.[105] But 'big names' were worth the trouble.

In attracting ordinary knights to Prussia, the Order relied both on the example of the princes, and on direct family ties within the regions covered by the German bailiwicks. Not just the landgrave, the margrave and the counts, but the whole military class of the area drained by the tributaries of the upper Elbe – Thuringia, Meissen and the Vogtland – was more-or-less closely concerned in it. This group provided nine grand-masters, an innumerable body of knight-brothers, and continuous donations.[106] If such knights wanted to give alms, or perform corporal acts of mercy, the three local hospitals of the Order gave them their chance; if their younger sons had to be provided for honourably, and their own church-patronage was inadequate, the local convent was the place to apply for admission as a priest-brother. If they wanted to migrate, the grand-master could offer them land; the Pleissenland provided the Order's most powerful family of lay vassals in Prussia, the von Stange, who had built their own settlement at Stangenburg, near Christburg, in 1285. If they wanted to crusade, Prussia was the obvious target. In a complex of relationships such as this, the bailiwick became a spiritual sponge, soaking up all the gentry had to give through the many orifices that led to atonement. It was the same at the confluence of the Main and the Rhine: Nassau, Falkenstein and Katzenellenbogen were so honeycombed with commanderies that local society automatically banked its contrition with the Order. In other areas – in the Breisgau, for example, and in Silesia and northern Switzerland – the Teutonic Order's place was taken by the Hospitallers, and until 1309 the Templars rivalled it in Brunswick and Halberstadt; but where the Order was well established it had the advantage over other religious houses by providing such a variety of routes to atonement.

In recruiting the plebeian crusader the Order relied mainly on the well-to-do, who could bring paid retinues, and partly on the general availability of the crusading vow as a means of atonement. To take an early example, in 1252 the count of Holstein sacked the city of Schleswig, and some of his troops broke into the church. This was by no means unusual in Scandinavian warfare, but, when one of the Holsteiners fell dead for no apparent cause, his companion, a crossbowman, was stricken with remorse. He went to the bishop, and swore that he would go to Prussia as a crusader and never fire a bolt at a Christian again.[107] Such moments of contrition must have accounted for many of the rank and file present on the Order's *reysen*; they were there because they needed that particular kind of war to pay off their debt to God, and this was the nearest theatre of operations.

Others went in for vicarious atonement. The burgher Lutbert of Rostock made a will in 1267 by which his property and a half-share in his ship were bequeathed to his son Jordan. If Jordan wanted to get the whole ship, he was obliged to make a voyage to Prussia or Livonia to obtain remission for his father's sins; and, if he preferred not to go, he must sell even the half-share he had, and use the money to pay someone else.[108] The plain penitents were encouraged to enlist in units directly under the command of the knight-brothers. The first regulations for such men were issued in 1292, and were based on the usages by which the Templars governed their native auxiliaries, the Turcopoles. In Germany they were called *Knechte*, or squires, and they could enlist either *in caritate* or for pay. In either case, they came under the same strict discipline as the knight-brothers themselves, living in the convent apart from their wives and incurring penance and correction for any breach of rules. On admission they had to swear loyalty and obedience, and promise not to go outside without leave or ever visit taverns; and, above all, none was to shed blood unless ordered to. Those *in caritate* had to trim their hair and beards like the knight-brothers, and got an honorarium of two bezants for their first year, rising to four if they stayed on.[109]

By this means the Order could skim off the cream of the more indigent crusaders, and make sure that their poverty was not allowed to hinder their military efficiency. If they were not needed in war they could be found war duties in any convent, and they would earn their remission in either role. On the march they were expected to act as an advance guard, and as flankers, and in battle they formed up round the baggage under the marshal's standard while the knight-brothers charged. Like the half-brothers, who did the manual work, they were not actually members of the Order, but they were essential to its military performance.

Thus Prussia provided crusaders of all ranks with opportunities for effective military service. Why they went there depended on who they were. It would be idle to claim that all or most of them were high-minded champions of Christendom, risking their lives for God's forgiveness. When Froissart pointed out that 'men-at-arms cannot live on pardons, nor do they pay much attention to them except at the point of death', he knew what he was talking about, and, indeed, the grand-masters were known to stimulate interest in their war by offers of wages to those who took the cross. At the same time, nobody seems to have made a fortune out of fighting the Lithuanians, and most appear to have given more than they got. The forty English knights who decided in 1349 to build a castle and chapel on the Lithuanian frontier, to receive converts and deter the heathen,[110] may have been misguided, but they can hardly have been cynical profiteers. A hostile poet, Heinrich de Teichner, dismissed the *Praussenvart* as a waste of resources better spent at home.

WARS AND POLITICS, 1304–1409

With the help of the crusaders, the Order began to gain ground. The new arrivals of 1304 took part in the *winter-reysa* early in 1305. They rode to the Niemen, devastated the territory round Grodno, and camped opposite Gediminas's new fort, displaying their banner from dawn to noon as an act of provocation. Under the banner, the count of Homberg and the other crusaders were ceremonially knighted by the commander of Brandenburg. Next year they destroyed the town by the stronghold of Grodno, and made an unsuccessful attempt on the fort with 100 brothers and 6000 knights. More crusaders arrived in 1307, with the new Prussian master, Henry von Plotzke, and in the following years the Lithuanians of Carsovia submitted and their three forts were destroyed. There were retaliatory raids into Prussia in 1308 and 1311, but on the last Vytenis was defeated at Woplauken (near Rastenburg), and the pressure on his Niemen lands never relaxed. One raid penetrated over fifty miles into enemy territory, reaching Salcininkai, just south of Vilnius; others probed every territory along the Lithuanian border, and they were sent out every year from 1313 to 1320.

Gediminas, grand-prince since his brother's death in 1315, then prepared his knock-out blow. In 1322, instead of replying directly to the Prussian *sommer-reysa*, he sent a force to devastate the bishopric of Dorpat in Livonia, and opened negotiations with the pope, the king of Poland and the burghers of Riga – all, for different reasons, then at odds with the Order. The early weeks of 1323 were intensely cold, and the crusaders were unable to set out on a *winter-reysa*. While Gediminas's brother David, now prince of Pskov, kept the Livonians busy by invading Estonia, the main Lithuanian army went on an unopposed expedition down to the mouth of the Niemen and took the town of Memel. In August he devastated Samland, in September Dobrzyn; in October the Order sent to Vilnius and concluded a truce. It was estimated that the Lithuanians had killed or captured 20,000 Christians in the previous year and a half.

The Order made an alliance with Novgorod, reopened hostilities along the frontier with the help of a new batch of crusaders, and began six new castles to secure the interior of Prussia. The new grand-master,

Werner von Orseln, arrested Gediminas's envoy and persuaded John XXII to issue a crusading Bull offering full remission of sins to all who fought Russians, Tartars and heathens during the next three years (20 June 1325). Gediminas replied by invading the Order's allies, Brandenburg and Mazovia, in concert with King Wladyslaw of Poland, and then in 1329 the city of Riga summoned him to Livonia to help them overthrow the knight-brothers. The result was another breakthrough by the Lithuanians in the north; but, while Gediminas stripped the interior, the Livonian master, Eberhard Monheim, laid siege to Riga, which fell the following year, and Grand-Master von Orseln led a large force of crusaders, including King John of Bohemia, on a *sommer-reysa* against Poland. With Riga in its power, the Order could hold out against Gediminas and retaliate against Lithuania from the north; in the south, King Wladyslaw was forced to make peace in 1332, and the knight-brothers were safe for ten years. That is, they were secure enough to carry on the frontier war of devastation, siege, castle-building and ambush, both from Livonia and from Prussia, without suffering any massive breakthrough by enemy forces. Gediminas even signed a peace with Livonia in 1338.

By the end of this phase, both sides were again preparing for total war. Gediminas was dead and his son Algirdas became ruler of Pskov, so that Livonia was once more threatened all along her frontier. The grand-master was authorized to conquer the whole of Eastern Europe by the emperor Lewis; the Prussian knight brothers began to construct three military highways into Lithuania, summoned more crusaders from Germany, and were reinforced by the king of Bohemia's son, Margrave Charles of Moravia. In 1342 Algirdas and the Pskovians invaded Livonia, got as far down the Dvina as Üxküll, and were held and counter-attacked by a combined force of Livonians and Estonians; but the following year the Estonian peasantry revolted against their landlords, the king of Denmark's vassals, and the Livonian master Burchard von Dreileben had to send for a reinforcement of 630 Prussian brothers to help suppress the rising. Civil war between Gediminas's sons prevented the Lithuanians from taking immediate advantage of this crisis, but, once Algirdas and his brother Kestutis had gained control of Vilnius, in 1345, they launched the big attack. That year, Grand-Master Ludolf König was unable to stop the Lithuanians ravaging Samland, and went mad with grief when the crusaders blamed him for the disaster; for the invaders then turned north, crossed the Dvina not far from Riga, and ravaged central Livonia, returning home with 600 prisoners. There was a further raid into Samland in 1346, launched as soon as Grand-Master Dusmer's defensive patrol had gone off duty, and in 1347 two more invasions under Kestutis and his brother Narimont which pushed southwards into Barthia. By this time the number of captives driven from Prussia into Lithuania was being reckoned in thousands, and the frontier lay open; if the raids had continued, the knight-brothers might well have been forced to submit.

However, they were saved by an *annus mirabilis* of victories in 1348, and by the Black Death. The victories were secured by 'preventive strikes' into Lithuania; crusaders had arrived from England and France, and the marshal and Grand-Commander von Kniprode were able to lead out a destructive *winter-reysa* which defeated a Russo-Lithuanian pursuing force by the frozen river Strawen, east of the Niemen. Meanwhile, master von Hercke of Livonia ravaged and depopulated the northern district of Samogitia, round Siaulai, and reinforced his defences south of the Dvina. A *sommer-reysa* by Grand-Master Dusmer brought back 1500 baptized prisoners from Welun (Veliuona) on the Niemen to settle in Prussia, and the Lithuanians were unable to retaliate until 1352. By then, the plague had weakened both sides, and the Lithuanians' opportunity for pressing home the incursions of 1345–7 had passed. Algirdas and Kestutis still meant to conquer the Order's lands, but Winrich von Kniprode was now grand-master and was prepared to hold his own.

He spent his thirty-one years of office strengthening his frontier and home commanderies with new and rebuilt castles, recruiting more and more crusaders, particularly from Western Europe, and maintaining constant pressure on the defences of Lithuania. His large investment in masonry and entertainment has been described as symptomatic of his Order's inward corruption, and he has been blamed for turning the crusade into a cruel chivalric entertainment. But von Kniprode was a realist; he was only putting into practice the military lessons he had learnt as marshal and grand-commander of Prussia in the 1340s. He was fighting a war of attrition in which he had two advantages: a more advanced technique of siegecraft and fortification, and a reserve of unpaid military manpower. His enemy had greater resources, spread over a vast area, and could inflict proportionally greater damage on the Order than the Order could inflict on Lithuania, provided his armies got through the wilderness that separated the two powers. This had happened often enough in the past, and it happened again early in von Kniprode's grand-mastership: from 1352 to 1354 the Lithuanians reached the Frische Haff and devastated Warmia, only thirty miles from Marienburg, and in 1356 they destroyed seventeen villages near Allenstein (Olsztyn). Therefore the ways in had to be blocked; the Niemen had to be cleared of Lithuanian forts up to the confluence with the Viliya, and the Masurian lakes had to be studded with castles wherever they could be bypassed. This would leave a no-man's-land of about ninety miles' breadth between the Lithuanian forts on the upper Niemen and the safeguarded Prussian region. No large invasion force could hope to get through the bogs and forest which filled that area; therefore the Order could concentrate its energies on the lower Niemen and raid either northwards into Samogitia, or eastwards into Lithuania proper. The object of these raids was to extend the no-man's-land as far as possible, by depopulating or at least devastating the countryside, and to keep Lithuanian armies pinned down in their own territories.

Von Kniprode was also extremely successful in weakening his enemies through diplomacy. The alliance of the Poles and Lithuanians, and the continuing independence of the archbishop of Riga and his suffragans, had endangered the Order in the past, and had to be provided against. King Casimir of Poland made peace with Lithuania in 1357, and in 1350 a papal award confirmed the archbishop in possession of the whole city of Riga apart from the castle. Nevertheless, von Kniprode managed to prevent active co-operation between Poles and Lithuanians, mainly by keeping up alliances with the Polish dukes, who were opposed to the increasing power of King Casimir; and in 1366, by the peace of Danzig, he brought about an agreement between the Livonian brothers and the archbishop of Riga which gave the brothers the right to exact military services from the citizens.

The Lithuanian princes attempted to outmanoeuvre him. In 1358 Kestutis sent to the emperor, Charles IV, offering to accept baptism provided that the Order hand back all the lands it had conquered from him and his brothers, but Charles was too deeply committed to the Order to take the offer seriously. Divisions within the Lithuanian dynasty gave von Kniprode the opportunity of effective countermeasures. In 1365 he won over a son of Kestutis, and had him baptized with great rejoicing at Marienburg, and from 1380 he was allied with Jogaila, the son of

Algirdas (died in 1377) and fought with him against Kestutis. He was quite prepared to deal with his enemies amicably when anything could be gained by it – as when in 1372 he made a treaty involving the exchange of prisoners with Algirdas and Kestutis, and in 1379 concluded a ten years' truce with Kestutis. He knew this old pagan very well, as he had been fighting him since the 1340s, and had held him prisoner at Marienburg for eight months in 1361. Bargaining with God's enemies was risky, since the Holy War was theoretically unending, but it could be defended as the only way of winning that war; in any case, von Kniprode could hardly forswear a weapon used so astutely by the other side.

Von Kniprode's success made his grand-mastership the golden age of the Order in Prussia, and his contemporaries in Livonia, masters von Hercke, Vietinghof and Vrimersheim, benefited accordingly, since the wars on the Niemen meant that their main enemy had one hand tied. They were able to stabilize their south-eastern frontier with new castles, and conduct raids deep into Samogitia from the north, often in concert with their Prussian brothers. In 1346 Grand-Master Dusmer had loaned them the 19,000 marks they needed for the purchase of Estonia from the king of Denmark, and von Kniprode did not press for repayment; after 1376 he let them off with a quarter of what they owed. Their incursions into Pskov, Polotsk, and Lithuania were of more use to him than their money.

Only once after 1356 were the enemy able to penetrate Livonia to within easy reach of Riga (in 1361); and only once was the interior of Prussia threatened by a raid down the Niemen. On this last occasion, in 1370, Kestutis was caught at Rudau in Samland and forced to retreat after a bloody battle which cost the lives of twenty-six of the brothers, including Marshal Henning Schindekopf. By the time von Kniprode died, in 1382, Kestutis had launched his final incursion, which got as far as Tapiau (Gvardeysk), twenty-five miles east of Königsberg; but that summer the Order's troops occupied Trakai, fourteen miles west of Vilnius, and Vilnius itself was taken by the Order's ally Jogaila, who was supposed to be on the point of baptism. Kestutis surrendered to his nephew, and was murdered in August. The interminable crusade against the Lithuanians appeared to be drawing to a close.

Under von Kniprode's successors, this illusion of triumph was threatened by two developments. The first was the introduction of cannon, used on the *winter-reysa* of 1381 by the Order, and given to Jogaila as a present during the detente of the following year. These heavy 'bombards' could only be transported long distances by water, which meant that the power upriver had the advantage of the power downriver when it came to sieges; the Lithuanians could get their cannon to the Order's forts quicker than the Order could haul its cannon to Lithuania. In 1384, when Jogaila and Witold (Vytautas), his cousin, were again at war with the Order, Grand-Master Zöllner von Rothenstein spent the summer building a new brick castle called Marienwerder, on the site of Kaunas. When he had gone home, Witold said to Jogaila, 'You have the land, you have the people; bring up the guns and we shall take it in no time with our army.' Jogaila said, 'Perhaps the master will attack us.' 'Not within a month', replied his cousin. 'He will not be able to; and meanwhile we shall get what we want.'[111] Marienwerder fell after six weeks, as it happened, even though the garrison had a cannon of their own, which was so well handled that it shattered the counterweight of one of the old-fashioned Lithuanian ballistas 'like an egg'. Zöllner could do nothing. The following year he found himself opposed at a crossing of the Viliya by Prince Skirgaila (Jogaila's brother) 'with innumerable bombards', and in 1388 he was repulsed from Skirgaila's fort on the lower Viliya by artillery. The great *sommer-reysa* of 1390 to Vilnius, which included Henry Bolingbroke, earl of Derby, and lasted eleven weeks, only managed to take one of the outlying forts of the city; while Jogaila recaptured Grodno, before relief could arrive, that same year.

The other development was Jogaila's breach with the Order in 1383 (when he became convinced that Zöllner meant to divide Lithuania between him and Witold), and his election to the throne of Poland in 1385. This *coup* did not produce a Polish–Lithuanian super-power, since the rulers of the two countries pursued separate and often antagonistic policies for the next fifty years at least, but it resulted in the baptism of the leading Lithuanian nobles; Jogaila's own baptism (as Wladyslaw IV) did revive Polish hopes of regaining territory lost to the Order, and enabled the Poles to reopen the offensive against the Order which had been suspended by Casimir III. By 1392 Witold had come to terms with Wladyslaw, who let him keep the lands of his father, Kestutis, including Vilnius. The Order could only continue its crusade against Lithuania by ignoring the fact that its ruler was a baptized Christian, who professed to be baptizing his subjects.

At the same time, the old quarrel with Riga broke out once more.

Archbishop John IV left the city for Lübeck and appealed to the pope and King Sigismund of Bohemia for protection. The Order seized his castles, and Sigismund occupied the Order's land within his kingdom; the master of Livonia, Wennemar Hasenkamp von Brüggeneye, was summoned to the Curia to answer the archbishop's charges.

Under grand-masters Conrad von Wallenrod (1391–3) and Conrad von Jungingen (1393–1407) the Order responded to these reversals of fortune by a policy of territorial expansion. Since the old frontier was now inadequate, it was decided to push it out as far as possible, both by war and by purchase. Between 1390 and 1395 the Order bought the duchies of Dobryzn and Opole, on Wladyslaw's northern and south-western frontier, from the dukes who owned them, and between 1400 and 1402 the whole of Brandenburg Neumark, which hemmed him in to the north-west. Repeated campaigns against Lithuania by larger and larger armies, which included both crusaders and mercenaries, convinced Witold that it was worth buying off the Order to avoid becoming dependent on his cousin, and in 1398 he agreed at Sallynwerder to surrender his rights over Samogitia in return for a 'perpetual peace' and a strip of wilderness west of the lower Niemen.

The boyars of Samogitia were not a party to this transaction, and were still unbaptized. Campaigns against them continued for the rest of Conrad von Jungingen's grand-mastership, sometimes with the help of Witold and sometimes not, but in 1406 they submitted, and the following year applied for permission to live under the town law of Prussia – in vain. Wladyslaw had been placated by the return of Dobryzn, and for three years he, Witold and the Order co-operated against the newly risen power of Muscovy. Grand-Master Conrad von Jungingen's brother Ulrich succeeded him at a time when it appeared that only the schismatic Russians were left to fight.

However, neither Poland nor Lithuania had relinquished its hopes of regaining its lost lands, and the rulers of both countries were aware that the price of the Wallenrod–Jungingen expansion had been discontent with the Order's rule within Prussia. Burghers and kingly vassals were expressing discontent with war taxation and military service, and crusaders had been in short supply since 1396, when the prospect of fighting the Turks had diverted French, English and German knights from the Lithuanian front to the crusade of Nicopolis. In 1409 the Samogitians revolted, with the support of their former prince, and Grand-Master

Ulrich retaliated against Poland by reoccupying Dobrzyn and harrying Mazovia. This action was in accordance with the policy stated by his brother in a letter to the German electors in 1397; all who gave aid to the heathen would be treated as enemies of the Order.[112] But were Samogitians still heathen? And, if so, what had the Order been doing in their country for the last decade? That August, Wladyslaw and Witold combined to produce a public manifesto against their common enemy. In it they stated that the Samogitians were laudable converts, whom they had themselves baptized, while the native Prussians were still semi-pagan after nearly 200 years of rule by the Teutonic Knights. They claimed that the brothers were not interested in conversion, only in aggrandizement at the expense of their neighbours; unless God stopped them, they would subjugate all the princes in the world.[113]

This rhetoric prepared the way for a combined Polish–Lithuanian invasion with an army strong enough to overcome any forces the Order could send against it. From this point, the character of the war changed. It was no longer a fight against the heathen pursued by a strategy that involved the seizure of land from Christian neighbours: it became a war waged by Poland and Lithuania for the reconquest of lands the Order had taken. It was pursued both in the field and by an intellectual assault on the concept and function of monastic knighthood.

STRATEGY AND TACTICS

The war against pagan Lithuania has been described as a war of attrition, but this gives little idea of how it was conducted. Since it lasted for more than a hundred years, during which both combatants grew steadily richer and more powerful, neither the Order nor the heathen can be said to have achieved the aim of a war of attrition. There was some kind of fighting almost every year from 1283 to 1406, vast expenditure of labour and money, and a continuous record of atrocities and devastation: both war-machines were effective enough to leave the enemy's resources undestroyed.

To explain this paradox, it is necessary to look at the geography of the region. At this period, as was pointed out in chapter 1, most of it was covered by a dense deciduous forest, reaching from the Baltic coast to the Beresina, and from the Pripet marches to the Dvina. In the middle of this area, on the upper Niemen, Viliya, and upper Dvina, the

Lithuanians and their Russian tributaries had cleared enough land to support sizeable populations; but this still left a belt of uncleared land, almost 100 miles wide, between them and the Order's settled zones in Prussia and Livonia. Within this belt, the going was very tough: not only trees, undergrowth and the thickets left as *hege* or barriers all round Samogitia, but also marsh, bog, lake and the innumerable tributaries of the great rivers, presented problems of logistics and transport which medieval armies were ill equipped to solve. There survives a compilation of routes between Prussia and Lithuania (*Die Littauischen Wegeberichte*, made 1348–1402)[114] which gives a clear picture of the difficulties. For example, if you had got to Betygala, near the upper Dubysa, which flows into the Niemen from Samogitia, and you wanted to proceed to Vandziogala, north of Kaunas, twenty-one miles as the crow flies, thirty-five by modern by-roads, the following route (twenty-seven miles) was offered: first there was a *damerow*, or patch of scrubland, with a track; then a great wood where you had to clear your way (*rumen*); then there was a heath; then another wood, 'the length of a crossbow shot, and there you have to clear your way too'; then a heath; then another wood (more trail-blazing for over three miles). That was on the edge of the true *Wiltnisse*: the route from the Prussian lowlands to the upper Niemen crossed the middle of it. One way which was found by a native Prussian scout was described in a letter that was copied into the *Wegeberichte*, and dated from Insterburg (Chernyakhovsk) on the Pregolya. It begins,

Dear Lord Marshal,

Take notice in your wisdom that by God's grace Gedutte and his company have got back in safety and have completed everything you sent us to carry out and have marked the way so far as 4½ miles this side of the Niemen, along a route that crosses the Niemen and leads straight into the country.[115]

They had travelled a distance of less than seventy miles as the crow flies, in nine stages, each marked by a 'night-camp' at the end of a day's journey; and these were experienced rangers, carrying out a mission as quickly as possible. They reported that they had 'found a lot of peoples and a lot of houses in the waste', and alternative routes listed in the *Wegeberichte* suggests that there was no lack of 'good and secret' tracks, if only people knew where they were; but nothing like a public road that could be used by armies and merchants. Knights who left the track, or failed to travel in parties, were sure to be killed or die of starvation;

armies were constantly getting lost or failing to make contact with the enemy. A good day's journey through the *Wiltnisse* was about twelve miles; it took a week to get from Kaunas to Vilnius (fifty-five miles apart as the crow flies), four days from Merkine to Trakai (forty-three miles), six days from Trakai to Traby (fifty-two miles). Only the Niemen and the Dvina provided sure methods of bulk transport through these forest zones, and both rivers were often used in support of military operations – for bringing up supplies, bricks, siege-machines, horses, reinforcements – but there were still problems. The upper Dvina is a fairly rapid river in places, running between steep banks, and therefore river-borne armies had a hard pull upstream: only once did the Livonians get to Polotsk by water. The southern tributaries that flowed from Lithuania were short and shallow. The Niemen is remarkably placid and winding. So extravagant were its meanders that it was said in the fifteenth century that boatmen could spend a day going round one of these bends and light their evening fire by walking a short distance over to the embers left in yesterday's camp.[116] Progress this slow would not matter when there was a castle to be built, or when, as before 1283, the enemy was only a few miles away, but it became a severe handicap when a campaign had to be fought a long way up- or downriver; and weather conditions made speed essential. Both Prussians and Lithuanians kept prams and longboats on the Niemen, and sometimes they raided and fought in them; they were essential for keeping the Order's castles above Tilsit (Sovetsk) supplied; but it was not practicable to float large invasion forces to the mouth or headwaters of the river within the 'real time' available to summer campaigners. Short-cuts were sometimes found: thus in 1376 the commander of Balga had six-man boats built on the banks of the Niemen when he got there by the overland route, and in 1393 the marshal carried his boats thirty-six miles on waggons. But these stratagems were only ways of cutting down a marginal difference between two very slow and cumbersome ways of travelling. On the whole, the mounted expedition guided by expert woodsmen (*leitzlute*) remained the only effective way of getting into enemy territory where there were tracks; while, where there were none, one could only go on foot.

The climate placed further restrictions on such expeditions. Then as now, the region was liable to heavy rains and heavy snowfalls, and, since there were no roads, the effect of either was to make movement impossible. Sheer cold made it impossible for the Order to invade

Lithuania in the winter of 1322–3; the common soldiers fell dead on the march, and many of the fruit-trees that had been planted in Livonia and Prussia never recovered. In February 1376 the snow was so deep that a Livonian expedition had to ride out in single file, and that March the Lithuanians lost a thousand horses from hardship. In other years, as in 1387, the snow lay so thick that no one attempted to get through. But a 'weak winter' was even worse: unless the ground froze – 120 days of frost is the modern average – it would not support men or horses, and there could be no fighting. The rain swelled the rivers and soaked the soil. When the snow melted, and the ice broke up on the rivers (any time during March and April), communications were again impossible, and autumn rainfall could be intolerably heavy. However eager the enemies were to fight each other, they were always apt to be kept apart by the weather. Thus in 1394 Duke Philip of Burgundy wrote to the grand-master asking whether there would be a *reysa* the following year, and Conrad von Jungingen had to write back,

we cannot offer any consolation or certain hope in a matter of this kind to the glorious lord himself, or to any man living, because it is impossible to provide a truthful forecast of future contingencies, especially since on our expeditions we are obliged to go across great waters and vast solitudes by dangerous ways ... on account of which they frequently depend on God's will and disposition, and also on the weather.[117]

There were only two sets of weather conditions which would allow serious campaigning, and neither could be expected to last for more than two months at the outside. One was a 'hard' or 'good' winter: not too cold for a man to relieve himself in the open air, or too snowy for riding, but just sharp enough to congeal the bogs, harden the ground and freeze over the rivers. As in 1364, for example: 'This year winter was hard, and it lasted three months, so that we had several good *reysen* ...'[118] The other set of favourable conditions was provided by a hot sun and drying winds, so that land and water transport could be used in combination. This could happen any time from April to October, or not at all, and was unlikely to last for more than a month. In both cases, a sudden change in the weather could prove disastrous. Floods in summer or thawing ice in winter could trap an army without hope of relief, as when King Wladyslaw III of Poland was caught between two swollen lakes at Mazowsze in August 1332, or when the thawing of the

Strawen made it impossible for the fleeing Lithuanians to escape from Marshal von Kniprode in February 1348. The effect of these risks was to confine all large-scale operations to areas along the Niemen and Dvina, where there were tried and tested escape-routes, and where warfare took the form of siege and castle-building. It was also prudent, when more ambitious invasions were attempted, to split up the invading army into detachments so as to reduce the chances of disaster. This was grasped from an early date by the Order, which had fewer men to lose.

Different weathers and seasons imposed different types of campaign on the belligerents. The *winter-reysa* had to be a rapid foray of some 200-2000 men, carrying both rations and fodder at the back of their saddles; the object was to loot, devastate and depopulate a given area as quickly as possible. On reaching enemy territory, they would put up simple cabins, or *maia*, to store their provisions and plunder, then spread out and do all the damage they could without taking or building forts, or spending long enough to invite a serious counter-attack. After each day's plunder they would return to headquarters and camp for the night, moving on the next day. A good *winter-reysa* had to arrive without warning, and retire before the enemy could mobilize or the weather changed. Hermann of Wartberg records one such success in 1378: the Livonians went into Lithuania in February, stayed there for nine *suwalky* (overnight camps) and came back with 531 head of cattle and 723 horses.[119] Meanwhile the Prussians also had *una bona reisa*, according to Wigand of Marburg, and returned with 100 prisoners. There were usually two *winter-reysen*, one in December, one in January or February, leaving a gap for the Christmas festivities, when the seven-hour day left too little time for raiding. This, at any rate, was the custom of the Teutonic Knights, who appear to have campaigned in winter more regularly than the Lithuanians, perhaps because their bases were nearer the Baltic coast and less snow-bound than the Lithuanian heartlands. The Lithuanians did make great winter incursions, notably in 1322-3, when the cold was too great for the Order to attack Lithuania, and in 1356, 1370 and 1382 under Kestutis, but for the most part they seem to have calculated that their frontier garrisons were likely to do more harm to the raiders than they would inflict on the Order by going out themselves. Like Nicholas I, they put their trust in generals Janvier and Février.

The *sommer-reysa* was usually a bigger affair, when the masters of Prussia and Livonia mobilized all their resources for a full *hervart* (offensive expedition), and the grand-prince set out with a *karias* (large army) of boyars, castellans and their levies. It was usually intended to secure new ground by destroying an enemy fort or building a new one in enemy territory, but it always involved devastation, plunder and harassment as well, and was sometimes preceded by smaller incursions intended to 'soften up' and impoverish the area round the fort marked out for attack. The Order's marshal appears to have collected reports on the enemy's state of readiness, and to have made his plans accordingly; thus in the *Wegeberichte* there is information about places forty miles to the east of Grodno (Dubitshki, Vasilishki, Zheludok and Volkovisk), which 'lie thirty-six, forty-five and fifty-four miles apart from each other, and are full of arable estates, and they report that no armed force has yet been to that part of the country.'[120] And, when von Kniprode went to besiege Kaunas in 1362, he was acting on the reports of a reconnaisance made the previous year.

Since there was always a wilderness to cross, the summer campaigners had to carry their food with them, as in winter, and in 1365 von Kniprode insisted on a full month's supply for every man. However, they could expect to find grass for their horses on the march, and the routes marked by the *leitzlute* went through places where there was 'good water and fodder'. Even if no forts were taken, there would always be hauls of people and animals; as in 1376, when Kestutis returned from the Pregolya with fifty mares and sixty stallions from the stud farm at Insterburg and 900 prisoners, and in 1378, when the commander of Ragnit carried off forty waggon-loads of spoil from Samogitia. However, the quest for plunder could sometimes go too far. In September 1314, Marshal Henry of Prussia pushed over 100 miles east of Grodno to Novogrudok, leaving his loaves and packhorses at *maia* along the return route, and discovered that the castellan of Grodno, Gediminas's brother David, had swooped on them before he could reach them; his troops had to eat their own horses, and any herbs and roots they could find, on the way back to Prussia, and many died of starvation.[121]

It was always safer to raid lands adjacent to the Dvina and the Niemen, within reach of river-boats, castles and bailey-bridges, and it was here that most of the fighting took place. Each side was trying to hold (in the case of the Dvina) or gain (in the case of the Niemen) a stretch of river that could be fortified and garrisoned so as to serve as a reliable entry into enemy country beyond the wilderness. This meant lavishing more and more resources on territory that had little intrinsic value and could not be properly settled or cleared for as long as hostilities lasted. Raids into fertile country, if successful, did something to replenish the supplies of men and material that were constantly being reduced by sieges and castle-building along the rivers and frontiers, but for most of the fourteenth century this served to prolong, rather than conclude, the fighting. It was only after von Kniprode had managed to win control of the Niemen up to the confluence of Kaunas that one side gained a definite advantage, and could begin continuous raiding with a view to winning and holding the homelands of the other; and even then the advantage was to some extent counterbalanced by the introduction of cannon. The process took so long – ninety-three years to advance from Ragnit to Kaunas, a distance of seventy-five miles as the crow flies – because the armies were wearing themselves out on the terrain, rather than annihilating each other, and were constantly drawing strength from expanding economies a long way behind the front.

The destructiveness of the raids is hard to assess, because estimates always come from chroniclers or advocates interested in blackening the enemy and emphasizing the achievements of their own side. When the Order's own annalist Wigand of Marburg records of a *reysa* in 1364 (which included English crusaders) that it attacked an unprepared territory, which they devastated inhumanly,[122] it seems fair to conclude that the peasant population suffered more than usual. But those who lived in areas liable to attacks would naturally become skilled at hiding and escaping, and it was usually more profitable to take them prisoner, and drive them home over the wilderness, than simply to massacre them. It was the garrisons of outlying castles that were most likely to be killed to the last man, but, after King John of Bohemia had insisted on sparing the 6000 Samogitians who surrendered in Medewage in 1329, this kind of slaughter became less common. No count was kept by the Order of the peasants killed on its *reysen*, however, and it can only be assumed that the death-toll was sufficiently high to deter settlers from the wilderness and balance losses inflicted by the Lithuanians. These lose nothing in the telling. According to the Order's sources, the great raids of Prince David of Grodno in 1322–3 were responsible for the death or capture of 4000 in Estonia, 10,000 in Dobrzyn (of whom 8000–10,000 were killed) and 2000 in Mazovia. Kestutis was supposed to have carried off over 2000 in 1352, 500 in 1353, 900 in 1376 – figures which are not incredible, even if they are unlikely to be accurate. On the whole, it seems that captivity was a much more likely fate than death for a peasant caught by invaders, simply because he was worth more alive than dead. Nevertheless, the Order was quite prepared to massacre as a way of bringing about political submission, as had been proved during the conquest of the Prussians, and again in the 1390s during the war for Samogitia. The lives of prisoners might very easily be sacrificed on the march. Thus in 1311 Commander Gebhard von Mansfeld slaughtered all his captives and cattle to prevent their falling into the hands of a Lithuanian army, and in 1377 the commander of Balga murdered 200 prisoners because it was too much trouble to take them back through an unexpected thaw – unlike the hundred horses and thousand steers with them. It would be wrong to deduce that this war was more inhumane than others fought at the same time in France and Spain; but the fact that the displacement of civil populations was part of the strategy of both sides made it more likely that the defenceless would die.

In addition to the *reysen* there were constant small raids by enterprising frontier commanders and castellans, or by bands of native guerrillas. Thus Wigand of Marburg reported of the commander of Insterburg in 1372:

He goes into the wilderness with a hundred picked men to plunder and harass the pagans. They dismount at the Sesupe, eat and drink, re-mount and cross the Niemen, entering four villages that were not warned of their coming and putting to the sword whoever they find beginning their night's sleep, men, women and children.[123]

Small companies of Old-Prussian irregulars, called *latrunculi* or *strutere*, had been allowed to terrorize the wilderness and adjacent lands since the 1260s, and, since they acted as guides and auxiliaries to the Order's *reysen*, their dirty deeds were recorded with approval. Murdering Lithuanians in their bath-houses, or at their feasts, or in bed, was reckoned sport. Since the *strutere* knew all the secret paths, and often went on foot, creeping up to villages through the forest, no settled community was safe from them.

On the other hand, the warriors tended to develop a certain consideration for each other as the century wore on. In theory, it was a fight to the death, with no quarter given or asked, and there were always some dedicated heroes who lived up to the theory, holding out to the last man and refusing mercy when it was offered. Such were Nicholas

Windekaym, of Old-Prussian stock, vainly jabbing at Kestutis, who was safe inside his armour, and asking, 'Why should I not take my revenge on the pagans?', and the warriors who murdered Captain Gastot on the march back home in 1363, when Marshal Schindekopf had given him his hand.[124] But this was not how the knights of Western Europe treated each other, and the more the Order relied on these auxiliaries the more it had to accept the usages of war which they respected. By 1350 both sides were ransoming prisoners, and in von Kniprode's time there were ceremonious parleys on the field of battle and truces involving the exchange of captives; the Order undertook to advance money for the release of all crusaders who fell into enemy hands, even if they were captured by brigands outside Prussia. But, if crusaders or mercenaries captured any Lithuanian over the rank of knight, they were obliged to sell him to the Order for a fixed sum: the tariff in the indenture made with the lords of Strammel and Manteuffel in 1390 specified 500 Prussian marks for a king, 100 Prussian marks for a duke, and 50 for a count. Not very much, considering that they were paying these two freelances 5400 Prussian marks for a year's service with their retinues; the grand-master would make a handsome profit on the resale.[125]

Such conventions protected the rich, but not the common soldiers, and still allowed the wholesale slaughter of garrisons in castles taken by assault. Lithuanians could sometimes buy their lives by promising to accept baptism, but, considering the ultimate purpose of the war, it is surprising that there are not more references to such bargains; either there were many convinced pagans, or the blood-lust of the Order's armies was too often uncontrollable.

Nor were the Crusaders from the West reluctant to wage war as destructively as possible, provided they saved their own skins. The apparatus of chivalry – heralds, truces, challengers, ransoms, picnics in armour – was inseparable from the military profession to which they belonged, but it still allowed them to kill, burn and destroy the civilian population without remorse or pity, whether in France or in Lithuania. For many, the attraction of a *reysa* was that it provided military training and experience, rather than remission of sins. The Sire de Boucicaut went to Prussia three times as a young man, 'because it seemed to him that there was a great lack of warfare in France at that time ... and he had been told that there was bound to be *belle guerre* that season' in Prussia. In 1390 he wanted to go on crusade with the duke of Bourbon in the Mediterranean, but the king forbade him, and let him undertake a *reysa* instead; he had to wait a whole year for Conrad von Wallenrod's first campaign, but he enjoyed it very much, because 'he saw that it was a grand affair, and *moult honorable et belle*', what with the 'great assemblage of knights and squires and noblemen, from both the kingdom of France and elsewhere'.[126] For this kind of knight-errant, the Lithuanian crusade had very little religious importance; Boucicaut's biographer hardly bothers to use even the rhetoric of the Holy War in describing his deeds. Yet for the Teutonic Knights and their subjects the rhetoric was inescapable, because they were a religious Order with political powers vested in them solely as a means of carrying out this crusading mission. It was essential that Latin Christendom should accept that fighting in Prussia was good for the soul. Thus, when the chronicler of the Cistercian Abbey of Oliva heard of the terrible casualties at Crécy, he wrote, 'Would that all these men had been stained in waves of their own blood by infidels, on behalf of the celestial kingdom and for the defence of the Catholic Faith!' In that case, the citizens of heaven would rejoice; but since they had merely been killed for the sake of the earthly kingdom 'it is to be feared that there was rejoicing at this event among the citizens of Hell'.[127]

The contrast between the way the war was fought, and the way the Order justified it became increasingly apparent after 1386, and by 1409 was one of the strongest weapons in the hands of Witold and Wladyslaw. Between these dates, the Order followed a policy that has been called 'illusionist': pretending that Lithuanians were Saracens, for the sake of keeping up the influx of crusaders and gaining territory from Christian powers. However, it should not be forgotten that all the combatants made use of illusion to gain their ends. In the case of Poland, it was the political illusion that the king had ultimate sovereignty over all the lands that his predecessors had alienated, and that the interests of justice and Christianity would best be served by the expansion of the Polish state. In the case of Lithuania, it was the illusion that Witold was concerned more for the souls than the territory of the Samogitians, and that he had not, in the past, co-operated with the Order whenever it suited him. All his insistence on the immortality of the Order's occupation of Samogitia could not conceal the fact that it was the Order's support which had compelled Wladyslaw to recognize him as a grand-duke of Lithuania in 1392. The real question was, which illusion had the strongest army?

7

THE CRUSADE AGAINST NOVGOROD,
1295–1378

While the Teutonic Order was waging a war without end on the frontiers
of Livonia and Prussia, the princes and merchants of north Germany
and Scandinavia were involved in a complicated and uneasy relationship
with the Russian 'schismatics' of Novgorod and Pskov, and this, for
limited times and purposes, turned into another kind of crusade. Chapter
5 has related how the thirteenth-century popes came to entrust the
waging of this crusade to the kings of Sweden in particular; this chapter
tells the story of how these kings saw fit to carry out their mission in
the fourteenth century.

THE DEBATABLE LANDS

The Swedish conquest of Finland brought the frontier of Catholic
Europe to the edge of the sub-Arctic region. In the immense land-mass
that rings the Gulf of Bothnia from the Lofoten Islands in the west to
the White Sea in the east, the battle for survival continued to take
precedence over all other conflicts, even the war between the Catholic
and the Orthodox faiths, and the rivalry between Novgorod and the
kingdoms of Norway and Sweden. Disadvantages of climate, soil and
vegetation made it difficult to expand the political and religious structures
that were needed for the waging of full-scale wars. Nevertheless, the
attempt was made, and the crusade played an essential part in nerving
these kingdoms to fight each other continuously and unprofitably over
some of the most sterile and desolate country in Europe.

Both Novgorod and Sweden derived an increasing share of their wealth
from the Far Northern hinterland, and depended for their prosperity on
contacts with affluent traders from more favoured regions. They therefore
stood to gain by jockeying for position along the main routes of access
in both directions, and, once Sweden had got Viborg (Viipuri), the

jockeying grew fiercer. It became possible to wage war for possession of Lake Ladoga, and even for Novgorod itself. And, if neither side had the resources to conquer and annex Far Northern territories beyond Ladoga, it was still feasible to get more out of the system by which these territories were exploited.

This system was a way of getting animal products from a region beyond the reach of the merchants who paid high prices for them in the main Baltic markets. It involved great hardships, and several intermediary stages, but it was worth it because, the colder the climate, the better animals are protected against it by fur, skin and fat; and, the smaller the human population, the more numerous the beasts and birds. Arctic varieties of fox, hare and weasel are found even on the mountains where the snow never melts, with whiter, denser and finer fur than their downhill cousins'. There, also, lives the glutton, whose pelt 'gleams with a tawny blackness, variegated with figures like cloth of Damascus; and is made more beautiful to look at by skilful artifice, and coloured to match whatever kind of garment it be joined to. Only princes and magnates use this fur as winter clothing, and they have it made up like tunics.'[128] Lower down the mountains there were sable, marten, otter, beaver and ermine – the last also a mark of noble ostentation, as when St Bridget of Sweden's son Charles was presented to the pope wearing 'a mantle on which were sewn whole ermine skins from top to bottom, so that when he walked it looked as if ermines were running all over him; and each ermine's head had a little gilded bell hung about the neck and a gold ring in its mouth.'[129] 'You are a son of this world', said the pope – accurately, no doubt, but ermine was a lot cheaper in Sweden. The beaver gave a more serviceable pelt, was good to eat and easy to catch; it was being trapped and hunted to extinction in the Scandinavian lowlands in this period, and the pursuit of fresh stocks was what brought dealers and trappers to the Far North in greater numbers about the turn of the thirteenth century. As all furs, except plain squirrel, grew harder to find further south, these pioneers increased in number and importance.

The immense summer congregations of birds on Enara (Inari) and other lakes, which had been plundered for meat and feathers at least since King Alfred's time, continued to supply a valuable secondary staple to fur, and met an increasing demand from affluent burghers aping the noble preference for soft mattresses, eiderdowns and cushions. The northern gyrfalcon was sought after all the more as the techniques and elaboration of hawking spread among the knightly classes. The seals and whales of the Arctic Ocean became the only cheap source of oil for Northern Europe when the offshore fisheries of the Baltic and North Sea were hunted bare. And the teeming fish of the Bothnian rivers and Lapland lakes, which had formerly been exportable in a small way when wind-dried, smoked or soused, became a profitable food-crop once a new method of salting had been brought to the Bothnian gulf by the Dutchman Benkelszoon towards the end of the fourteenth century. In the course of the next hundred years, Tornea (Tornio) became a great international fish-market, where Russians, Lapps, Karelians, Finns, Swedes, Norwegians, and Germans came with or for their herring, mackerel, pike and salmon: the herring small, the salmon sometimes seven-foot long; the pike dried hard, and broken up with hammers.

As these animals preyed on each other, so did the men who got their living by them, each group exploiting and being exploited for the ultimate satisfaction of the fur-clad pickled-herring eaters lolling on the feather-beds of Western Europe and Russia. At the lowest end of the scale came the Lapps, who were classified into sea-, forest- and fell-Lapps, according to whether they lived on the Arctic Ocean, the Bothnian rivers, or the mountain range that came between them. As immigrant settlers edged them away from the coasts of the Bothnian Gulf and the White Sea, which they had inhabited before the fourteenth century, more of them took to living off the reindeer as herdsmen and hunters in the interior, and increased the range of their migrations to get access to the now more valuable fisheries and hunting grounds of the Far North. They moved over a wide arc stretching from the Dovre Fjell in central Norway to the tip of the Kola peninsula, a distance of some 1200 miles, wherever climate and altitude made life too arduous for others, but they were bound by economic interest to the settled communities on the fringe of this area. For centuries they had paid tribute to, and exchanged furs for cloth and metal with the northern Norwegian landowners who ran the *Finnferth*, under licence from their king, and the agents of Novgorod in the east; then in the thirteenth century the *Finnferth* was discontinued and a new wave of entrepreneurs moved in, among whom the Karelians were dominant. These intruders could offer improved hunting techniques, and better prices for furs, in return for higher yields and a closer personal dependence. Those Lapps who visited lands on the edge of the wild were bound to immigrant farmers as a kind of intelligent livestock, paying furs and meat in exchange for the use of nearby grazing grounds and some form of protection. Thus their lives were changed both by the demands of the European market and by the influx of newcomers to the fringes of the arable world. These contacts also changed the way in which the neighbouring peoples looked at the Far Northern world – no longer as the alien wilderness of Adam of Bremen's geography, but as a reserve of potentially valuable land. To the Norwegians the whole region was still their Finnmark, open to Norse traders and fishermen and coastal settlers because the Finns, as they called the Lapps, were in some sense their men. But in the thirteenth century the citizens of Novgorod began to call the Kola peninsula their province of Ter, and the Lapps, or Sam, the dependants of their Karelians. In the fourteenth century, contacts between Swedish middlemen settled at the mouths of the Bothnian rivers – the *birkarlar* – and their Lapp clients led Swedish kings to refer to the upriver region as their Lappmark, over which the crown had those mysterious rights which European rulers had pretended to possess over wilderness since Merovingian times. But Finnmark, Lappmark, Karelia and Ter were not defined areas: they were names applied to roughly the same area by virtue of a common pursuit carried on within it – exploiting the Lapps.

Next in the scale of exploitation came the Karelian Finns, the people able to move most freely in and out of Lapland and compete as trans-humant grazers and hunters with the Lapps. While out on their seasonal journeys, the Karelians appear to have taxed, and traded with, dependent Lappish groups all the way from the Norwegian mountains to Kola; but the homesteads from which they came lay on the edge of Swedish Finland and Novgorod, and by 1295 were subject to either one or the other tributary system. Like Lapps, they handed over furs and other produce to their overlords, but unlike Lapps they were well-enough armed and organized to conduct raids on each other and on neighbouring settlements, and could bring their gains direct to market in Finland, Sweden or Russia. In 1252 the king of Norway and the prince of Novgorod agreed to leave the Far North open to tax-collectors and traders from both countries, but the result was not concord: Norwegians were under sporadic attack from Karelian raids from then onwards, and the competing Russian and Swedish interests within settled Karelia gave marauders increased scope for action. Thus the Karelians served as an electric current passing between the colonial settlements and the sub-Arctic world, transmitting shocks from one to the other whenever local conditions gave rise to friction.

Alongside the Karelians, from the late thirteenth century onwards, came frontiersmen of other nations: land-hungry peasants from Finland and Sweden, pushing up the eastern and western shores of the Bothnian Gulf; Germans on the rivers at the northern end; Norwegian fishermen, farmers and traders along the Arctic Ocean (as far as Vardø by 1307); Russian 'boat-men' and peasants making for the shores of the White Sea by way of lakes Ladoga and Onega. Hunger and greed drove them into a region so inhospitable that their hopes of survival were always more or less bound up with the running of the fur, fish and Lapp trade, as trappers, hunters or dealers.

Therefore they were inextricably bound to the more organized and stratified societies they had left behind them, which provided them with their only profitable markets and asserted political mastery by taxes and military obligations. They paid less in *skatt* and tithe, and could claim free ownership of the land they brought under cultivation; they could recoup by such levies as the *birkarlaskatt*, contributed by the Lapps to the *birkarlar*; but, still, they paid, and could only maintain their position on the fringes of Lapland by virtue of the grain, butter, salt and metals that came in from the south.

While the Novgorodian, Swedish and Norwegian realms were prime consumers of sub-Arctic produce, and were governed by prosperous elites most of whose wealth was securely based on arable farming, they were not at the top of the hierarchy of exploiters. By 1300 all three were to some extent dependent for their economic survival on the goodwill of the Hansa, the association of German traders based on the cities of northern Germany and the south-east Baltic, which had gained a privileged position – in Norway a monopoly – as importer and exporter of the main international commodities. Hanseatic merchants were the essential middlemen between the North and the consumers of England, France, Flanders and Germany, and in the course of the fourteenth century they were able to safeguard their privileges by naval and military action. As lords of the Baltic trade-route, they were courted by Russians and Swedes, and resisted in vain by the kings of Norway and Denmark; they alone had the organization, the resources and the credit to bring the great trading-areas together.

This system worked, but not smoothly or peaceably. There were many possibilities of conflict, from the casual ambushes of trappers and tax-collectors round the North Cape to the full-scale war of armies and fleets in the Baltic. There were two main types and areas of warfare. One was the result of competition between the basic suppliers of produce, fought out by small raiding parties over the whole of Lapland, Karelia and Bothnia; the other was a battle for control of the territories at the head of the Gulf of Finland, fought by the techniques of devastation, siege, castle-building and amphibious invasion. These territories were the provinces (*volost* or *gislalagh*) of Savolaks (north-west of Lake Ladoga), Jääskis (between Ladoga and Viborg) and Äyräpää (the coastland from Viborg to the Neva), which were peopled by Karelians; Ingria, or Izhora, south of the Neva; and Vod, or Watland, on either side of the river Luga, sometimes known as the province of Koporye. These lands were the gateway through which Lapland produce and the Baltic trade reached Novgorod and Novgorod exported to the West. Whereas the battle for the Far North was for access to hunting grounds, fisheries and nomadic camps, and could not be simplified by the drawing of boundaries, the battle for the Neva and Ladoga did involve a fixed frontier between empires and the imposition of political control on settled populations.

Political control meant religious affiliation, since there were few other forms of cultural identity between rulers and ruled. As has been described earlier, the conversion of the Vods, Ingrians and Karelians had been a way of staking political claims. The types of Christianity to which they had been converted remained the sign of whom they belonged to, and both sides followed up the thirteenth-century missions with attempts to incorporate the neophytes into their distinctive church organizations.

With the Latins this meant attaching as many Karelians as possible to the very few frontier churches that were founded outside the fairly tight grouping of forty to fifty parishes in south-west Finland, and subjecting them to a fixed food rent in lieu of tithe under the arrangement known as the 'Law of Kyrö'. What part the Dominicans of Åbo played in this can only be surmised; neither friars nor bishops appear to have been adventurous in taking their authority and doctrines to the periphery of the diocese, once the forms of allegiance had been accepted. If a new bishopric had been established for the Karelians and Ingrians, as had been planned in the thirteenth century, the picture might have been different; but, as it was, Finnish Catholicism concentrated its resources in one corner of the country, where the population was densest, and maintained its hold on the frontier lands largely through its administrative machine. There were no new religious houses until the Franciscans appeared at Viborg in 1402-3.

With the Greek-Orthodox Russians, on the other hand, the winning of new underpopulated lands meant an opportunity for fulfilling the monastic and missionary vocations experienced by many believers in the centuries of Mongol supremacy. There were already at least seventeen monasteries in or near Novgorod by 1250, not including the abbey of St George at Old Ladoga, and in the succeeding years the number grew, especially in the provinces. Before 1329 a community was established on the island of Valamo (Valaam), at the north end of Lake Ladoga, and other 'black clergy' had moved into Karelia, Ingria and Vod. By the end of the fifteenth century there were ten monasteries among the Russian Karelians, and seven parishes; the total number of churches was twenty-six. As Novgorod grew increasingly independent of princely authority, the archbishop took on more of the powers of head of state, and was well placed to bring the provinces into his fiscal system. The groups of powerful boyars who shared the government with him were concerned both with exploiting the frontiers economically, and with enhancing their prestige by church-building and endowments. As in the West, conversion and colonialism went hand-in-hand.

Thus the distinction 'Greek' and 'Latin' which had been somewhat arbitrarily imposed on the political divisions of the thirteenth century by popes and crusaders, took on greater significance in the subsequent period, especially in the debatable lands between the castellany of Viborg and the Novgorodian outposts of Ladoga and Koporye.

THE MAKING OF A RUSSO-SWEDISH FRONTIER, 1295-1326

The raids that plagued these lands in the period 1295 to 1314 resulted from Marshal Tyrgils Knutsson's determination to use his new fort of Viborg as a springboard for the conquest of the whole Neva-Ladoga region, and were conducted for the purpose of bringing each district under the rule of new military outposts.

In 1295 the marshal sent a fleet up the Neva and into Ladoga, where the Swedes built a fort at Keksholm (the Finnish Kekkisalmi, now

Priozersk) on the western shore; the whole garrison and its captain, one
Sigge Loba, was wiped out by a Novgorod counter-attack the same year,
and the site was taken over by the Russians. It was clearly impossible
to maintain a force some 200 miles away from Viborg castle by water
(although only fifty by land) and the next Swedish thrust was better
conceived. The marshal led over a thousand warriors to the mouth of
the Neva, near where St Petersburg was to stand, and made a new fort
which he called Landskrona. That was in 1299; the following year the
Landskrona garrison sent out raids north and south, into Lake Ladoga,
Karelia and Ingria, but again the Swedes were beaten by the problem
of supply, and in 1301 the fort was besieged and taken by Novgorod.
Tyrgils fell from power in 1305, and was later beheaded. The site of
Landskrona remained unoccupied by either side; but the Novgorodians
safeguarded themselves to the north and south of the Neva by new
fortifications at Koporye (1297) and what had been Keksholm, where a
new 'Karelian town' was built in 1310. Then a new prince, Dmitri
Romanovich from Briansk, led a seaborne Russian raid along the coast
of Swedish Finland to a point halfway between Helsinki and Viborg,
and ravaged the settlements along the connecting land-route. Another
raid westwards in 1313 brought the Swedes back to Lake Ladoga, plundering and burning, and for a brief period in 1314 an anti-Russian rising
among the Karelians enabled them to reoccupy Keksholm; but they
were soon driven out, and the 'Karelian town' remained a Novgorodian
outpost in the hands of a friendly Karelian boyar. Marshal Tyrgils's
design remained half-completed, with Viborg as the easternmost bastion
of Swedish power, the Neva open to all comers, and Novgorod firmly
in control of Lake Ladoga and the adjoining coastlands.

In the Far North there was no opportunity for a parallel consolidation
of power by either side, since there were no sea-routes along which to
supply outposts, and the population remained too mobile and small to
pin down or dominate. There were merely inconsequential raids and
retaliations by roaming war-bands of Karelians, Russians and Norwegians, such as are noted in the Icelandic Annals under the years 1271,
1279, 1302, 1303 and 1316, with Karelians asserting their prowess in the
mountain-region of Lapland, and Norsemen defending their settlements
along the northern coastline.

Then in 1319 simultaneous political changes in Russia and Scandinavia
began to prepare the way for further hostilities. On the deaths of King

Birger of Sweden and King Håkon V of Norway, both kingdoms were inherited by Håkon's grandson and Birger's nephew, Magnus II and VII. As he was only two years old, for the next ten years power lay with the regent, his mother, Ingeborg, and with the councils of Norway and Sweden. By the time he was proclaimed of age – a carefully educated Swedo-Norwegian monarch – his nobles and bishops had secured a controlling interest in government which he was never quite able to dislodge. There was conflict throughout his reign between king, or regent, and these great men; but one of the issues over which they were least divided was the pursuit of war with Novgorod, and the continuation of this struggle therefore became especially important for the stability of the dual monarchy.

The Swedish archbishop and bishops favoured aggression in the East for several reasons. One was the prevalence of the crusading ideal: the belief that it was their spiritual duty to bring Russians, Karelians, Ingrians and Vods into the Catholic fold, in accordance with the abortive papal policy of 1223–57. Another was the prospect of increasing their revenues and patronage, of enriching the see of Åbo, and possibly creating a new diocese for Karelia; more converts meant more tithe – in 1329 the council of Sweden ordered all Karelians and Tavastians to contribute – and more territory meant the chance of more estates. These opportunities began to seem particularly attractive after 1309, when the Avignon papacy began a series of fund-raising campaigns which meant levying crusading tithes on the clergy of Northern Europe ostensibly for the purpose of financing a new crusade to the East. The money was actually used for a variety of political purposes, such as fighting the Visconti in Italy, and the popes were realistic enough to pay for the privilege of getting it by conceding a share of the proceeds to the kings within whose realms the collecting nuncios and financiers were allowed to operate. These agents were tireless and sometimes very effective, drawing taxes from as far off as Iceland and Greenland; it was natural that the clergy should begin to feel that, if they were paying money for general crusading purposes, the king and his warriors should be encouraged to undertake that particular sort of crusade which would bring them some immediate advantage.

The magnates and lesser nobles of Sweden also stood to gain by the increased number of fiefs and offices which might follow from a war of conquest. Finland was already a source of profit and power for the great and the adventurous. There was the prefecture of the Duchy, and the captaincies of Åbo, Tavastehus and Viborg; there were advocacies, bailiwicks and fiefs. Such men as Lyder of Kyren, the brothers Sune and Peter Jonsson, Matthias Kettilmundsson, Karl Näskonungsson and Gerhard Skytte were doing well out of areas conquered in the thirteenth century, where there was little chance of too much interference by the Crown; they would do even better further east. Moreover, landowners were now interested in promoting settlement within the hunting and raiding grounds still crossed regularly by Karelians under Russian rule. Under the regency, Archbishop Olof of Uppsala granted hereditary tax exemption on all land newly brought into cultivation by settlers in Lapland, and the king's high steward freed all settlers on the Ulea river from tax until the king came of age.[130] Such concessions would only be worthwhile if the new lands were brought under effective Swedish rule, and this meant military action.

Norwegian settlers and crown officers in the Far North were eager to retaliate against what they saw as Russo-Karelian poaching within their Finnmark, and to compensate themselves for the unfavourable economic conditions which increasingly beggared their country from the mid thirteenth century. Norway had lost half of her western dependencies to Scotland in the 1260s, and drew little profit from Iceland, Greenland and the Orkneys; Finnmark could still be retrieved, however, as the German trade monopoly was not effective in the Far North. Moreover, the most powerful baron in the country, Erling Vidkunnson, was a great landowner and trader in Hålogaland, the most northerly province, and had a direct interest in promoting Norwegian concerns in this direction; as high steward from 1323 to 1332, and as a friend of the regent and King Magnus, he was in a position to get things moving.

Meanwhile, there were changes at Novgorod which made the city's rulers more than ever determined to defend and if possible expand their colonial dependencies. In 1318 the Mongols appointed Prince Yury of Moscow great-prince of the Russians, and Yury sent his brother to Novgorod, presumably to claim the allegiance of the city in preparation for the war for supremacy with the prince of Tver. In the ensuing years, Yury had to prove his worth to the suspicious Novgorodians by giving them military assistance and leadership when they needed it. This gave the boyars and archbishop the chance of waging war with larger and better equipped forces than they could raise on their own account, and their own levies had already proved themselves able to match the Swedes at raiding by land and sea. In 1318 they had got as far west as Åbo, where they landed, pillaged the district and burned down the cathedral. There was no immediate retaliation from Sweden, but it was evident that neither the Novgorodian nor the Swedo-Norwegian regime was prepared to rest content with the *status quo* of 1292 much longer.

The first signs that something amounting to a crusade was under way came in 1320, when the regent reaffirmed Sweden's ties with the Teutonic Order by granting a generous immunity to the Swedish estates of the Order, which were grouped under the commandery of Årsta on the coast south of Stockholm. Soon after this the pope was asked to allow his annual revenue from Peter's Pence to be used for the defence of the realm against the Russians and their allies, and in 1321 a Swedish force made another unsuccessful attempt to recapture the Karelian town on the site of Keksholm. Reinforced by Prince Yury, the Novgorodians reacted with an imposing show of strength. In 1322 they arrived at Viborg, laid siege to the castle for a month, hanged a number of captives and went home; the following year they secured Lake Ladoga by building a new fort on Orekhov island (Nöteborg in Swedish, later Oreshek, now Petrokrepost), where the Neva leaves the lake, and dispatched a raiding force from Karelia across Lapland to harry the Norwegians of Håloga-land. Earlier that year, Pope John XXII had encouraged the Norwegians to fight back by promising full crusading privileges to all who fell in battle against the 'pagans called Finnar'.[131]

However, the building of Orekhov put an end to the fighting on the Neva. Prince Yury decided he had done enough, and the Novgorodians had more pressing quarrels (with the Lithuanians and the tribes on the northern Dvina) to pursue; the Swedish council and the regent found that in future their raiding parties would be unable to sail into Lake Ladoga without first besieging the new fort at Orekhov, and thus there was no hope of a cheap victory. They had evidently launched their futile raid on Keksholm in the belief that Prince Yury would be too busy fighting the prince of Tver to assist Novgorod; now that they had been proved wrong, it was time to make peace, and on 12 August 1323 a treaty was concluded which now goes by the three names of Nöteborg, Orekhov and Pekkinsaari (Pähkinäsaari).

The Swedes and the Novgorodians agreed to stop fighting and to observe peace 'on the old terms', and versions of these terms survive in

Swedish, Russian and Latin transcripts of a lost original charter.[132] The Novgorodians ceded to King Magnus the three western provinces of Karelia (Savolaks, Jääskis and Ayräpää – see map 6), and both sides agreed to build no more castles anywhere in Karelia. They also agreed to observe what looks like a frontier, a line running in a northerly direction from the Gulf of Finland, near the mouth of the Neva, towards central Finland, and then over to the north end of the Gulf of Bothnia. But what this frontier represented was not specified, and remains obscure. It can be precisely reconstructed only at the southern end, where it delimits the Karelian provinces recognized as Swedish, but it does not correspond with the existing and future limits of Swedish and Russian overlordship towards the north. If it is a territorial boundary in the political sense, it gives Novgorod a vast area of northern Karelia already penetrated by Swedes and by Finns under Swedish lordship. In 1323 it probably represented the limit of the open country within which Russian Karelians had free access to their traditional hunting and fishing grounds, regardless of territorial ownership. By 1500 the Swedes had built the new castle of Olufsborg in Savolaks, and had established territorial claims well inside this country; but for the time being there was some sort of truce.

Sweden was thus out of the war. The Norwegians, under Erling the Steward, were slower to come to terms, but in 1326 they also agreed to make peace and observe 'the old boundaries'. These boundaries – probably those agreed on in 1251 between Alexander Nevsky and Håkon the Old – were certainly not a dividing line between two powers, but the outer limits of a region within which both enjoyed restricted fiscal rights. From the Lyngen Fjord, east of Tromsø, to the southern shore of the Kola peninsula both rulers were entitled to collect up to five white squirrel furs a year from each 'bow' – that is, from each adult male Lapp. At the eastern end of this region, the Norwegians were entitled to take their tribute from Karelians with Lappish mothers.

Thus neither treaty changed the political situation. The only new development was the strengthening of Novgorod's hold on Lake Ladoga and its shores by the building of Orekhov, and this meant that future expeditions by the Swedes would have to be bigger and better equipped than they could afford for the time being. The fighting was merely suspended.

THE CRUSADES OF KING MAGNUS

For over twenty years neither Sweden nor Novgorod was ready for a full-scale war on the Neva. In 1326 Novgorod turned from Moscow to Lithuania for a protector, and in 1333 handed over the wardenship of her western provinces to Prince Narimont, son of Gediminas. Although Prince Simeon of Moscow was able to reassert authority over the city in 1340, Narimont's son Alexander kept the governorship of Koporye until the end of the decade, and neither the Lithuanians nor the Muscovites were inclined to embark on aggressive policies towards Sweden; they were too suspicious of each other. The territorial ambitions of the Regent were satisfied by the acquisition of Scania from Denmark in 1332, and the magnates of Norway and Sweden were kept busy after that with internal struggles. The maturing King Magnus was eager both to restore the power of the crown at home and, until 1343, to secure further territory from Denmark. In such conditions, trouble along the Russo-Swedish frontier was merely an irritating distraction to the two governments.

Therefore, when the enterprising Swedish captain of Viborg co-operated with the Karelians in an anti-Russian revolt in 1337, the Novgorodians' attitude was restrained; they first negotiated with him, at Orekhov, and only when Captain Sten persisted in helping the Karelians to raid Lake Onega and the town of Ladoga did they retaliate. The Russians raided Swedish Karelia, and Sten was beaten off while attacking Koporye. But the situation was not allowed to get out of hand: a Russian delegation to King Magnus patched up a peace in 1339, and took the wind out of Sten's sails. 'If our Karelians flee to you', they declared, 'kill or hang them all. If your Karelians flee to us, then we will treat them in the same fashion, so that they shall not give rise to discord between us.'[133] Independent action by frontiersmen merely interrupted the profitable flow of trade without gaining the ground or lordship which would counterbalance the cost of war.

However, if political expediency favoured peace, the embers of the crusade were kept alive in the meantime. Papal collectors continued to raise money from both kingdoms for crusading purposes, and in 1324 they repeated the deals they had made with the kings of France and England by granting the king of Sweden a half-share for his own use. By 1329 they had raised £4340 sterling, of which they handed over £2158 to the regent; and, when in the 1330s their yields dropped, it became clear that they would need firmer royal backing to raise the level of future levies – which would mean handing over a larger share. The tax-paying clergy therefore continued to show interest in the possibility of bringing the crusade nearer home. A note in the Register of Uppsala refers to 'the preaching of the cross against the Karelians'[134] among the topics to be brought to the attention of the faithful during the festivals of 1340. And during the 1340s the court was being reminded of this as well as other religious duties by the king's cousin Bridget, who had charge of the queen's ladies-in-waiting and was beginning to win fame as a prophetess.

Bridget's posthumously compiled Revelations contain several thoughts on the subject of crusades which must have been expressed in the period 1344–8.[135] Her main object was to reform and purify the upper class, and, like St Bernard in his day, she saw the Holy War as the best possible way in which kings and knights could carry out their God-given social duty of fighting. After King Magnus had tried and failed to get possession of the kingdom of Denmark in the early 1340s, she informed him that his warriors had lost their lives in this fruitless enterprise because God did not wish him to increase his territories at the expense of other Christian kingdoms. It would be far better 'to send his vassals and people to those heathen parts where it is possible to increase the Catholic faith, and charity'. Rather than vex his subjects with taxes to pay for wars that were hateful to God, the king should raise money only for self-defence or for attacking unbelievers. When she asked Christ whether he were going to give the order for Magnus to begin the crusade, Christ replied, through his Mother,

If the king wishes to go forth against the heathen, I advise him – I do not command him – first, that he have a good heart, and a sound body. His heart will be good provided his only motive in setting out be the love of God and the salvation of souls. And his body will be fit if he be regular in fasting and labour. Secondly, let him take pains to ensure that he have vassals and knights who are volunteers, and men of righteousness ... because whosoever aspires to bring others to the kingdom of heaven, must begin by correcting his own errors.

Christ also advised the king to enlist learned clerics, who would be able to reach the minds of the pagans, and insisted that the crusading army must be small and select. A mass army would be sure to contain sinners, and sinners would not be allowed to enter the Promised Land. According to the rhyme-chronicle called the *Förbindelsedikt*[136] which was produced in patriotic circles about 1452, the Virgin also admonished the king to let no foreigners accompany him, but it appears from the Revelations that what Bridget actually objected to was mercenaries in general, rather than aliens.

This picked body of conscientious volunteers was to be marshalled under two banners: one of the Passion, signifying peace, and one of the Sword of Justice, signalling war. It was essential that the heathen should first be offered peace, faith and liberty, by having banner number one displayed to them, and only if they rejected the offer were the army to move on to battle under number two. Once defeated, they could be compelled to accept baptism into the Latin faith, on pain of death. If they were killed, it was surely better for their souls than being left to drag out their lives in sinful error.

Armchair crusaders were not uncommon in the fourteenth century, and this war-cry from the boudoir seems no more fatuous than other appeals of the time. Bridget's views were given added force by her social position and connections; her brother Israel Byrghisson was one of the king's ablest servants, and the bishop most concerned with the eastern provinces, Hemming of Åbo, was a friend and a promoter of her canonization. However, the decision to declare war on Novgorod was the king's own, and, since he was not such a fool as Bridget pretended, he was moved by political calculation, rather than religious zeal.

For Novgorod appeared to have fallen between two stools. In 1346 Prince Algirdas of Lithuania had subjugated the city's southern lands, and Simeon of Moscow had failed to intervene; the citizens were divided between competing boyar factions, and were reduced to executing their own ex-mayor for offending the Lithuanians. On the other hand, the Swedes and the Norwegians were now at peace with each other, and with King Valdemar IV of Denmark. Valdemar himself had set an example of conspicuous piety by going on a pilgrimage to Jerusalem. Magnus had assured the succession by having his son Eric elected king of Sweden and Scania, and his son Håkon recognized as heir to Norway. He had settled his internal difficulties for the time being, and was drawing up a national law-code. He had brought the administration of Sweden under the control of a nominated royal justiciar, the 'official-general'. It was time for a successful war of conquest, but it was generally accepted that the king could only call out the full military strength of his kingdoms for service overseas if he got the consent of his magnates first. Thanks to the propaganda of the clergy and landowners concerned with Finland and the Far North, a war with Novgorod was likely to command that consent; and, when Magnus broached the project to the Norwegians in 1347, and met with some opposition, he overcame it by declaring the enterprise a full crusade. He sailed over to Finland in the autumn, and remained there for the winter, while his envoys prepared the way for next year's invasion.

It is slightly surprising to read in the Novgorod Chronicle that Magnus's message to the Russians was

Send your philosophers to a conference, and I will send my philosophers, that they may discuss about the faith and ascertain whose faith is better; if yours, then I will join it, but if ours, then you will enter our faith, and we shall all be as one man. But if you do not agree to uniformity then I will come against you with all my forces.[137]

It is usually assumed that the chronicler misrepresented the substance of the Swedish embassy, and that the real object of the mission was to discuss boundaries and lay claim to new territory. Perhaps; but there is nothing improbable in the story as it stands, since Magnus would obviously increase his chances of getting the war authorized by a crusading Bull from Avignon if he gave public notice that his aim was to extend the Latin faith. This was how Bridget had advised him to begin his campaign, by peaceful persuasion; and in any case, what the faiths represented on the river Neva was primarily a difference between two rival colonial systems. Whether Magnus also hoped to be accepted at Novgorod as prince protector, in succession to the Lithuanian and Muscovite rulers, is unknown; certainly he could not have chosen a less likely method of seducing the Novgorodians than challenging their beliefs. They replied that if he were really interested in theology he ought to apply to the patriarch of Constantinople. Instead, he returned to Sweden and assembled an army which (according to the *Förbindelsedikt*) included Danish and German auxiliaries, and Henry of Rendsburg, one of the counts of Holstein. Henry had already campaigned against the Lithuanians very briefly in 1345, and seems to have been ready to go anywhere for money and loot; he got a pension from Edward III of England in 1355, and acted as his intelligence agent for the Baltic. The army set sail on 8 June 1348, and had reached Viborg when envoys from Novgorod arrived to resume negotiations. Again Magnus is alleged by the Russian sources to have insisted on his religious mission: 'I have no grievance whatever against you. Adopt my faith, or I will march against you with my whole force.'

The envoys hurried back to Orekhov, and the crusaders flooded up the Neva behind them, offering the inhabitants the choice of death or baptism into the Latin church. According to the Russian sources, many were baptized and 'had their beards shaved', as the *Förbindelsedikt* put it;[138] the garrison at Orekhov was cut off and besieged, and some of the invaders moved south into Ingria and Vod. The siege began on 24 June; a month later, a Novgorodian raiding party defeated the Swedes near Koporye, but the besiegers sat tight, and the fortress surrendered on 6 August. Ten boyars were held prisoner, and the rest of the Russo-Lithuanian garrison was allowed to march home.

These successes were made possible by the lack of unity between Novgorod and her allies. The Lithuanians, who were still supposed to be defending the province of Koporye, were fully occupied at home with the Teutonic Knights, and made no move to reinforce Orekhov during the siege. The Muscovite prince Simeon was delayed by business with his overlord, the Khan of the Golden Horde. His brother Ivan arrived late. Magnus also appears to have had the advantage of numbers, since he was using both levy-troops and foreign auxiliaries; but this advantage was short-lived. One summer's campaign was enough for most of his men. The king himself retired to Sweden soon after Orekhov fell, and left behind a garrison that was small enough for the Novgorodian city forces to tackle with the help of a detachment from Pskov. The fort was besieged. Winter set in. The Pskovians marched home, to the amusement of the Swedes, but the Novgorodians stayed, and in February 1349 they took the fort and killed or captured all the defenders.

Why had Magnus allowed this to happen? He knew that there would be no hope of relieving his men once winter set in; he knew that Novgorod would not allow him to occupy the Neva lands without a struggle. It is possible that he expected help from the Livonians, who did attack Izborsk that winter. It is possible that he expected the Russians to send an embassy to Sweden to negotiate, before they counter-attacked. In either case, he was mistaken; but he would hardly have done better if he had recruited only pious warriors to fight the war, as St Bridget later claimed, or if he had simply massacred the whole Orthodox population, as the *Förbindelsedikt* suggested a century later.[139] His only chance of success seems to have been lost when he sailed back to Sweden rather than pressing onwards to Ladoga and Novgorod; but it took him a long time to understand this.

In 1349 the Black Death reached Sweden and made it impossible to avenge the loss of Orekhov for the time being, at least by military action. Instead, Magnus tried to raise money by appealing to his subjects to send a penny each to their cathedrals, and pray that the Virgin would avert the plague; he tried to weaken the Russians by forbidding his Hanseatic allies to trade with Novgorod. He seems to have interpreted the plague as a mark of divine anger at his not having persisted with the campaign against the heathen; at all events, it made him more rather than less determined to continue the war in better times. There was still a lack of unity or leadership among the Russian states, and it was clearly impossible for Novgorod to hold out against an effective economic blockade from the West. If the Teutonic Order, the Livonian bishops and the Hansa could be persuaded to co-operate, such an embargo might be brought into effect. Pope Clement VI was bound to favour the enterprise and another expedition would oblige him to offer a crusading tax and crusading Bulls. The Norwegians were attacked by a Russian raiding force during the plague year – it reached the steward's own estate at Bjarkey – and would be more eager to assist their king than before.

By August 1350, when the first harvest of plague-victims had been buried, another army of crusaders had been scraped together, and the king sailed back up the Neva to Orekhov. What he did on this occasion is entirely ignored by surviving contemporary sources; apart from one reference in the Icelandic Annals,[140] the whole story of the 1350 expedition rests on the fictitious 'Testament of King Magnus' composed by a Russian monk a century later.[141] Without placing much confidence in this document, modern historians tend to assume that it contains an outline of events no more misleading for 1350 than for 1348; in which case it can be deduced that Magnus retired baffled from Orekhov, and continued his voyage south to Koporye. He may have tried to take this fort instead, but was again frustrated, and continued westwards to the mouth of the river Narva; there his fleet was hit by a storm and dispersed. This may not have been as great a failure as it sounds, since the purpose of the expedition may have been harassment rather than conquest. Magnus must have had fewer men with him than in 1348, and was evidently hoping to achieve victory by interrupting trade, rather than by direct invasion. However, the loss of his ships was obviously a grave setback, as it placed the success of his anti-Russian campaign entirely in the hands of his German allies. Instead of returning to Sweden, the king remained in Estonia and Livonia for the winter of 1350–51 trying desperately to persuade or compel the Order, the bishops and the merchants to keep up the blockade, while his agents at the Curia got the pope to place the full weight of his authority behind a new campaign.

On 15 January 1351 the merchants at Dorpat reported to Lübeck that Magnus had spent Christmas at Reval and had insisted that the Livonian authorities should arrest all who had ignored his embargo and impound their goods. When the burghers of Reval and Dorpat demurred, he 'told them they should be ready to give him satisfaction for the injury done him by the merchants'. In reply, two of them asked the king whether he wished to accuse the merchants in common, or one or more of them individually. To which the king replied, 'We do not know what a merchant in common is, but we accuse all those visiting Novgorod.'[142] He was put off with delays and soft answers, and it is unlikely that the Russian trade was ever seriously affected by his ban. Nevertheless, he was able to make a thorough nuisance of himself. He was able to enforce the seizure of all Hanseatic cargoes bound for Novgorod in Swedish ports; he was able to remind his hosts in Livonia that he had a slight claim to the duchy of Estonia, which they had bought from King Valdemar of Denmark not long before; he asserted his influence by granting an insubstantial privilege to Riga, and a meatier charter to the Cistercians of Padis in Estonia, giving them patronage, land and fisheries in Finland. By this time it was spring, and there was good news from Avignon and Sweden. Clement VI had agreed to let Magnus collect and borrow half of a four-year crusading tithe to pay for the forthcoming campaign. The archbishops and bishops of the North were instructed to begin preaching a full crusade against the Russians as soon as the plague abated.[143] The Teutonic Order was told to give its full assistance,[144] and the purpose of the enterprise was set out in rhetoric calculated to appeal to all the faithful.

According to Clement's Bull of 14 March 1351, certain peoples called Karelians and Ingrians had recognized the error of their infidelity and had especially called on Magnus to help them receive the Christian faith. Magnus had reached out his strong hand to protect them from the injuries and oppressions with which the Russian enemies of the Catholic faith were wont to afflict them. But, once they had received baptism and the faith, those same Russians, yearning to exterminate them now that the king had withdrawn, unexpectedly invaded both their country and other parts of Christendom, with bestial savagery. Some of the Catholics they slew with the sword, others by hanging from trees, others by exposure to the gnawing of dogs, and others by unbelievable varieties of torture, and so compelled the now cruelly enslaved survivors among the Karelians and Ingrians to turn again to their original blind error, while the king was prevented by the plague from expelling the invaders. So let all true believers rise up and rescue these unfortunate peoples! And to lend colour to these fictions came the news that the Russians had taken the offensive again, invaded Finland, besieged Viborg, and returned home unmolested after devastating the district.

The response of the Scandinavian clergy was magnificent; they had little chance of refusing to contribute to the tithe, once their bishops in synod at Jonköping had agreed to the papal loan. In 1351–2, the king's high stewards and other royal officers acting for the nuncio fleeced them of £2937 sterling – more than the contribution for 1324–9. But nobody else showed any interest in helping Magnus to continue the war, which had ended with an exchange of prisoners in June 1351; the magnates of Norway and Sweden showed themselves increasingly hostile to his regime, and his friend Pope Clement died in 1352. Just at the moment when the quarrel with Novgorod appeared to have been raised to the status of something high and holy, it became apparent to almost everyone concerned that the whole enterprise was impractical, unprofitable and fraudulent. In 1355 the Curia suddenly asked for its money back, perhaps in response to the machinations of King Valdemar IV of Denmark. Next year, a revolt against the king broke out in Sweden; he was compelled to share his kingdom with his son Eric, and he spent the rest of his reign overwhelmed by political crises. He lived to see Scania reconquered, and the union between Norway and Sweden dissolved. His final humiliation took place posthumously, when an unknown fifteenth-century Novgorod scribe wrote the document attached to the Fourth Novgorod Chronicle which is known as the 'Testament of King Magnus'. According to this writer, Magnus had ended his life as Gregory, a monk and convert to the Orthodox faith in the monastery of Valamo on Lake Ladoga, where he had been received after being deposed and shipwrecked. Now that death approached, the ex-king addressed his son and an imaginary brother with a stern warning against ever attempting to invade Russia, and pointed the moral by recapitulating the history of Russo-Swedish relations since 1240.

In the disasters by land and sea which had befallen his people for the last hundred years, the penitent king was made to see clear evidence of God's anger, and his own lamentable history was recited as final proof that no good could come of crusading against the Orthodox Russians. Therefore his successors must

live in peace and charity, avoid all manner of treachery and untruth, renounce luxury and drunkenness and all devilish play, do wrong to no man nor violence to any, break no agreement sealed by the kissing of the cross, and go not over to the land of Russia as long as peace prevail and the cross be kissed, for we gain no joy in this life therefrom, and we lose our souls thereby . . .

Excellent advice; but Magnus could only have given it if he had indeed been a convert to the Orthodox faith. In his Latin world, fighting the Russians was a meritorious act, and if he had had any doubts on the subject they would have been stilled by his visionary kinswoman Bridget. Even after the crusade had failed, Bridget continued to claim that Christ expected the king and his archbishop to conquer and convert the 'heathen'. The first attempt had failed because her instructions had not been properly obeyed, but Christ's words were plain: 'I consign this part of the earth to your hands, and I require you to answer for it.'[145] Bridget expected such high moral standards from her crusaders that no actual expedition against the Russians could ever have satisfied her. If only the pure in heart were allowed to fight for Christ, the Orthodox of Novgorod were safe.

The eclipse of Sweden and Norway under alien rulers for the century after Magnus's death meant that there could be no further attempts to turn local disputes along the eastern frontier into wars of conquest and conversion. The Mecklenburger and Danish dynasts who held power gained more by trade with the Russians than they could hope to get by fighting. King Albert of Sweden made an alliance with the Teutonic Knights of Livonia in 1375, and in 1378 Pope Urban VI authorized the Swedish bishops to grant indulgences to all who fought in, or paid for, a further crusade against the Russians;[146] but nothing happened. Swedish and Finnish frontiersmen attempted small campaigns in 1395, 1396 and 1411, but got nowhere. Russian and Karelian raiders clashed with Norwegians in the 1440s, but the Copenhagen government did little. When, towards the end of the century, a group of Swedish nobles managed to assert their independence of the Danish king by supporting Sten Sture as regent, the situation changed. Muscovite expansion to the west, and Sten's ambition to consolidate his rule by reasserting Swedish power in Finland and, if possible, Livonia, brought about a state of war in the North. On 22 June 1496, Pope Alexander VI issued the last crusading Bull for the recruitment of warriors in Sweden, but in vain: the Bull was intercepted by the regent's enemy, King John of Denmark, and Sture was deposed before he could push the war to a conclusion. Even in the Baltic the maintenance of the *status quo* was more important than the Holy War. In the 1540s, the exiled Swedish archbishop Olaus Magnus recalled the good old days, when Swedish kings had dubbed 'golden knights' after their coronations, and had sworn them to defend the church; 'and they used to observe this oath so faithfully and strictly that once they had heard war proclaimed against the enemies of the faith, especially against the Muscovite schismatics on the eastern limits of the kingdom . . . at once, at their own expense, they went off to war in a strong armed band to fight the Lord's battle . . .' But the next Swedish crusader was to be Gustavus Adolphus.

8

SYSTEMS OF GOVERNMENT

The Latin crusaders devised three ways of ruling their conquests in the Baltic region. As systems by which outside authorities controlled new countries, they met with varying success. Sweden and Finland remained together for nearly 600 years. The Teutonic Order kept Prussia and Livonia for nearly 300. The king of Denmark was suzerain of northern Estonia for little more than a century. No one factor decided how long they lasted, but logistics, economics, density of colonization, and cultural assimilation all counted as much as administrative efficiency.

The shortest-lived regime was the least intrusive. The king of Denmark intervened decisively in Estonia only twice: to conquer the province, in 1219, and to impose a land settlement, in 1238–42. After that, he sent out a captain and a bishop to Reval as overseers of royal and church interests, and left his vassals to pay tithe and land-tax and do homage to new kings. In theory, Valdemar II had the same royal powers over Estonia as over Denmark; in practice, his successors had limited rights, and delegated power to their Saxon tenants, the *Ritterschaft*, while their governors acted within a framework of consultation and legal process. In 1248 the *Ritterschaft* and the burghers of Reval were already acting as a legislative body for certain purposes, and in 1252 some vassals were granted automatic hereditary succession to their lands according to German feudal law. Danish inheritance customs never took root. By 1282 a council of vassals was advising the captain, and in 1315 the whole *Ritterschaft* was allowed to live, inherit and rule its fiefs according to its own law-code. It was established that the duchy belonged to the crown, and the king minted the money, but the efforts made by Danish rulers to maintain and extend their powers against their church and baronage in the period 1242–1319 bore no fruit in Estonia. The loyalty of the province's landowners rested on economic self-interest and guarantee of tenure.

This arrangement might have lasted longer but for the disintegration of the Danish monarchy in the 1330s, and the financial difficulties of Valdemar IV, its restorer, in the 1340s. Beset by pressing problems at home, and unable to break the Hanseatic trade monopoly at sea, Valdemar calculated that he would get more by selling the province than by hanging on to what was left of his rights as suzerain; he accepted 10,000 marks from the Teutonic Knights, and Estonia became a dependency of the grand-master, loosely federated with the Livonian province. Reval and the corporation of vassals kept their constitutional privileges, but the rule of the master of Livonia proved more effective and exacting than the distant hegemony which had released them. In effect, Danish power had been undermined by peasant revolt which the Order had crushed (see p. 212).

In Finland, on the other hand, the kings of Sweden tried to assimilate the new country to the old; their control was based on a greater variety of links, built up over a much longer period of conquest, and consolidated by closer contact. A community of Swedish immigrants and Finnish converts already existed in the south-west of the country before Birger Jarl asserted royal power in the 1240s, and this community served as a prototype of colonial society. Its members lived like the freeholding mixed farmers of Sweden, observing similar laws and obeying a Swedish bishop; the king and his captain at Åbo could build up their authority here, as at home, and gradually extend it beyond the pale as more Suomi and Tavastians were converted.

The majority of native freeholders were not consigned to the rule of a feudal baronage, as were the Estonians; rather, the whole population of Finland, except the slaves (*orja*) formed several more or less privileged groups, each directly connected with the king. There were magnates, but they were not a distinct order, and their status was determined by their usefulness as administrators. The royal castles established at Åbo, Tavastehus and Viborg were centres of authority to which estates and fiscal rights were attached, and were granted for a term to vassals who acted as captains or advocates and appointed subordinate prefects and bailiffs. Thus in 1340 King Magnus II empowered Daniel Nilsson to hold

our castles of Åbo, Tavastehus and Viborg, with lands, provinces, and all other
of their appurtenances to keep and rule in our name for four successive years
... on condition that he send over in full every year our tribute from Finland
and Åland, in various furs, ready money, butter, cattle, and 'king's bushels', and
he may hold back the annual residue of what comes from other rights and our
pleas there emerging, without rendering any account, for the building of the
said castles and for the costs and charges both of himself and of the castellans.[147]

This leasing out of royal lands and rights on conditional tenures, as
län, was a way of binding Swedish magnates to their king, in Sweden as
in Finland, and assisted their development into a powerful unifying
caste; it meant that Swedish nobles could thrive in Finland, and that the
two countries shared the same elite. Thus the king's brother governed
as captain and duke in 1284–91 and 1302–18, and at Viborg members of
the families of Bielke, Stålarm, Grip, Vase, Bonde and Tott were installed
between 1320 and 1483, employing bailiffs from the Sparres and Natt och
Dags, among others.

The military retainers of these magnate–governors and of the bishops
were boarded out among the freeholders, and in time some of them got
land, intermarried with the better-off natives and colonists, and were
recognized as *frälse*, or nobles: men of rank with hereditary tax-
exemptions. They were the leaders of local society in Finland proper
and Tavastia in peace and war, with defensible halls, manors, coats-of-
arms and seals, but not an all-powerful corporation and not exclusively
Swedish. They co-operated with the king's officers in administration
and warfare, and dominated the local assemblies of freeholders, but were
sharers in the commonwealth rather than political monopolists.

Beside them stood the clergy, heavily concentrated in south-west
Finland, but recruited both from Swedes and Finns and enjoying the
same privileges as the clergy in Sweden. In 1291 a Finn called Magnus
became bishop of Åbo and in the same century priests and friars of
Swedish, Finnish, English and German origin co-operated in advancing
the conversion. Their work strengthened royal authority, at first by
accustoming all Christians to pay tax – which the king took over from
the bishop – and later by involving Sweden and Finland in the common
enterprise of the anti-Russian crusade. Their wealth came largely from
tithe (which was levied in three varieties, according to the density and
economy of settlement), and the spread of this imposition, and canon

law, helped to bring a very loosely knit province within a single political framework.

By 1400 the burghers of the new towns established at Ulfsby (Björneborg or Pori), Rauma, Åbo, Borgå (Porvoo), Viborg and Pernå (Pernaja) formed another privileged group looking to the king for protection; and the settlers of Nyland were organized into localities with law-meetings and social customs similar to those of Sweden. The general body of rural freeholders lived under public law: whether the recognized code was Finnish or Swedish, they participated in open assemblies and were linked directly to the crown by contributing tax and military service. This diversity of political arrangements was also reflected in the difference between the castellanies of East and West Finland, for at Viborg the captain's main duties were defending a frontier, and keeping track of thinly scattered and vagrant subject populations. He dealt with the head-men of Karelian districts and war-parties, and with fur-trading pioneers, who could not be fitted into the Åbo model of a Finno-Swedish society, and for whom royal authority meant little more than a poll-tax in furs and occasional leadership in war. West Finland, by contrast, was divided into parishes, hundreds and *snække laghar*, or levy-ship districts.

As a result of these many different contacts, royal authority could be exercised in Finland very much as in Sweden, and in some ways this country became simply the *Osterlande*, or eastern provinces, of one monarchy. In 1362 the 'law-man' of the *Osterlande* was summoned to bring a jury of clerks and laymen to take part in the election and acclamation of a new king in Sweden, alongside the seven law-men of the old country, and this participation became a valued privilege. The union flourished because the Scandinavian tradition of local self-government flourished – assisted by poor communications, sparse population, and cultural diversity. From the viewpoint of the ruling elite of king and magnates, this meant that Finland could not be governed very efficiently, and did not have to be, either. King Magnus's national law-code was not successfully exported there, the law-man was unable to perambulate and inspect all the law-meetings, and the governors of Viborg were very much their own masters. Under King Albert, the Swedish magnate Bo Jonsson Grip was able to build up a personal hegemony over all Finland, and it took his successor, the Danish queen Margaret, ten years to get control of it; but the effect of this ungovernability was not to separate the province from Sweden, but, rather, to encourage the growth of

Swedish institutions as a means whereby local interests could be protected. Hence the various law-meetings recorded in fifteenth-century documents (from the *lagmansting*, *vinterting*, *sommarting* and *häradsting*, to the *skatting*, and the *fiskting*) and the council of lay and clerical officials (*landzræth*), which met as a high-court at Åbo the week before St Henry's summer festival (18 June), from 1435 onwards.

Swedish rule therefore offered many, perhaps most, Finlanders, whether of Finnish or Swedish descent, personal and property rights, which were given additional force by the nature of the country. Among these rights was that of owning slaves, and the condition of the thrall or *orja* population was not manifestly improved under this system; but the bulk of the peasant farmers had no burdens other than tax, tithe and military service to complain of, and the *ting* gave them the opportunity of making their grievances heard.

Prussia and Livonia were run on a quite different system. There, government came through a complex administration staffed by a trained ruling class recruited from countries lying some 500 miles away. This administration was only part of the wider organization known as the Teutonic Order, and its shape was dictated by the monastic command-structure. Its purpose was not merely to govern and fight, but also to carry out a mission on behalf of the Western Church. After 1309, when the headquarters of the Order were established within Prussia, the system still meant that natives, colonists and outsiders from all over Europe were being exploited by one connecting hierarchy of officers committed to a cause rather than to a country. In some ways this turned out to be a very efficient method of government.

At the top, it ensured continuity and dedication. Neither Prussia nor Livonia was plagued with the recurring crises of medieval government, in the shape of disputed successions, minorities, regencies, and feckless or useless rulers. When a grand-master died, or became incapable, the Rule laid down an almost foolproof procedure for finding and installing an acceptable successor. The vice-master convened the leading regional commanders to an electoral chapter-meeting. The meeting nominated a president, the president nominated a college of twelve electors: seven knight-brothers, four serjeants and one priest-brother, selected by progressive co-option. Once a majority of electors had agreed on a candidate, the minority acceded in a unanimous acclamation. So, in 1303, when Grand-Master Hohenlohe abdicated in Prussia and tried to make a come-back in Germany, he met with no success; the election of his successor, von Feuchtwangen, was accepted by all. When Grand-Master von Orseln was murdered by a crazed brother in 1330, at a time when Prussia was at war with Poland, and the Order was discredited at the Curia and no crusaders were at hand to save the military situation, there was no crisis. The electors provided a new grand-master in three months, without undue haste, and the Order carried on as before. In 1345, when military disasters sent Grand-Master König temporarily insane, and König stabbed and killed a man for interrupting him at prayer, Vice-Master Dusmer simply confined him in Engelsburg castle, convened the electors, took office as grand-master, and immediately resumed hostilities against the Lithuanians. König later recovered his wits and returned to active duty, but never challenged Dusmer's authority.

The system also produced a high standard of ruler, owing to the practice followed until 1498 of always choosing men who had served as senior administrators and proved their worth. Luder of Brunswick, for example, had held high office for sixteen years before his election, and Dusmer, von Kniprode and Zöllner for ten. The wealth and importance of the families from which they came hardly seems to have influenced the electors. Even a prince such as Luder was not necessarily bound for the top: his peer Duke Albert of Saxony sweated out his service as a commander of the frontier without going higher. In the period 1309–1525 only one grand-master was deposed for misgovernment, and that was Henry von Plauen, who saved the Order from annihilation in 1410. Not all were model rulers. Several earned the epithets 'haughty', 'self-willed' and 'overbearing',[148] but none was found idle, indecisive or improvident.

This was important, because the constitutional checks on the grand-master's power which were written into the original Rule were never fully applied, and became a dead letter after 1309. After the move to Marienburg, he had personal lordship over Prussia, a private demesne in Pomerelia and, in the end, the revenues of four German bailiwicks attached to his own chamber or financial department. His hold on the Prussian commanders gave him control of the general-chapter of the Order, which met at Elbing, and he was able to use it simply to ratify the measures he proposed: new ordinances, senior appointments, and admissions. Its function was to set the Order's seal – half a Virgin and Child – on what he had done through his – a whole Virgin and Child.

The great officers of the Order (see above, chapter 3, first section) became the administrators-in-chief of Prussia. The grand-commander acted as castellan of Marienburg, and the treasurer also stayed close to the grand-master. The marshal took over Königsberg, the hospitaller Elbing, and the *Trapier* Christburg. As monks, they cohered and obeyed far more readily than the enfeoffed or salaried officials of lay kingdoms, and by the 1320s they had worked out ways of exploiting all the country's resources for the profit of the Order. Grain came under the *Gross-Schäfer* ('senior-manager') of the grand-commander at Marienburg, who supervised the corn-growing lands adjacent to the Vistula – the Oberland – and appointed agents called *Lieger* to buy or sell, depending on the state of the trade. The economy of eastern Prussia – the Niederland – came under the *Gross-Schäfer* of the marshal, at Königsberg, and his *Lieger* (three at home, one each at Lübeck and Bruges) and their commercial salesmen, or *Wirte*, were chiefly involved in the amber trade. The year's policy was dictated by Marienburg, and accounts were rendered annually to the treasurer; buyers and salesmen had to act within the scope afforded them by loans. Other sources of revenue – the common grain-tax, the forest, the mint, tolls, market dues, the profits of justice, fisheries and bath-houses – were exploited and developed by the grand-master and commanders within their spheres of jurisdiction, but for most of the fourteenth century the boroughs were not taxed directly. Instead, the grand-master received a share of the Hanseatic customs dues (the *Pfundzoll*) and became a member of the League himself.

To reinforce these economic controls, the Order divided Prussia into commanderies (*Kommende*), governed from castles by officers originally known as *preceptores*, and later as *Komturen* (commanders) or advocates, depending on whether they administered monks' or bishops' territory. These military abbots ruled for the grand-master by exercising political and military powers by and for the convent of brothers with whom they lived. Each house of Teutonic Knights was organized to function as a religious community, as a military cadre and as corps of officials. Many of these officials were fiscal specialists, accounting weekly to the commander for their departments, and while each convent was self-supporting, its efficiency was checked by monthly accounts rendered to a senior administrator. All fourteenth-century religious Orders were beset by secular concerns, and among the Cistercians and Benedictines the monk-wardens and numerous other estate agents were seen as signs of decay; but in an Order which accepted government as one of its prime duties such proliferation of officials was unavoidable and legitimate. Since most knight-brothers were not born into ruling families, it was desirable that administrative experience should be widely distributed, and the hierarchy of offices served as a promotion ladder on which the fittest climbed highest.

In the course of the fourteenth century, the ordinary knight-brothers in Prussia and Livonia became known as lords, rather than brothers, and had continually to be reminded of their monastic vows. New ordinances forbade them to wear fine, eccentric or tight clothing, to appropriate money left over from conventual purchases, to make frivolous journeys with excessive pomp; they were not to use private seals, to hoard money, to swear profanely, to plot, to canvass for office, to keep packs of hounds.[149] Since these things were forbidden, they were probably done. Nevertheless, the Order's system of inspection and punishment ensured that its members continued to live communal lives, obey orders and uphold the political system. They formed a true ruling caste, dedicated to keeping other people in their places and telling them what to do.

The military efficiency of this system may be judged from the Order's war record (see chapter 6); its economic performance is hard to assess, as there are no overall figures to show how much the Prussian government was making in the fourteenth century. However, the evidence of land-purchases, castle- and church-building, loans and campaigning suggests that it was doing very well. Not until the end of the century was it necessary to impose a general war-tax on Prussia, and not until the early fifteenth century are there signs of financial crisis and serious debt. The difficulties that convulsed Denmark, Sweden and the north-German principalities – declining state revenues, rebellious magnates, disintegrating territories – were avoided in Prussia and Livonia, or at least postponed.

This stability was not the result of rigid centralization or uniformity. The apparently similar hierarchies of the Order in Prussia, Livonia and Germany were actually performing rather different tasks, and remained largely separate in their political and economic working, although ultimately under the rule of the grand-master. In Prussia, the relatively subordinate position of the bishops of Samland and Warmia allowed the Order a free hand in state-building and administration. In Livonia, the master (appointed by the grand-master from the two candidates submitted by the Livonian commanders) was always preoccupied with the problems of a control shared with the much more independent bishops of Riga, Courland, Dorpat, and Ösel, and with the Estonian knights and bishop. After 1330, when Master Monheim occupied the whole city of Riga, the Order steered this commonwealth with a firmer hand, and the growing wealth and military effectiveness of the masters increased their independence. They, too, had their treasurers, marshals and great officers, and private estates in Germany, and, although they co-operated with the grand-masters, local concerns often came first: they could only be managed from Marienburg by tact and persuasion, and they could only rule with the assent of their provincial parliament, the *Landtag*, which met annually after 1422.

CONDITIONS OF MEN

(a) *Natives*

The conquerors of the eastern Baltic lands tried to reorganize the traditional patterns of society they found there. They wanted to make them more 'Christian' – that is, either more like the home countries, or more like an ideal Catholic model, and they wanted to make them manageable. They were all guided by the normal west European assumptions of the time, but they had to make concessions to pre-existing social patterns and to a variety of local difficulties: harsher climates, thinner populations, poorer soils, precarious economies and tenuous communications. By 1300 the makings of a new order were there: in each province there were laity and clergy, lords, peasants and burghers, administrators and subjects – categories that could not have been applied in 1200. However, as in other frontier lands, there were many people who could not be categorized in this way, and all categories had a peculiar east-Baltic flavour.

This was most noticeable in Finland, where social change was least planned and most gradual. A Finnish peasant with a holding of arable land on the west coast might appear similar in wealth and status to a Swedish peasant living near Stockholm, and be liable for the same forms of tax; but in fact he and the group to which he belonged might well derive most of their gains from inherited hunting rights fifty miles upstream, which could only be exploited by leaving their farms at certain times of year and letting their women do the work. In Karelia, most of the free population was so frequently engaged in hunting and trapping expeditions that a substantial and respected family might appear to the tax-collector to have no fixed abode; and when in 1316 King Birger insisted that all Karelian women should have the same rights as Swedish women,[150] he seems to have overlooked the fact that, while the she-Karelians were not allowed to inherit landed property, they were trained to hunt, fight and work alongside their men. A Lapp had no land, and might be bound to a farm like a slave; but he might only go to that farm once a year, and have the use of natural resources over an area bigger than an English shire. A parish as big as an Italian diocese might afford a bare living for one priest.

Further south, where there was a sharper distinction between conquerors and subjugated natives, and where lordship was already prevalent before the Germans came, the new rulers were able to reorganize society in their own image to a greater extent. One of the most pressing problems in the thirteenth century was how to adapt existing patterns of control without creating disorder and discontent. A native nobility already held sway; if the new regimes were to survive, they had to make use of it, and they were commissioned both by popes and by emperors to grant a measure of liberty to converted peoples.

At first, the treaty of Christburg (1249) laid down a number of civil rights which were to be enjoyed by all free members of the Prussian tribes which accepted Christianity. They could marry, bequeath property, trade, litigate, enter the Church and become knights; they could be disinherited only by due process of law. Any deviation from Christian law or custom carried the penalty of disenfranchisement, and the church courts run by the Teutonic Knights therefore constituted a method of political supervision; but, apart from this check, the treaty allowed much of the old order to survive under the new.

Then came the revolts and apostasies of 1260–83, during which many Prussians lost their lands, rights and lives, and many nobles emigrated. What emerged at the end was a more tightly regimented society, within which favoured natives enjoyed more clearly defined rights that raised them well above the level of ordinary freemen and aligned them with the German landowners who were beginning to settle among them. There was no one treaty to establish the position of this reorganized grouping, but its outlines can be deduced from the charters to individuals which were preserved in the Order's archive. One of the earliest was granted by *Landmeister* Rechburg to a certain Tropo in 1262, and its terms were remarkably generous.[151]

He received two tracts of land, and two settlements, with full rights of justice over both, to be held by him and his heirs of both sexes in perpetuity. He was freed from paying tithe or labour dues, and in addition he was given personal lordship over nine kin-groups in Samland. His only public obligations were to supply an unspecified number of men for three duties: *hervart* (offensive expeditions), *lantwern* (local defence) and *borchbuunge* (fortification). He probably already held the lands he was granted; the charter merely established the terms on which he could keep them, and, since he was evidently loyal, these enabled him to 'live like a lord'. Others got less, as witness the six Old-Prussian brothers named in *Landmeister* Baldersheim's charter of 1267.[152] They got forty-eight hides, and the tithe for which they were liable; but they were bound to pay *census* or grain-tax on all cultivated plots, let the Order have jurisdiction over their peasants, and let the peasants emigrate if they wanted to. They owed the three military services, and they also had to supply food to the Order's castles. Only if they agreed to this, runs the text, 'will we forgive them for the outrage they have done to the faith by their apostasy'. Loyalty paid: these men would cut a smaller figure in the neighbourhood than Tropo. There survives a document of 1299[153] in which the commander of Samland recorded the names of all the local *witingi* or nobles who had a clean record since the time of the apostasy, and Samland remained an area with a high proportion of Old-Prussian landowners. The more prosperous came to resemble German feudatories, with manors, manor-houses, town properties and coats-of-arms; they intermarried with immigrants and spoke their language. But many well-born Prussians who held their land by feudal tenure, and enjoyed rights over others which might be termed seigneurial, remained in practice unassimilated, sharing exiguous properties with kinsmen under the tribal law, and doing military service not as knights but in bands of rough-riders equipped 'with Prussian weapons' – shield and spear, rather than full armour. As long as the Lithuanian war lasted, such men were valuable; they were the vital link between the commanders and the rank and file, and the nature of the fighting ensured that they would not become too civilized.

In Livonia, where German settlement was sparser, fewer native warriors appear to have won the privileges of feudal tenure and noble standing, and the relatively backward state of the province allowed native society to remain unaltered for longer. In the fourteenth century, a recognized indigenous nobility survived in Courland, where it was protected by a 'Curonian feudal law' which allowed dozens of squireens to use the title of king as late as the eighteenth century. Elsewhere, the ascendancy of German knights absorbed a small number of loyal kinglets, and tended to degrade all other natives into the condition of a peasantry, from which the better-armed were recruited for the *reysa*. In Estonia, the battle for lordship between the king of Denmark and the Sword-Brothers led to the parcelling out of each *kilegund* or settlement-area among immigrant vassals; by the 1230s the king's list names only one landowner, Clement, as an Estonian.

The mass of the native populations paid the price for the privileges which were granted to their leaders. The treaty of Christburg let many Prussians be subjected to Polish law, and Polish law meant a rigorous seigneurial regime for the peasant. He owed his lord escort duty, transport services, the use of carts and carriers, varied labour services, bridge-building, boon works, attendance at his house, watch and ward over his property, hospitality, a tax on livestock, a plough-tax, two taxes on the value of his movable goods, and renders, on different occasions, of a cow, an ox and all dogs, beavers and falcons.[154] This was hard by any standards, and absurdly hard in a country where the government's prime requirements were military service and ready money; besides, it could only prevail in fully manorialized parts of the country. The tendency of the period 1250–1350 was for more Old Prussians to be brought under seigneurial control, but on much better terms than Polish law allowed. Landlords desperate for labour to develop their resources could only hope to attract tenants by imposing minimal dues and services, and the Prussians benefited from the favourable conditions granted to German and other immigrants.

The condition of those who lived in long-settled areas can be deduced from the law-code for the district of Pomesania, which was drawn up about 1340, in German.[155] These laws speak of two categories of people, free and unfree, and consign the unfree to the jurisdiction of their lords; they come under peasant law, *Gebauersrecht*, which is private. The freemen also include peasants, but they are peasants with rights, who cannot be sentenced to death in private courts and may demand trial by the written code. They live in households, under the authority of a responsible and hereditary head, and the community of householders forms the lowest court, regulating the economic life of the village. It exists in both free and unfree villages: in the former under a *Starost*, or head-man; in the latter under the lord's steward.

The unfree include various sorts. Some are just peasants, with farms of their own, who lack freedom because they owe suit of court to their lord, and are liable to be punished by his officers; they are not serfs or slaves, and they are allowed to answer for themselves in law-suits. Others are *gerthner*, smallholders living on plots belonging to the lord and liable to eviction; others are *Knechte*, hired labourers without personal rights, but with claims to a legal wage-rate. Evidently some lords were making money out of private justice, but their regime cannot have been harsher than that that was found in parts of England at the time and was much less oppressive than that of many French and German seigneuries: Pomesania had self-governing villages, and villeins with rights. The severest penalties were reserved for those who interfered with the machinery of justice: for refusal to appear in court, for forging charters, for bringing unsubstantiated charges against the lord's steward.

Nevertheless, the Teutonic Knights were clearly determined that Old Prussian peasants should be kept in their place. An appendix to the Pomesanian code stated that, when Prussians and Germans were drinking together, the Prussians must always drink first – in case of poison. If a Prussian were sentenced or acquitted under German law, he could not seek redress under his own law. If he killed a German, he paid twice as dearly as if he had killed a fellow-countryman. His best chance of improving his lot was to leave such prosperous districts as Pomesania and settle nearer the frontier under the more favourable conditions of German law. The relative freedom a man enjoyed within his ethnic grouping need not diminish the drawbacks of being a member of that group; the Order's policy of *Lasset Preussen, Preussen bleyben* (let Prussians stay Prussian) was not benevolent.

Many commentators, including St Bridget of Sweden,[156] were shocked at the way Prussian converts were left semi-pagan, uncouth and lawless, and they were probably right in deducing that this sort of neglect made the natives easier to manage from the military point of view – better fighters, and less apt to complain about their rights than German settlers. When they appeared in court and tried to testify, 'the Lords just sit and laugh', complained the Carthusians in 1428,[157] and Polish critics were never slow to point out that, even after 200 years of monastic rule, the Old Prussians were Christian only in name. In this as in other matters, the brothers acted as knights rather than as monks. And only two Old Prussians rose to high office in the church: Bishop James of Samland and the Grand-Master's chaplain Saul.

In Danish Estonia, some 80 per cent of the indigenous population was subject to immigrant seigneurs, and owed them 'tithe' and military duty. When landlords reacted to falling grain-prices by upping tithe during a political crisis, the Estonians lost patience. On 23 April 1343 they rose up and began killing their masters. German sources give an unlikely total of 18,000 dead as a result of this rebellion. The survivors within the Domburg at Reval appealed to Master von Dreileben of Livonia for help (the Danish captain was his prisoner); he restored order by killing many more thousands of rebels. They captured one of the kings whom the Estonians had elected to lead them, and, when von Dreileben asked him why they had revolted, he replied that 'they had been martyred and oppressed for so long that they could no longer submit or stand it.' But why had they massacred twenty-eight innocent Cistercian monks at Padis? 'They deserved what they got, sure enough; any German deserved to be killed, even if he were only two foot tall.' The rebels offered to obey the master of Livonia, provided they had no 'junkers or lords' over them, but the offer was rejected and the kings were hanged.[158]

Here was an example of what unrestricted 'colonialism' could lead to: grinding the faces of men who were equipped with weapons and obliged to perform military service was dangerous and self-defeating. However, there is no evidence that after the Order had bought Estonia in 1347 the natives were better treated; the likelihood of revolt had been diminished by the killing and degradation of all potential leaders, and that was enough. By the fifteenth century, the freer Estonians were either serving as agents of German barons, or they had emigrated to Reval to work for the German burghers as carters, porters, boatmen, watchmen, servants and journeymen. They could not join the *Ritterschaft*, and in the city they were denizens (*inwaner*) rather than full burghers. Most were smallholders or serfs or thralls (*drellen, ora*) some prosperous, some destitute. The prosperous were kept in their places by the public and private services they owed for their lands – *malewa* (the peasant equivalent of *hervart*), *census* and various dues to the lord, tithe and fees to the priest; the poor, by hereditary servitude or attachment to a manor or a trade. Whether most of them were worse off under German rule than they had been under their own warlords is impossible to assess, but there is evidence to suggest that many were. For example, in 1425 the friars of Reval complained that most poor Estonians were left in a state of uninstructed paganism by their bishop and parish clergy; but, if one of them died and were buried in consecrated ground before his family had paid the mortuary fee, the priest would have his corpse dug up and hung from the church door until the money was handed over.[159] This sort of indignity cannot have happened often, but it could not have happened at all before the conversion.

From 1350 to 1500 Estonia was an increasingly prosperous country within which the enjoyment of wealth and liberty was carefully confined to those who fell on the German side of the line separating *Deutsch* from *Undeutsch*. It is unlikely that the small minority of knights, priests and burghers could have maintained their hold without such a system of discrimination.

The Lettish and Estonian peoples of Livonia underwent a similar if somewhat less rigorous subordination to the German ascendancy. On the whole, indigenous nations did worse north of the Memel river and south of the Gulf of Finland, where there were fewest immigrants. It was the need to provide conditions fit for incoming peasants that made Prussia and Finland better places for conquered peoples to survive in.

(b) *Colonists*

In Finland there was little need for the crown to encourage colonization; hunger and new manorial exactions drove numbers of Swedes to the east. But in Prussia and Livonia the initial intractability of the land and the continuing harshness of the climate offered little inducement to settlers from Germany, especially as the whole of Central Europe lay open to them. The Teutonic Knights needed a secular nobility to hold down the countryside, and an influx of arable farmers to help develop it. They therefore made attractive offers to all Germans who chose to live under their rule.

Land-grants to knights could be extremely generous. In 1236 Hermann Balk enfeoffed one man with a fort, 300 Flemish hides with appendant fisheries, and tithe from three villages, to be held by him and by his heirs male or female in perpetuity. In return, the feoffee owed a pound of wax, a mark of silver and a tithe of grain every year; out of respect for his noble birth, he was not bound to perform any specific amount of knightly service, but, should he sell the land, the buyer would owe two knights and a squire, and all future settlers would be liable to serve.[160] That was in Prussia; in Livonia the Order was so hard-pressed for men that in 1261 the vice-master promised all knights and burghers who aided him against the Curonians fiefs of forty hides, with ten each for their squires, and tithe exemption for six years. In 1280 the Livonian master granted Andreas Knorring, a crusader, eight estates and an escheated inheritance with a marriageable heiress in return for only three horsemen a year.[161] The Knights of Estonia held their fiefs in return for military service fixed in 1350 at a flat rate of one German warrior and two Estonians per hundred *unci* (approximately 3000 acres) for the *hervart*. Such terms – and the enfeoffment of knights with tithe, rather than land – were the result of hurried occupation, and after the initial conquests, they no longer occur. However, the early grants did create a powerful baronage in Estonia, Livonia – especially episcopal Livonia – and parts of western Prussia, where the Order retained only the right of repossessing lapsed inheritances (*Heimfallsrecht*) or the option of buying back, if it wanted to curb baronial power. In Livonia the Lord had no right to take wardship, aid, scutage, marriage or relief; he could not prevent his vassal from alienating the fief he had granted, and had no say whether it was to be held in common or partitioned between brothers. Primogeniture – normal in Saxony by 1200 – was unknown.

In most of Prussia, feudal tenants were more strictly controlled. They had to perform more military services, and the Order kept greater residual rights over their fiefs. Not until the fifteenth century was the Prussian baronage able to combine as a class in a bid for greater political independence, as they achieved their partial success only with the assistance of the towns and the king of Poland.

Most German immigrants lived under municipal law – *Lübischer*, *Kulmischer*, or *Magdeburger Recht* – either in cities or villages, and these codes also offered the settler much better terms than he would get as a peasant in most parts of western Germany. As long as he paid an annual rent and did some form of military service, the newcomer was given virtual ownership of a sizeable town property or farm; the political independence of his community was restricted, but his personal and economic freedom were guaranteed.[162] His value as a warrior and a cultivator, rather than birth and tenure, determined his status.

The leading cities, Reval and Riga, were let off with fairly light military duties, but on the whole all burghers and peasants were expected to fight, both on *lantwern* and on *hervart*, either as fully armed knights or as light horsemen, according to whether they held forty hides or under. The plots of land given to peasant settlers were seldom smaller than a hide (about fifty-three acres) and sometimes much larger; they were lightly taxed, and were conceded initial tax-relief as an encouragement to clearance and building. They owed suit of court to the manor, but the law by which they were tried was the law of Kulm or Magdeburg, rather than private or seigneurial law; labour dues and renders in kind to the lord of the manor were few or none. Such conditions prevailed in all the colonized areas of Prussia during the period 1250–1400, and were applied to all who were prepared to live in them: at first Germans, then native Prussians, then Poles, Ruthenes and Lithuanians. They represent the fact that throughout the Holy War this was a seller's market for labour and fighting skills.

What the burghers got from the Order was above all the right to get rich. They were not subject to the tallages and town-aids which fleeced most north-European communities, they could trade within Prussia and Livonia without having to pay tolls, and they were allowed to join the Hansa of German towns while to some extent competing with other members. As long as Prussia was expanding, they, the feudal vassals, and the peasant settlers benefited from the rule of the Teutonic Knights, and co-operated with the Order, without being subjected to any rigorous state organization. Once the economic climate worsened and the Order began demanding more from its subjects, as in the period 1380–1410, the German community began to show signs of discontent; there were plots among disaffected townsmen, and a league among the west-Prussian knights was formed in 1397. In the fifteenth century, when the Order lost its military supremacy, and Polish armies began pushing down the Vistula, both burghers and Knights made bids for a greater degree of independence, and met with considerable success. In 1410 Prussia was still a lordship within which communities and individuals enjoyed privileges directly proportional to their usefulness to their monastic lords; by 1414 the Prussians were organized into estates of knights and burghers with constitutional rights and a share in government.

All three Baltic provinces thus followed different paths towards a broadly similar political condition: the sharing of power between authoritarian rulers and colonial interest-groups which had secured the right to assemble, deliberate and bargain. In Finland this right sprang from a long-established Scandinavian tradition brought over by immigrants and matured in a climate favourable to self-help and self-rule. In Livonia it came from the monopoly of power enjoyed by a small German elite divided among semi-autonomous lordships and obliged to co-operate by the demands of war and the threat of the indigenous majority. In Prussia, the complexity and diversity of the society created by the Order, and the wide distribution of freedoms that was the price of economic and military expansion, made autocratic rule increasingly difficult, and the efforts of the grand-masters to maintain it led to the social unrest and civil war of the fifteenth century. Nevertheless, while the going was good, the Order had established over ninety towns and a thousand villages in Prussia and Livonia.

CIVILIZATIONS

Conquest and conversion brought the eastern and western Baltic countries closer together, and both closer to the rest of Europe. In all the conquests, the distinctive forms of Latin civilization took root and seeded, but the extent to which they flourished varied greatly.

Catholic Finland resembled Catholic Sweden in many ways, but both countries remained culturally impoverished by the standards of the outside Catholic world. Where Sweden was poor, Finland was poorer – in educated men, in books, in churches, in towns, in arts, in schools. This was inevitable, considering the size and economy of the country; most of its inhabitants lived hard and primitive lives beyond the reach of ecclesiastical culture. In 1460, the friars and most of the priests were concentrated in thirty-six south-western parishes, and twelve more along the southern shore; there were only four churches in the whole of Swedish Karelia, outside Viborg. While the bishopric of Åbo was held by learned men, such as the Parisian graduate Hemming or the old Praguer Magnus Tavast (1412–52), the flock and its up-country pastors remained ignorant. Whereas in Sweden the fourteenth century was a time of literary and artistic flowering, when works in Swedish and Latin were being written by both clerics and laymen, Finland lacked both the patrons and the audience for such productions. The entourage of the bishop and the captain could not compare with the courtly and learned households of the king and the Swedish prelates, and the majority of the people spoke languages that were as yet unwritten; written texts were used only for the severely practical tasks of administration and saying the liturgy.

However, the success of the mission in attracting Finns to the priesthood (all the later medieval bishops, and most of the canons, were native-born) was in itself a striking achievement, unmatched in Prussia or Livonia. The enterprise to which these ordinands were called was largely that of making ends meet (chasing up parishioners for little bundles of fur, flax or hemp, tubs of butter, and, in the Åland Isles, the tenth seal); but they were also the key men who brought three cultures together – Finnish, Swedish and Latin.

The results of their work must not be looked for in great names or important books, or imposing buildings. The educational resources of the cathedral school at Åbo were fully stretched by the task of providing parish priests and sending the occasional high-flyer to the University of Paris (where the Finn Olaus Magnus was rector in the 1430s). Other schools existed, but it appears from a warning issued by Bishop Conrad Bitz in 1482 that they were so poorly endowed that the masters were apt to live off money, corn, and furs extorted from their pupils.[163] When the Russians burned Åbo cathedral and the bishop's castle of Kuusisto in 1318, they probably destroyed most of the books and records in Finland. Subsequent bishops built up a respectable library, as appears from the fragments preserved in Helsinki University Library, but the only large codices to survive the Middle Ages are about business: the *Registrum ecclesia Aboensis*, a collection of diocesan records compiled *c.* 1480–1560, and the Skokloster *Codex Aboensis*, a private copybook kept for Dean Särkilahti in the 1480s.[164] There are also the Tavastian 'Judgement-Books'[165] or records of law-meetings in central Finland between 1443 and 1510, and an extract from King Eric XIII's Tax-Book, drawn up in 1413. An Åbo service-book and a few religious texts complete the total; even allowing for subsequent centuries of fire and pillage, it appears that medieval Finland was nourished on intellectual field-rations.

The architects, sculptors and painters provided what was strictly necessary for worship and defence: the cathedral, two friaries, eighty pre-Reformation churches, the Brigittine convent at Nådendal, six castles, and shrines and frescoes in honour of the Virgin and St Henry. There were no chroniclers; only a few historical jottings survived to be worked into a *Chronicon episcoporum Finlandensium* by Bishop Juusten in the sixteenth century. The cult of Henry the Martyr gave the province its main indigenous literary theme: the story of the Swedish bishop murdered by a Finn, but devoted in heaven to the peace and welfare of Finland, which was celebrated both in the Latin *legenda*, office, hymn (*Ramus virens*) and sequence (*Ecce magnus presbyter*), and in the Finnish poem *Piispa Henrikin surmaruno*. Not an impressive total, by the standards of, say, medieval Ireland; but the starting-point was a mainly un-christian, illiterate and ungoverned world, which in two centuries became a recognizably Catholic society.

In Prussia and Livonia also, Christian civilization meant an attempt to reproduce Western models in unpropitious and sometimes stultifying circumstances; but, thanks to the nature of the conquests and settlements, the seeds were taken from a more florid stock than Sweden could provide, and nourished in a richer soil. As early as 1270, a Paris-trained schoolman, Maurice of Reval, was lecturing to the Dominicans in Estonia. Since the cultural innovators – Hanseatic merchants, friars, Teutonic Knights and mission-bishops – belonged to organizations rooted in Germany, their innovations were utterly German. Since they were either celibate or endogamous, they were resistant or hostile to the cultural forms both of their conquered subjects and of their Russian or Polish rivals. They generated a civilization which continued to express two things, Catholic supremacy and German solidarity, long after the Holy War had ceased to absorb their energies and aspirations. Its main determinants were war and the accumulation of wealth. Its nurseries and sanctuaries were the castle and the borough. Its vehicles were the German and Latin languages, and types of architecture and design derived from the family of cultures contained within the Empire.

The castle developed from the fortified tower, which replaced the timber blockhouse, and all its forms betrayed its pedigree. The most elaborate was Marienburg, which was not only a fort but also a palace, a monastery, a parliament-house, a government office, an arsenal and a holy city, alerting the senses and awing the mind. The convent of knights and priest-brothers sang continual masses in the great chapel while the grand-master kept up the state of a prince, and the grand-commander and the treasurer conducted the business of the Order in their own suites. The inner citadel – the *Mittel-* and *Hochschloss* – covered over five acres of land by 1400, and at either end lay an outer castle and a sizeable town. The Sire de Lannoy, who went there in 1412, reported that Marienburg contained arms and provisions enough to 'maintain a garrison of a thousand persons for ten years or ten thousand for one year'.[166] This all-purpose structure merely elaborated a pattern found all over Prussia and Livonia on a much smaller scale: a tower and a fortified quadrangle.

The square keep, or *Stock*, as it was called in Livonia, contained the bare essentials of military and monastic life: a chapel, a refectory (*Remter*), a dormitory and the commander's chamber. The central quadrangle was a fortified yard containing kitchen, stables, workshops, armoury and sometimes parish churches. The need to preserve all the components of religion, wealth and authority behind walls led to rebuilding and enlargement in pacified areas, and this meant either emphasizing the cubic unity of the buildings or diversifying the parts by raising towers and roofs, and duplicating the quadrangle to form a rectangle. Most rebuildings of this kind took place in the fourteenth century, under the supervision of imported German architects, and in the more secure parts of Prussia the ingenuity and simplicity of their work expresses the supremacy of their masters in the plainest terms. From outside, the people saw only smooth cliffs of brick, soaring up from the *parcham*, or levelled terraces, and presenting blind surfaces almost as far up as the battlements. The gateways defied entry, and the fortified latrines, or *dansker*, which projected from the top of the walls like truncated viaducts proclaimed to a humiliated world, 'As for the dregs thereof, all the ungodly of the earth shall drink them' (Psalm 75.10). The immense vaulted chambers of the interior, made necessary by the collective life (for example, the *Remter* of Marienburg, Arensburg, Heilsberg, and Allenstein), suggested rooms fit for giants, and the complexity of the roof-lines indicated a 'city builded upon a hill'.

The forts along the Prussian frontier were much simpler in plan, and in Livonia, where stone was the usual building-material, the four-square layout was the commonest, without much elaboration. Even at Riga, the *Ordensschloss* remained a single massive quadrangle defended by two squat towers. But, wherever the Order and the mission-bishops ruled, their power and their culture shared the same intimidating barracks.

Outside the castles, the symbols of this imported culture were concentrated in towns – sizeable along the Vistula and the coast, otherwise small and, in Livonia, sparse. Here were the cathedrals, collegiate churches, hospitals, town-halls, guildhalls, friaries and chapels, all modelled on the prevailing patterns of Westphalia or the north German coast and simplified or coarsened to fit in with the defensive system. Tall spires signalled to the seafarer and reminded the burghers of the Lübeck Marienkirche, which many must have visited. Massive gatehouses defied unauthorized entry, and, if the community expanded (as at Elbing), each new parish was walled and stockaded to localize the two perpetual dangers – fire and enemy attack. All public buildings spoke of Germany, and the Holy War.

The builders both of castles and of churches tended to emphasize two simple shapes: the rectangle and the triangle. In Prussia and Livonia, they are displayed with economy and directness. The cathedrals of Frauenburg and Königsberg, the large churches of Danzig, Braunsberg, Wormditt and Rössel, and the smaller churches of Santoppen and Falkenau, are long boxes, weatherproof, secure and structurally sound. Their towers advertise their presence to the surrounding countryside, and their patterned, stepped and turreted gables reassure the citizens that there is money to spend on triangles of fancy brickwork as well as on rectangles of plain wall. But solidity is never risked by wide 'Perpendicular' windows or by outgrowths of aisle or chapel, or by finicky Frenchified buttresses. Elegant brickwork is used like corrugated iron. The result is both perfect and perfunctory.

Inside, the wood- and stone-carvers worked to instruct, delight and welcome. The light denied on the outside of the castles streamed in through the many windows of the inner quadrangles, and the rooms were sometimes blazing with paintwork and encaustic tiles. Subterranean furnaces sent hot air circulating below the floors, and the cloisters offered comfort and delight to the stroller. If the Teutonic Knights used architecture to intimidate others, they used interior decoration to please themselves and their guests, and, beginning at Marienburg, the fashion for elaborate painting, carving and tile-work spread to other leading castles and to the churches and the halls of the burghers. Donors commissioned craftsmen from Silesia, Thuringia, Poland and Prussia itself to beautify their places of worship with crucifixes, triptychs, carved panels, images, friezes and ornamented capitals. For most of the fourteenth century, they were producing stocky, bright, and lifelike effigies which enacted the doctrines and legends of the church in blunt tableaux with widely opened eyes. There was nothing sinuous, stylish or sophisticated about this work. *Hausfrau* madonnas and square-jawed archangels referred directly to the gospel text and to the street, rather than to the canons of elegance and ideal form which stamped the contemporary images of northern France and East Anglia. The poor remnant of these figures collected in the museum at Gdansk (Danzig) gives the impression of a modest and devout congregation posing in its best clothes. The faith ringed and sheltered by awesome defences reveals itself as homely and approachable, fully bearing out the description of Prussian piety penned on the eve of the Reformation by the great Dominican historian Simon Grunau. By then, fashions had altered, and the artists were infusing their work with extremes of feeling.

Such were the cradles and the images of Christian civilization in the Order's dominions. They stood out like knots in a net of roads and colonized reclamations that was spread out into the underlying forest, marsh and scrub. The net was full of holes and interstices, where alien subjects lived unredeemed lives within sight of the steeple and the battlement, and it stopped short at the wilderness to the east. Between Prussia and Livonia, Christian culture was a strip of coast road, squeezed between the Baltic and the primeval forest. In Livonia, the net resembles a cobweb, stretched to breaking point between the quays of Reval and Riga, and the frontier outposts. It is not surprising that the people who lived on these flimsy structures expressed themselves in forms of worship and literature that joined them to the mainstream of Catholicism, rather than making concessions to what they thought of as barbarism.

The dominant cult was that of the Mother of God, patroness of the Teutonic Order, of the see of Riga, of Livonia and Prussia. The Order impressed her stamp on all it did. The military routine was geared to her feasts; *winter-reysa* normally began on the Purification (2 February), *sommer-reysa* on either the Assumption (15 August) or the Nativity of the Virgin (8 September). Grand-Master von Kniprode was renowned for the redoubled observances in her honour which he ordered before every campaign, and Grand-Master von Feuchtwangen ordered a *Salve regina* or an *Ave* to be said by every member of the Order every hour of the day, as early as 1309. The Conception, at that date a feast more generally observed by the Eastern than by the Western Church, was instituted as a feast of the Order by Grand-Master von Altenburg in 1340, and in 1390 Zöllner von Rothenstein authorized the Visitation to be kept throughout Prussia on 2 July, as a sign of his adhesion to the Roman papacy during the Schism. In the thirteenth century, the castles of Marienburg, Marienwerder and Frauenburg were named after the Virgin Mary; in the fourteenth, another Marienburg and Marienwerder on the Niemen, and a Marienburg and Marienhausen in Livonia.

For the Teutonic Knights, she was mainly a war-goddess. The Livonians inherited this belief from Bishop Albert and the Sword-Brothers, and embroidered her icon on the master's battle-flag, but the Prussians also claimed her as protectress, and set up an eight-foot outdoor mosaic of her on the apse of the *Hochschloss* chapel at Marienburg, to watch over the countryside. (It was destroyed in 1945.) She turned defeat into victory. In 1330 she appeared to King Wladyslaw of Poland and demanded, 'Why do you destroy my country?' The miraculous triumphs of Strawe (1348) and Rudau (1370) were attributed to her personal intervention. Von Kniprode rewarded her for Strawe by building a Cistercian nunnery at Königsberg, and for Rudau by founding a house of Austin friars at Heiligenbeil.

The favourite male saints were the soldiers Sebastian, Laurence, Maurice and George, and the missionaries Andrew and Bartholomew; their cults reflected the Order's main concerns, but were not restricted to it. St Maurice was seen as the patron of the young Hanseatic merchants lodging in Livonian towns, and they formed a guild in his name which was called the *Schwartzenhaupter*, after their Moor's-head emblem. And, as in the rest of Europe, it was Christ the victim, rather than Christ the victor or the judge, who received most attention here, particularly in the cults of Corpus Christi and the Five Wounds. In the 1330s Grand-Master Luder of Brunswick insisted on hearing the mass of the Passion every Friday, and the image of the lacerated body was an emotive symbol for the wounds sustained by Christendom at the hands of the heathen – among other things (see p. 62 above).

These were the most visible forms taken by the faith in the Order's colonies, apart from acts of war. The number and intensity of the cults is not surprising, in countries run by monks and bishops, and the comparatively rich literature produced here between 1290 and the Reformation was also the work of the Teutonic Order.

The knight-brothers were seldom scholars, and were often derided for their illiteracy; but illiteracy meant ignorance of Latin. There is evidence that many knight-brothers were practised artists in their own language, and that among priest-brothers there were always good Latinists and teachers. The need to instruct non-Latinists in the faith, and the pleasure of rhyming in German led to the growth of a vernacular literature inside the Order, but outside Prussia, by the 1290s; from then onwards, Prussian convent libraries, schools (at Elbing and Torun) and writers appear. Mary and the Old Testament are the dominant themes of their German verse. By 1300 there was a *Passional,* a collection of saints' lives and passions adapted to praise the Virgin, and *Der sûnden widerstreit,* in which Lady Spirit triumphs over Lady Sin thanks to Mary's assistance. Then came a number of poems associated with Grand-Master Luder, himself author of a verse legend of St Barbara (now lost; a Latin version survives), who commissioned a series of verse renderings of biblical texts: Maccabees, Daniel, Ezra, Nehemiah and Esther. These were continued under Grand-Master von Altenburg with a paraphrase of Job, and a *Historien der alden ê,* an abridgement of the Old Testament and ancient history in 6000 verses. Such works were probably read aloud at common meals to inspire the knight-brothers with the scriptural prototypes of war-heroism.

The most remarkable religious work of Luder's time was *Von siben ingesigelen,* dedicated to the grand-master and written by Tylo, a canon of Samland, in 1331, at the rate of seventy-eight verses a day. This was a translation of the *Libellus septem sigillorum,* expounding the seven manifestations of Christ from the Incarnation to Judgement Day, and like all such poems was marked by extravagant and sentimental praise of his Mother, who is symbolized as the burning bush, Solomon's crown, Aaron's rod, the fruitful almond, Gideon's fleece, the ark, the ladder, the linden-tree, the grape and the phoenix. To read of God the Father as 'the kisser', the Holy Ghost as 'the kiss', and the Son as 'the mouth surpassing all delights' is to taste the modish exuberance which permeated the Order's spirituality. This was an international literary convention, but it went with successful attempts to turn the Word of God into vigorous German prose. Such were the translations of the Prophets by the Franciscan Claus Cranc, commissioned by Marshal Dahnfeld of Prussia in 1347–59, the 'History of the Apostles', and the 'Prose Apocalypse' (based on the verse apocalypse written by Commander Hesler in Thuringia before 1312). And the prose tradition continued in Prussia with the Middle High German Marco Polo (late fourteenth century) and the *Leben der Seligen Frawen Dorothee* (1401–17), which in 1492 became the first book printed in Prussia.

The story of the conquests and crusades also inspired a number of remarkable works, both in Latin and in German. All provided a record of heroic deeds, combined with praise of the Virgin and a justification of the Order's mission in terms of biblical prototypes, notably the Maccabees. Henry of Livonia led the way, with his history of the founding and expansion of the Riga mission, and his example was followed in Prussia by a Latinist who composed a now lost account of the early wars of the Teutonic Order. This was used and continued down to 1326 by the priest-brother Peter of Dusburg, who apparently was writing his *Chronicon terrae Prussiae* at Königsberg from 1324 to 1330. The Annals of Torun and Oliva, and the historical works of John of Posilge (fl. 1360–1405), Conrad Bitschin (fl. 1430–64) and Laurence Blumenau (d. 1484) continued the tradition of Latin historiography well into the fifteenth century, by which time the need for polemicists, lawyers, and envoys had made Prussia the seat of all varieties of Latin learning. Grand-Master Zöllner von Rothenstein's attempt to turn Chelmno school into a university was not successful, but, there and at Torun, Elbing and Königsberg, masters trained men for the higher education provided at Prague, Leipzig and the new German universities.

The most distinctive form chosen by the Baltic historians – in Scandinavia and north Germany as well as in the Order's provinces – was the verse-chronicle, invented by the Anglo-Norman writer Gaimar in the mid twelfth century and well suited to combine both epic and annals, for the entertainment of both learned and unlearned. The first was the Livonian Rhyme-Chronicle, written in the 1290s either by a knight-brother or by a bloodthirsty priest, under the influence of the great Middle High German narrative poems. This powerful but clumsy work related the history of Livonia down to 1291, and the story from 1315 to 1348 was taken up by Bartholomew Hoeneke's Low German 'Younger Livonian Chronicle', which survives only in a later prose recension. After that, no rhymes from Riga; but meanwhile the history of Prussia had been versified by Grand-Master Luder's chaplain, Nicholas of Jeroschin. His *Kronike von Pruzinlant* is a vast expansion of Dusburg's Latin work, but more verbose and passionate in tone, and it was continued down to 1394 by the Order's herald, Wigand of Marburg, who concentrated on the details of sieges and expeditions. Most of the original is lost, but it survives in a Latin translation made on the orders of the Polish historian Dlugossius in 1464.

The purpose of these works is the same as that of the Latin chronicles: to create and affirm a sense of historical mission, by providing foundation myths, an heroic epos, and proofs of divinely ordered destiny. They buttress the Order's power by emphasizing its international reputation, its sacrifices, its collective courage and the barbarity and ruthlessness of its enemies. Behind these, as behind all the manifestations of Christian culture in the Baltic provinces, lies a strong determination not to become part of the world that the thirteenth-century newcomers had conquered, but to change it.

The change was more strongly marked in some places than in others. On the lower Vistula, for example, in the years between 1362 and 1394, it was possible for the daughter of an immigrant Dutch farmer, Dorothea of Montau, to win a reputation for outstanding holiness in a wholly German and Catholic society. As a craftsman's wife at Danzig, and as a widow and recluse at Marienwerder, she dreamed dreams, saw visions and gave advice, which earned the respect of people of all ranks, from the grand-master to the peasant. She was the flower of Prussian piety, a middle-class St Bridget whose voice and miracles were proof that God and his Mother were deeply interested in the daily doings of the province, and despite her criticism of the Knights the Order worked hard to get her canonized. However, among the 260 deponents who testified to her sanctity, only one was an Old Prussian, although it was claimed that she had done good work among Prussian converts. It is clear from her well recorded life and utterances that she belonged almost exclusively to the world of the castle, the cathedral and the township, where Catholicism was thoroughly 'at home'; not to areas where her Church confronted Old Prussian 'superstition', Lithuanian paganism or Greek Orthodoxy.

Yet many, perhaps most, of the Order's subjects lived in such areas. In Prussia, the eastern wilderness acted as a barrier against schismatic and pagan influence, although rural heathenism survived to the west of it, and Jews and Hussites reached the coast down the Vistula. In Livonia, the much-crossed Russian frontier let in the Orthodoxy the Order was fighting against. There were Russian communities at Riga, Dorpat, Reval and Narva, with their own priests and churches, and, however much Greeks and Latins referred to each other as 'dogs' and 'godless ones', they shared many beliefs, festivals and cults: in particular, the cults of the Mother of God, Holy Cross and St George. Thus, at Reval in 1425, the bishop and parish clergy included the Russian Church among the stations of their Rogationtide procession, but ignored the Dominicans, whom they despised for 'eating bran and chaff like pigs'.[167] In Dorpat, for all its sovereign bishop, cathedral, churches, nunnery and two friaries, too much Catholicism was bad for business and endangered the peace; a city so dependent on Russian merchants had to make room for their religion and culture. Out in the country, the indigenous population seems to have remained, if not heathen, then only halfway Catholic. In Estonia the old beliefs and the new combined in the popular festival of *Hinkepeve*, when the spirits in the sky were venerated under the guise of All Souls. In Livonia a similar legacy of pre-Christian myth and ritual survived in the midsummer vigil of St John, down to the present day.

To describe such cults as 'one form of ideological struggle against foreign oppressors', or to claim that because paganism survived 'there are no grounds for speaking of a cultural mission on the part of the German crusaders affecting the local population' (Mugurevics) is to ignore the layering of faiths throughout central Europe, the Balkans and Russia into modern times, quite irrespective of Germans or crusaders. The synthesis of Christianity and other religions has been in progress far too long for any particular significance to be applied to the 'double faith' of the Baltic. The phrase 'cultural mission' is no doubt sinister, Teutonic, and somewhat moth-eaten; but the success of the 'foreign oppressors' in setting up a predictably and characteristically imperfect medieval church system ought not to be denied.

9

THE WITHERING OF THE CRUSADE,
1409–1525

TANNENBERG AND AFTER, 1409–14

Grand-Master Conrad von Jungingen, the conqueror of Samogitia, died on 30 March 1407. According to Laurentius Blumenau, he was both a martyr and a prophet: a martyr because he hastened his own death by refusing to have intercourse with a woman, which his doctor had prescribed as a sure remedy for gallstones; a prophet because he warned his brother knights not to elect his brother Ulrich as his successor, since he was an incurable Pole-hater.[168] But Blumenau was writing fifty years after the event, and there is no contemporary evidence for either story. Ulrich was elected grand-master, and two years later declared war on Poland: not because he hated King Wladyslaw, but because his brother's policy of playing off Poland against Lithuania had broken down. The Samogitians had revolted; Grand-Prince Witold had supported them, and Wladyslaw had refused to restrain Witold. Evidently he was no longer wary of defying the Order; the invasion of Dobrzyn and other of his lordships in 1409 was a logical, if unintelligent, way of forcing him to change his mind.

Ulrich miscalculated: he did not expect Witold and Wladyslaw to combine against him effectively, and he expected his own ally, King Sigismund of Hungary, to play an active part in any further hostilities against Poland. In fact, Witold and Wladyslaw stuck together, and raised armies larger than the Order's total Prussian strength, while Sigismund accepted money and did nothing. After a nine-months' truce, it became clear that Lithuania and Poland were going to attempt nothing less than the reconquest of Kulm, and that none of the grand-master's friends was going to help him; even Master von Vietinghof of Livonia had agreed not to attack Witold without three months' warning.

On 1 July 1410 Wladyslaw and Witold made contact at Czerwinsk on the Vistula, and soon afterwards began a rapid march northwards with an army of Polish and Lithuanian levies, reinforced by Czech, Moravian, Wallachian and Crim Tartar mercenaries. They were met a few miles inside the Prussian frontier by the grand-master's combined force of Prussians and crusading volunteers, and on 15 July, at Tannenberg/ Grünwald, von Jungingen committed his troops to battle. He was presumably hoping that the Virgin would once more save her disciples by granting them victory against overwhelming odds; but by the end of the day, the entire high-command and the bulk of the field army of the Order in Prussia had been annihilated. The grand-master, the marshal of the Order, the grand-commander, the treasurer, several commanders and 400 brothers lay dead on the field of battle; the rest of their army was either killed, captured or routed. At one stroke, the allies appeared to have destroyed their enemy and made Prussia defenceless.

However, the Order was saved by the strength of its citadel, and by the losses of the allies at Tannenberg. One of the Henries von Plauen,[169] who had been entrusted with the defence of Pomerelia, took charge of the remaining forces, and held out at Marienburg for fifty-seven days. While the Prussian bishops and their vassals submitted to Wladyslaw, von Plauen refused to come to terms; he was waiting for bad weather, disease, the arrival of reinforcements from Livonia, or action by King Sigismund. On 19 September, Wladyslaw raised the siege. His artillery had not proved effective, his troops had dysentery, there was news of Livonian troops on the move, Sigismund had made an attack on his allies in Silesia, and he could no longer afford to pay his Bohemian mercenaries. On the way home he captured the new marshal of the Order, Michael Kuchmeister von Sternberg, but his chance of reconquering the Kulmerland in one campaign had vanished. On 1 February 1411 he agreed to a peace at Torun by which the Order kept all it had held before 1409 except Samogitia, which was to pass to Witold and Wladyslaw for the length of their lives. The Order was also bound to pay an indemnity amounting to £850,000 – ten times the average annual income of the King of England.[170]

The Teutonic Knights had suffered other great defeats in the past, but in those days the enemy had been the heathen and death in battle had been interpreted as martyrdom. The blood of slain knights had served to glorify the Order and to stimulate the recruitment of new members and crusaders. Tannenberg would not have been such a disaster if it had been possible to view it as a blow against Christendom, because it would then have brought in a rush of volunteers eager to save Prussia, but the Order found difficulty in propagating this view. Although it was emphasized that Wladyslaw had employed Tartars and schismatic Russians to bring about his victory, the rest of Europe was not outraged; contemporary references to the battle describe it as a lamentable tragedy, but a tragedy for which the Order was partly to blame. A Lübeck chronicler claimed that the Teutonic Knights had been defeated by God's will, because of their pride, and 'because they became too harsh towards their poor subjects, so they say'.[171] An English commentator, used by Walsingham and translated by Capgrave, wrote that the 'kyng of Crakow' had asked the 'heres of Pruse' to help him against the Saracens, but instead they had

set upon him on the other side only to destroy him. Behold what zelatouris thei were of oure feith! Here religion was ordeyned to defende the feith; and now covetise stereth hem to destroye it! The Kynge that was newly Cristis child, thoute it was best first to fite ageyn these religious renegatis. He faute with hem and put hem to flite and conquered al the cuntre, suffering hem to use her eld lawes and customes.[172]

There had been no lack of German crusaders in von Jungingen's army. There had been the usual mixed company under St George's banner, and separate companies of volunteers from Westphalia, Swabia, Switzerland and the Rhineland. The reaction to the defeat within the Empire was favourable to the Order, and reinforcements began to arrive soon afterwards, led by the bishop of Wurzburg. However, non-German crusaders had been in short supply for ten years before Tannenberg (where, according to Monstrelet, there were a few knights from Normandy, Picardy and Hainault), and the lack of response from England and France after the battle showed that the international standing of the Order had declined. King Henry IV, an old Prussian crusader who always posed as a good friend of the Order, and who had laughed at the Polish manifesto against it in January 1410, suddenly lost interest in paying damages to Prussia for shipping taken by English privateers. Never had the Order needed £10,000 more urgently; but the king felt that the likelihood of Prussia's falling to the 'infidels' made it inexpedient to meet the debt.[173]

One company of Burgundians, including Sire Gilbert de Lannoy, set out 'pour aller en Prusse contre les mescreans' in 1412, and saw service against Wladyslaw in the *reysa* of 1413, but this appears to have been the last time non-German crusaders fought for the Order. They stopped coming partly because the outbreak of war between England and France kept them fully employed in the West for the next generation, and partly because Witold and Wladyslaw were successful in convincing the rest of Europe that they were Catholic princes and neither 'miscreants' nor 'Saracens'. It was widely felt that any further crusade against the heathen – the Russians and the Tartars – ought to be undertaken by Prussia, Lithuania and Poland in concert; there could be no merit in weakening Christendom by helping Catholic powers against each other. Thus the treaty of Torun contained a clause by which Witold and the Order agreed that in future they would convert or conquer the infidels as a joint enterprise. As long as the three Catholic powers of Eastern Europe remained at enmity with each other, this was unlikely to happen.

This was one of the more serious consequences of Tannenberg, as far as the Order was concerned; in future, it had to rely almost exclusively on Germany for allies and volunteers, and this meant showing increased deference to the wishes of German princes – in particular, to Sigismund, who was crowned king of Germany in 1414. Another was the crisis within Prussia, where the burghers and secular knights and bishops began to object to the Order's monopoly of political power, and Danzig declared war on the Knights. Grand-Master Henry von Plauen (elected in November 1410) tried to placate his subjects by summoning a *Landesrat* of representatives from the cities and landowning class to consult with him over matters of policy, but the policy he favoured was striking back at Poland as soon as possible. Neither his commander, nor his bishops, nor his lay vassals were willing to risk another Tannenberg; he forced them into a brief campaign in September 1413, but was quickly deposed by his own marshal with the connivance of the Estates. Thereafter the government of Prussia was shared between the Order and the Estates, each increasingly resentful of the other. Internal disunity increased the chances of a successful Polish invasion.

Wladyslaw had accepted King Sigismund as arbiter in all his outstanding differences with the Order, but when in 1414 the king's Award of Buda ordered the Poles to rest content with the peace of Torun, and make no further claims on ancient Polish territory within Prussia, Poland went to war once again. A large army marched north and laid siege to Strasburg (Brodnica) on the Drweca; the new grand-master, Michael Kuchmeister von Sternberg, cut Wladyslaw's supply line, and for the Poles the campaign degenerated into the 'Hunger War'. Pope John XXIII's envoy arranged a truce and the invaders withdrew.

Grand-Master Kuchmeister was a tall, corpulent man with a taste for study and a talent for political calculation, a ruler better suited to the times than the two impetuous war-heroes who had preceded him.[174] The war of 1414 convinced him that, if Prussia were to be saved from conquest by Poland, it would be necessary to redress the balance of power by an appeal to the crusading instincts of the rest of Europe. Pope John would never sanction a public crusade against Catholic Poland on his own account. King Sigismund and the well-disposed German princes were unwilling to risk open war on the Order's behalf. However, in November 1414 the powers and the prelates of Catholic Europe met together at Constance to take measures for combating the Hussite heresy, reunifying the papacy and reforming of the church; if an ecumenical council could be persuaded to guarantee the Order's right in Prussia, and reaffirm its support for the Order's crusading mission Wladyslaw would be deterred from pursuing his claims. A victory in the propaganda war would save the Order from the real war which it was no longer strong enough to win. In December 1414 the Order's delegation, under the *Deutschmeister* and the archbishop of Riga, arrived at Constance with eleven wagons and an appeal from the Grand-Master's proctor, Peter Wormditt.

CONFRONTATIONS AT CONSTANCE, 1414-18

Wormditt's memorandum[175] began with a historical introduction. He reminded his audience that Satan's armies beset Christendom on all sides, and that the Teutonic Knights had been appointed like Maccabees to fight God's war against the heathen. They had saved Poland from the Prussians and the Lithuanians, and the whole Catholic world had been eager to offer them assistance; Prussia had become a Christian country, and their Order had become a training-ground for all the nobility and knighthood of Europe. However, their prosperity had aroused the envy and hatred of ungrateful Poland, and the king had allied himself with Witold and the pagans to destroy them. He had failed, and had apparently agreed to a firm peace and an end to all contention by the treaty of Torun.

But what had come of it? Wormditt then went through the articles of the treaty, showing how Wladyslaw had infringed them all, either in spirit or in letter. His bishop had laid a complaint against the Order at Rome; his envoys had spread slander against the Teutonic Knights all over Europe. He had failed to release his prisoners-of-war as agreed, he had plotted to subvert Prussia with the deposed Grand-Master von Plauen, he had violated the frontier and intercepted merchants. He had then defied King Sigismund's sentence, and once more inflicted all the horrors of war on the unlucky subjects of the Order. These horrors Wormditt found it difficult to describe, but he made the attempt: murder, infanticide, 'presbitericide', enslavement by Tartars, rape, abortion, arson and sacrilege, the work of an obdurate Pharaoh at the head of a semi-pagan army.

In days of old, when the faith was in danger, all men had risen up to defend it. 'But now it is not so. For nowadays no man takes heed of another's loss, if it leaves him untouched. No man is concerned with distant perils. As long as he can live at ease, each man thinks he is fortunate enough and perfectly safe.' Nevertheless, says Wormditt, the Council would do well to look to the defence of Prussia, for it was Holy Ground, purchased by the blood of their ancestors, of which Virgil might have written (quoting Eclogue 1, 70–72):

> Did we for these Barbarians plant and sow,
> On these, on these, our happy Fields bestow?
> Good Heav'n, what dire Effects from Civil Discord flow!

Do not desert us now, in our time of trouble, he implored the Council – 'lest in the annals of your pontificate and in the chronicles of your royal reigns a place be found to describe this dire disaster: that the Order itself was destroyed in your days'.[176]

Wormditt presented his case with ingenuity and pathos, but the pope was anxious not to antagonize the Poles before they had even arrived at Constance, and shortly afterwards he made what amounted to a declaration against the Order by appointing Witold and Wladyslaw his vicars-general, or protectors of all Catholics, in Novgorod and Pskov. He also abrogated the Order's claim to Lithuania, hoping no doubt to remove discord between the parties, and enlist Poland and Lithuania in the crusading cause. But this was not exactly what either side wanted. On 5 July 1416, the Polish canon-lawyer Paul Vladimiri (Wlodkowic) delivered a reply to the Order's charges which systematically challenged all the assumptions on which Wormditt's appeal had been made, even the legality of the crusade itself. Vladimiri's standing as rector of the University of Cracow, and pupil of the famous canonist Zabarella, enabled him to adopt an independent stance and carry the argument to a more rigorous intellectual level.

His speech – later published as the *Tractatus de potestate pape et imperatoris respectu infidelium*[177] – began with a historical introduction rather different from Wormditt's, in which he contrasted the Order's record of waging war not only on the aggressive heathen, but also on Christians and pagans living in peace, with Poland's achievement in bringing the Lithuanians to the Church by peaceable conversion. He then investigated the title-deeds by which the Teutonic Knights held their power: first their claim that they were acting for the pope, then their commission from the emperor.

Obviously, the pope could not grant the Order powers which he did not himself possess, and documents in which he appeared to do so would be null and void. The Knights could only do what the popes had specifically ordered them to do, and what the popes were entitled to command; no more. The main question was, 'Could Christians lawfully be commanded by their pope to attack sovereign infidel nations?' Yes was the answer, but only in the case of the Holy Land, where Christ himself was born and lived; otherwise, any infraction of the property rights of any unoffending neighbour, be he pagan or Christian, was a violation of natural law which not even the papacy could sanction. Granted, the pope had jurisdiction over all men, and could order infidels to be punished; but not for offences against laws of which they were ignorant. Could he then order Christians to convert infidels by force? No: force is incompatible with the free choice which the Scriptures and canon law regard as inseparable from genuine conversion. The end does not justify the means. Therefore the Bulls on which the Order based its right of dominion were either invalid, or valid solely as justifying the waging of defensive war against infidels who infringed the natural rights of Christians. And in that case the Order had gone much too far.

As for the imperial charters of 1226 and 1245, which instructed the Teutonic Knights to convert, punish and rule the heathen, they were founded on the mistaken assumption that the emperor had an independent responsibility for the spreading of the faith, when in fact all modern authorities were agreed that his duty was to assist missions, not to initiate them. 'O Lord Emperor, the preaching of the Gospel is not committed to thee!' These charters certainly granted the Order the right to wage offensive war against unoffending pagans, and to annex their territory; but the emperor had no right to authorize unjust war, and had no legal power over peoples living at peace outside the recognized limits of the Empire. Frederick II had therefore trespassed on the pope's own sphere of jurisdiction, and violated the natural property rights which it was his duty to uphold. 'O! how generous that emperor was with other men's property.'

In this initial broadside, Vladimiri's ammunition was drawn from the 200 years of vigorous legal study which had elapsed since the Teutonic Order was given its commission. Under the influence of a succession of teachers, from the twelfth-century 'school of St Victor' to Zabarella, the idea of natural law had grown stronger and more widely respected, and the doctrine of the Just War had been established with far greater precision. If the Order could appeal to tradition, and to documentary evidence, Poland could appeal to reason and Aristotle. However, embedded in the heart of canon law there remained a comment which the great decretalist Henry of Susa, bishop of Ostia ('Hostiensis'), had made on a passage in Gregory IX's Decretals (III, 34, 8) in the period 1245 to 1254. He had argued at some length that

on the birth of Christ all honour, and all sovereignty, and all dominion and jurisdiction ... was removed from all infidels and conferred on believers. That this was done for a just cause is proved by Ecclesiasticus 10.8: 'Because of unrighteous dealings, injuries, and riches got by deceit, the kingdom is translated from one people to another.' ... And this sovereignty over *regnum* and *sacerdotium* the Son of God committed to Peter and to his successors.[178]

Therefore the popes did have dominion over the heathen, and they were entitled to confer this on the Teutonic Knights, as every trained canon-lawyer in the Council must have been muttering when Vladimiri concluded his speech on 5 July. But Vladimiri was prepared; on 6 July he came out with the refutation which he later expanded into the tract known as *Opinio Ostiensis*.[179]

He admitted that Hostiensis had indeed laid down that infidels were wholly incapable of exercising lawful political power, and that Hostiensis had many followers – Giles of Rome, Oldradus, Andreae, and Peter de Anchorano, who had recently stated that 'Christians may lawfully steal, purloin, rob, seize and invade the lands and goods of infidels who do not recognize the Roman Church or Empire, even if they wish to live peacefully with us.' If this was so, Christians were not required to obey either divine or natural law in their dealings with the heathen; but Vladimiri, speaking 'not as an ambassador, but as a doctor', undertook to give fifty-two conclusions that proved Hostiensis wrong. He used Scripture to show that God had commanded the pope to feed and protect, rather than destroy, the heathen, and Roman law to establish that property rights were always to be respected; he quoted Aquinas to prove that infidel property and authority were as inviolable as Christian. He justified the exception of the Holy Land by claiming that Titus had conquered Palestine as the result of a Just War, and that therefore the pope, as inheritor of the dominion of Rome, had the right to restore it to Christian rule. And all lands wrongly taken from Christians by Muslims could be rightly recovered, but only after the illegality of the dispossession had been established by process of law. The pope had the right to judge and punish infidels, but only for offences against natural law – idolatry, sodomy, attacks on Christians, and refusing to admit missions to their territory; and he should proceed to dispossess them only as a last resort, to avoid imminent peril to Christendom. And, if he did so, and conferred dominion over them on a Christian ruler, their property rights must still be respected.

Moreover, the pope's powers over infidels were certainly never granted directly to the Christian emperors, and their charters to the Teutonic Order therefore remained null and void. Conversion could only be brought about by persuasion and kindness, and therefore the Teutonic Knights and their crusading friends were not only mistaken, but also in sin, when they waged war to extend the faith. Those who died in the Northern crusades were surely damned, unless they repented, for it was the duty of the Christian knight to ascertain the justice of the cause for which he fought. Those wars fulfilled none of the five necessary conditions for a Just War, and in addition they involved the crusaders in breaking fundamental prohibitions against fighting on Sundays and feast days. What was gained by such sinful aggression was stolen property, and ought not to be kept by the aggressors. Innocent IV had decreed that an infidel was entitled to have stolen goods restored to him by the sentence of a Christian judge. Moreover, it was perfectly lawful for a Christian ruler (such as Wladyslaw) to use heathen allies to defend his country: had not the Maccabees made an alliance with the Romans? On all conceivable grounds, it was clear that the heathen had natural rights, and that their rulers were entitled to exercise lawful power over them; therefore it was the duty of all Christians to reject the opinion of the bishop of Ostia, and rather follow Innocent IV, who had written that 'there can be lawful dominion and jurisdiction among infidels' and that 'infidels ought to be compelled to the faith'.

It was a powerful argument, but it was challenging rather than persuasive; Vladimiri was not trying to make friends, just seeking to make points. 'You're a good advocate for pagans against Christians' reads a gloss in one of the manuscripts of the *Opinio*; for them, that is, against us – and this must have been how most of his audience reacted. Some had themselves been on *reysen*, and many more believed that heathens were bad and Christians good. Civilians were convinced that the emperor's authority was virtually limitless, and canonists that papal power could be extended far wider than Vladimiri allowed. However, the Council had other business to attend to: the condemnation and burning of John Huss, to begin with. And Vladimiri and Witold had less theoretical arguments to use against the Order. On 28 November 1415 a Polish deputation had arrived, in company with some indignant figures who announced themselves as authentic Samogitians anxious to join the Roman Church but afraid to do so because of the continuing hostility and aggression of the Teutonic Knights. At last, the pagans were in the witness box. And at the same time King Wladyslaw informed the Council by letter that he would have begun a crusade against the Turks if he had not been held up by fear of an attack from Prussia.

The Samogitians presented their complaints in February 1416, and a week later the Polish and Lithuanian ambassadors made a formal appeal for justice against the wrongs inflicted on their countries by the Teutonic Knights. No immediate decision was taken. Then the Order's advocate, Ardecino de Porta of Novara, asked that the Council excuse it from answering further charges; an attempt was made to read out a recapitulation of all the points at issue between Poland, Prussia and Lithuania, but the text was far too long to be heard in one session, and the Council suspended the reading and turned to investigating the heresies of

Jerome of Prague. It was evidently going to be difficult to swing the assembly either way; but the Samogitian deputies had made some impact, and the Order had no easy way of discrediting them. It was suspected in Prussia that they were simply the tools of Witold, and had in fact no intention of becoming Catholics; but how could this be proved? The answer, as too often with the Teutonic Knights, was an act of violence: in March the Samogitians were arrested on their way back from the Council, and held prisoner contrary to all international law and convention.

That September, both Wladyslaw and the grand-master wrote to the Council reassuring delegates that they had no intention of waging war on each other for the time being, but their intellectual troops were fully engaged. Vladimiri was composing a more detailed attack on the Teutonic Knights (*Articuli contra cruciferos*), proving not only that their political powers were unjustified, but also that their scandalous conduct was inconsistent with the profession either of knight or of monk. Dr Dominic of San Gemignano attempted to refute Vladimiri's refutation of Hostiensis, and Dr John Urbach asserted once again the right of the pope to authorize offensive war in order to bring about the conversion of the heathen – there was no lack of texts to support him.[180]

Urbach was a paid polemicist of the Order, but he was not the fiercest opponent of the Polish king. That same autumn, the Dominican John Falkenberg was completing his own 'Book on the Doctrine of the Power of Pope and Emperor' in order to convict Vladimiri of heresy and error before the Council. Objecting to the Pole's dismissive view of the powers of the emperor, he used Aristotle to prove that the civil power had a legality older than, and independent of, that of the papacy, and went on to claim that the emperor was God's vicar in temporal matters, and therefore had a duty to repossess in God's name that part of his earth that was occupied by those who defied him by disbelief, idolatry, schism and heresy. These were God's enemies, regardless of whether they made war or peace with the rest of the world, and Augustine and Isidore proved that it was for the emperor, not the pope, to make war on them. Of course, love was necessary; but since the object of fighting the heathen was to protect Christians, such wars were the result of love. 'And therefore, it is more certain than certain that to protect the faith by making war against infidels out of love is to deserve the kingdom of heaven.' After that, it followed that the Teutonic Knights and the Northern crusaders were wholly justified in all that they had done, because they had acted in obedience to the doctrines of the Church and in vindication of the legal rights of the emperor; they were entitled to wage war on the Feasts of the Virgin for the same reason that Christ had healed on the Sabbath – 'are ye angry at me, because I have made a man every whit whole on the Sabbath day?' (John 7.23).

But, when the Poles made use of unbelievers to devastate a Christian country, it was not only an outrage, it was heresy to pretend otherwise. Augustine and Chrysostom were agreed: it is never right to make friends with the devil. Therefore all Christians who helped Wladyslaw in the wars of 1410 and 1414 merited eternal damnation, and the whole Polish nation was liable to be condemned by the Church to lose both its political independence and life itself. Since Wladyslaw and Witold had made it clear that they intended to conquer Prussia and then overwhelm the rest of Central Europe to the Rhine, they must be condemned by the Council forthwith.

The Conciliar movement had given intellectuals a prominence in the conduct of political business which they had seldom previously enjoyed. Whether anyone benefited from this is doubtful; certainly not Falkenberg. His work suggests he was a clever man; his conduct proves that he was too clever by half. Attacking Vladimiri was fair game, but attacking Wladyslaw, and attacking him gratuitously, was folly. Moreover, at the same time as he published his *Liber de doctrina*, his much more scurrilous work, known as the *Satira*, was submitted to the professors of the Sorbonne. This was an exercise he had written some five years earlier, after moving from Poland to Prague to Magdeburg, where he was an inquisitor. He maintained that 'Jaghel', i.e. Wladyslaw, was a mad Lithuanian 'dog' who had persecuted Christians abominably, and was unworthy to be king even of Poland. He was merely an 'idol', and all Poles were idolators. Because Poles were idolators, they were apostates and heretics, and all who attacked them deserved eternal life. Because they threatened the Church from within, they were worse than pagans; to prevent them spreading their heresy, true Christians ought to exterminate all or most of them, along with their king, and if they did so they would certainly go to heaven.[181]

What appears to modern readers as a satire on the concept of the crusade, or on medieval thought in general, was neither meant nor taken as either: Falkenberg used his treatise as ammunition in the campaign against Wladyslaw, and, since it was manifestly slanderous, Wladyslaw had him dealt with. In the course of the year 1417, he was arrested, imprisoned, and condemned both by the Dominican Order and by the Council as the author of a scandalous libel. His flirtation with the doctrine of tyrannicide made him a public menace, but his more generally pro-imperial and anti-Polish propositions earned him a certain amount of sympathy, especially among the German nation. The Polish delegation found it more difficult to deal with the ideas than with the man; despite a detailed refutation by Vladimiri, and despite urgent appeals to the Council and Martin V, the new pope, there was no formal conviction of Falkenberg for heresy. Just before the Council dispersed, on 14 May 1418, he had the satisfaction of hearing a committee of three cardinals report that, although his *Satira* deserved to be 'torn apart, ripped to shreds, and trampled underfoot', it was not heretical. He was then carried off to spend six years in prison in Florence and Rome.

This uncalled-for intervention by Falkenberg had helped neither party. The Order's chances of getting the Council to take some kind of action against Poland were reduced by the publication of what amounted to a caricature of what the grand-master wanted; the Poles' determination to make a heresy out of Pole-hatred, and convict the Teutonic Knights of having briefed Falkenberg, roused considerable opposition even among those delegates not otherwise hostile to Wladyslaw. The heresy conviction was prevented by the English and the Spaniards. In the course of 1417 a number of polemicists expressed open support for at least two of Falkenberg's conclusions: that it was legitimate and meritorious to wage offensive war on the heathen in certain circumstances, and that it was damnable to use heathen allies against a Christian people. In January the advocate Ardecino de Porta of Novara published a *Tractatus*[182] pointing out some of the inconsistencies in Vladimiri's reasoning, and advancing a quaint anti-pagan argument of his own: since God had enfeoffed the heathen with the lands they occupied, they were obliged to keep his law; since by their idolatry they broke it, they ought to be disseised by God's vicar, the pope. Ardecino was paid by the Order for his efforts, as was Urbach for the official reply to Vladimiri that appeared in June. But there also appeared two opinions in favour of the Order's case by powerful independent thinkers who enjoyed widespread respect: Cardinal Pierre d'Ailly, bishop of Cambrai, an old exercised theologian and advocate of church reform; and the Benedictine Andrew Escobar, bishop of Ciudad Rodrigo and former student at Vienna University.

D'Ailly tried to simplify the debate by reducing it to two questions: 'May Catholics wage a just war on Christians with the assistance of pagans?' and 'Are the Teutonic Knights entitled to wage war on infidels in order to acquire their lands?' He concluded that there was no absolute prohibition against using heathen allies against Christians: a man was expected to fight for his lord, be he Christian or pagan. And, on the other hand, either pope or emperor was entitled to order Christians to make war on pagans, for one of three reasons: to regain lost Christian territory, to repress aggressive pagans, and to punish those who 'shamed the Creator' and seduced Christians by their unnatural way of life. Otherwise, peaceful infidels should be left in peace and their rulers and property should be regarded as lawful. Thus, if Wladyslaw's pagans were his subjects, he was justified in using them against the Order; if the Order's charters authorized the Knights to wage war for one of the three good reasons, their way was just. And then D'Ailly added that Falkenberg's conclusion that Wladyslaw and the Poles ought to be killed by all Christian princes for heresy, idolatry and persecution of the Church was perfectly correct – provided that they had been tried, convicted and sentenced for these crimes by a legitimate authority. This brief opinion[183] was meant to take some of the wind out of both sets of sails, but it was harder on Vladimiri than on the Order.

Escobar produced a rousing and very traditional vindication of the crusade in general and the Teutonic Knights in particular. He repeated the history of Poland's relations with the Order down to 1414 in such a way as to convict Wladyslaw of hindering a lawfully constituted religious Order in its work. Then he tackled in some detail the question of forcible conversion. Vladimiri had argued that missionary work and the waging of war were incompatible, because men cannot be compelled to the faith. But the purpose of waging war was not to drive men to baptism at the point of the sword, but to deter them from their own blasphemous and idolatrous practices as a preliminary to the change of heart that must lead to conversion. We are all God's children; if some of his children insult him by denying the true faith, it is the duty of the rest to correct them for the good of their own souls, and this is what the Teutonic Knights had been commissioned to do, and had done – because they love their neighbours, as well as loving God. And if the king of the Poles chose to call in pagans to help him assert territorial claims against these good men, he deserved to lose both his claims and his crown;

and all good Christians should go to the assistance of the Order.[184]

Against such arguments as these, Vladimiri's contention that the Order was guilty of something called the 'Prussian heresy', and deserved to be treated as an illegal organization, carried little weight. So radical was his approach that it would have been impossible to condemn the Order for the reasons he gave, without impugning the good name of the papacy, the Empire and most Christian princes. However carefully he strove to distinguish between the Northern, the Spanish and the Palestinian crusades, the flaws in the distinction appeared obvious. Crusaders (and would-be crusaders) tended to stick together. However, the Council would never have decided for or against either side unequivocally, if only because it had far more important business to attend to. The new pope, Martin, concluded the last session by imposing silence on the king of Poland's advocate; and then appointed Witold and Wladyslaw as his vicars-general in Russia. Their catholicism was loudly reaffirmed.

THE SURVIVAL AND EXTINCTION OF THE ORDER IN PRUSSIA, 1418–1525

The Order had little reason to be dissatisfied with what had happened either, since the Council had showed itself in general to be in favour of crusades, and, in part, friendly towards the Teutonic Knights. It had avoided being tarred with the same brush as Falkenberg, whose doctrines were not formally condemned until 1424, and appeared to have won the war of words. Or so the continuator of Posilge's Prussian Chronicle wrote in 1418: 'the king's envoys had cast reproaches at the Order with many great lies against the pope and the whole council before the Romish king and the electors, and in every plea they made they were overcome by the truth since they persisted in their lies'.[185] The Knights would obviously be justified in continuing to uphold the rights guaranteed them by the treaty of Torun.

But the fact was that they were no longer strong enough to do so. From 1418 to 1422, Kuchmeister confronted Wladyslaw's demands for his western territories with a perfectly respectable series of charters, and answers that satisfied the imperial tribunal at Breslau (Wroclaw); but, when Wladyslaw lost patience with the negotiations and invaded Prussia once more, the Order was compelled to come to terms after a campaign that lasted less than two months. By the treaty of Lake Melno (Meldensee)

Kuchmeister's successor, Paul von Russdorf, surrendered various scraps of frontier territory to Poland, and resigned the Order's residual claim to Samogitia for ever. Von Russdorf had appealed to the Empire for help, but the Polish advance had been so rapid that the war was over before any crusaders arrived. A month after the treaty, on 27 October 1422, Count-Palatine Lewis of the Rhine, and Archbishop Dietrich von Moers of Cologne led their men into Prussia. They spent the winter there, and then went home. They were the last crusaders to Prussia, even from Germany; in future the Order had to rely on its own members, or on mercenaries (whom it could ill afford), or on Prussian levies (who no longer wanted to serve).

Even when Poland and Lithuania drifted apart, as in the period 1422 to 1447, the Order was unable to gain any lasting advantage from the division. Grand-Master von Russdorf – a pious intriguer, with a smile and a winning word for every occasion, who was known in Poland as the Holy Ghost[186] – grew friendly with the ancient Witold, and with his successor Svitrigal (Svitrigaila, Swidrigel, etc.), but his intervention in the Lithuanian succession dispute of 1431–5 was not a success. The king of Poland struck back by sending an army of Hussites to the mouth of the Vistula; the Hussites devastated western Prussia for four months, and by December 1435 von Russdorf was compelled to make peace. His country was demoralized and discontented, his Catholic army had been trounced by a gang of heretics; his conqueror had incurred excommunication for using them, and the Order's privileges had been confirmed by the Council of Bâle: but in vain.

The plight of Prussia was bemoaned to Europe by a friend of the Order, the accomplished Latinist Conrad Bitschin. In his *Epistola ecclesie deplanctoria*[187] he heaped abuse on the enemy – 'O execrable Poland, O dullard nation, O nation crazed! How could you be so forgetful of your own salvation that you chose so nefarious an ally?' – and drew attention to the wanton spoliation of his country: 'Lament, O delicate Prussia, thou who until of late wast opulent in fruit and fish and all manner of delightful food . . .' He then appealed for military assistance: 'Take heed, you Catholic knights and soldiers who have hitherto come from the frontiers of distant lands to receive generous wages; take heed, I implore you, of your calling, for in this affair you are summoned not merely to receive wages, but to do battle, and the wages of battle are paid in Grace.' Not enough, it seemed; nobody came. The estates grudged their military service and their taxes, and the knights of Catholic Europe stayed at home. Only the Livonians fought on, and they were defeated (see below, p. 249).

After the peace of Lake Melno, therefore, it was only a matter of time before the Order was compelled to surrender all that the Poles wanted. It took over forty years, and the struggle involved repeated arbitration, polemic, litigation, and warfare, culminating in a thirteen years' civil war that tore Prussia in half; but in the end the superior resources of the Polish–Lithuanian monarchy were bound to prevail. By the second treaty of Torun (19 October 1466) Grand-Master Lewis von Erlichshausen was compelled to disgorge all he held on either side of the Lower Vistula – the lands taken from Poland since 1309, and the Prussian Oberland conquered before 1250, including Marienburg castle itself. The east Prussian rump, which he continued to rule from Königsberg, remained an independent principality, but the grand-masters were expected to take personal oaths of loyalty to the kings of Poland to guarantee their good conduct.

These wars were in no sense a continuation of the Northern crusade, despite the efforts of the Order and its publicists to attract crusading assistance. The only 'heathen' left to fight were the Russians, and the struggle with Poland prevented the Prussians from undertaking such action. If they had combined, such a crusade might well have taken place; but, as long as they remained bitterly hostile, the Holy War was suspended.

The idea survived the reality, however, because it was the official *raison d'être* of the Prussian government, which remained in the hands of professed monks until 1525. As long as the rest of Europe paid lip-service to this idea, there was some hope that it might be manipulated to the advantage of the lords of Prussia. Until 1411, belief in the crusade had been a powerful cohesive force, joining the Order, its subjects and 'guests' in pursuit of a common political goal, however mistaken or indefensible; afterwards, it became a private obsession of the Order, nerving its members to hold untenable positions as long as possible – not only against the Poles, but also against their own burghers and junkers and bishops. This dedication to a mission that could never again be carried out, at least in Prussia, helped to keep the old system of government going, but did not prevent the brothers becoming odious to their subjects, quarrelsome among themselves, and disobedient both to their Rule and to their grand-master. They were now recruited exclusively from the impecunious lesser nobility of western Germany; no burghers or mere knights need apply, and in Germany their numbers fell by a third between 1400 and 1450. Those who went out to Prussia were seen as 'Outlanders' by the rest of Prussian society, and treated the 'Inlanders' with resolute lordliness, enforcing their powers as *gebittiger* (officials) with slights and mockery. When their subjects complained to a knight in office, he would strike his head and say, 'Look you here, this is the *Hochmeister* sitting here! I will be all the *Hochmeister* you need, so get down, you sons of bitches!'[188] Their vassals looked back to the good old days of Dusmer and von Kniprode, when settlers were treated with respect. As the junkers of the Kulmerland and Torun pointed out to the Order in 1438, 'Although it was your predecessors who brought a part of the country to the Christian faith, how did that come about, other than by the strength and might of *our* forefathers?'[189] 'We won you with the sword' was the answer to all such questions, until in 1454 the burghers and vassals took the sword into their own hands and turned to the king of Poland for assistance.

This attitude was not the result of the impatience of unworldly with worldly men. The system of administration and business which had developed in the fourteenth century absorbed more of the Order's energy in the fifteenth, when they were brought into fierce competition with other Prussian interests; and there was much less written evidence of spiritual or intellectual exercise, at least among the Prussian brothers. There was now no need for the sumptuous entertainment which had made Marienburg attractive to crusaders in the past, but the remorseless conviviality of these snobbish bachelors served to pass the time and remind the colonials who was boss. They did not even bother to recite the Hours, and they scarcely even knew the Paternoster, complained the Carthusians in their 'Admonition' of 1428: 'while men sing in church, the lords sit in the cellar and take their ease and make merry ... Thus there is no more delight in the Offices, and there is no spirituality in the convents, neither in their lives nor in their dress.'[190] In peace they domineered, made money, feasted and philandered; in war they fought as vigorously as ever, but the outcome now depended on their ability to pay their mercenaries, rather than on knightly prowess. Nor could they bring themselves to agree with each other: from 1410 there were continual quarrels between the various 'tongues' into which they were divided. Grand-Master Henry von Plauen tried to advance Low Germans, and met with hatred and conspiracy among the High Germans, who had come to regard Prussia as their preserve; von Russdorf patronized Rhinelanders, but met with bitter opposition from the Swabians, Bavarians, and Franconians, who claimed a monopoly of offices. Yet, while the brothers grew more incorrigible and less manageable, political power slipped from their hands, as a corporation, into those of the grand-master: at first, by the connivance of the Prussian estates, who paid their homage to Conrad von Erlichshausen personally on his election in 1441; and later, when dread of Poland led the brothers to appoint 'outside candidates' from reigning German dynasties: Frederick of Saxony in 1498, Albert of Brandenburg–Ansbach in 1511 – princes who made use of the Order to promote their family interests.

After 1466, all the grand-masters tried to reform the Order, but none succeeded in convoking the general-chapter which was seen as a necessary preliminary. The problem of the Prussian knight-brothers was never considered in isolation; it was approached as an aspect of the decay of the whole Order, and, since the masters of Livonia and Germany could not be brought to co-operate in a general reform, it was never successfully tackled.

A far-sighted reformer might have considered two radical solutions to this dilemma. One was to remain true to the crusading tradition, face the fact that the Northern crusade was over, and pull out of Prussia; the Order would then have been able to fight against the real menace confronting Catholic Europe, the Ottoman Turks, and could have reformed itself into a true fraternity of military celibates, unhampered by the cares of government and politics. The other was for the Prussian brothers to cut their ties with the Order, renounce their vows, marry, and settle down as members of a secular Prussian ruling class.

In the fifteenth century the first of these courses had its advocates. The Emperor Sigismund – still king of Hungary – was anxious to halt the Ottoman conquest of the Balkans, and at the conference of Lutsk (1429) proposed that knight-brothers be placed in charge of military operations on this front; a section from Prussia, under Commander Claus von Redewitz, reoccupied the lands in Transylvania which the Order had held from 1211 to 1225, and stayed there until half were wiped out by a Turkish invasion in 1432. By 1437 Sigismund was suggesting that the whole Order be resettled in this area by the joint authority of himself, the pope and the Council of Bâle. After the grand-master had submitted to Poland in 1466, it was the Poles who favoured the idea. In 1497 Grand-Master von Tiefen marched from Königsberg to Halicz on the Dniester to assist King John Albert against his rebellious vassal, the *voivot* of Wallachia; but he fell sick with dysentery as soon as he got there, and died at Lwow. His army of 4000 men went home immediately, and the ensuing election of Frederick of Saxony was a victory for those brothers who disliked co-operation with Poland and wished to strengthen their ties with Germany. Saving Europe from the Turks was one thing; leaving Prussia was another. It was not until Prussia had left the Order that the knight-brothers could think of seriously devoting themselves to the Eastern Front, and it was not until 1595, with the first Habsburg grand-master, the Archduke Maximilian, that they actually did so.

By contrast, holding on to Prussia remained a popular and practical policy within the Order, even after 1466 – half was better than none. In the relatively peaceful days that followed the submission to Poland, the province flourished; in the time of Grand-Master von Tiefen, wrote Paul Pole in his sixteenth-century Prussian Chronicle, 'Prussia appeared no less than a pleasure-garden of the Lord', and the equable von Tiefen prided himself on the fine clothes and rich diet of his burghers and peasants, whom he refused to vex with taxes and wars.[191] It was a country worth keeping, even if the task made the knight-brothers bad monks. Until the Reformation, when the whole idea of monasticism came under attack, nobody suggested that they should cease to be monks altogether; for this apparently simple solution raised insuperable difficulties. In the first place, only the pope could dissolve a religious Order, and successive popes and grand-masters persisted in believing that the Teutonic Knights could reform. Secondly, the social function of Prussia and Livonia as 'asylums' for the indigent nobility of Germany could only be preserved if the ruling elites of these provinces needed constant replenishment. The rule of celibacy guaranteed this. And, finally, secularization was by no means a certain method of keeping Prussia. How would renegades be able to renounce their Rule without renouncing their lands and privileges?

In the end, secularization was imposed on the Prussian brothers by the grand-master. They had elected Albert, son of the margrave of Brandenburg, as a promising young soldier whose powerful connections would deter the King of Poland from increasing his influence over

Prussia. Albert took the monastic vow, and with the support of the Emperor Maximilian refused to do homage to Poland. When Maximilian deserted him, he prepared for war. Master von Plettenberg of Livonia refused to co-operate, but Albert placed his hopes in the hiring of German mercenaries and alliances with Denmark or Muscovy – or the Tartars. When the Poles declared war, he went through with the traditional invocation of the Virgin, making a barefoot pilgrimage to her shrine near Rastenburg and holding solemn processions at Königsberg. But the fighting went badly for Prussia; cannon were floated down the Vistula from Cracow, and one by one the Order's castles were besieged and captured. The Emperor Charles V arranged a truce in 1521, and, although the question of homage was referred to arbitration, there was little chance that Albert would be able to avoid making his submission.

To make matters worse, the internal peace of Prussia was threatened by the spread of Lutheran opinions among the laity and some of the secular clergy. This meant riot and confusion in most German principalities, but in ecclesiastical lordships it threatened the very existence of the state. Albert lacked the resources to wage civil war for the maintenance of the old order, especially as several of his commanders and his own bishop, Polenz of Samland, favoured the heresy; he met Luther at Wittenberg in 1522, and found a way out. In Luther's view, it was the duty of all Teutonic Knights to renounce their vows and marry, and it was Albert's duty to establish a secular duchy for himself in Prussia. These measures would reconcile Albert to his anti-monastic Lutheran subjects, and preserve his standing as a territorial ruler. After he had secured peace with Poland, by persuading King Sigismund to enfeoff him as hereditary duke of Prussia, and his own Estates and bishops had ratified the agreement, those knight-brothers who objected to the change had no means of stopping it. Albert had allowed all the great offices to fall vacant and had run down the total strength of knight-brothers in Prussia to fifty-five. He summoned only a minority of these to Königsberg in May 1525 to approve his decision. Most of them were intimidated by the hostility of the burghers and egged on by Albert's entourage. Only seven stood by their vows. After a few days' hesitation even these gave their consent, and cut the crosses from their habits for fear of being lynched.

It was not the spiritual decadence of the Order, or the decline of the crusading ideal, that put an end to the rule of the Teutonic Knights in Prussia. The subsequent reform of the German bailiwicks under Grand-Master Kronberg, and the part played by the Knights in the Habsburg offensives against the Protestants and the Turks indicate that armed monks still had a place in European politics long after 1525, and the survival of the Order in Livonia until 1562 proves that the Baltic convents still had life in them. It was the failure of the Prussian knight-brothers to come to a satisfactory political settlement with the Polish kingdom that put an end to the old Prussian system. By putting their trust in German princes, the Knights lost the power to preserve a monastic affiliation that was no longer essential to the military defence of the country and had become a contentious issue in the religious ferment of the 1520s. 'It happened with us lords of Prussia, as it happened with the frogs who took a stork as their king' – thus Brother Philip von Kreutz wrote a *Relation* of the whole 'dirty deal', as he called it. 'Now all the estates had done their homage, and I saw that there was no means by which the dirty deal could be changed, I did homage too, in order to save my property thereby, for I had a large sum of money in my employment [he was commander of Insterburg], more than any other Teutonic lord.' [192] It is interesting that, in the debate that accompanied the dissolution of the Prussian houses, the question of the morality of the crusade played little part: both the Teutonic Knights and their enemies preferred to argue about the morality of monasticism.[193]

The only Prussian brother who declared against the new duke was the commander of Memel, Eric of Brunswick-Wolfenbuttel, who was also the scion of a German territorial dynasty. The other Prussian convents accepted the change. The majority of those inside Germany remained deaf to Luther's 'Exhortation to the Lords of the Teutonic Order' (March 1523), but many of their estates were devastated in the Peasants' War, and subsequently confiscated by Protestant princes. In 1527 Master Kronberg of Germany became grand-master, and the Order embarked on a new career as an ally of the Habsburgs in the Wars of Religion.

LIVONIA AND THE RUSSIANS, 1400–1562

In Livonia, the Teutonic Knights held their ground during the fifteenth century with greater success than in Prussia. The country did well: the burghers at Reval and Dorpat cornered a fat slice of the Novgorod trade at the expense of the rest of the Hanseatic League, to which they belonged; Riga benefited from the continuing prosperity of Lithuania, and the knights of the Order and secular vassals profited by the export of rye. The country had been run on constitutional lines, with assemblies of estates deliberating with the master and bishops for much longer than had Prussia, but the demarcation lines between the authorities were now gradually redrawn in the Order's favour. The ancient triangular contest between the master, the archbishop and burghers of Riga, which appeared to have been solved for good in 1394, when Boniface IX ordered the chapter of Riga to adopt the habits and Rule of the Order, in fact recurred every generation until the end of the century, but these successive challenges by strong-minded prelates merely served to confirm the master as the predominant Livonian authority.

The troubles of the Prussian brothers obliged the Livonians to go to their help several times. In 1410 Conrad von Vietinghof marched south to help the grand-master after Tannenberg; Cisso von Rutenberg and Franke von Kersdorf went on long raids into Lithuania in 1433 and 1435, and Master John Osthof von Mengden made strenuous efforts to reinforce the grand-master in the war of 1454–66. But meanwhile the two provinces drifted apart. The Livonian Knights were recruited from the Low German areas disregarded in Prussia (Westphalia, Ruhr, and Netherlands) and their political outlook was different. The frontier with Lithuania was not under dispute, and the king of Poland had no claim on their lands; they derived no benefit from the grand-master's wars. When von Russdorf forced them to accept Franke von Kersdorf as their master in 1433, and von Kersdorf led them to a disastrous defeat at Wilkomierz (Pabaiskas on the Sventoji) two years later, they took future elections entirely into their own hands. They no longer let the grand-master choose their master from two elected candidates, and left him with the right to receive homage from a single nominee, who was always a Westphalian.

Not that the standards and lives of the Livonian brethren were either more spiritual or more strenuous than those of their colleagues. Their preoccupation with business, pleasure, rank and politics was equally marked, and their failure to produce or commission a single chronicle or history – even a rhyme-chronicle – has condemned them to obscurity. What they did has to be teased out of correspondence in the archives of the Order and the Hanseatic cities, and from Polish, Russian and

Scandinavian sources. They were dumb dogs, but at least they were able to bite.

In the fourteenth century the Livonians had been less ready than the Swedes to pick quarrels with the Russians, since the trading relation with Novgorod and Pskov was too valuable to be disturbed for long. Unrest along the frontier would lead to occasional raids and reprisals, as in 1341–2, 1368 and 1377, but, on the whole, differences were sorted out by discussion and treaty. Thus in 1362 the city of Pskov detained Hanseatic and Livonian merchants as a protest against encroachments by the bishop of Dorpat's subjects. In 1363 the Pskovians and Dorpaters met at Novgorod, deliberated, and separated without coming to terms. Then the Dorpaters detained merchants from Novgorod; but a committee of Novgorod boyars travelled to Dorpat, persuaded the Pskovians and the Dorpaters to agree, and all the merchants were released.[194] This may serve as an example of a long-continued passivity in matters connected with Russia; an attitude of watchfulness and mistrust, punctuated by skirmishes along the Narva, Luga and Velikaya, but no serious attempt by either side to conquer the other. Hence the reluctance of the Livonians to assist King Magnus of Sweden in his mid-century crusades; Swedes, Danes and Russians all had claims to Livonian territories, and the Order preferred to keep all three at arm's length. In any case, the Lithuanians presented a more immediate threat to the Catholic province than did the Russians.

In the fifteenth century, the conversion of Lithuania to Catholicism gave the Livonians an opportunity of renewing the attempt to subjugate the Russians, with the help of a powerful ally. Thus, in the period before 1409, when Witold was encroaching on Russian principalities and co-operating with the Order, Master Conrad von Vietinghof began to look again at Pskov – a small, prosperous commonwealth, no longer closely tied to Novgorod, remote from Moscow, and vulnerable to a combined Lithuanian–Livonian attack. As soon as Witold began raiding Pskov, Master von Vietinghof joined in; he made three *reysen* to the city, in 1406, 1407 and 1408, and destroyed the Pskovian army on the second, but on each occasion there was effective retaliation, and, when Witold lost interest in helping the Order, in 1409, the belligerents made peace.

Again, in 1443–8, Master Vinke von Overbergen, finding Novgorod torn between Muscovite and Lithuanian factions, and liable to succumb to either power, embarked on at least two ambitious *reysen* to the westernmost Novgorodian stronghold, at Yamburg on the Luga. He failed to take Yamburg in 1444, even with a train of bombards, but he devastated the Vod country up to the Neva, and imposed a trade embargo along his frontier.

These adventures came to nothing; or, rather, ended in a peace that was supposed to last for fifty years. The tie with Prussia prevented the Livonians from coming to a firm understanding with Lithuania, and obliged the masters to waste their resources in support of the grand-master during the war of 1454–66. Nevertheless, Livonia was prospering, and the military potential of the commonwealth was increasing, in both manpower and guns; the possibility of carrying through the failed crusade of 1242 still existed. The Russians had more men, and more guns, but depended on rivers and roads for moving them; Hanseatic shipping could bring both from Lübeck to Reval or Narva more quickly and cheaply. Thus, in about 1430 four Lübeck skippers supplied Reval with thirty-two cannon, powder, and 235 stone balls; a 'hulk' or merchant ship sold by a Danziger to a Reval burgher in 1462 carried six cannon, and three small Livonian convents inspected by visitors in 1442 contained six to eight cannon each.[195]

Moreover, a certain number of crusaders still came to Livonia. Thirteen noble volunteers were captured by the Poles at the battle of Wilkomierz, six of them close relations of the master, marshal or commanders. In 1439 the Lord of Gleichen (Thuringia) was serving as a 'guest' in Livonia. These errant lords may not have been much help from the strictly military point of view, but they were part of a wider affiliation with the society of the lower Rhine and Westphalia, where there was a general feeling that the Livonian knight-brothers did a useful job in protecting Hanseatic traders along the Novgorod route. The occasion of the war of 1443–8 was an outrage committed on an interpreter hired by the junker Gerard, uncle of the duke of Cleves, who was then negotiating between the master and the grand-master. Some Russians hacked off the man's feet, hands and head; the junker insisted on reparations from Novgorod, and five years later Master von Overbergen declared war in his name. As long as there was a risk of piracy, robbery and arrest along the north-eastern trade-route, the Livonian masters could count on German support for their occasional forays into Russia.

The *rapprochement* between the Eastern and Western Churches in the 1430s and 1440s did nothing to improve relations between the Livonians and the Russians. Among the Orthodox prelates who signed the decree of union between the churches at Florence in 1439 was the Russian metropolitan Isidore, but when Isidore came home he was not made welcome; 'he began the naming of the pope of Rome in his services, and other new things which we had never heard since the baptism of the Russian Land', complained the Novgorod chronicler,[196] and he was eventually hounded back to Rome. His protector, Pope Eugenius IV, wrote to Grand-Master von Erlichshausen advising him that now the Order 'is not troubled by infidels' the money collected for the purposes of reconciliation with the Orthodox Church ought to be spent on subjugating or exterminating the archbishop of Riga and others who supported the authority of the council against that of the papacy. 'Destroy them, or they will destroy you', was the pope's message.[197] Nevertheless, the Livonians pressed on with the war against Novgorod.

The outcome of that war was an armistice that left Novgorodian and Livonian garrisons eyeing each other across the river Narva. Upstream, and on either shore of Lake Chud, the antagonists were the Order and the bishop of Dorpat to the west, and Pskov to the east. Fort and counter-fort marked the frontier; the Order's Nyenslot, and the Russian Nyenslot, on the upper Narva; the bishop's Nyenhus (Neuhausen) and Izborsk, south of the Lake; the archbishop of Riga's Marienhausen, and the Pskovian outposts at Vishegorodok and Ostrov, on the Velikaya. The fact that this frontier was held against Pskov by three different and sometimes discordant authorities gave the Russians a certain advantage; it was possible to raid Dorpat without necessarily offending the master of Livonia. In 1458, Master von Mengden's involvement with the war in Prussia encouraged Pskov to begin raiding the Livonians, and in 1463 the Russians laid siege to Nyenhus with 'mennigerleye wunderlike instrument'[198] and took the castle. Von Mengden sent an emissary speeding to Italy to warn the pope that the province was in great danger, but the situation in Prussia was even worse; the bishop of Dorpat's lost marcher land could not be recovered while the master was husbanding all his resources to save the grand-master from the Poles.

Behind the assertiveness of this small Russian frontier-state lay the growing power of the great eastern principality of Moscow, where Pskov was seen as a useful check on both Novgorod and the Lithuanians. A formal alliance was concluded soon after the fall of Nyenhus, and Muscovite troops arrived to secure the surrounding territory. Hitherto, the grand-princes of Moscow had intervened in this area only at the request of Novgorod, and in dire emergencies such as the Swedish crusade of 1348. Normally they were too busy with their Mongol overlords to pursue an aggressive policy towards their western neighbours, and distance delayed and limited their military expeditions. It was over 350 miles from Moscow to Novgorod, and another 140 to Pskov, so that no invading army could accomplish more than a short season of devastation.

The situation changed when Grand-Prince Ivan III, now virtually free of Mongol supremacy, began the 'gathering in of patrimonial lands' – that is to say, the annexation of all surviving Russian principalities under Muscovite rule. His ancestors had been called in to save Novgorod from the Swedes in the 1320s and in 1348, but the Novgorodian commonwealth had retained and reasserted its independence thereafter, despite occasional Muscovite intrusion. By 1471 Ivan was ready to put an end to this unsteady relationship, and make use of his gigantic military strength to incorporate the oligarchy of boyars into his autocracy. His ultimate design of wresting former Russian lands from the Lithuanian grand-duchy made it essential to root out the pro-Lithuanian faction within that oligarchy, and in that year he invaded Novgorod, overwhelmed the city's forces, and compelled the boyars to submit and hand over those who were designated friends of 'the Latin king' of Poland– Lithuania. From 1471 to 1489 Ivan reduced Novgorod by stages to a humbled and demoralized dependency of Moscow, without a parliament or a policy of its own; Pskov was his willing collaborator, and all the resources of north-west Russia could be pressed into the service of his great war with Lithuania. The Teutonic Knights of Livonia found themselves confronted by an Orthodox super-power, able to take action against them as masterfully as the king of Poland had dealt with Prussia. Moreover, the Muscovites, like the Livonians, interpreted their expansion as a crusade; a crusade to save the western and northern Russians from the godless rites of the Latin Church.

The danger was understood as early as 1471, when Master Wolthus von Herse wrote to the grand-master that, if Pskov and Novgorod were to join forces with Moscow, 'we shall then have to make peace on their terms, and resign to them all they extort from us, or else we will have to wage war against them all'.[199]

Wolthus planned an anti-Russian alliance with Lithuania, but he was deposed before he could go to war. His successor, Bernard von der Borg, reacted to Novgorod's second submission to Ivan in 1478 by attempting to gain control of Pskov on his own. On New Year's Day 1480 he led a full muster of the Livonian army to the Velikaya and attacked the city of Pskov, but had to retire without doing more than sacking Vyshegorodok. On 20 January he reached Pskov again, and ravaged the country thereabouts while another force raided Gdov, on the east bank of Lake Chud. The Pskovians sent to Ivan for assistance, and in February a Muscovite army under Prince Andrew Obolensky retaliated with a rapid but devastating thrust through the bishopric of Dorpat and the Order's commandery of Fellin. Then he went home; he was needed elsewhere. The master hit back with a *reysa* to Izborsk, round Pskov, and over to the other side of the lake, where he was said to have killed over 3000 Russians at Kobyliye.

But he failed to take Pskov, or Izborsk, and Ivan's refusal to be drawn into an extended war suggests that there was little chance of his doing so. Master von der Borg was deposed by his commanders, after quarrelling with both the archbishop of Riga and his own knights, and incurring the ban of Pope Sixtus IV. His successor, Johann Freitag von Loringhoven (1483–94), was too much occupied with Riga to take action against the Russians, but he succeeded in crushing the burghers so decisively that by the end of his mastership Livonia was a more disciplined commonwealth than before. At the same time, Ivan III decided to establish a permanent Muscovite presence on the Livonian border, and built the great fort of Ivangorod to overlook the Estonian frontier town of Narva from the east bank of the river. The *afspröke* (agreement) of Wolmar in 1491, between Order, bishops and burghers, made it possible for the Livonians to wage war again; Ivangorod, the year after, made war both possible and probable, although the immediate consequence was a renegotiated peace treaty.

The new master, Wolter von Plettenberg, was a typical product of the Livonian system. His family were landowners near Soest, in Westphalia, from where so many knights and merchants had travelled to the eastern Baltic since the twelfth century. They had branches in Westphalia, branches in Livonia, and members in the Order. He went out to the fort at Narva when he was ten, and worked his way up the hierarchy of offices until he became marshal. Having hammered the burghers of Riga with success, he was elected master in 1494, while in his forties; a quiet, shrewd, decent and experienced man, so it was said. For the first seven years of his mastership, Livonia was under the shadow of impending invasion. Each side committed offences against the other that were held to justify a breaking of the peace at any time.

The grand-prince closed down the Hanseatic office at Novgorod and imprisoned the German merchants trading there – not such a bad thing for Livonia, which would then became the main centre of North-Eastern trade, but some of the imprisoned merchants were Livonians. The citizens of Reval expressed their feelings by executing two Russians – one for passing bad money, one for buggery. The master got the Emperor Maximilian to appeal to the German princes for help for Livonia; a few volunteers took ship for Riga. Next year, 1496, Ivan was at war with the Swedish regent, Sten Sture, and a Swedish armada sailed over from Viborg and took Ivangorod; some Estonians helped them pillage the fortress, and, when the Swedes left, they bequeathed the place to the Order. Soon afterwards, the Russians were preparing a bridge to cross the Narva, and skirmishing broke out along the frontier. Von Plettenberg had to face the fact that Livonia, with a total levy strength of under 10,000 men, was drifting into war with a power that could mobilize several armies of up to 20,000.

He began his search for allies by approaching King John of Denmark–Norway (and, for the time being, Sweden); but John would help only in return for the former Danish duchy of Estonia. His father, Christian I, had reassumed the title of duke of Estonia in 1456, but to demand the country itself was asking too much. Then Wolter turned to the king of Poland's brother, Grand-Duke Alexander of Lithuania, Ivan's chief enemy, and after a visit to Vilnius concluded the offensive alliance known as the treaty of Wenden, on 21 June 1501. He persuaded the estates to pay for the hire of mercenaries, and 2000 German cavalrymen and *lanzknechte* arrived on the boat from Lübeck. He was matching a corps of heavy-armed professionals, backed by an amateur levy of squires and native tenants, against a threat of incalculable but superior strength: an old formula, which had not always proved successful in the past, and was now to be tested to the limit. The dream of a joint Latin invasion of Russia might now be revived – provided the Lithuanian and Livonian armies could be brought to act in concert.

This was not what happened. Alexander was detained by the unexpected death of his brother and the need to secure the throne of Poland for himself. Von Plettenberg marched to Izborsk, won a victory on the Seriza with his field-guns, and then waited in vain at the appointed rendezvous at Ostrov on the Velikaya. He destroyed Ostrov (7 September 1501) and marched home. His war of conquest had become a struggle for survival; Muscovite armies were *en route* for Livonia, and von Plettenberg had to face them on his own with the knights of his Order – some 430 – and a reduced number of hired men. The Russians arrived in November, and for six weeks central Livonia was systematically devastated by three separate armies, which von Plettenberg could do nothing to stop. When he summoned a *Landtag* to Wolmar in January, three of the bishops and the vassals of Estonia failed to attend. The commonwealth was divided, half the country in ruins and the other half demoralized; another Russian invasion followed, this time assisted by 7000 Tartars and 1600 tracking dogs to nose out fugitives. When the master sent to Lithuania begging for help, his ally merely told him to fight on.

That he did so was for centuries a source of pride and self-congratulation to the German ascendancy in the Baltic, and won for von Plettenberg the status of a hero among German nationalists. There is no disputing his skill as a general; but it might be worth inquiring whether his policy of waging offensive war against Moscow was not simply a disastrous mistake. The Lithuanian alliance might well have proved a source of strength, but the risk of defeat or non-co-operation was always present, and for Livonia this could mean extinction, or at least subjugation. On the other hand, war with Moscow appeared inevitable by 1500, and neither an offensive nor a defensive strategy seemed to offer much chance of success; von Plettenberg was seizing his only opportunity of doing something. He could in theory have submitted to Ivan, but in practice the training and attitudes of the Livonian Knights made this unthinkable: they had too much to lose, and the long tradition of the crusade against the schismatics forbade them. The master had little choice in carrying on with his last-ditch stand. It was fortunate that in his mercenary troops, his field- and handguns, he had the same technological advantage that his predecessors had so often exploited against superior numbers in the past.

In August 1502, the frightened Estates met and agreed to mobilize the country for one more campaign. For three days after the Nativity of the Virgin (8 September) Livonia fasted and prayed; then von Plettenberg marched on Pskov with all his knight-brothers, some 3500 hired foot and horse, a train of guns and the Livonian levy-troops. At Lake Smolina, on the eve of the Exaltation of the Cross (14 September), he fought his way through the Muscovites by gunfire and cavalry charges; both armies limped away from the battlefield, but there were no further invasions of Livonia that or the following year. It was alleged that the master had seen the Virgin in a vision, and had promised her a pilgrimage to Jerusalem in return for victory. A curiously old-fashioned story,[200] in the circumstances; for only in a superficial sense was von Plettenberg re-enacting the Livonian past.

Russians had invaded Lithuania before, and small armies, or forts, had resisted and repelled these invasions. Livonia's chances of conquering or being conquered by the schismatic easterners had in those times aroused concern and intervention from Rome, Germany and Scandinavia. The province of St Mary had then had a standing and importance of its own, as an outpost of the Latin faith. In 1502 the antagonism which had formerly been concentrated into the Livonian–Russian frontier had been extended into a war between much greater powers – Muscovy and Lithuania–Poland, neither much concerned with the future of Livonia except as a possible dependency. As far as the pope was concerned, the danger to Livonia was far less important than the danger of the Ottoman advance into Europe. From 1495 to 1503 the Order's proctor at Rome continually begged for a crusading Bull on behalf of von Plettenberg, but to no effect: Alexander VI was anxious to get the Russians as allies against the Turks. The last serious plea for a Northern crusade – in the tract entitled *Eyme schonne hysthorie* – fell on deaf ears. Ivan III made peace with von Plettenberg at Pskov in 1503, and the province was granted another fifty years grace before the serious invasions began; it had become a counter in a game played by more successful imperialist powers, any one of which could deploy far more men and guns than the Livonians. The local marcher warfare between Baltic colonists, which had been conceived of as a confrontation between the Greek and Latin faiths, had been superseded by a struggle for power between Muscovy, Poland and Sweden in which the medieval concept of the Holy War had no importance, except to the Russians.

The Livonian Knights, who personified that concept, held on to their position as a Catholic corporation garrisoning the strongholds of a partly Lutheran colony for as long as their more powerful neighbours allowed. A series of invasions beginning in 1557 annihilated their diminutive army and obsolete castles, and after the last master, Kettler, had renounced his vows and become a secular duke (on 5 March 1562) the old commonwealth was partitioned between Muscovy, Poland, Sweden and Denmark. When the Prussian knights had done this, the Livonian nobles had advised Master Plettenberg to follow their example and secularize the province. He had refused, because in his opinion the Livonians were too weak and divided to resist the Muscovites without reinforcement by the German Order. When he was proved right, Catholic apologists wrung their hands and pointed to the backsliding of the Knights themselves. 'As long as the knightes of the Order in Lifelande kepte and maintained the Catholike faith ... ten thousand coulde in open filde put to flighte fourescore thousand of the Moscovites: but sens that the same worshypfull Order put downe the awncient religion, ... all the victory hath enclined to our adversaries' – so F. Staphylus, in *Apologia Recens* (Cologne 1562), translated for English readers by Thomas Stapleton, as a warning against the demoralizing effects of 'the newe ghospell of Luther'.

A broadsheet published at Nuremberg advertised the plight of the martyred Livonian Germans to their fellow-countrymen. The coloured woodcut showed furry Muscovites firing arrows into three naked women hanging from a bough, to which the hearts of their children have been tied. The little bodies lie below them on the grass. The imagery is that of old-time crusading rhetoric (see above, pp. 124, 196) but the responses were cool or calculating. The appeal and the apparatus of Holy War had been diverted by other causes more pressing than the defence of 'the old soiourne and retire of the Saxon Nobilite'.

CONCLUSION

In this survey, the Northern crusades have been treated as the result of a change in outlook which took place among the Scandinavian and German peoples during the twelfth century. Their rulers began looking at their eastern neighbours in a new and religious light, similar to the light in which other Europeans had already come to view the Muslims of Palestine and Spain. Their wars took on a new meaning, and led to unprecedented results. And these results – the complex of innovations which made up the Latinized east Baltic – confirmed and elaborated the outlook from which they sprang. For most of the Middle Ages, a powerful body of Catholic opinion saw the Baltic provinces as a Christian frontier held by armies of the true faith against a hostile outer world of heathendom and schism.

This approach in no way overlooks the fact that the wars against the heathen of the North were fought for the same reason as other wars. The belligerents wanted to capture trade-routes, to win land for the land-hungry, to increase the revenues and reputations of princes and prelates, to prevent piracy, to secure larger shares of natural resources, or any share at all of loot. These motives were always present. But they do not explain why the fighting was construed as a crusade, or why it was necessary to set in motion the machinery of preaching, privilege and redemption. If it was all about fish, fur and wax, or Danish, Swedish and German expansion, there was no need to pretend that it was holy. Moreover, there was no reason why so many outsiders, from the popes to the knights of England, France and Burgundy, should join in. The kings and monastic knights of the Baltic stood to gain more in material ways than those outsiders, but, even with them, the profit motive is not a convincing explanation. They were certainly profiteers, but among their means of getting wealth crusading wars cannot have ranked high. The risk of failure and the cost of warfare were too great, and the practical gains too meagre, to make the books show a profit.

To present these wars as false – either as matters of interest disguised as matters of conscience, or simply as misnamed events – is too easy. This type of judgement is itself fraudulent. It avoids the unavoidable question of why men who were never reluctant to wage war for profit, fame, vengeance or merely to pass the time, without any disguise or pretext, nevertheless chose to claim that certain wars were fought for God's honour and the redemption of mankind. The answer must be that this claim was regarded at the time as no less real than, say, Edward III's claim to France, or the king of Denmark's claim to Estonia, or the baronage of England's claim to represent the community of the realm: logically unsound, perhaps, but worth fighting for, and usually worth a sum of money as well.

There is little point in trying to distinguish between crusades undertaken for pure or spiritual motives and those that were political, papalist, perverted or corrupt in aim, execution or effect (between the First Crusade, and the Fourth, to take the commonest example). Such criticisms were made throughout the Middle Ages and applied to all crusades. They spring rather from the essential ambiguity of the idea, rather than from any measurable failure of idealism. It was never possible to convince all Catholics that crusades were a good thing, nor was it necessary. Holy Wars, like monasteries, provided an outlet for some, but not for all. A crusade was both a religious movement and (after *c*. 1185) an enterprise that had to conform to certain legal restrictiojns: it had to be decreed by the pope, preached by the Church, dignified by the granting of privileges and indulgences to recruits, and justified by reference to the interests of Christendom. The Northern crusades were inspired by intermittent local enthusiasm; by appeals from Rome, and by the commission to wage perpetual Holy War which was granted to the Teutonic Knights. It therefore seems legitimate to treat 300 years of diverse warfare as the story of one recurrent phenomenon, and to deal more with the ideas and organization that provided the unifying theme than with the other motives and concerns of the crusaders. Nor is there space for more.

From this point of view, the Northern crusades began as a consequence of the closer involvement of the Baltic world with the civilization of Latin Christendom in the twelfth century. During this period the idea of the Holy War was grafted onto Baltic affairs to meet a need felt by those who wanted to conquer or convert the heathen coastlands, and who had been schooled in or touched by the Jerusalem crusade. These men were not one group, and their aims were not identical, but, in so far as they had a common cause, the Holy War defined it and gave it a structure and a meaning. After the experiments which were tried from the 1140s to the 1200s, a variety of crusading institutions took root: the German monastic Orders of knighthood, the monastic and episcopal states, the papal legations, the cross-wearing kings and kingdoms, and the colonies in conquered lands. Out of the conquests of 1200–1300 two of these institutions emerged as the strongest: the Teutonic Order and the Swedish kingdom. From the 1270s onwards the continuance of the Holy War was entrusted to these two in particular by the papacy. Neither succeeded in overthrowing the non-Catholic powers against which the war was directed, Lithuania and Novgorod–Pskov. Yet both preserved the gains of the thirteenth century against counter-attack, and kept alive the idea on which the enterprise was founded.

Sweden ceased to play a part in this movement after the dying out of the Folkung dynasty in the 1360s and the incorporation of the kingdom into Queen Margaret's Scandinavian Union. The defining of the Russo-Swedish frontier continued to be a cause of friction under the Union, and occasionally of concern to the papacy, but generated no more crusades. When a Russian war broke out again in the 1490s, the cause of Catholicism was invoked, but in vain.

The Teutonic Order was outmanoeuvred in Prussia by the Polish–Lithuanian alliance, and during the fifteenth century found it increasingly difficult to sustain the crusade tradition in this area, owing to the fact that the Turk had replaced the Lithuanian as the leading non-Catholic power confronting Eastern Europe. The tradition was adopted to justify the defence of Prussia against Catholic foes and the maintenance of the *status quo* inside the province, but could not attract the outside support that was needed for survival.

In Livonia, the Order and its partners kept up the intermittent war on Russian Orthodoxy for longer, but the rise of Muscovy and the near-disaster of 1501–2 made it clear that the price of continuing this war would be annihilation. Both here and in Prussia the driving out of devils by armed force in the thirteenth and fourteenth centuries had raised up devils seven times stronger.

The start of the Northern crusades had marked a phase in the bringing together of peoples into a common Catholic civilization. Was their end a symptom of the dissolution of that civilization? No. The Baltic was still a Catholic lake in 1500, and the Baltic states were thoroughly integrated members of the Catholic family, some two generations after the crusading had ended. Catholic interests could no longer be served by continuing the Holy War in this region; that was the difference. The rise of Muscovy, Lithuania–Poland and the triple monarchy of Scandinavia was a political revolution which meant that the defence, and extension, of the faith in North-East Europe depended almost wholly on relations between these powers, and the Teutonic Order in Prussia and Livonia was (after 1466) too feeble to count as more than a makeweight.

FURTHER READING

This list is meant for the student with no knowledge of German, or any of the Slav or Scandinavian languages.

I. NORTH-EAST EUROPE ON THE EVE OF THE CRUSADES

The contemporary sources of geographical information, Adam of Bremen's *Gesta Hammaburgensis ecclesiae pontificum*, Helmold's *Chronica Slavorum*, and the lives of Otto of Bamberg by Ebbo and Herbord have been translated, the first two by F. J. Tschan – *The History of the Archbishops of Hamburg–Bremen* (New York, 1959) and *Chronicle of the Slavs* (New York, 1935) – and the last by C. H. Robinson, as *The Life of Otto, Apostle of Pomerania* (London, 1920). *Olaus Magnus: A Description of the Northern Peoples* vol. 1, ed. Peter Foote (London, 1996) is a translation of books 1–5 of *De Gentibus Septentrionalibus*. W. R. Mead, *The Historical Geography of Scandinavia* (London, 1981) is the most concise and informative survey, especially chapters 2 and 3, and on Denmark and Sweden in this period see Birgit and Peter Sawyer, *Medieval Scandinavia* (Minneapolis, 1993). Not much of the recent literature on West Slav civilization has been translated into English, but on their towns see Helen Clarke and Björn Ambrosiani, *Towns in the Viking Age* (Leicester, 1991 and 1995), chapter 6, and on their origins Pavel Dolukhanov, *The Early Slavs* (Harlow, 1996). The creation of Russia has been ably reconstructed by Simon Franklin and Jonathan Shepard in *The Emergence of Rus 750–1200* (Harlow, 1996). M. Gimbutas, *The Balts* (London, 1963) remains useful on the early history and religion of this group. R. E. Burnham, *Who are the Finns? A Study of Prehistory* (London, 1946), and A. Sauvageot, *Les Anciens finnois* (Paris, 1961). On the Lapps (Sami) see Knut Odner in *Norwegian Archaeological Review*, XVIII (1985), and Inger Storli in the same journal, XXVI (1993); also Inger Zachrisson in *Social Approaches*, ed. Ross Samson (Glasgow, 1991), 191–9.

Janet Martin has investigated the medieval fur-trade in *Treasure from the Land of Darkness* (Cambridge, 1986) and the concept of a 'circumbaltic' culture (Nylen) colours several articles in *Society and Trade in the Baltic during the Viking Age*, ed.

Sven-Olof Lindquist (Visby, 1985). For new approaches to medieval Baltic navigation see C. Westerdahl, 'The use of maritime space', *Medieval Europe*, 11 (1992) (York). For trading and military interaction with the East: Thomas S. Noonan, 'The Nature of Medieval Russian–Estonian relations 850–1015', *Baltic History* (1974) was seminal.

2. THE WENDISH CRUSADE IN THEORY AND PRACTICE, 1147–85

On the genesis of the crusading movement in general, see C. Erdmann, *The Origin of the Idea of Crusade*, trs. M. W. Baldwin and W. Goffart (Princeton, 1977); and for an alternative view, C. Tyerman, 'Were there any crusades in the twelfth century?', *English Historical Review*, CX (1995) and J. Riley-Smith, *The First Crusade and the Idea of Crusading* (London, 1995). On the Pomeranian missions, R. Bartlett, 'The Conversion of a Pagan Society in the Middle Ages', *History*, LXX (1985), and for Slav–Dane relations T. Damgaard-Sørensen, 'Danes and Wends' in *People and Places* (Woodbridge, 1991), ed. I. Wood and N. Lund. A sketch of the mission–crusade connection is in Elizabeth Siberry, 'Missionaries and Crusades' in *The Church and War*, ed. W. J. Shiels (*Studies in Church History*, XX (1983)).

Sources for the 1147 campaign are Helmond (trs. Tschan, as above); book XIV of *Saxo Grammaticus* (trs. E. Christiansen, British Archaeological Reports int. ser. 84 and 118): and *Knytlinga Saga*, trs. H. Palsson and Paul Edwards (Odense, 1986). On Saxo, see Inge Skovgaard-Petersen, 'Saxo, Historian of the Patria', *Mediaeval Scandinavia*, 11 (1969) and B. Sawyer 'Valdemar, Absalon and Saxo', *Revue Belge de Philologie et d'Histoire*, LXIII (1985), 685–705.

For a new archaeological perspective on the crucial development of Lübeck, see Günter P. Fehring, 'Origins and Development of Slavic and German Lübeck', *From the Baltic to the Black Sea*, ed. D. Austin and L. Alcock (London, 1990). Work by Friedrich Lotter, Hans-Dietrich Kahl and Tore Nyberg has superseded earlier interpretations of the Wendish wars and crusades, and Lotter's is abridged as 'The Crusading Ides and the Conquest of the Region East of the Elbe' in *Medieval Frontier Societies*, ed. R. Bartlett and A. Mackay (Oxford, 1989). See also *The Second Crusade and the Cistercians*, ed. M. Gervers (New York, 1991), for H.-D. Kahl, 'Crusade Eschatology as Seen by St Bernard' and K. Guth, 'The Pomeranian Missionary Journey of Otto of Bamberg and the Crusade Movement'.

3. THE ARMED MONKS: IDEOLOGY AND EFFICIENCY

Malcolm Barber, *The New Knighthood* (Cambridge, 1994) is unmatched on the Templars. A. Forey, 'The Emergence of the Military Orders', *Journal of Ecclesiastical History*, XXXVI (1985), and *The Military Orders* (London, 1992) shed light on the German Orders, as does the useful Helen Nicholson, *Templars, Hospitallers and Teutonic Knights: Images of the Military Orders* (Leicester, 1993); and for valuable work on the recruiting of lay crusaders, James M. Powell, *Anatomy of a Crusade* (Philadelphia, 1986). But the essential work on the Teutonic Knights and their mission is in German. Lotter, Wippermann, Paravicini, Boockmann, Kahl, Nowak, Benninghoven, Hellmann and Sarnowsky have all published books or articles over the last twenty years, and have superseded earlier research. The series *Quellen und Studien zur Geschichte des Deutschen Ordens* is now over fifty volumes long, and continues to debouch from Marburg.

However, Heldrungen's eyewitness account of the amalgamation of the Sword-Brothers and the Teutonic Knights is translated from a sixteenth-century German version in Jerry Smith and William Urban's indispensable *The Livonian Rhymed Chronicle* (Bloomington, Indiana, 1977). And a caustic view of the Order's rule appears in Indrikis Stern, 'Crime and Punishment among the Teutonic Knights', *Speculum*, LVII (1982).

On German eastward emigration, the best survey is C. Higounet, *Les Allemands en Europe centrale et orientale au Moyen Age* (Paris, 1990); the German version has no index. The debate on the Order's relations with the emperor is summarized in English by Marian Dygo in 'The German Empire and the Grand Master of the Teutonic Order in the Light of the Golden Bull of Rimini', *Acta Poloniae Historica*, LX (1990).

For a general theory of west-European expansion in the Middle Ages, with particular reference to eastern Europe, there is Robert Bartlett, *The Making of Europe: Conquest, Colonization, and Cultural Change* (Princeton, 1993), chapters 2–3, 5–9.

4. THE CONQUEST OF THE EAST BALTIC LANDS, 1200–1292

J. A. Brundage, *The Chronicle of Henry of Livonia* (Madison, Wis., 1961), provides the indispensable source for the subjugation of Estonia and Livonia and Jerry Smith and William Urban have translated *The Livonian Rhymed Chronicle* (Bloomington, 1977) with brief but excellent notes.

Livonia: A rapid sketch is contained in E. Johnson, 'The German Crusade in the Baltic', *A History of the Crusades*, ed. K. M. Setton, III (Madison, Wis., 1975), and a detailed account of the Livonian wars in W. Urban, *The Baltic Crusade* (De Kalb, Ill., 1975). See also W. Urban, 'The Organization of the Defense of the Livonian Frontier in the Thirteenth Century', *Speculum* (1973), and his much expanded second edition of *The Baltic Crusade* (Chicago, 1994).

Prussia: On Danish involvement with the mission, Stella Szacherska, 'Valdemar II's expedition to Pruthenia', *Mediaeval Scandinavia*, XII (1988).

For the conquest of Prussia, see K. Gorski, 'The Teutonic Order in Prussia',

Medievalia et humanistica, XVII (1966), and 'L'Ordre theutonique: un nouveau point de vue', *Revue historique*, CCXXX (1963); also M. Biskup, 'Teutonic Order State Organization', *Acta Poloniae historica*, III (1960). There is no translation of the main source, Peter of Dusburg's Chronicle, which is in *Scriptores rerum Prussicarum*, ed. T. Hirsch, M. Toeppen and E. Strehlke (Leipzig, 1861–74), 1, and was reprinted at Darmstadt in 1984 with introduction, notes and German translation by C. Scholz and D. Wojtecki.

Estonia: P. Rebane, 'Denmark, the Papacy and the Christianization of Estonia' is in *Gli inizi del Cristianesimo in Livonia–Lettonia*, ed. A. Weiss, *et al.* for Pontificio comitato di Scienze Storiche, Atti e Documenti (Vatican, 1989–90).

Finland: For the Swedish background see Sawyer and Sawyer, *Medieval Scandinavia* (see above, chapter 1) and John Lind, 'Early Russian–Swedish Rivalry', *Scandinavian Journal of History*, XVI/4 (1991); for the Finns, *A History of Finland*, ed. E. Jutikkala (London, 1962), chapters 1–3 (by K. Pirinen). On St Eric, there is a fine analysis of the evidence by J. E. Cross, 'St Eric of Sweden', *Saga-Book*, XV pt 4 (1961), with a translation of the 'standard legend'. On the early missions, see C. L. A. Oppermann, *The English Missionaries in Sweden and Finland* (London, 1937), and J. Gallén, *La Province de Dacia de l'Ordre des frères prêcheurs* (Helsinki, 1946).

5. THE THEOCRATIC EXPERIMENT, 1200–1273

Standard works on the theory of papal monarchy (by Ullmann, J. A. Watt and B. Tierney) deserve sceptical assessment in so far as they stress the consistency and coherence of papal political initiatives. There is little in English on the relations between Rome and this region, but chapters 1–3 of J. Muldoon, *Popes, Lawyers and Infidels: the Church and the Non-Christian World 1250–1550* (Liverpool, 1979) are useful for canonist doctrine on missions and the heathen. There is a brief but useful note on 'Crusade and Mission' in Colin Morris, *The Papal Monarchy* (Oxford, 1989), 479–89. There are no English works on what the legates did in North-East Europe, or on the papal attitude towards the northern Russians. On these subjects, and the anti-Russian crusade, see W. Urban, *The Baltic Crusade* (De Kalb, Ill., 1975), 127–71, and M. Purcell, *Papal Crusading Policy* (Studies in the History of Christian Thought, XI, Leiden, 1975). *Preaching the Crusade* by Christoph Maier (Cambridge, 1994) covers the role of friars.

6. THE LITHUANIAN CRUSADE, 1283–1410

The broad history of this period is efficiently summarized in Jean W. Sedlar, *East Central Europe in the Middle Ages 1000–1500* (Washington, DC, 1994). William Urban's *The Samogitian Crusade* (Chicago, 1989) mostly concerns wars against Lithuania; see Giedroyc in *Journal of Baltic Studies*, XXII/4 (1991).

The rebirth of Lithuanian historical writing includes the outstanding contributions (in English) of M. Giedroyc (esp. in *Oxford Slavonic Papers*, XVIII (1985) and XIX (1987), S. C. Rowell (whose *Lithuania Ascending* (Cambridge, 1994) gives a detailed account of Lithuanian princely policies from the 1290s to the 1350s) and R. J. Mazeika, whose 'Of Cabbages and Knights', *Journal of Medieval History*, XX/1 (1994) concerns trade between the combatants. Rowell and Mazeika collaborate in 'Zelatores Maximi' (*Archivium Historiae Pontificiae*, XXXI (1993)) on the problems of co-ordinating Baltic missions in the period 1305–40. On Jogaila's conversion, nothing surpasses Giedroyc's 'Lithuanian Options prior to Kreva' in *La Cristianizzazione della Lituania* (Pontificio Comitato, Vatican, 1990): a collection with English contributions by Gimbutas, Urban, and Mazeika.

William Urban shed new light on Bacon's views of Holy War in 'Roger Bacon and the Teutonic Knights', *Journal of Baltic Studies*, XIX/4, 363–70, and see Muldoon (above, chapter 5). On the crusaders from the west, and their illusions, consult: L. Toulmin-Smith, *Expeditions to Prussia and the Holy Land made by Henry Earl of Derby*, Camden Society, 2nd Ser., LII (London, 1894); and F. du Boulay, 'Henry of Derby's Expeditions to Prussia 1390–1 and 1392', *The Reign of Richard II*, ed. F. du Boulay and C. Barron (London, 1971), 153–72 and Maurice Keen, 'Chaucer's Knight, the English Aristocracy, and the Crusade' in *English Court Culture*, ed. V. Scattergood (London, 1983). On notions of Lithuanian heathenism see Helmut Biorkhan, 'Les Croisades contre les paiens de Lituanie et de Prusse' in *La Croisade: réalités et fictions*, ed. D. Buschinger (Göppingen, 1989).

On peripheral subjects, see R. Cazelles, *Jean l'Aveugle* (Paris, 1947); P. W. Knoll, 'Wladyslaw Lokietek and the Restoration of the *Regnum Poloniae*', *Medievalia et humanistica*, XVII (1966); and his *The Rise of the Polish Monarchy: Piast Poland in East Central Europe 1320–70* (Chicago, 1972).

The essential source for Russo-Lithuanian relations in the thirteenth century has been edited and translated, with notes, by G. A. Perfecky as *The Hypatian Codex Part Two: The Galician–Volynian Chronicle*, Harvard Series in Ukrainian Studies, XVI/1 (Munich, 1973).

7. THE CRUSADE AGAINST NOVGOROD, 1295–1378

The various Novgorod chronicles (down to 1446) were merged by R. Michell and N. Forbes as *The Chronicle of Novgorod*, Camden Society, 3rd ser., XXV (London, 1914), and for the Russian side there is J. Fennell, 'The Campaign of King Magnus Eriksson against Novgorod in 1348: An Examination of the Sources', *Jahrbücher für Geschichte Osteuropas*, I (1966), rectified with needless acerbity by John Lind in 'The Russian Sources of King Magnus Eriksson's Campaign', *Mediaeval Scandinavia*, XII (1988). Fennell's *The Emergence of Moscow* (London,

1968) is still the best account of fourteenth-century politics, to be prefaced by reading his *The Crisis of Medieval Russia* (London/New York, 1983) and C. J. Halperin, *Russia and the Golden Horde* (London, 1987).

For Magnus's reign in Sweden, see F. D. Scott, *Sweden: The Nation's History* (Minneapolis, 1977), 69–79, and, on St Bridget, C. Bergendorff, 'A Critic of the Fourteenth Century: St Birgitta of Sweden' in *Medieval and Historiographical Essays in Honour of James Westfall Thompson*, ed. J. Cate and E. Anderson (Chicago, 1938), 3–18. For Norway's part in the war, see K. Selnes, 'Un conflit norvégo-russe au Moyen Age', *Scando-Slavica*, VIII (1962).

There are relevant articles in English by Häme (on the Far North in sagas), Julku (on the treaties of 1323 and 1326) and Vahtola (on Karelian mobility) in the first volume of *Nordkalotten i en skiftande värld*, ed. K. Julku Rovaniemi, 1987/88.

Thomas Noonan, 'Medieval Russia, the Mongols, and the West. Novgorod's relations with the Baltic 1100–1350', *Medieval Studies*, XXXVII (1975) remains indispensable. For the involvement of Livonia in these wars, consult William Urban, *The Livonian Crusade* (Washington, DC, 1981), which concerns the period 1300–1583.

8. THE CRUSADING STATES OF NORTH-EAST EUROPE

On the Order and the Hansa, consult P. Dollinger, *The German Hansa*, trs. D. S. Ault and S. H. Steinberg (London, 1970), and M. Postan, *The Cambridge Economic History of Europe*, II (Cambridge, 1952), 223–32, and E. Lönnroth, ibid., III (Cambridge, 1963), 361–96. See also A. von Brandt, 'Recent Trends in Research in Hanseatic History', *History*, XLI (1957).

On Livonia, see J. Leighley, *The Towns of Mediaeval Livonia*, University of California Publications in Geography, VI, no. 7 (1939), and Z. Ligers, *Histoire des Villes de Lettonie et d'Esthonie* (Paris, 1946). A Schwabe, *Agrarian History of Latvia* (Riga, n.d.) is useful but rare.

On Danish Estonia see T. Riis, *Les Institutions politiques centrales du Danemark 1100–1332* (Odense, 1977), 323–36, and P. Rebane, 'The Danish Bishops of Tallinn 1260–1346', *Journal of Baltic Studies*, V (1974) and Niels Skyum-Nielsen, 'Estonia under Danish Rule' in *Danish Medieval History: New Currents*, ed. Skyum-Nielsen and N. Lund (Copenhagen, 1981). On the merging of beliefs among native Estonians: Ivar Paulson, *The Old Estonian Folk Religion* (Bloomington, 1971), and for a nationalist survey of the period: E. Uustalu, *The History of the Estonian People* (London, 1952), 49–66: 'Estonia under the rule of the Teutonic Order'.

The vast German literature on Prussia under the Order is almost entirely untranslated; pp. 52–89 of F. L. Carsten, *The Origins of Prussia* (Oxford, 1954) – a good outline of the settlement. An informative illustrated survey of the whole range of the Teutonic Knights' achievements is F. Benninghoven's catalogue for the 1990 Berlin exhibition: *Unter Kreuz und Adler* (Berlin, 1990).

There is a collection of good photographs of the Order's castles in Prussia and Livonia in A. Winnig, *Der Deutsche Ritterorden and seine Burgen, Die Blauen Bücher* (Königstein im Taunus, n.d.); the text is wholly unexplanatory. For sculpture, see K. H. Clasen, *Die Mittelalterliche Bildhauerkunst im Deutschordensland Preussen*, 2 vols (Berlin, 1939); and C. Wünsch, *Ostpreussen, Die Kunst im Deutschen Osten* (Berlin, 1960), includes many illustrations. On the Order's literature, the standard works (W. Zeisemer, *Die Litteratur des deutschen Order in Preussen* (Breslau, 1928); C. H. G. Helm and W. Zeisemer, *Die Litteratur des deutschen Ritterorden* (Giessen, 1951) are naturally in German, but there is M. E. Goenner, *Mary-Verse of the Teutonic Knights* (Washington, DC, 1943), and Marian Dygo, 'The political role of the cult of the Virgin Mary in Teutonic Prussia', *Journal of Medieval History*, xv (1989). On the ideology of the Order as a whole, see the excellent Mary Fisher, *Die Himels Rote: the Idea of Christian Chivalry in the Chronicles of the Teutonic Order* (Göppingen, 1991).

9. THE WITHERING OF THE CRUSADE, 1410–1525

G. C. Evans, *Tannenberg 1410: 1914* (London, 1970), is a good read. C. R. Jurgela, *Tannenberg* (New York, 1961), reconstructs the battle from a Lithuanian point of view, and the subject of Prusso-Russo-Lithuano-Polish relations is broadly covered in O. Halecki, *Borderlands of Western Civilization* (New York, 1952) 117–46, and G. Vernadsky, *The Mongols and Russia* (New Haven, Conn., 1953), chapter 4.

The sequence of events at Constance is best studied in the sources translated in *The Council of Constance: The Unification of the Church*, ed. J. H. Mundy and K. M. Woody, Records of Civilization LXIII (New York, 1961), and P. Glorieux, *Le Concile de Constance* (Ciresio's diary) (Tournai, 1964). On the Polish case against the Order, see S. F. Belch, *Paulus Vladimiri and His Doctrine Concerning International Law and Politics*, 2 vols (The Hague, 1965) – ardently Vladimirian. His works were published with Polish and English translations by Ludwik Ehrlich in 3 volumes as *Pisma Wybrane Pawla Wlodkowica* (Warsaw, 1968–9), and the infamous *Satira* of his opponent by H. Boockmann in his definitive *Johannes Falkenberg* (Göttingen, 1975), 312–53. There is an outline of the dispute between Poland and the Order in Muldoon (see above, chapter 5), 106–19, and for medieval theories of war, see F. H. Russell, *The Just War in the Middle Ages* (Cambridge, 1975).

For the narrative history of Prussia and Livonia from 1410 to 1525 there is still nothing outside German other than the antiquated Sieur de Wal, *Histoire de l'Ordre teutonique* (Paris, 1784–90), iv – vii; but for the social and political problems of Prussia there is the matchless Michael Burleigh, *Prussian Society and the German Order* (Cambridge, 1984) and his satellite articles: 'History, Privilege and Conspiracy Theories in Mid-fifteenth Century Prussia', *European History Quarterly*, XIV (1984), and 'Anticlericalism in Fifteenth Century Prussia: The Clerical Contribution Reconsidered', *The Church in Pre-Reformation Society*, ed. C. M. Barron and C. Meyer-Boll (Woodbridge, 1985). These are marred by partisanship on behalf of the Order's vassals, but remain the only readable work on the subject in any language. On relations with England, J. H. Wylie, *History of England under Henry the Fourth*, 4 vols (London, 1884–98) is worth consulting; also E. F. Jacob, *The Fifteenth Century* (Oxford, 1961), 356–60, and M. M. Postan, 'Anglo-Hanseatic Economic Relations', *English Trade in the Fifteenth Century*, ed. E. E. Power and M. M. Postan (London, 1933). A fuller treatment is in T. H. Lloyd, *England and the German Hanse 1157–1611* (Cambridge, 1991).

For the ascendancy of Moscow in the North, see J. Fennell, *Ivan the Great of Moscow* (London, 1961), and his 'Russia 1462–1583', ch. 18 of *The New Cambridge Modern History*, II (Cambridge, 1957), see also J. Raba, 'The Fate of the Novgorodian Republic', Slavic and East European Review, XLV (1967), and W. Westergard, 'Denmark, Russia and the Swedish Revolution 1480–1503', *Slavic and East European Review*, XVI (1937). There is a good map of the Russo-Swedish war of 1495–7 (map no. 30) in *Suomen Historian Kartasto*, ed. E. Jutikkala (Porvoo and Helsinki, 1959). For the ecclesiastical crisis within Novgorod, see J. L. Wieczynski, 'Archbishop Gennadius and the West', *Canadian–American Slavic Studies*, VI (1972). For an excellent study of the Livonian problem in the sixteenth century, consult W. Kirchner, *The Rise of the Baltic Question* (Newark, 1954) and David Kirby, *Northern Europe in the Early Modern Period* (Harlow, 1990); parts 1 and 2 contain the best summary of the relations of the Order and other powers in the sixteenth century.

The indiscipline of the Livonian knights is discussed by I. Sterns in *Speculum*, LVII (1982) as above, chapter 3.

In addition to the works in the above reading list, there are collections of Latin sources, which the reader will find listed below, in the 'References to Sources' section, under 'Abbreviations'. Those who know German are advised to consult the great bibliographies Dahlmann-Waitz, *Quellenkunde der Deutsche Geschichte*, 10th edn, vol. 1 (Stuttgart, 1969), section 26, nos 1153–75, and *Lieferung* 22–3 (*Estland und Lettland. Litauen*) and 27–8 (*Slaven*); Gebhardt, *Handbuch der deutschen Geschichte*, 9th edn, 4 vols (Stuttgart, 1970–6), esp. 1, 380–2 and 579–606; and Wattenbach-Schmale, *Deutschlands Geschichtsquellen im Mittelalter*, 1 (Darmstadt, 1976), esp. 419–41. *Documents on the Later Crusades*, ed. Norman Honsley (Basingstoke, 1996) includes translations from some sources used above: Wigard (no. 13), Eric Olai (no. 23), Capgrave (no. 24), Boucicant (no. 33), Vladimiri (no. 35) and Falkenberg (no. 36).

REFERENCES TO SOURCES

ABBREVIATIONS

Brundage   *The Chronicle of Henry of Livonia*, trs. J. Brundage (Madison, Wis., 1961).

CDP   *Codex diplomaticus Prussicus*, 6 vols, ed. J. Voigt (Königsberg, 1836–61).

CPD   *Codex Pomeraniae diplomaticus*, ed. K. Hasselbach, J. Kosegarten and F. von Medem (Greifswald, 1843–62).

DD I / II   *Diplomatarium Danicum*, ser. 1, 11, ed. L. Weibull, N. Skyum and H. Nielsen (Copenhagen, 1963).

DD I / III   *Diplomatarium Danicum*, ser. 1, 111, ed. C. A. Christensen, H. Nielsen, L. Weibull (Copenhagen, 1976).

DS   *Diplomatarium Suecanum*.

EK   *Erikskrönikan*, ed. R. Pipping, Samlingar utgivna av svenska fornskriftsällskapet CLVIII (Uppsala, 1921).

FD   *Förbindelsedikten*, ed. G. K. Klemming as 'Sammanfogningen mellan Gamla och Nya Krönikan' in *Svenska Medeltidens Rim-Krönikar* (Stockholm, 1865), 171–92.

FHL   *Fontes historiae Latviae medii aevi*, ed. A. Svabe (Riga, 1937–48).

FMU   *Finlands Medeltidsurkunder*, ed. R. Hausen, 1 (–1400) (Helsingfors, 1910).

LEKU   *Liv-, Esth-, und Curländisches Urkundenbuch*, 12 vols, ed. F. G. von Bunge (Reval and Riga, 1853–1910).

LR   *Livländische Reimchronik*, ed. F. Pfeiffer (Stuttgart, 1844).

MGH SS   *Monumenta Germaniae Historica: Scriptores rerum germanicarum*, ed. G. H. Pertz, T. Mommsen *et al.* (Hanover, Berlin &c) 1826–.

MPH   *Monumenta Poloniae historica*, 4 vols, ed. A. Bielowski (Lwow, 1864–84).

NC   *The Chronicle of Novgorod 1016–1471*, trs. R. Michell and N. Forbes, Camden Society, 3rd ser., XXV (London, 1914).

Perfecky   *The Hypatian Codex Part Two: The Galician–Volhynian Chronicle*, ed. and trs. G. A. Perfecky (Munich, 1973).

Perlbach   *Die Statuten des Deutschen Ordens*, ed. M. Perlbach (Halle, 1890).

PUB   *Preussisches Urkundenbuch*, 2 vols, ed. A. Seraphim, M. Hein and E. Maschke (Königsberg, 1909–39).

Saxo   Saxo Grammaticus, *Saxonis gesta Danorum*, ed. J. Olrik and H. Ræder (Copenhagen, 1931).

SMHD   *Scriptores minores historiae Danicae medii aevi*, 2 vols, ed. M. Gertz (Copenhagen, 1917–20).

SRP   *Scriptores rerum Prussicarum*, 5 vols, ed. T. Hirsch, M. Toeppen and E. Strehlke (Leipzig, 1861–74).

SS   E. Weise, *Die Staatschriften des Deutschen Ordens*, Veröffentlichungen der Niedersächsischen Archivverwaltung XXVII (Göttingen, 1970).

Tschan   *The Chronicle of the Slavs by Helmold, Priest of Bosau*, trs. F. J. Tschan (New York, 1966).

Trevisa   John Trevisa, *On the Properties of Things*, 2 vols, ed. M. C. Seymour (Oxford, 1975).

REFERENCES

NB. References made to translations of texts do not imply that the translation has been quoted; merely that the translation given corresponds to the passage referred to.

1. *NC*, 11.
2. *NC*, 76.
3. *Oeuvres de Ghillebert de Lannoy*, ed. C. Polvin and S. C. Houzeau (Louvain, 1878), 33.

4.   Pisces salsos et foetentes apportabant alii
    Palpitantes et recentes nunc apportant filii ...

Galli Chronicon, 11, 27 (*MPH*, 1, 447).
5. *Knytlinga Saga*, ch. 32, a mid-thirteenth-century source using twelfth-century statistics. C. af Petersen and E. Olson, *Sǫgur Danakonunga* (Copenhagen, 1919–25) 79–81.
6. Saxo, 497.
7. Herbord, *Vita Ottonis* (*MPH*, 11, 78).
8. Saxo, 357, 392.
9. *Corpus iuris Sueo-gotorum antiqui*, ed. H. Collin and C. Schlyter (Stockholm, 1827), 1, 300–1.
10. Roskilde Chronicle, ch. 17 (*SMHD*, 1, 30).
11. Charter to Lund cathedral, 6 Jan 1135 (DD 1/11, no. 63).
12. *Two of the Saxon Chronicles*, 2 vols, ed. C. Plummer and J. Earle (Oxford, 1952 reissue), 1, 221.

13. Herbord (*MPH*, 11, 88).
14. Saxo, 488.
15. Ebbo, *Vita Ottonis*, 111, 18 (*MPH*, 11, 67).
16. Saxo, 464–5.
17. Snorri Sturlason, *Magnuss Saga Blinda*, ch. 10, trs. L. M. Hollander, in *Heimskringla* (Austin, Tex., 1964) 726.
18. *De proprietatibus rerum*, xv, ch. 87 (Trevisa, 777).
19. Sturlason, *Heimskringla* (see note 17 above), 147.
20. Brundage, 190.
21. *De proprietatibus rerum*, xv, ch. 125 (Trevisa, 822).
22. *NC*, 36–7.
23. Gallus, *MPH*, 1, 455.
24. Saxo, 390.
25. Saxo, 419.
26. Tschan, 180.
27. '. . . non efficaciter set tamen obedienter complevimus' – Epistle 150 *Monumenta Corbeiensia*, ed. P. Jaffé, Bibliotheca rerum Germanicarum, 1 (Berlin, 1865), 245.
28. Vincent of Prague's Annals, Written 1167–71, *MGH SS*, xvii, 663.
29. Herbord, *MPH*, 11, 118.
30. Saxo, 432.
31. Saxo, 413.
32. Saxo, 458–9.
33. Tschan, 187–8.
34. Saxo, 395.
35. Tschan, 280.
36. Saxo, 551.
37. *DD* 1/11, no. 189. No copy of this Bull is dated by year.
38. *CPD*, no. 50.
39. *CPD*, no. 36.
40. *DD* 1/111, no. 27.
41. *Opera omnia*, 4 vols, ed. J. Mabillon (Paris, 1839), 1 (1252–78). See also his letter to his uncle Andrew, a Templar: B. S. James, *The Letters of St Bernard of Clairvaux* (London, 1953), 479.
42. *La Chanson de Roland*, ed. L. Gautier (Paris, 1920), lines 95–101.
43. M. Tumler, *Der Deutsche Orden im Wenden, Wachsen, und Wirken bis 1400* (Vienna, 1955), 603ff.
44. Cf. H. de Curzon, *Le Règle du Temple* (Paris, 1886); and Perlbach.
45. Other important thirteenth-century crusaders all came from central or eastern Germany; only Count Engelbert I of Mark (round Dortmund), in 1262, was from the Rhineland.
46. Tumler, *Der Deutsche Orden*, 389–90, 607–10.
47. Perlbach, 127.

48. *CDP*, III, nos. 48 and 96.

49. T. Dzyalinski, *Lites ac res gestae inter Polonos Ordinemque*, 2 vols (Poznan, 1855), I, 117, 121, 136, 150, 182, 194–205.

50. *Chronica terre Prussie*, ed. M. Toeppen (*SRP*, I, 151).

51. *SRP*, I, 149.

52. *PUB*, I, no. 105.

53. Brundage, 50.

54. 'Cognoscimus Deum vestrum maiorem diis nostris...' Henry of Livonia *Chronica*, XIV, 11.

55. *LR*, lines 4238–40.

56. *Chronica Alberici monachi trium fontium*, *MGH SS*, XXIII, s.a. 1232.

57. Hartmann von Heldrungen's *Relation*, *FHL*, 212.

58. *Magistri Vincentii Chronicon Polonorum*, *MPH*, II, 373.

59. *SMHD*, II, 465–7.

60. Brundage, 189.

61. Matthew Paris, *Chronica majora* (ed. H. R. Luard, Rolls Series, VII (1872–1883)), IV, 9.

62. *NC*, 17–18.

63. The text of the *Vita* of St Eric is in *Erik den Helge*, ed. B. Thordeman (Stockholm, 1954).

64. *FMU*, no. 52.

65. *Bullarium Danicum*, ed. A. Krarup (Copenhagen, 1931), 73.

66. *DS*, I, nos 127–9 and 133.

67. *NC*, 68–9, records the expedition; the Pushkin Codex adds the baptism.

68. Ed. Rolf Pipping (Uppsala, 1921), with a *Kommentar till Erikskrönikan*, Svenska litteratursällskapet i Finland, CLXXVII (Helsingfors, 1928).

69. *EK*, lines 101–32.

70. *EK*, lines 137–42.

71. *EK*, lines 143–56.

72. *LEKU*, I, no. 559.

73. *EK*, lines 1795–6; *NC*, 115.

74. *FHL*, 204.

75. Innocent III to Folkwin, 25 Jan 1212, *FHL*, 65.

76. H. Hildebrand, *Livonica* (Riga, 1887), no. 12 (19 Nov 1225).

77. *LEKU*, I, nos 202–4, 209.

78. Brundage, 222.

79. *LEKU*, I, no. 58.

80. *NC*, 86–7

81. *LEKU*, I, no. 281 (12 Mar 1255).

82. *SRP*, I, 147.

83. Volhynian Chronicle, s.a. 6770 (Perfecky, 82).

84. Galician Chronicle, s.a. 6760 (Perfecky, 62).

85. Galician Chronicle (Perfecky, 63).

86. *LR*, lines 6379–410.

87. Galician Chronicle, s.a. 6766 (Perfecky, 73).

88. C. Hartnoch, *Selectae dissertationes* (Frankfurt, 1679). See also the report on paganism in fifteenth-century Samogitia by Hieronymus of Prague, as given to Aeneas Silvius, *SRP*, IV, 238–40.

89. See, for example, *SRP*, I, 185 (Dusburg), and *SRP*, II, 638 (Wigand).

90. *LEKU*, I, no. 538.

91. For these complaints, see *LEKU*, I, nos. 585 (Riga), 584 (Archbishop John III), 586 (Bishop Conrad of Ösel), 603 (bishop of Courland), and 616 (archbishop in 1305). For the eventual papal inquiry (in 1310), see A. Seraphim, *Das Zeugenverhör des Franciscus de Moliano* (Königsberg, 1912).

92. *LEKU*, II, 15–20.

93. Alexander IV, 6 Aug 1257, *LEKU*, II, no. 3029.

94. *LEKU*, II, no. 630.

95. Dusburg (*SRP*, I, 178).

96. *Opus maius*, I, ch. 3; III, ch. 14; and VII, ch. 4/1. See the translation by R. B. Burke, *The 'Opus majus' of Roger Bacon* (Philadelphia, 1928).

97. For Humbert's *Opusculum*, see E. Brown, *Appendix ad fasciculum rerum expetendarum et fugendarum* (London, 1690) 185ff.

98. The *Relatio* of the Bishop of Ormutz is in 'Analecta zur Geschichte Deutschlands und Italiens', *Abhandlungen der historischen Classe der K. Bayerischen Akademie*, IV (1846).

99. Continuation of Volhynian Chronicle, s.a. 6813.

100. Warden Nicholas to John XXII, 25 Nov 1323 (*PUB*, II, no. 429).

101. Abbots Paul of Oliva and Jordan of Pelplin.

102. *PUB*, II, no. 638 (12 Mar 1329).

103. *Le Confort d'ami*, lincs 3032–45, in *Oeuvres de Guillaume de Machaut*, 3 vols, ed. E. Hoepffner (Paris, 1908–21), III, 106–7. For a prose tale of the same campaign, written down 1395–99, see *Chronique et Geste de Jean des Preis*, 6 vols, ed. A. Borgnet (Brussels, 1867–87), VI, 412–16.

104. L. Toulmin-Smith, *Expeditions to Prussia and the Holy Land Made by Henry Earl of Derby* (Camden Society, 1894), provides the fullest possible analysis of Henry's accounts.

105. *SRP*, II, 595.

106. For a good map, see H. and G. Mortensen and R. Wenskus, *Historische geographischer Atlas der Preussenlandes* (Wiesbaden, 1968), sheet 1.

107. *SRP*, V, 581.

108. *LEKU*, VI, no. 3040.

109. Perlbach, 140.

110. *Calendar of entries in the Papal Register: Petitions*, I, ed. W. H. Bliss (London, 1896), 176 (29 Sep 1349).

111. Wigand of Marburg, *SRP*, 11, 632.

112. *LEKU*, IV, 1449 (26 Apr 1387).

113. H. von der Hardt, *Magnum oecumenicum Constantiense concilium*, 7 vols (Frankfurt, 1696–1742), III, 6–8.

114. *SRP*, 11, 662ff; *Die Littauischen Wegeberichte*.

115. Ibid., no. 57.

116. Dlugossius, *Annales*, ed. J. Dabrowski (Warsaw, 1964–   ), 1, 86.

117. *CDP*, V, no. 57.

118. Wigand of Marburg, *SRP*, 11, 544.

119. *SRP*, 11, 115.

120. *Wegeberichte*, no. 84.

121. Peter of Dusburg, *SRP*, 1, 180–1.

122. *SRP*, 11, 545.

123. *SRP*, 11, 572.

124. Wigand of Marburg, *SRP*, 11, 530 and 540.

125. *CDP*, III, no. 72.

126. *SRP*, 11, 786.

127. *SRP*, V, 618.

128. Olaus Magnus, *Historia de gentibus septentrionalibus* (Rome, 1555), VI, ch. 21.

129. J. E. Rietz, *Scriptores Suecici medii aevi cultum culturamque respicientes* (Lund, 1845), III, 208 – from Abbess Margaret of Vadstena's *De Sta. Birgitta Chronicon* (in Swedish).

130. *FMU*, no. 465.

131. *FMU*, no. 309.

132. *FMU*, no. 313.

133. *NC*, 133.

134. *FMU*, no. 473.

135. *Revelationes S. Brigittae*, ed. C. Durantus (Antwerp, 1611), 101, 103 (on knighthood), 596 (on need for crusade), 600, 603 (on taxes), 612–13 (Christ's advice), and 614 (need for new see).

136. *FD*, lines 133–5.

137. *NC*, 141.

138. *FD*, line 167.

139. *FD*, lines 181–2.

140. Lögmannsannáll, s.a. 1351, *FMU*, no. 573.

141. For a Latin translation see M. Akiander, 'Utdrag ur Ryska annalen', *Suomi*, VIII (1848), 101–4.

142. *DS*, no. 4669.

143. *FMU*, no. 588.

144. *FMU*, no. 589.

145. *Revelationes S. Brigittae*, 701.

146. *Acta literaria Sveciae* (Uppsala, 1724), 593.

147. *FMU*, no. 470.

148. For example, Conrad von Wallenrod ('sere gefurcht' – *SRP*, III, 170), Ulrich von Jungingen ('radix malorum' – *SRP*, IV, 58), Conrad von Erlichshausen ('eyn scharffer man' – *SRP*, IV, 414) and Ludwig von Erlichshausen ('hochmuttig und egen koppisch' – *SRP*, IV, 427).

149. Perlbach, 146-56.

150. *FMU*, no. 275.

151. *PUB*, I, no. 173.

152. *PUB*. I, no. 262.

153. *PUB*, I, no. 718.

154. For example, Duke Mestwin of Pomerelia's privilege to the Cistercians of Byszewo, 29 Sep 1292: *Pomerellische Urkundenbuch*, I, no. 487.

155. Text in *Jura Prutenorum saeculo xiv condita*, ed. P. Laband (Königsberg, 1866), and in V. T. Pashuto, *Pomezaniya* (Moscow, 1955).

156. *Revelationes S. Brigattae*, II, ch. 19.

157. *SRP*, IV, 460–1.

158. *Die jüngere Livländische Reimchronik*, ed. K. Höhlbaum (Leipzig, 1872), 22.

159. *LEKU*, VII, no. 355.

160. *CDP*, I, no. 46.

161. *LEKU*, I, nos 362 and 466.

162. Cf. *Kulmischer Handfeste*, *CDP*, I, no. 105.

163. R. Hausen, *Registrum ecclesiae Aboensis* (Helsingfors, 1890), no. 680.

164. *Codices medii aevi Finlandiae*, 2 vols, ed. J. Jaakkola (Copenhagen, 1952), I.

165. Ed. R. Hausen (Helsingfors, 1881–2).

166. *Oeuvres de Ghillebert de Lannoy* (see above, note 3), p. 22.

167. *LEKU*, VII, no. 355.

168. *SRP*, IV, 56.

169. From a branch of the ruling family of the Vogtland (between Thuringia and Bohemia), which has named all its males Henry since the twelfth century, and provided five senior officers of the Order in Prussia between 1328 and 1499. This Henry, and his brother, the commander of Danzig, were remote cousins of the later grand-master Henry Reuss von Plauen.

170. E. Weise, *Die Staatsverträge des Deutschen Ordens*, 2nd edn, 2 vols (Marburg, 1970), I, 85–9.

171. The Rufus Chronicle, in *Die Chroniken der Niedersächsischen Städte: Lübeck, 5* vols, ed. C. Hegel and K. Koppman (Leipzig, 1884–1911), III, 52.

172. *SRP*, II, 795.

173. J. H. Wylie, *History of England under Henry the Fourth*, 4 vols (London, 1884–98), IV, 13–15.

174. *SRP*, III, 59 and V, 266.

175. *SS*, 65–III.

176. *SS*, 108–10.

177. *SS*, 118–20.

178. *SS*, 44–64.

179. *SS*, 121–62.

180. Dominic, *SS*, 248–64; Urbach, *SS*, 276–308.

181. H. Boockmann, *Johannes Falkenberg* (Göttingen, 1975), 312–53.

182. *SS*, 228–47.

183. *SS*, 265–70.

184. *SS*, 391–406.

185. *SRP*, III, 374.

186. *SRP*, IV, 381.

187. *SRP*, III, 512–18.

188. Brambeck, *SRP*, VI, 414.

189. *SRP*, IV, 411.

190. *SRP*, IV, 448–65.

191. *SRP*, V, 207, 208–9.

192. *SRP*, V, 374.

193. For a Lutheran apology by one of Albert's ex-knight-brothers see F. zu Heydeck, *An der Hochwurdigen Fürsten unnd Herren Hern Walther vonn Blettenbergh. . . . Eyn gar Christlich Ermänung* (Königsberg, 1526).

194. *NC*, 149, 150.

195. *LEKU*, VIII, no. 386 (*c.* 1430); XII/I, no. 125 (1462); IX, no. 804 (1442).

196. *NC*, 197, 198.

197. *LEKU*, IX, no. 1015 (16 Nov 1443).

198. *LEKU*, XII, no. 214.

199. Cited by O. Stavenhagen in 'Johann Wolthus von Herse', *Mittheilungen aus der Livländische Geschichte*, XVII, 29.

200. Cf. accounts by Bredenbach (1563) and Herberstein (*c.* 1549) in *Rerum Moscoviticorum autores varii*, ed. C. Marnius and J. Autorius (Frankfurt, 1600), 227 and 88.

INDEX

(The following abbreviations are used throughout: P: pope, E: emperor, K: king, Abp: archbishop, Bp: bishop, G M: grand-master, M L: master of Livonia, D: duke, C: count.)

<u>Follow up</u>　　　　　7space trades

- Continuous AoA ✓　DOTMLPF

- Development Planning WG
　　　Judith - govccard
　　twce　email to David J　AFit

· Mission based SE
　　　govccard - will connect
　　　mission thread linkages

· Stuart Booth - common tool infrastructure
　　　↳ bridge CBA — SE (DP phase - Problem)

· SEI for linking assessment models
　　to ISP tagging.

READ MORE IN PENGUIN

In every corner of the world, on every subject under the sun, Penguin represents quality and variety – the very best in publishing today.

For complete information about books available from Penguin – including Puffins, Penguin Classics and Arkana – and how to order them, write to us at the appropriate address below. Please note that for copyright reasons the selection of books varies from country to country.

In the United Kingdom: Please write to *Dept. EP, Penguin Books Ltd, Bath Road, Harmondsworth, West Drayton, Middlesex UB7 0DA*

In the United States: Please write to *Consumer Services, Penguin Putnam Inc., 405 Murray Hill Parkway, East Rutherford, New Jersey 07073-2136.* VISA and MasterCard holders call 1-800-631-8571 to order Penguin titles

In Canada: Please write to *Penguin Books Canada Ltd, 10 Alcorn Avenue, Suite 300, Toronto, Ontario M4V 3B2*

In Australia: Please write to *Penguin Books Australia Ltd, 487 Maroondah Highway, Ringwood, Victoria 3134*

In New Zealand: Please write to *Penguin Books (NZ) Ltd, Private Bag 102902, North Shore Mail Centre, Auckland 10*

In India: Please write to *Penguin Books India Pvt Ltd, 11 Community Centre, Panchsheel Park, New Delhi 110017*

In the Netherlands: Please write to *Penguin Books Netherlands bv, Postbus 3507, NL-1001 AH Amsterdam*

In Germany: Please write to *Penguin Books Deutschland GmbH, Metzlerstrasse 26, 60594 Frankfurt am Main*

In Spain: Please write to *Penguin Books S. A., Bravo Murillo 19, 1°B, 28015 Madrid*

In Italy: Please write to *Penguin Italia s.r.l., Via Vittorio Emanuele 45/a, 20094 Corsico, Milano*

In France: Please write to *Penguin France, 12, Rue Prosper Ferradou, 31700 Blagnac*

In Japan: Please write to *Penguin Books Japan Ltd, Iidabashi KM-Bldg, 2-23-9 Koraku, Bunkyo-Ku, Tokyo 112-0004*

In South Africa: Please write to *Penguin Books South Africa (Pty) Ltd, P.O. Box 751093, Gardenview, 2047 Johannesburg*

READ MORE IN PENGUIN

ARCHAEOLOGY

The Penguin Dictionary of Archaeology
Warwick Bray and David Trump

The range of this dictionary is from the earliest prehistory to the civilizations before the rise of classical Greece and Rome. From the Abbevillian handaxe and the god Baal of the Canaanites to the Wisconsin and Würm glaciations of America and Europe, this dictionary concisely describes, in more than 1,600 entries, the sites, cultures, periods, techniques and terms of archaeology.

The Complete Dead Sea Scrolls in English Geza Vermes

The discovery of the Dead Sea Scrolls in the Judaean desert between 1947 and 1956 transformed our understanding of the Hebrew Bible, early Judaism and the origins of Christianity. 'No translation of the Scrolls is either more readable or more authoritative than that of Vermes' *The Times Higher Education Supplement*

Ancient Iraq Georges Roux

Newly revised and now in its third edition, *Ancient Iraq* covers the political, cultural and socio-economic history of Mesopotamia from the days of prehistory to the Christian era and somewhat beyond.

Breaking the Maya Code Michael D. Coe

Over twenty years ago, no one could read the hieroglyphic texts carved on the magnificent Maya temples and palaces; today we can understand almost all of them. The inscriptions reveal a culture obsessed with warfare, dynastic rivalries and ritual blood-letting. 'An entertaining, enlightening and even humorous history of the great searchers after the meaning that lies in the Maya inscriptions' *Observer*

READ MORE IN PENGUIN

RELIGION

The Origin of Satan Elaine Pagels

'Pagels sets out to expose fault lines in the Christian tradition, beginning with the first identification, in the Old Testament, of dissident Jews as personifications of Satan ... Absorbingly, and with balanced insight, she explores this theme of supernatural conflict in its earliest days' *Sunday Times*

A New Handbook of Living Religions
Edited by John R. Hinnells

Comprehensive and informative, this survey of active twentieth-century religions has now been completely revised to include modern developments and recent scholarship. 'Excellent ... This whole book is a joy to read' *The Times Higher Education Supplement*

Sikhism Hew McLeod

A stimulating introduction to Sikh history, doctrine, customs and society. There are about 16 million Sikhs in the world today, 14 million of them living in or near the Punjab. This book explores how their distinctive beliefs emerged from the Hindu background of the times, and examines their ethics, rituals, festivities and ceremonies.

The Historical Figure of Jesus E. P. Sanders

'This book provides a generally convincing picture of the real Jesus, set within the world of Palestinian Judaism, and a practical demonstration of how to distinguish between historical information and theological elaboration in the Gospels' *The Times Literary Supplement*

Islam in the World Malise Ruthven

This informed and informative book places the contemporary Islamic revival in context, providing a fascinating introduction – the first of its kind – to Islamic origins, beliefs, history, geography, politics and society.

READ MORE IN PENGUIN

HISTORY

The Vikings Else Roesdahl

Far from being just 'wild, barbaric, axe-wielding pirates', the Vikings created complex social institutions, oversaw the coming of Christianity to Scandinavia and made a major impact on European history through trade, travel and far-flung colonization. This study is a rich and compelling picture of an extraordinary civilization.

A Short History of Byzantium John Julius Norwich

In this abridgement of his celebrated trilogy, John Julius Norwich has created a definitive overview of 'the strange, savage, yet endlessly fascinating world of Byzantium'. 'A real life epic of love and war, accessible to anyone' *Independent on Sunday*

The Eastern Front 1914–1917 Norman Stone

'Without question one of the classics of post-war historical scholarship' Niall Ferguson. 'Fills an enormous gap in our knowledge and understanding of the Great War' *Sunday Telegraph*

The Idea of India Sunil Khilnani

'Many books about India will be published this year; I doubt if any will be wiser and more illuminating about its modern condition than this' *Observer*. 'Sunil Khilnani's meditation on India since Independence is a *tour de force*' *Sunday Telegraph*

The Penguin History of Europe J. M. Roberts

'J. M. Roberts has managed to tell the rich and remarkable tale of European history in fewer than 700 fascinating, well-written pages . . . few would ever be able to match this achievement' *The New York Times Book Review*. 'The best single-volume history of Europe' *The Times Literary Supplement*